Parental Guidance, State Responsibility and Evolving Capacities

Parental Guidance, State Responsibility and Evolving Capacities

Article 5 of the United Nations Convention on the Rights of the Child

Edited by

Brian Sloan
Claire Fenton-Glynn

BRILL
NIJHOFF

BRILL | NIJHOFF

With the exception of Chapters 2, 5, 7 and 10 and the Introduction, all chapters of this book were previously published as a special issue in Brill's journal *The International Journal of Children's Rights*, Volume 28, issue 3 (2020).

Library of Congress Cataloging-in-Publication Data

Names: Children's Rights: Families, Guidance and Evolving Capacities (Conference) (2019 : University of Cambridge) | Fenton-Glynn, Claire, editor. | Sloan, Brian, 1984- editor. | Convention on the Rights of the Child Implementation Project, sponsoring body. | University of Cambridge, host institution.
Title: Parental guidance, state responsibility and evolving capacities : Article 5 of the United Nations Convention on the Rights of the Child / edited by Claire Fenton-Glynn, Brian Sloan.
Description: Leiden ; Boston : Brill Nijhoff, [2020-2021] | Includes index. |
Identifiers: LCCN 2021037190 (print) | LCCN 2021037191 (ebook) | ISBN 9789004446861 (hardback) | ISBN 9789004446854 (ebook)
Subjects: LCSH: Convention on the Rights of the Child (1989 November 20). Article 5—Congresses. | Parent and child (Law)—Congresses. | Children (International law)—Congresses. | LCGFT: Conference papers and proceedings.
Classification: LCC K700.A6 C45 2019 (print) | LCC K700.A6 (ebook) | DDC 346.01/7—dc23
LC record available at https://lccn.loc.gov/2021037190
LC ebook record available at https://lccn.loc.gov/2021037191

Typeface for the Latin, Greek, and Cyrillic scripts: "Brill". See and download: brill.com/brill-typeface.

ISBN 978-90-04-44686-1 (hardback)
ISBN 978-90-04-44685-4 (e-book)

Copyright 2020-2021 by Brian Sloan and Claire Fenton-Glynn. Published by Koninklijke Brill NV, Leiden, The Netherlands.
Koninklijke Brill NV incorporates the imprints Brill, Brill Nijhoff, Brill Hotei, Brill Schöningh, Brill Fink, Brill mentis, Vandenhoeck & Ruprecht, Böhlau Verlag and V&R Unipress.
Koninklijke Brill NV reserves the right to protect this publication against unauthorized use. Requests for re-use and/or translations must be addressed to Koninklijke Brill NV via brill.com or copyright.com.

This book is printed on acid-free paper and produced in a sustainable manner.

Contents

Notes on Contributors VIII

Introduction 1
 Brian Sloan and Claire Fenton-Glynn

PART 1
Decoding Article 5

1 The Enigma of Article 5 of the United Nations Convention on the Rights of the Child
 Central or Peripheral? 13
  Elaine E. Sutherland

2 The Scope and Limitations of the Concept of Evolving Capacities within the CRC 36
  Gerison Lansdown

3 Assessing Children's Capacity
 Reconceptualising Our Understanding through the UN Convention on the Rights of the Child 52
  Aoife Daly

PART 2
Article 5 and Domestic Legal Systems

4 'Evolving Capacities' and 'Parental Guidance' in the Context of Youth Justice
 Testing the Application of Article 5 of the Convention on the Rights of the Child 83
  Ursula Kilkelly

5 Parental Guidance in Support of Children's Participation Rights
 The Interplay between Articles 5 and 12 in the Family Justice System 104
  Nicola Taylor

PART 3
Parental Responsibility and Evolving Capacities

6 Do Parents Know Best? 129
   John Eekelaar

7 From Reasonable to Unreasonable
   Corporal Punishment in the Home 148
   Trynie Boezaart

8 Parental Responsibilities and Rights during the "Gender Reassignment" Decision-Making Process of Intersex Infants
   Guidance in Terms of Article 5 of the Convention on the Rights of the Child 172
   Lize Mills and Sabrina Thompson

PART 4
The Impact of Article 5 in Adoption Proceedings

9 Children's Capacities and Role in Matters of Great Significance for Them
   An Analysis of the Norwegian County Boards' Decision-Making in Cases about Adoption from Care 199
   Amy McEwan-Strand and Marit Skivenes

10 Children's Views, Best Interests and Evolving Capacities in Consenting to Their Own Adoption
   A Study of NSW Supreme Court Judgements for Adoptions from Care 232
   Judy Cashmore, Amy Conley Wright and Sarah Hoff

11 Article 5 of the Convention on the Rights of the Child and the Involvement of Fathers in Adoption Proceedings: A Comparative Analysis 257
   Brian Sloan

PART 5
Case Studies on the Application of Article 5

12 Article 5: The Role of Parents in the Proxy Informed Consent Process in Medical Research Involving Children 281
   Sheila Varadan

13 Scotland's Named Person Scheme
   A Case Study of Article 5 of the United Nations Convention on the Rights of the Child in Practice   307
      Gillian Black

14 New Zealand Case Studies to Test the Meaning and Use of Article 5 of the 1989 United Nations Convention on the Rights of the Child   323
      Mark Henaghan

   Index   347

Notes on Contributors

Gillian Black
Professor of Scots Private Law, University of Edinburgh, United Kingdom

Trynie Boezaart
Emeritus Professor, University of Pretoria, South Africa

Judy Cashmore
Professor of Socio-Legal Research and Policy, University of Sydney, Australia

Amy Conley Wright
Associate Professor of Social Work and Policy, University of Sydney, Australia

Aoife Daly
Lecturer, School of Law, University College Cork, Ireland

John Eekelaar
Emeritus Fellow, Pembroke College, University of Oxford, United Kingdom

Mark Henaghan
Professor of Law, University of Auckland, New Zealand

Sarah Hoff
Research Assistant, University of Sydney, Australia

Ursula Kilkelly
Professor of Law, University College Cork, Ireland

Gerison Lansdown
International Children's Rights Consultant

Amy McEwan-Strand
Research Assistant, Centre for Research on Discretion and Paternalism, University of Bergen, Norway

Lize Mills
Senior Lecturer in Law, Stellenbosch University, South Africa

Marit Skivenes
Professor, University of Bergen, Norway

Brian Sloan
Fellow in Law, Robinson College, University of Cambridge, United Kingdom

Elaine E. Sutherland
Professor, University of Bergen, Norway; Visiting Professor, Edinburgh Napier University, United Kingdom; Professor Emerita, University of Stirling, United Kingdom; Distinguished Professor of Law Emerita, Lewis & Clark Law School, Portland, OR, USA

Nicola Taylor
Professor of Law, University of Otago, New Zealand

Sabrina Thompson
LLM candidate, Stellenbosch University, South Africa

Sheila Varadan
PhD Candidate, Leiden University, The Netherlands

Introduction

Brian Sloan and Claire Fenton-Glynn

The papers in this Edited Collection follow on from a colloquium held in Cambridge in July 2019, as part of the United Nations Convention on the Rights of the Child Implementation Project. The fifth event in this series (with previous events covering Articles 12, 6, 3 and 2), the colloquium brought together international experts in the fields of law, sociology and neuroscience to analyse the implementation of Article 5 of the United Nations Convention on the Rights of the Child, which reads:

> States Parties shall respect the responsibilities, rights and duties of parents or, where applicable, the members of the extended family or community as provided for by local custom, legal guardians or other persons legally responsible for the child, to provide, in a manner consistent with the evolving capacities of the child, appropriate direction and guidance in the exercise by the child of the rights recognized in the present Convention.

Held across two days, the aim of this colloquium was to explore the challenges faced by legal systems in giving effect to this internationally-agreed standard. Contributions covered such issues as residence disputes, gender identity and bodily integrity in the context of religious and cultural practices, the significance of environment and play on the evolution of children's capacity, and parental control of access to knowledge of origins. All participants were invited to submit papers for a Special Edition of the International Journal of Children's Rights, from which a small number of articles were selected. Serendipitously, Aoife Daly also submitted a paper to the journal during this period, focusing on Article 5, which we were delighted to be able to include in the Special Edition.

We felt, however, that there was still more that could be added to the literature in this area. We therefore sought permission of the Editors of the International Journal of Children's Rights to expand the Special Edition into an Edited Collection, which would add five more contributions to the nine contained in the journal. We thank the Editors for their support in this project, as well as the publisher for recognising the importance of further academic research into this often over-looked article of the Convention.

Part 1   Decoding Article 5

In the first contribution, Elaine Sutherland appropriately seeks to explore what the drafters of Article 5 sought to achieve with this provision and highlight the most controversial issues, including the tension between protecting the family from the state and protecting the child from the family (or indeed the wider community). She notes that Article 5's themes pervade the rest of the Convention, potentially leading to the conflicting arguments that Article 5 serves no independent purpose or should be recognised as a general principle. This conflict is arguably reflected in the fact that, as Sutherland observes, the Committee on the Rights of the Child rarely makes specific reference to Article 5 obligations, albeit that she considers the likely explanation to lie in the Convention's reporting process. It also is telling that Sutherland reports the absence of real discussion among the drafters about what the term 'evolving capacities' actually means, since its elusiveness remains apparent in some of the other contributions to this volume. She ultimately concludes, however, that Article 5 makes 'a vital contribution to the realisation of children's rights', in squarely addressing the need to balance the roles of parents and the state respectively, and in adopting the necessary broad notion of evolving capacities.

Gerison Lansdown, author of the seminal UNICEF report on Article 5 (*The Evolving Capacities of Children*, 2005), explores how understanding the concept of evolving capacities requires an analysis of how the CRC differs from other human rights treaties in its treatment of autonomy. She explains how the application of this principle poses a profound challenge to traditional assumptions about the relationship between the child, parents and state in respect of the exercise of rights. Application of the concept of evolving capacities of the child in the context of their rights necessitates integration of three approaches to the child: respect for the emerging entitlement of the child to exercise rights on their own behalf, respecting the child's right to appropriate protections in view of their relative vulnerability and youth and the creation of environments that allow for the optimum fulfilment of the child's potential.

Aoife Daly's chapter seeks to reconceptualise approaches to assessing children's capacity, particularly in light of Article 5. Having critically examined some previous attempts to articulate the nature of capacity in the case of children, including in English medical law, she advocates a more explicitly rights-based approach constructed around the CRC. The model Daly proposes encompasses four concepts: Autonomy (linked to Article 12 and its protection of the child's right to be heard); Protection (linked to Article 3 and its safeguarding of best interests and rights to protection from harm, with varying implications for different types of decisions); Evidence (linked to Article 2, which on her analysis requires sufficient understanding on the part of decision-makers to avoid discriminating against children as a group or against particular groups of children); and Support (linked to Article 5 and its protection of the right to receive guidance in order to maximise capacity and of relational decision-making). Importantly, her framework is thus not *limited* to Article 5, and she usefully shows how it can be linked to other provisions of the Convention. Daly argues that an insistence on understanding capacity through a children's rights lens will at least prompt challenging questions going to the heart of what it is to respect children as equals, and to respect their life experience as crucial to their best interests.

Part 2:   Article 5 and Domestic Legal Systems

In Part 2 of the book, authors explore the application of Article 5 in domestic legal systems – both in relation to juvenile justice (Kilkelly) and family justice (Taylor).

Ursula Kilkelly explores the application of Article 5 in the context of children in conflict with the law. She links the concept of 'evolving capacities' in Article 5 with the concept of 'responsibility' in the criminal justice system, and argues that there is no great clarity in the distinctions between the concepts of autonomy, capacity and responsibility from a children's rights perspective. She notes that criminal responsibility is the only area of the Convention where an age-based approach is mandated, requiring states to establish a minimum age, although she suggests that the choice of this age is often a political decision rather than one that is determined by children's capacity. The downside of the concept of evolving capacities in the context of youth justice, she argues, is that the child will not always be protected from full responsibility, and she questions whether this can be compatible with the requirement to provide to children greater protection than adults on account of their special status and vulnerability. Finally, Kilkelly turns to the exercise of parental responsibility in relation to children in the youth justice system, and notes that although international instruments rely heavily on families in preventing children coming into conflict with the law and becoming involved in criminal activities, it is unclear what role they should play in decision-making around criminal responsibility. She concludes by arguing that to truly enable the exercise of the child's rights in youth justice in line with Article 5, parental responsibility should be exercised to promote mandatory independent representation for children in criminal proceedings.

Nicola Taylor, in her chapter, examines the interplay between Articles 5 and 12 of the UNCRC in the context of decisions about post-separation parenting arrangements. She argues that this is a previously under-considered, yet promising, avenue in family dispute resolution in that it focuses on how best to enhance parental responsibilities, rights and duties in support of child-inclusive practice. Shifting the emphasis to incorporate parents, aided by the sociocultural concept of scaffolding, has the benefit of widening the family justice frame of reference for child participation beyond the existing statutory provisions, professionals' roles and court processes that currently feature so prominently. She presents the findings of a nationwide study with 655 separated parents and 364 family justice professionals, following the 2014 reform of New Zealand's family justice system, which confirms the significance of parental engagement with children when post-separation parenting arrangements are being made and provides encouraging evidence of the scope and impact of such child participation in intrafamilial decision-making contexts.

Part 3: Parental Responsibility and Evolving Capacities

The contributions in Part 3 of the book focus on parental responsibility, and how this should be exercised in the light of children's evolving capacities.

The title of John Eekelaar's contribution poses a distinctly blunt question going to the heart of debates on Article 5: 'do parents know best?'. His particular concern is situations where parents make use of a court on a matter where children's interests are relevant but no query is raised about those interests because the parents are in apparent agreement about what those interests require. Eekelaar draws a distinction between situations where children are in an intact family and where the child's parents are separating. In the former situation, he regards it as generally appropriate for a legal system to emphasise the norms protected in article 5, namely the parents' abilities to decide between themselves how best to guide the child. He considers the situation to be very different, however, where the parents separate and the 'joint project' has failed. In such circumstances, Eekelaar regards it as potentially insufficient protection for best interests that the parents have apparently agreed arrangements for post-separation parenting between themselves, since the appearance of agreement does not necessarily indicate an absence of conflict and a more optimal solution for the child may exist. With particular reference to the policy emphasis on accepting what separating parents have agreed in England and Wales, he highlights the potentially countervailing Article 18 obligation on states to 'use their best efforts' to ensure that, in exercising their responsibility, 'the best interests of the child will be [the parents'] basic concern'.

The focus of Trynie Boezaart's chapter is also on the wider question of parental responsibility, but she focuses her attention on the corporal punishment of children by their parents. She argues that the unreasonableness of corporal punishment in the home is evident: it is not right for children if parents assault them when they are supposed to sensitively direct and guide them, nor is it right for children if their parents undermine, instead of respect, their inherent dignity. Drawing on the recent jurisprudence from the South African courts, she critically evaluates the position of the Constitutional Court against international benchmarks, and analyses the progress of this jurisdiction towards achieving protection for children from violence in the home

Lize Mills and Sabrina Thompson consider the application of Article 5 in the context of surgical interventions on intersex infants. Focusing on the interaction between parental decision-making and state authority in deciding whether to perform life-altering operations, Mills and Thompson argue that states have a duty to assist parents to make decisions in their children's best interests, and to provide appropriate direction and guidance in this respect. In doing so, they note the difficult choice faced by parents – in a world where a binary concept of gender is the norm, sex alteration surgery may prevent the child from being ridiculed, bullied and ostracised. However, they contend that the state has a duty to provide the parents of intersex infants with sufficient knowledge and support and an enabling environment that will allow them to leave the decision to be made by their child, as well as ensuring that the stigma of being born intersex is diminished within society. Finally, Mills and Thompson provide a useful overview of a number of jurisdictions that have started to implement measures to aid parents in this regard, focusing in particular on Colombia, Malta and the United States. Despite recognising that development is piecemeal and limited, these examples nevertheless provide hope for the future.

Part 4: The Impact of Article 5 in Adoption Proceedings

In their contribution, Amy McEwan-Strand and Marit Skivenes explore children's capacities through an analysis of decision-making in cases concerning adoption from care. Drawing on an empirical study which examined all 169 judgments made relating to such adoptions in Norway from 2011–2016, they conclude that many children are absent in the decision-maker's justification and conclusion about whether adoption is appropriate. The study suggests that age is used as a proxy for competency and maturity, and that while young children do not have their capacity assessed at all, older children undergo a superficial assessment at best. McEwan-Strand and Skivenes conclude that decision-makers may often be unaware of their obligations in this respect, or do not have sufficient competency in assessing children's capacities, leading to a failure to implement children's rights in line with the UNCRC.

Judy Cashmore, Amy Conley Wright and Sarah Hoff also consider the issue of children's capacity and consent in relation to their own adoption, focusing on New South Wales. They identify a clear recognition of children's evolving capacities in some reported judgments, particularly in relation to older children. They note, however, that despite a formal *prima facie* consent requirement in relation to a child aged 12 or older, some judges emphasised that a child's views about the adoption itself or post-adoption contact would not be treated as determinative. While the authors accept that such an approach may valuably protect children from the burden of the decision, they note the danger that a child's view is more likely to be considered 'rational' when it accords with that of the judge. Cashmore and her colleagues also highlight the possible pitfalls of relying on the evidence of assessors in adoption proceedings as compared to granting the relevant child independent representation, although they are somewhat more positive in their conclusions about approaches to evolving capacities in New South Wales than McEwan-Strand and Skivenes are about Norway.

Brian Sloan argues in favour of the relevance of Article 5 to the involvement of fathers in adoption proceedings. In particular, he considers that such involvement can constitute 'appropriate direction and guidance' to the child or her representatives, when coupled with the child's identity-related rights in, *inter alia,* Articles 7 and 8 of the CRC. In the course of his analysis, Sloan undertakes a detailed critique of the work of Jill Marshall, a strong advocate for a mother's right to anonymous birth and relinquishment for adoption. Sloan accepts that a mother's advocacy for adoption (without paternal involvement) may also constitute 'appropriate direction and guidance' for Article 5 purposes. He suggests, however, that these conflicting implications of that article lead to a conclusion that neither mothers nor fathers have an unfettered right to mandate or forbid adoption in the absence of an independent assessment of welfare. He then tests the law of England and Wales, Scotland and Ireland against that conclusion. He argues that, despite a very difficult history on matters surrounding adoption, Irish Law potentially fits best with his analysis because it has enshrined the presumptive involvement of a potential adoptee's father in primary legislation. In closing, he highlights the inevitable difficulties with a child-centred Convention in a context where some might consider Marshall's arguments to be normatively valid.

Part 5: Case Studies on the Application of Article 5

Sheila Varadan examines the involvement of children in medical research and experimentation, and their right to informed consent. Although the proposed paragraph on medical decision-making was left out of the final draft of the UNCRC, she suggests that a number of provisions continue to have relevance for the protection of children involved in medical research, including Article 3, 12, 13, 18, 36 and – the focus of this contribution – Article 5. This article, she argues provides a framework to navigate the relationship between the proxy decision-maker – for example, parent or guardian – and the child, in light of their developing autonomy. She suggests that parents are obligated not only to involve their children in the informed consent process, but to foster the exercise of their rights, by enabling them to assume progressive agency and responsibility over decision-making.

The topic of Gillian Black's chapter might be considered unusual, in the sense that it concerns a government scheme that had been abandoned, following a successful court challenge, without ever having been implemented by the time she finalised her text. The initiative in question was the Scottish Government's 'Named Person' scheme, whereby every child in Scotland who would be allocated a particular adult, generally a health visitor, teacher or headteacher, who would be a single identified point of contact, who knew the child, and could help support and advise the child and parents. As Black explains, the scheme was dogged by controversy from the outset, with potential Named Persons concerned about resourcing, independence and liability, and parents' groups protesting against state interference even where there was no reason to believe that a child was at risk, as well as violations of privacy and data protection rights. Black nevertheless argues that the abortive scheme provides a valuable case study, in that the scheme was clearly highly pertinent to the rights protected in Article 5 but did not apparently take specific account of its requirements. She accepts that the Article 5 implications of the scheme were arguably variable. On the one hand, it could have supported children in recognising that parents' child-raising rights are fettered, and also helped parents in exercising their responsibilities. On the other, the wholesale and mandatory operation of the scheme arguably failed to respect children's evolving capacities. It is a recurring theme of the papers in this volume that Article 5, in common with the rest of the Convention, does not necessarily provide clear answers.

The final chapter, by Mark Henaghan, analyses the wording of Article 5 and four New Zealand case studies to test the possible interpretations of Article 5. He argues that Article 5 – like all international instruments – is not designed to provide prescriptive answers to challenging problems where there is a clash of which rights should prevail for children in particular situations. The central theme of Henaghan's paper is that where there is a clash of a child's rights the tiebreaker should be which right in the particular situation will best enhance the unique identity of a particular child. He argues that the purpose of a child's rights framework is so the child can construct their individualised identity which is authentic and real for that particular child. The New Zealand case studies have been chosen to exemplify particular aspects of Article 5 and see how they are played out in particular court settings and whether the outcome enhances or inhibits the child's opportunity to develop their unique identity.

Concluding Thoughts

Overall, we hope that this Edited Collection will add to the understanding of this important and sometimes overlooked article of the UNCRC, and lead to further scholarship in this area. Such scholarship, we hope, will ultimately lead to greater awareness and recognition of Article 5's requirements and implications in the wider world. This is true even if it remains impossible conclusively to resolve conflicting interpretations and priorities within the UNCRC, not least the inevitable tensions involved in recognising the rights *inter alia* of parents and families within a children's rights convention. We must also acknowledge the limitations of attempting to focus on one CRC article at a time in light of its considerably and deliberately interconnected nature.

Of course, the papers included in this Edited Collection provide only a sample of the wide variety of papers given at the colloquium. In particular, we are aware that the papers provide a predominantly European perspective, and that there is a preponderance of family-law focused pieces. This was not intentional: as discussed above, the colloquium itself in fact drew participants from a range of disciplines and jurisdictions. Having said this, we think that the chapters provide an interesting snapshot of our discussions, and we hope that they provide fascinating insights for scholars working in this area. We are pleased to have been able to include papers focusing on parental involvement *per se* as well as on evolving capacities.

It remains for us to thank some people and organisations without whom this volume could not have been published: all authors, colloquium participants and anonymous reviewers for lending their energy and expertise; Elaine Sutherland for her inspirational leadership of the CRC Implementation Project and her trust in allowing us to coordinate the Article 5 iteration; Laura Lundy, Helen Stalford and the whole editorial board of the International Journal of Children's Rights for selecting the Article 5 project as the topic of the special issue, and allowing us to build on this for the Edited Collection; the catering and conference team at Robinson College for their help in organising the colloquium there; Cambridge Family Law Centre, the Cambridge Socio-Legal Group, the University of Cambridge Strategic Research Initiative on Public Policy and Robinson College, Cambridge for generous financial and moral support; Siôn Hudson for invaluable editorial assistance; and the team at Brill for their highly professional production process.

PART 1

Decoding Article 5

CHAPTER 1

The Enigma of Article 5 of the United Nations Convention on the Rights of The Child

Central or Peripheral?

Elaine E. Sutherland

1   Introduction

Some 30 years ago, the General Assembly of the United Nations set the gold standard for children's rights when it adopted the Convention on the Rights of the Child[1] ("CRC" or "Convention"), a comprehensive statement of the civil, political, social, economic and cultural rights of children and young people. It is familiar territory that the Convention came into force more quickly than any other human rights instrument, less than a year after its adoption, and has now been ratified by every country in the world save the United States.[2]

Since most children live in families, recognition of their rights has implications for the responsibilities and rights of other family members, most notably their parents. The CRC recognises the importance of the family, describing it in its Preamble as 'the fundamental group of society' and various articles elaborate on the role of parents and the state's obligations to them. Article 5 seeks to regulate the relationship between the parties – the child, the parents (and, sometimes, the wider family or community) and the state – in this triangular relationship.[3] To that end, it requires States parties to respect the responsibilities, rights and duties of parents to provide direction and guidance to the child

---

1   United Nations Convention on the Rights of the Child, 1577 UNTS 3, adopted 20 November 1989, entered into force 2 September 1990.
2   The failure of the US to ratify the Convention is a sad irony given its considerable contribution to the drafting process (Cohen, 2006).
3   E/CN.4/1989/48, paras. 188 and Office of the United Nations High Commissioner for Human Rights (2007). *Legislative History of the Convention on the Rights of the Child. New York: United Nations (hereinafter "Legislative History")*, Vol. 1, 362. The Legislative History was published in two volumes and can be found at: www.ohchr.org/Documents/Publications/LegislativeHistorycrc1en.pdf *and* www.ohchr.org/Documents/Publications/LegislativeHistorycrc2en.pdf [accessed 31 October 2019]. See also, Detrick, with Doek and Cantwell, 1992.

in exercising Convention rights. Parental authority is not unfettered, however, and the obligation applies only to parental direction and guidance that is both appropriate and provided in a manner consistent with the evolving capacities of the child.

There is no equivalent of Article 5 in the Declaration of the Rights of the Child which inspired the CRC and it did not feature in the early Polish drafts of the Convention. While the US delegation was motivated to propose its inclusion by a desire to emphasise the importance of the family in the child's life and protect the family from undue state intrusion, others saw the value of Article 5 as protecting the rights of the child in the family setting. Yet numerous other articles in the Convention seek to achieve each of these goals, calling into question whether Article 5 adds anything.

The United Nations Committee on the Rights of the Child (UNCteeRC), the body responsible for monitoring implementation of, and compliance with, the Convention, has not classified Article 5 as one of the four general principles underpinning the CRC, that honour being confined to Articles 2 (non-discrimination), 3(1) (primacy of the child's best interests), 6 (the child's right to life, survival and development) and 12 (the child's participation rights) (General Comment No. 5: para. 12). However, the impact of Article 5, like that of the four general principles, is pervasive in so far as it applies across the sectoral rights set out in the Convention, begging the question whether it should be accorded the same status.[4]

This chapter sets the scene for those that follow in this volume, exploring what the drafters of the Convention were seeking to achieve in Article 5 and highlighting issues that they found particularly controversial.[5] Using textual analysis and the work of the UNCteeRC,[6] other human rights bodies and

---

4   As Tobin and Varadan note (2019: 185), despite the UNCteeRC's reluctance to identify Art. 5 as one of the general principles, 'its jurisprudence increasingly suggests that this is precisely how the Committee views' the principle of evolving capacities. For further exploration of this thesis, see, Varadan, 2019.
5   While the work of the drafters provides a backdrop to understanding the Convention, it is worth remembering Tobin's warning (2019: 9) that, '[t]oo often engagement with the Convention is unaccompanied by any explanation as to the methodology being employed to generate the meaning of its provisions' and his injunction (2019: 10) that its interpretation should be 'principled, practical, coherent and context sensitive.' At the heart of principled interpretation, lies the Vienna Convention on the Law of Treaties, 1155 U.N.T.S. 331, adopted 23 May 1969, in force 27 January 1980, Art. 31(1), requiring that a 'treaty shall be interpreted in good faith in accordance with the ordinary meaning to be given to the terms of the treaty in their context and in the light of its object and purpose.' The remainder of Art. 31 elaborates on that theme, while Art. 32 addresses supplementary means of interpretation, either to confirm the results of applying Art. 31, or to deal with remaining ambiguity and the like.
6   While the Committee's *General Comments* provide immensely helpful guidance on what it understands the various Convention provisions to mean, strictly speaking, these interpreta-

2 Drafting

Unlike many of the other provisions in the Convention, there was no early version of Article 5 in the First Polish draft, nor did its content feature in the views received on that draft (E/CN.4/1324, Corr.1 and Add.1–5, and *Legislative History*, Vol. 1, 357). Rather, the seeds of what became Article 5 were planted by the Danish delegation, in 1981 (HR/(XXXVII)/WG.1/WP.21 and *Legislative History*, Vol. 1, 357),[7] with a more detailed version being put forward by the NGO Ad Hoc Group in 1984 (E/ CN.4/1985/WG.1/WP.1 and *Legislative History*, Vol 1, 357).[8] These saplings informed a proposal put to the Working Group by Australia and United States, in 1987, and the following year the Working Group discussed this amended version of the Australian-US text which was supported by Austria and the Netherlands:

> The States Parties to the present Convention shall respect the rights and duties of the parents and, where applicable, legal guardians, to provide direction to the child in the exercise of his or her rights enumerated in the present Convention in a manner consistent with the evolving capacities of the child, having due regard to the importance of promoting the

---

tions are not binding on States parties, since the UN Convention, like other human rights treaties, does not give the relevant treaty body express power to adopt binding interpretations of the treaty (International Law Association: Committee on International Human Rights Law and Practice 2004: paras. 16 and 18). However, it is widely accepted that the views expressed in *General Comments* are 'non-binding norms that interpret and add detail to the rights and obligations' (Alston 2001: 775).

7 The text is as follows: 'Parents or other guardians have the main responsibility for the child. Every State Party has, however, the responsibility to satisfy the needs of the child and ensure the child the rights set forth in this Convention.'

8 The text is as follows:
1. The protection of the child's interests cannot be dissociated from the protection of the child's natural family.
2. The responsibility of parents is to do everything in their power to ensure their children's well-being and harmonious development. Parents shall participate in all decision-making and orientation with regard to their children's education and future.
3. The States Parties to the present Convention undertake to recognize, support and protect the family unit in every way to enable it to carry out its function as provider of the most suitable environment for the child's emotional, physical, moral and social development.'

development of the skills and knowledge required for an independent adulthood (E/CN.4/1988/WG.1/WP.22 and *Legislative History*, Vol. 1, 360).[9]

The observer from Australia emphasised that the proposed text brought together, 'two important general concepts', the child's evolving capacities and the rights and duties of parents (E/CN.4/1988/28, para. 28 and Legislative History, Vol. 1, 360), but it was clear from the outset that support for the proposal was motivated by quite distinct priorities.[10] For the United States delegation, the central feature of the provision was the extent to which it protected the place of the family and particularly parents in the child's life while, for others, it was the acknowledgement of the child's emerging agency that was important, with the issue of parental authority proving particularly contentious. In addition, there were those amongst the drafters who doubted that there was any need for Article 5, taking the view that other provisions afforded sufficient protection for the family in the child's life (E/CN.4/1987/25: para. 103 and Legislative History, Vol 1, 358).

2.1   *The Role of the Family*

The US delegation focussed on the protection afforded to the family by Article 5, arguing that there should be a provision early in the text of the Convention, recognising the central role of the family, 'in order to emphasize its importance and relationship to all the other rights' set out in it (E/CN.4/1987/25: para. 101 and *Legislative History*, Vol. 1, 358).[11] In this, it drew support from the International Covenants on Economic, Social and Cultural Rights and on Civil and Political Rights, both of which refer to the family as 'the natural and fundamental group unit of society'.[12] It fell to the observer from Canada to point out that,

---

9   What became Article 5 was known as Article 5 bis throughout First and Second readings. For simplicity, provisions will be referred to in this chapter by their number in the final text of the Convention.

10 For Kamchedzera (2012: para. 22), the innovation in Art. 5 emanated 'from three bases': 'the need to take into account the evolving capacities of the child when providing appropriate direction and guidance'; 'the centrality of a child rights' rather than a 'welfarist' approach; and 'the need to delineate the scope of parental authority and discretion'.

11 'The representative of the United States explained that his country attached great importance to the family as the natural and fundamental group unit of society' explaining that 'the family should be explicitly protected'.

12 International Covenant on Economic, Social and Cultural Rights, 993 U.N.T.S. 3, adopted 16 December 1966, entered into force 23 March 1976, Art. 10(1) ('The widest possible protection and assistance should be accorded to the family, which is the natural and fundamental group unit of society, particularly for its establishment and while it is responsible for the care and education of dependent children …') and the International Covenant on Civil and Political Rights, 999 U.N.T.S. 171, adopted 16 December 1966, entered into force 3

while the Covenants sought to protect the family from the state, there was a need to ensure, as Article 5 sought to do, that:

> in protecting the family from the State, the family must not be given arbitrary control over the child. Any protection from the State given to the family must be equally balanced with the protection of the child within the family (E/CN.4/1987/25: para. 106 and *Legislative History*, Vol. 1, 358).

2.2 *The Child's Evolving Capacities*

Recognition of the child's evolving capacities can contribute to protecting the child from arbitrary family control. In the course of the drafting process, the concept was discussed in the context of a number of articles, including Articles 13 (freedom of expression), 14 (right to freedom of thought, conscience and religion) and 15 (freedom of association and peaceful assembly) (*Legislative History*, Vol. 1, 446, 467 and 470, respectively), leading some delegations to conclude that it had been addressed sufficiently and that Article 5 was unnecessary (E/CN.4/1987/25: para. 103 and Legislative History, Vol. 1, 358). Others pressed for a general provision dealing with the child's evolving capacities.[13] In the event, there was no separate provision and reference to the concept only found its way into Articles 5 and 14 of the final text of the Convention.

Given the importance that some of the drafters attached to the concept of the child's evolving capacities, it is curious that there was no real discussion of what the term actually means. The Australian-US proposal made reference to 'promoting the development of the skills and knowledge required for an independent adulthood', but that speaks to the goal of recognising the child's evolving capacities rather than its content. It is not clear why that elaboration did not make its way into the final text, but its omission may be no bad thing since it could be read as implying that children are valued as potential adults rather than – as the drafters intended – valued in their own right, as children. It may be that the failure to discuss the content of the child's evolving capacities was prompted by recollections of the disagreement that arose during discussions of the related matter of parental authority.

January 1976, Art. 23(1) ('The family is the natural and fundamental group unit of society and is entitled to protection by society and the State.').

13   Canada, supported by Finland, raised the issue in 1987, but was content to leave the matter until after other substantive articles had been addresses: E/CN.4/1987/25: para. 104 and *Legislative History*, Vol. 1, 358. *Legislative History*, Vol. 1, 446. Canada and Norway raised the possibility during discussion of Article 13: *Legislative History*, Vol. 1, 446.

2.3 Parental Authority

While various delegations emphasised different aspects of Article 5, they were all clear that it sought to balance the rights of the child, the parents and the state. That led some to express concern that its effect would be to curtail parental authority and, in order to offset that risk, the Federal Republic of Germany proposed inclusion in the Convention of the following provision:

> Nothing in this Convention shall affect the right and the duty of parents and, where applicable, legal guardians to take measures as are required for the upbringing and well-being of the child (E/CN.4/1988/WG.1/WP.22, para. 29 and *Legislative History*, Vol. 1, 360).[14]

When the matter was raised in relation to Article 5, one gets a sense that some delegates were anxious to avoid revisiting an issue that, it was emphasised, had been 'discussed at length' in the context of article 14 (E/CN.4/1988/WG.1/WP.22: para. 30 and *Legislative History*, Vol. 1, 360), when a sharp division emerged between states that insisted on children being raised in their parents' (or father's) religion and those that saw scope for the child to exercise freedom of choice (*Legislative History*, Vol. 1, 458–459).[15] Consensus proved elusive and the final text simply requires the States parties to respect both the child's right to freedom of thought, conscience and religion and the rights of parents (and others) to provide direction to the child in a manner consistent with the child's evolving capacities.

The nature of the child-parent relationship was also addressed when the representative of Senegal[16] proposed the addition of the following article:

---

[14] The proposal was to insert this provision into what became Article 41 (respect for higher standards) of the final text. No such provision was inserted.

[15] The Permanent Representative of Bangladesh wrote to the UN Office in Geneva requesting that a paper be annexed to the report of the Working group in 1986: E/CN.4/1986/39, annex IV. It contained the following statements: 'Article 7 (bis) [later Article 14] appears to run counter to the traditions of the major religious systems of the world and in particular to Islam. It appears to infringe upon the sanctioned practice of a child being reared in the religion of his parents. We believe that the article as presently drafted will give rise to considerable difficulties in application and appears also to be in conflict with Article 8.' The Permanent Representative of Morocco made a similar request in respect of a paper noting that, in Morocco, the child is raised in the father's religion: E/CN.4/1987/WG.1/WP.35.

[16] The representative of Senegal proposed, but later withdrew, another new article requiring States parties to 'provide, in case of need, appropriate assistance to the family with a view to helping it to assume its responsibilities for the harmonious development of the child', E/CN.4/1989/WG.1/WP.17 and *Legislative History*, Vol. 1, 363.

> The child has the duty to respect his parents and to give them assistance, in case of need (E/CN.4/1989/WG.1/WP.17 and *Legislative History*, Vol. 1, 363).[17]

While that proposal garnered a degree of support, some of the drafters who were sympathetic to the sentiment it articulated felt that the obligation on a child to respect his or her parents was a moral, rather than a legal, one. The representative of Senegal accepted the Canadian suggestion that this matter might more appropriately be explored in the context of education and, in the event, what became Article 29 (aims of education) states, as one of the objectives of education, 'the development of respect for the child's parents' (Article 29(1)(c)).

2.4 Beyond Parents

The early drafts of Article 5 focussed on the role of the child's parents and legal guardians and, during the technical review in 1988, concern was expressed that the draft Convention as a whole, 'may not adequately recognize the role of the extended family and community when parental care is not available', noting that 'cultures, traditions and customs in many countries and areas provide for such a role' (E/CN.4/1989/WG.1/CRP.1/Add.1, para.13 and *Legislative History*, Vol. 1, 361). That concern was taken on board during the Second Reading (1988–1989) and, while some disquiet was voiced over the extent to which inclusion of the broader group would alter 'the traditional triangular responsibility for the child', there was no strong opposition to amending the text to accommodate this aspect of cultural diversity (E/CN.4/1989/48, para. 180 and *Legislative History*, Vol. 1, 362). In this, the inclusion, where applicable, of 'members of the extended family or community as provided for by local custom' reflects recognition of the broader group and of its possible role both when parental care is present and when it is absent.

Article 5, as adopted by the General Assembly on 20 November 1989, provides:

> States Parties shall respect the responsibilities, rights and duties of parents or, where applicable, the members of the extended family or community as provided for by local custom, legal guardians or other persons legally responsible for the child, to provide, in a manner consistent with the evolving capacities of the child, appropriate direction and guidance

---

17 A provision along these lines is found in the African Charter on the Rights and Welfare of the Child, Art. 31(a). See further, Sloth-Nielsen and Mezmur, 2008.

in the exercise by the child of the rights recognized in the present Convention.

3 The Content of Article 5

As we have seen, Article 5 seeks to regulate the roles of the parties in what is a triangular relationship. At the apex of the triangle, sits the child and the focus of Article 5 is the exercise, by the child, of his or her Convention rights. At one corner of the base, are the parents and, sometimes, the wider family or community, with the right to provide appropriate direction and guidance to the child in a manner consistent with the child's evolving capacities.[18] At the other corner, is the State party, with the obligation to respect the parents' right to provide that direction and guidance. Couched in these terms, Article 5 presents as a neat, conceptual, legal structure, but what does this tidy formulation really mean and does it make a difference beyond what is achieved by other provisions in the Convention?

Bearing in mind the 'universal, indivisible, interdependent, and interrelated' nature of human rights,[19] understanding the content of Article 5 requires situating it in its wider human rights context, reading it alongside other human rights instruments and other provisions in the CRC itself and, in particular, its general principles. While the work of other human rights bodies and the abundant scholarly literature in the field are of assistance in amplifying the obligations under the CRC, it is the UNCteeRC that makes the major contribution to understanding the substance of a particular provision. First, through its *Days of Discussion* and its *General Comments*, it clarifies what it regards as being required by the various provisions.[20] Secondly, it provides feedback to States parties in its *Concluding Observations* on their periodic reports. In addition,

---

18 Kamchedzera (2012: para. 23) characterises Art. 5 as reflecting the child's right to receive appropriate direction and guidance, placing a correlative duty on parents to provide it. While Tobin and Varadan (2019: 161) endorse that characterisation, their detailed analysis of the duty owed by States parties to parents (164–169), reflects acknowledgement that a right (at least, vis à vis the state) is bestowed on parents by Art. 5.

19 Vienna Declaration and Programme of Action UN Doc A/CONF.157/23, adopted 12 July 1993, para 5. See also, Committee on the Rights of the Child, *General Comment No. 7* (2005) *Implementing child rights in early childhood*, CRC/C/GC/7/Rev.1, para. 3 ('The Committee reaffirms that the Convention on the Rights of the Child is to be applied holistically in early childhood, taking account of the principle of the universality, indivisibility and interdependence of all human rights.').

20 In this chapter, selective examples of *Concluding Observations* from the last five years are used by way of illustration.

since 2014, it has been empowered to receive "communications", as they are known – essentially, individual complaints about alleged violation of Convention rights by a State party that has ratified the Third Optional Protocol – and to make determinations thereon.[21] Yet only 2 of the 22 cases decided under the complaints procedure thus far raised an Article 5 issue and, even then, only alongside numerous other Convention provisions.[22] Of the 65 cases pending, only three do so, again, alongside many other Convention provisions.[23] Before we drill down into the content of Article 5, using these various resources to inform a textual analysis, it may be helpful to reflect upon it in the context of a criticism levelled at the CRC more generally.

3.1 The Convention, the Family and Parental Authority

Critics of the CRC sometimes argue that recognising children as right-holders makes them autonomous, undermining the family and parental authority and leaving children unprotected and burdened with responsibilities they are not equipped to assume (Hafen and Hafen, 1996).[24] Yet the CRC recognises the importance of the family, with its Preamble echoing the reference to protecting the family 'as the fundamental group of society', found in earlier human rights instruments, and elaborating on that theme with the addition of the words 'and the natural environment for the growth and wellbeing of all its members and particularly children.' The important role of parents in the child's life is reflected in numerous articles in the Convention, including Article 5.[25] Nor are children left to their own devices, with their best interests being accorded primacy by Article 3(1), States parties being required to ensure their care and

---

21 *Optional Protocol to the Convention on the Rights of the Child on a Communications Procedure*, A/RES/66/138 (2011). Communications may also relate to breaches of the First and Second Optional Protocols to the Convention where the State party complained of has ratified the relevant Protocol.
22 These figures state the position as at 6 August 2019. The two cases, *S.H. v. Finland* CRC/C/81/D/6/2016 and *J.S.H.R. v. Spain* CRC/C/81/D/13/2017, fell on admissibility grounds.
23 Case no. 30/2017 against Paraguay (lack of access to child allegedly abducted by mother, residing in Paraguay, by father residing in Argentina); Case no. 75/2019 against Germany (right to maintain personal relations and regular contact with both parents); Case no. 87/2019 against Finland (family reunification, parental deportation).
24 In contrast, Kamchedzera (2012: 30–39) criticises the 'obsession with "families", parenthood and adult-centred liberal relativism' in analysing Art. 5 and provides six reasons why this emphasis is misleading (in terms of his 'progressive dignified life' approach).
25 See also, Articles 3(2) (care and protection, taking account of the duties of parents), 9 (separation from parents), 10 (family reunification), 14 (freedom of thought, conscience and religion), 18 (parental responsibilities), 27(3) (provision of assistance to parents) and Article 29(1)(c) (development of respect for the child's parents).

protection by Article 3(2) and through the application of concepts like "the child's age and maturity" and "the child's evolving capacities".

Since its earliest days, the UNCteeRC has stressed the central role of the family, with a Day of General Discussion, in 1994, being devoted to, "The role of the family in the promotion of the rights of the child". There, the Committee recognised that, whereas 'traditionally, the child has been seen as a dependent, invisible and passive family member', the child now had a higher profile with the right to be heard and respected. In this context, it stressed the central role of the family as 'an essential agent for creating awareness and preservation of human rights, and respect for human values, cultural identity and heritage, and other civilizations' and acknowledged the need to find 'appropriate ways of ensuring balance between parental authority and the realization of the rights of the child.'[26]

Reflecting the fact that, in many societies, the wider kinship group plays an important part in nurturing and raising children,[27] the obligation placed on States parties under Article 5 extends, not simply to the child's parents, but also, where appropriate, to members of the extended family or community as provided for by local custom. In its elaboration on what this means, the UNCteeRC has taken an inclusive approach, reaching beyond the traditional to embrace more recent developments by referring to 'the nuclear family, the extended family, and other traditional and modern community-based arrangements' (*General Comment No. 7 (2005)*, para. 35). When it turned its attention to children in street situations, it noted that many retain contact with their families but, for those who do not, it recognised that the community becomes all the more important and endorsed support being provided by 'trustworthy adults associated with civil society organizations' *General Comment No. 21 (2017)*, para. 35).

In its *Concluding Observation* on States parties' periodic reports, the UNCteeRC has expressed concern that many are not doing enough to combat the obstacles some families experience in parenting, highlighting the particular difficulties faced by those impacted by poverty[28] and in indigenous, minority and Roma communities, where children are at higher risk of family separation and

---

26　Committee on the Rights of the Child, Report on the fifth session, January 1994, CRC/C/24, Annex V, p. 63.

27　Examples of wider family groups include the African, First Nation Canadian and Native American tribe, the Hawaiian *'ohana* and the Maori *whānau*.

28　See, for example, UNCteeRC *Concluding Observations* on Argentina, CRC/C/ARG/CO/5-6, 2018, para. 36; Australia, CRC/C/AUS/CO/4, 2012, para. 50; Brazil, CRC/C/BRA/CO/2-4, 2015, para. 46; Honduras, CRC/C/HND/CO/4-5, 2015, para. 51; Mongolia, CRC/C/MNG/CO/5, 2017, para. 26; Pakistan, CRC/C/PAK/CO/5, 2016, para. 42; Senegal, CRC/C/SEN/

institutionalisation.[29] It has been troubled by the prevalence of children without parental supervision who serve as heads of household and are vulnerable to abuse, neglect, and other rights violations.[30] Numerous countries have been criticised for not doing enough to help working parents[31] and the Committee has repeatedly recommended that States parties take account of the effect on children of parental incarceration.[32] It has noted the continuing impact of gender inequality on parents, in some countries and, where this applies, has recommended that mothers and fathers be given equal legal responsibility for children[33] and an end to the practice of taking children away from their mothers' care at a certain age in the event of parental divorce.[34] It is clear, then, that

---

CO/3-5/, 2016, para. 44; Switzerland, CRC/C/CHE/ CO/2-4, 2017, para. 52; Timor-Leste, CRC/C/TLS/CO/2-3, 2015, para. 38; and Uruguay, CRC/C/URY/CO/3-5, 2015, para. 45.

29 See, for example, UNCteeRC *Concluding Observations* on Bulgaria, CRC/C/BGR/CO/3-5, 2017, para. 35; France, CRC/C/FRA/CO/5, 2016, para. 53; Ireland, CRC/C/IRL/CO/3-4, 2016, para. 43; New Zealand, CRC/C/NZL/CO/5, 2016, para. 27; Norway, CRC/C/NOR/CO/5-6, 2018, para. 21; Pakistan, CRC/C/PAK/CO/5, 2016, para. 42; and Romania, CRC/C/ROU/CO/5, 2017, para. 28.

30 See, for example, UNCteeRC *Concluding Observations* on Kenya, CRC/C/KEN/CO/3-5, 2016, para. 41; Mongolia, CRC/C/MNG/CO/5, 2017, para. 25; South Africa, CRC/C/ZAF/CO/2, 2016, para. 42; and Tanzania, CRC/C/TZA/CO/3-5, 2015, para. 48.

31 See, for example, UNCteeRC *Concluding Observations* on Australia, CRC/C/AUS/CO/4, 2012, para 49 (latest available); France, CRC/C/FRA/CO/5, 2016, para 55; Gambia, CRC/C/GMB/CO/2-3, 2015, para 52; Jamaica, CRC/C/JAM/CO/3-4, 2015, para 36; Maldives, CRC/C/MDV/CO/4-5, 2016, para 50; Peru, CRC/C/PER/CO/4-5, 2016, para 45; Suriname, CRC/C/SUR/CO/3-4, 2016, para 23; and the United Kingdom of Great Britain and Northern Ireland, CRC/C/GBR/CO/5, 2016, paras 50-51.

32 See, for example, UNCteeRC *Concluding Observations* on Bangladesh, CRC/C/BGD/CO/5, 2015, para. 50; Brazil, CRC/C/BRA/CO/2-4, 2015, para. 49–50; Dominican Republic, CRC/C/DOM/CO/3-5, 2015, para. 45; Guinea, CRC/C/GIN/CO/3-6, 2019, para. 32; Iran, CRC/C/IRN/CO/3-4, 2016, para. 63; Malawi, CRC/C/MWI/CO/305, 2017, para. 31; Mauritius, CRC/C/MUS/CO/3-5, 2015, para. 47; Norway, CRC/C/NOR/CO/5-6, 2018, para. 21; Qatar, CRC/C/QAT/CO/3-4, 2017, para. 27–28; Samoa, CRC/C/WSM/CO/2-4, 2016, para. 39; Sweden, CRC/C/SWE/CO/5, 2015, para. 36; Switzerland, CRC/C/CHE/ CO/2-4, 2017, para. 52; United Arab Emirates, CRC/C/ARE/CO/2, 2015, para. 51; and the United Kingdom of Great Britain and Northern Ireland: CRC/C/GBR/CO/5, 2016, para. 54.

33 See, for example, UNCteeRC *Concluding Observations* on Bhutan, CRC/C/BTN/CO/3-5, 2017, para. 28(a)(b); Central Africa Republic, CRC/C/CAF/CO/2, 2017, para. 47, Gambia, CRC/C/GMB/CO/2-3, 2015, para. 51; Senegal, CRC/C/SEN/CO/3-5/, 2016, para. 44; and Iraq, CRC/C/IRQ/CO/2-4, 2015, para. 50.

34 See, for example, UNCteeRC *Concluding Observations* on Gabon, CRC/C/GAB/CO/2, 2016, para. 40; Gambia, CRC/C/GMB/CO/2-3, 2015, para.51; Iraq, CRC/C/IRQ/CO/2-4, 2015, para. 50; Kenya, CRC/C/KEN/CO/3-5, 2016, para. 39; Oman, CRC/C/OMN/CO/3-4, 2016, para. 43; Pakistan, CRC/C/PAK/CO/5, 2016, para. 32; Saudi Arabia, CRC/C/SAU/CO/3-4, 2016, para. 32; United Arab Emirates: CRC/C/ARE/CO/2, 2015, para. 47.

the UNCteeRC is alert to the importance of the family environment and of parental involvement with children.

There is no denying that the Convention brought a radical change in the recognition of children's rights. That, after all, was its purpose. It will be recalled that, during the drafting of the Convention, a small number of states sought the addition of a provision that would have secured for parents almost-unfettered authority over their children.[35] Happily, they did not prevail because, had they done so, the rights guaranteed to children by the Convention would have been downgraded from entitlements to privileges, available only at the discretion of their parents. Instead, the Convention places limits on parental authority, through its general principles, sectoral rights and the balancing exercise embodied in Article 5.

Article 5 does not, however, pose a threat to healthy families. It and other provisions in the Convention aim to secure respect for the rights of children and to prevent families from becoming havens for tyrants, just as the United Nations Convention on the Elimination of Discrimination Against Women[36] sought to end the scope for the tyranny that can flow from gender-based inequality in families. Parents and others who find these developments threatening should, perhaps, ask themselves why.

---

35   See footnotes 15–16, above, and the accompanying text. A small number of States parties have shown a strong attachment to the notion of parental authority, entering declarations or reservations on the matter when they ratified the Convention. See, "Declarations and Reservations" at: https://treaties.un.org/Pages/ViewDetails.aspx?src=TREATY&mtdsg_no=IV-11&chapter=4&clang=_en [Accessed 31 October 2019]. The following declaration is one example: 'The Republic of Kiribati considers that a child's rights as defined in the Convention, in particular the rights defined in Articles 12–16 shall be exercised with respect for parental authority, in accordance with the Kiribati customs and traditions regarding the place of the child within and outside the family.' The last *Concluding Observations* on Kiribati were in 2006, CRC/C/KIR/CO/1, when the UNCteeRC urged withdrawal of the declaration, and the second report from Kiribati, lodged on 13 February 2019, notes its withdrawal. Poland made a similar declaration and the Holy See has entered a reservation that it 'interprets the articles of the Convention in a way which safeguards the primary and inalienable rights of parents, in particular insofar as these rights concern education (articles 13 and 28), religion (Article 14), association with others (Article 15) and privacy (Article 16).' See, UNCteeRC *Concluding observations* on Poland, CRC/C/POL/CO/3-4, 2015, paras. 6–7 (urging withdrawal of a declaration in similar terms) and on the Holy See, CRC/C/VAT/CO/2, 2014, para. 31 (welcoming plans to re-examine its reservations).

36   1249 U.N.T.S. 13 (1979), adopted 18 December 1979, entered into force 3 September 1981.

3.2 The State Party's Obligations to the Child

By requiring States parties to respect the responsibilities and rights of parents to provide direction and guidance to the child in exercising Convention rights, Article 5 does not absolve the state itself of its other responsibilities to children, including the obligation, under Article 3(2), to ensure to the child such protection and care as is necessary for his or her well-being, an obligation amplified in Article 19 (prevention of abuse and neglect) and other articles.[37] The UNCteeRC has made quite clear that, while recognition of the evolving capacities of young people means they have increased levels of agency to take responsibility and exercise their rights, this does 'not obviate States' obligations to guarantee protection', since 'engaging adolescents in the identification of potential risks and the development and implementation of programmes to mitigate them will lead to more effective protection' (*General Comment No. 20 (2016)*, para. 19).

The importance of this obligation to ensure that children are protected, as well as recognition of the family as the optimum environment for children-rearing and the state's role in supporting parents, is reflected in the UNCteeRC's *Concluding Observations* on States parties' periodic reports. It has noted, with approval, examples of states that offer guidance to families and caregivers on child rearing[38] or provide additional support to families living in poverty.[39] Numerous countries have been praised for making reform of the child care system a governmental priority,[40] while others have been recognised for their progress in deinstitutionalising out-of-family care of children;[41] for promoting

---

37 See also Articles 34 (sexual exploitation and sexual abuse), 35 (sale, trafficking and abduction) and 36 (other forms of exploitation).
38 See, for example, UNCteeRC *Concluding Observations* on Australia, CRC/C/AUS/CO/4, 2012 (last available), para. 49; Bhutan, CRC/C/BTN/CO/3-5, 2017, para. 28; Chile, CRC/C/CHL/CO/4-5, 2015, para. 52; Jamaica, CRC/C/JAM/CO/3-4, 2015, para. 36; Oman, CRC/C/OMN/CO/3-4, 2016, para. 43; and Switzerland, CRC/C/CHE/ CO/2-4, 2017, para. 44.
39 See, for example, UNCteeRC *Concluding Observations* on Jamaica, CRC/C/JAM/CO/3-4, 2015, para. 43; Peru, CRC/C/PER/CO/4-5, 2016, para. 45; and the United Arab Emirates, CRC/C/ARE/CO/2, 2015, para. 6.
40 See, for example, UNCteeRC *Concluding Observations* on Jamaica, CRC/C/JAM/CO/3-4, 2015, para. 38; Oman, CRC/C/OMN/CO/3-4, 2016, para. 45; Romania, CRC/C/ROU/CO/5, 2017, para. 28; and the United Kingdom of Great Britain and Northern Ireland, CRC/C/GBR/CO/5, 2016, para. 50.
41 See, for example, UNCteeRC *Concluding Observations* on Bulgaria, CRC/C/BGR/CO/3-5, 2017, para. 34; Georgia, CRC/C/GEO/CO/4, 2017, para. 26; Nauru, CRC/C/NRU/CO/1,2016, para. 5; Timor-Leste, CRC/C/TLS/CO/2-3, 2015, para. 32; Serbia, CRC/C/SRB/CO/2-3, 2017, para. 39; Turkmenistan, CRC/C/TKM/CO/2-4, 2017, para. 36; and Uruguay, CRC/C/URY/CO/3-5, 2015, para. 37.

family-based and general foster care;[42] and for increasing the number of children with disabilities and special needs being adopted.[43]

Conversely, the UNCteeRC has noted, with concern, that a small number of countries lacked any cohesive, consistent legal framework for alternative care and foster care[44] while, in others, insufficient human, technical and financial resources were allocated to the child protection system.[45] Many states have been urged to establish adequate safeguards and clear criteria for determining whether children should be placed in alternate care;[46] to provide support and facilitate family-based care for all children;[47] and the UNCteeRC has repeatedly recommended that material poverty should never be the sole justification

---

42 See, for example, UNCteeRC *Concluding Observations* on Antigua and Barbuda, CRC/C/ATG/CO/2-4, 2017 para. 36; Barbados, CRC/C/BRB/CO/2, 2017, para. 41; Mauritius, CRC/C/MUS/CO/3-5, 2015, para. 43; South Africa, CRC/C/ZAF/CO/2, 2016, para. 41; and Tanzania, CRC/C/TZA/CO/3-5, 2015, para. 48.

43 See, for example, UNCteeRC *Concluding Observations* on Serbia, CRC/C/SRB/CO/2-3, 2017, para. 41 and Yemen, CRC/C/YEM/CO/4, 2014, para. 53.

44 See, for example, UNCteeRC *Concluding Observations* on Mauritius: CRC/C/MUS/CO/3-5, 2015, para. 43; Nepal, CRC/C/NPL/CO/3-5, 2016, para. 43; and Switzerland, CRC/C/CHE/CO/2-4, 2017, para. 49.

45 See, for example, UNCteeRC *Concluding Observations* on Barbados, CRC/C/BRB/CO/2, 2017, para. 44; Cameroon, CRC/C/CMR/CO/305, 2017, para. 31; Estonia, CRC/C/EST/CO/2-4, 2017, para. 26; Georgia, CRC/C/GEO/CO/4, 2017, para. 26; Iraq, CRC/C/IRQ/CO/2-4, 2015, para. 53; Lebanon, CRC/C/LBN/CO/4-5, 2017, para. 26; New Zealand, CRC/C/NZL/CO/5, 2016, para. 27; Saint Vincent and the Grenadines, CRC/C/VCT/CO/2-3, 2017, para. 38; Slovakia, CRC/C/SVK/CO/3-5, 2016, para. 35; South Africa, 2016, CRC/C/ZAF/CO/2, para. 42; Suriname, CRC/C/SUR/CO/3-4, 2016, para. 24; United Kingdom of Great Britain and Northern Ireland: CRC/C/GBR/CO/5, 2016, para. 53; and Zambia, CRC/C/ZMB/CO/2-4, 2016, para. 42.

46 See, for example, UNCteeRC *Concluding Observations* on Chile, CRC/C/CHL/CO/4-5, 2015, para. 55; France, CRC/C/FRA/CO/5, 2016, para. 54; Gambia, CRC/C/GMB/CO/2-3, 2015, para. 53; Honduras, CRC/C/HND/CO/4-5, 2015, para. 54; Jamaica, CRC/C/JAM/CO/3-4, 2015, para. 39; Japan, CRC/C/JPN/CO/4-5, 2019, para. 29; Kenya, CRC/C/KEN/CO/3-5, 2016, para. 42; Nauru, CRC/C/NRU/CO/1, 2016, para. 37; Nepal, CRC/C/NPL/CO/3-5, 2016, para. 43; New Zealand, CRC/C/NZL/CO/5, 2016, para. 27; Oman, CRC/C/OMN/CO/3-4, 2016, para. 46; Samoa, CRC/C/WSM/CO/2-4, 2016, para. 34; Slovakia, CRC/C/SVK/CO/3-5, 2016, para. 35; and Zambia, CRC/C/ZMB/CO/2-4, 2016, para. 42.

47 See, for example, UNCteeRC *Concluding Observations* on Argentina, CRC/C/ARG/CO/5-6, 2018, paras 27–28; Belgium, CRC/C/BEL/CO/5-6, 2019, para. 28; Colombia, CRC/C/COL/CO/4-5, 2015, para. 34; Democratic Republic of the Congo, CRC/C/COD/CO/3-5, 2017, para. 31; France, CRC/C/FRA/CO/5, 2016, para. 54; Gabon, CRC/C/GAB/CO/2, 2016, para. 43; Ireland, CRC/C/IRL/CO/3-4, 2016, para. 44; Italy, CRC/C/ITA/CO/5-6, 2019, para. 24; Japan, CRC/C/JPN/CO/4-5, 2019, para. 29; Lebanon, CRC/C/LBN/CO/4-5, 2017, para. 26; Qatar, CRC/C/QAT/CO/3-4, 2017, para. 27–28; Saudi Arabia, CRC/C/SAU/CO/3-4, 2016, para. 33; Suriname, CRC/C/SUR/CO/3-4, 2016, para. 24; Timor-Leste, CRC/C/TLS/CO/2-3, 2015, para. 41; and Uruguay, CRC/C/URY/CO/3-5, 2015, para. 38.

THE ENIGMA OF ARTICLE 5 OF THE UNITED NATIONS CONVENTION   27

for removing a child from parental care.[48] It is clear, then, that numerous States parities are falling short in respect of their child protection obligations, although whether that stems from undue deference to parents, rather than a lack of resources or commitment, is a more complex issue that is outwith the scope of this chapter.[49] Certainly, in some countries, an appreciation of the value of family-based care – whether through support of the child's own family or by securing an alternative family environment – is lacking.

In each case, the UNCteeRC rarely makes specific reference to the obligation on States parties under Article 5, anchoring its observations and recommendations to other aspects of the Convention. To some extent, that is a product of the reporting process itself. The UNCteeRC has issued guidelines to States parties on the form and content of their periodic reports, most recently, in 2015.[50] States parties are directed that the treaty-specific portion of their report 'should not exceed 21,200 words' and that information about compliance with specific articles in the Convention should be provided under various headings – or "clusters" – which group cognate articles together, and address particular points.[51] Article 5 is clustered with Articles 9–11, 18(1) and (2), 20, 21, 25 and 27(4). While States parties are directed to address, 'Family environment and parental guidance in a manner consistent with the evolving capacities of the child (Art. 5)', as one of ten enumerated points for the cluster, many of the other points, like 'Separation from parents (Art. 9)', 'Children deprived of a family environment (Art. 20)' and 'Adoption (Art. 21)' may require more explanation. Bearing in mind the word limit, States parties may say little (or nothing) about Article 5, devoting attention to the other points. When the UNCteeRC publishes its *Concluding Observations*, the format mirrors this model based on the clusters and, while there are subdivisions within each of the clusters, it is

---

48 See, for example, UNCteeRC *Concluding Observations* on Colombia, CRC/C/COL/CO/4-5, 2015, para. 33; Dominican Republic, CRC/C/DOM/CO/3-5, 2015, para. 42; Lebanon: CRC/C/LBN/CO/4-5, 2017, para. 26; Malawi, CRC/C/MWI/CO/3-5, 2017, para. 29; Mauritius, CRC/C/MUS/CO/3-5, 2015, para. 44; Pakistan, CRC/C/PAK/CO/5, 2016, para. 41; and Romania, CRC/C/ROU/CO/5, 2017, para. 29.

49 For a forthright and comprehensive analysis of the shortcoming of the child protection systems in Aotearoa New Zealand, Australia, Canada and the United Kingdom, see, Cleland (2016: 131–146).

50 *Treaty-specific guidelines regarding the form and content of periodic reports to be submitted by States parties under Article 44, paragraph 1 (b), of the Convention on the Rights of the Child*, CRC/C/58/Rev.3, 2015. In addition, the Committee has made the Simplified Reporting Procedure available to States parties whose periodic reports are due from 1 September 2019 onwards: see, https://ohchr.org/EN/HRBodies/CRC/Pages/ReportingProcedure.aspx [Accessed 31 October 2019].

51 *Treaty-specific guidelines*, above, paras. 10 and 17, respectively.

in the nature of the issues other than the obligation under Article 5 that they tend to attract greater comment.[52] Nonetheless, there is the sense that, had Article 5 been absent, the important issues would still have been addressed, raising the question whether the drafters who thought it unnecessary might have had a point.

3.3 Respecting the Right of Parents and Others to Direct and Guide the Child

The underlying function of Article 5 is to mediate the relationship between the parents and States parties in facilitating the exercise, by the child, of Convention rights. In this, it applies not only to the exercise of rights within the family, but also to their exercise in all other settings: at school, in the medical arena (Mills and Thompson, in this volume), in adoption proceedings (Sloan, in this volume); in the child protection context (Black and McEwan-Strand/Skivenes, in this volume), in the public sphere and so forth (Henaghan, in this volume).[53] By requiring States parties to respect the rights and responsibilities of parents to direct and guide the child in exercising rights, Article 5 acknowledges their important role in the child's life. It does not, however, signal acceptance of unfettered parental authority. First, the obligation placed on States parties is one of respect, not mandatory deference.[54] Secondly, it applies only where the direction and guidance is both appropriate and provided in a manner consistent with the child's evolving capacities. Ultimately – and aside from cases where the communications procedure under the Third Optional Protocol is invoked – it will be for the State party to decide whether parental authority is being so exercised. What, then, is the import of these various qualifications?

3.3.1 Direction and Guidance

Does direction differ from guidance? It can be presumed that it does since, if the drafters had thought that the terms meant the same thing, there would

---

52   It is worth noting that, following the General Assembly resolution on *Strengthening and enhancing the effective functioning of the human rights treaty body system*, A/RES/68/268, adopted 9 April 2014, the UNCteeRC, at its 1928th meeting, agreed to 'reduce the word length of concluding observations by 20% of the current average length by the end of 2015'.

53   Addressing Art. 5 in the context of the child's choice of hair length; cultural identity; possible right to be breastfed; and right to be protected while maintaining bonds with parents.

54   As Tobin and Varadan note (2019: 165), the obligation to respect reaches beyond 'a negative obligation to refrain from interfering' to encompass 'a positive burden for states to take measures to ensure the effective enjoyment of a right'.

have been no need to use them both. The UNCteeRC does not elaborate on the distinction but, applying ordinary linguistic interpretation, it is reasonable to posit that direction takes the form of an instruction to the child, whereas guidance denotes something less peremptory and more in the nature of advice. Indeed, rather than being a dichotomy, direction and guidance can be viewed as something of a continuum.

3.3.2 "Appropriate" Direction and Guidance

What constitutes "appropriate" direction or guidance will be context-specific and other chapters in this volume explore what it means in particular settings.[55] However, some general observations may be made. Given the pervasive application of the general principles, direction or guidance that conflicts with any of them is unlikely to be deemed to be appropriate, always bearing in mind the scope for conflict between the principles themselves.[56] Thus, for example, direction that promotes or perpetuates discrimination prohibited by Article 2 would not be regarded as "appropriate" and the UNCteeRC has not been slow to criticise States parties for failing to do enough to tackle social and cultural norms and persistent patriarchal attitudes that present females as inferior to males.[57] Similarly, since Article 3(1) has been characterised by the UNCteeRC as both a substantive right and a fundamental interpretive legal principle,[58] parental guidance that does not accord primacy to the child's best interests would not be regarded as "appropriate".[59] Direction or guidance that

---

[55] While Tobin and Varadan (2019: 171 *et seq.*) predict that the 'meaning of "appropriate direction and guidance" will remain contentious', they note that this 'does not mean … that its contours are without limit', offering helpful analysis of how this plays out in various contexts.

[56] See, for example, the scope for conflict between Articles 3 and 12, discussed by Sutherland (2016: 34–35).

[57] See, for example, the *Concluding Observations* on Bhutan, CRC/C/BTN/CO/3-5, 2017, para. 28; Fiji, CRC/C/FJI/CO/2-4, 2014, para. 22; Gabon, CRC/C/GAB/CO/2, 2016, para. 41; India, CRC/C/IND/CO/3-4, 2014, para. 33; Iran, CRC/C/IRN/CO/3-4, 2016, para. 61; Iraq, CRC/C/IRQ/CO/2-4, 2015, para. 51; Jordan, CRC/C/JOR/CO/4-5, 2014, para. 17; Oman, CRC/C/OMN/CO/3-4, 2016, para. 43; Senegal, CRC/C/SEN/CO/3-5/, 2016, para. 43; Venezuela, CRC/C/VEN/CO/3-5, 2014, para. 27; and Yemen, CRC/C/YEM/CO/4, 2014, para. 29.

[58] Committee on the Rights of the Child, *General Comment No. 14 on the rights of the child to have his or her best interests taken as a primary consideration* (2013), CRC/C/GC/14, para. 6, describing Article 3(1) as a "threefold concept", the third element being that it is a rule of procedure.

[59] That point is reinforced by Article 18(1), recognising the primary responsibility of parents or legal guardians for the upbringing and development of the child and that 'the best interests of the child will be their basic concern'.

does not reflect respect for the child's right to life, survival or development, as required by Article 6, would, again, be inappropriate. So, for example, when the UNCteeRC turned its attentions to physical punishment of children, it roundly condemned the practice, finding that it not only violated Article 5, but also Articles 3, 6 and 19.[60] The fourth of the general principles, the Article 12 obligation to take account of any views the child wishes to express, is discussed more fully below in the context of the evolving capacities of the child.

Beyond applying the general principles, the open-ended nature of the word "appropriate" suggests that there may be scope for a State party to evaluate the quality of the parental direction or guidance. Arguably, that does not permit it simply to refuse to respect parental input with which it disagrees where the parental position falls within a range of reasonable views on the matter at hand. Direction or guidance that exposes the child to harm would, clearly, never be appropriate and there will be other instances where parental direction is so far outwith normal parameters that the State party may treat it as inappropriate. It is also worth bearing in mind that a loving, committed parent may, nonetheless, be a person whose judgment, generally or on a specific issue, is abysmal and it is the responsibility of the state to shield the child from it (see further Eekelaar, in this volume).

3.3.3   Evolving Capacities of the Child

States parties are only required to respect the parental right to direct and guide the child where the direction and guidance is provided in accordance with the child's evolving capacities. What, then, is meant by "evolving capacities"?[61] The UNCteeRC explains that the term:

> refers to the processes of maturation and learning whereby children progressively acquire knowledge, competencies and understanding, including acquiring understanding about their rights and about how they can best be realized (*General Comment No. 7 (2005)*, para. 17).

Its use reflects that fact that the CRC applies to all children and young people, from infants to 17 year-olds.[62] Like Articles 3 and 12, it acknowledges the unique

---

60   Committee on the Rights of the Child, *General Comment No. 13: The right of the child to freedom from all forms of violence* (2011), CRC/C/GC/13, developing what it said in *General Comment No. 8: The right of the child to protection from corporal punishment and other cruel or degrading forms of punishment* (2006), CRC/C/GC/8.

61   For a very full analysis of the discussion of "evolving capacities" in the UNCteeRC *General Comments*, see, Varadan (2019: 316–328).

62   Article 1, defining the child as 'every human being below the age of 18 years'.

nature of each child and the need for individualised assessment of their capacities. The UNCteeRC acknowledges that all children have capacities and makes clear that the concept should not be used as 'an excuse for authoritarian practices that restrict children's autonomy and self-expression' (*General Comment No. 7 (2005)*, para. 17).[63] In various *General Comments*, it expands on the different capacities of children, citing the example of the ability of an infant to recognise a parent or caregiver and bond with that person as the foundation of the child's development (*General Comment No. 7 (2005)*, para. 16). Beyond infancy, it counsels that parental direction and guidance will 'compensate for the lack of knowledge, experience and understanding of the child' but that, as the child develops in these respects, the parent will 'have to transform direction and guidance into reminders and advice and later to an exchange on an equal footing' (*General Comment No. 12*, para. 84). The child's evolving capacities are not determined simply by age, since children of the same age may differ one from another, and a given child may demonstrate greater competency in some situations than in others, with economic, social and cultural factors playing a part in the child's opportunity to develop his or her abilities (*General Comment No. 7*, para. 17). In this, evolving capacity both overlaps with, and is broader than, the concept of "age and maturity" found in Article 12.

Gerison Lansdown's (2005: x) much-cited conceptual framework of evolving capacities as a developmental concept, a participatory or emancipatory concept and a protective concept highlights the considerable overlap between evolving capacities and the general principles embodied in Articles 3 and 12. (see also Kilkelly, in this volume) As we have seen, Article 5 does not absolve States parties of their obligation, under Article 3(2), to ensure to the child such protection and care as is necessary for his or her well-being.[64] Does Article 5 do anything more? While both Articles 3(2) and 5 acknowledge the role of parents and states, article 3(2) is confined to the child who may be in need of protection when, it can be assumed, the child's capacities would be an inherent part of assessing the need for protection and the form of any protection required. Article 5 is broader in scope and covers the role of parents, and the State party's obligation to respect it, in any exercise of rights by the child.

Turning to the participatory or emancipatory nature of evolving capacities, does Article 5 add anything to the obligation, embodied in Article 12, to take

---

63 See also Committee on the Rights of the Child, *General Comment No. 20* (2016), para. 18, describing "evolving capacities" as 'an enabling principle that addresses the process of maturation and learning through which children progressively acquire competencies, understanding and increasing levels of agency to take responsibility and exercise their rights.'
64 See footnotes 37–50, above, and accompanying text.

account of any views the child wishes to express, in all matters affecting the child, in accordance with the child's age and maturity? Again, Article 5 is broader, since it is not confined to the child's views, extending to the child's agency, more generally.

4 Conclusions

Article 5 seeks to facilitate the exercise, by children and young people, of the rights guaranteed to them by the Convention. For some of its drafters, its importance lay in protecting the family from undue state intrusion, enabling parents and, sometimes, the wider kinship group, to provide the child with direction and guidance in exercising rights. Others emphasised the need to protect children within the family in order to secure their opportunity to exercise Convention rights. Yet other of the drafters, however, thought Article 5 to be unnecessary.

In so far as Article 5 regulates the power balance between parents (and, where appropriate, members of the extended family or community) and the state, it can certainly be argued that article 18(1) protects parents from undue state interference by acknowledging that they 'have the primary responsibility for the upbringing and development of the child,' albeit, it makes no mention of the wider kinship group. Similarly, it can be argued that children are given a degree of protection within the family by numerous of the Convention's provisions, in particular, Articles 3 and 12. Perhaps the nay-sayers had a point.

Yet Article 5 makes a vital contribution to the realisation of children's rights. First, it addresses squarely the place of parents and the state in the exercise of rights by the child, providing the criteria to be applied in striking the crucial balance between their respective roles. As we have seen, its low profile in *Concluding Observations* is, in all probability, a function of the reporting process itself. Nor can the fact that Article 5 has yet to feature prominently in cases decided under the CRC communications procedure be regarded as significant. The procedure itself is in the early days of operation and few cases have been decided under it. Not only is Article 5 cited in pending cases, but there is the, as yet, unrealised possibility of it being used in domestic courts once the jurisprudence on it under the communications procedure develops. In that, its full potential has still to be realised, something explored in other chapters in this volume when it is applied in a variety of specific contexts.

Secondly, had Article 5 been omitted, the concept of the child's evolving capacities would have been confined to the narrow ambit of their right to freedom of thought, conscience and religion, guaranteed by Article 14. It now has a central place, applying to the exercise of rights by the child across the board where parents seek to offer direction and guidance. As a result, the UNCteeRC has taken the opportunity, in numerous *General Comments*, to expand upon its content, elaborating on what it means both conceptually and in particular contexts, and the body of academic literature is growing. These contributions would not have been anything like as extensive without Article 5. Like the capacities of children themselves, our understanding of Article 5 and the scope for its application are evolving.[65]

By providing explicitly for balancing of the rights of the various players and articulating the pervasive application of the evolving capacities of the child, Article 5 makes a central contribution to the understanding and implementation of children's rights. In this, it reminds us, in the words of the UNCteeRC *General Comment No. 8* (2006), that, 'The child is not a possession of parents, nor of the State, nor simply an object of concern.'

Acknowledgement

My thanks go to Kaitlin Kelly, a Lewis and Clark Law School alumna, and to Poppy Prior, a Stirling Law School graduate, for their valuable research assistance.

References

Alston, P., "The historical origins of the concept of 'General Comments' in human rights law" in L. Boisson de Chazournes and V. Gowlland-Debbas, *The International Legal System in Quest of Equity and Universality: Liber Amicorum Georges Abi-Saab* (The Hague: Matinus Nijhoff, 2001).

Black, G., "Scotland's Named Person scheme: a case study of Article 5 UNCteeRC in practice", in this volume.

Boisson de Chazournes, L. and Gowlland-Debbas, V., *The International Legal System in Quest of Equity and Universality: Liber Amicorum Georges Abi-Saab* (The Hague: Matinus Nijhoff, 2001).

Cohen, C. P., "The Role of the United States in the Drafting of the Convention on the Rights of the Child", *Emory International Law Review* 2006 (20(1)) 185–198.

---

65 As Kamchedzera notes (2012: para. 75), 'the notion of the child's evolving capacities has only recently started to gain recognition as a principle applicable to all other rights in the CRC.'

Cleland, A., "A Long Lesson in Humility? The Inability of Child Care Law to Promote the Well-Being of Children" in E. E. Sutherland and L-A.B. Macfarlane (eds.), *Implementing Article 3 of the United Nations Convention on the Rights of the Child: Best Interests, Welfare and Well-being* (Cambridge: Cambridge University Press, 2016), 131–146.

Detrick, S. (ed.) with Doek, J. and Cantwell, N., *The United Nations Convention on the Rights of the Child: A Guide to the "Travaux Préparatoires"* (Dordrecht: Martinus Nijhoff, 1992).

Eekelaar, J. "Do Parents Know Best?", in this volume.

Hafen, B. C. and Hafen, J. O., "Abandoning Children to their Autonomy: The United Nations Convention on the Rights of the Child", *Harvard International Law Journal* 1996 (37(2)), 449–492.

Henaghan, M., "New Zealand Case Studies to Test the Meaning and Use of Article 5 of the 1989 United Nations Convention on the Rights of the Child", in this volume.

International Law Association: Committee on International Human Rights Law and Practice, *Final Report on the Impact of Finding of the United Nations Human Rights Treaty Bodies* (London, 2004).

Kamchedzera, G., *A Commentary on the United Nations Convention on the Rights of the Child, Article 5: The Child's Right to Appropriate Direction and Guidance* (Leiden: Martinus Nijhoff, 2012).

Kilkelly, U., "The limits of evolving capacity from a children's rights perspective", in this volume.

Lansdown, G., *The Evolving Capacities of The Child*, Innocenti Insights Series (Florence: UNICEF Innocenti Research Centre, 2005).

McEwan-Strand, A. and Skivenes, M., "Article 5 and children's role in cases of adoption from care", in this volume.

Mills, L. and Thompson, S., "Parental responsibilities and rights during the 'gender reassignment' decision-making process of intersex infants", in this volume.

Sloan, B., "Article 5 of the Convention on the Rights of the Child and the Involvement of Fathers in Adoption Proceedings: A Comparative Analysis", in this volume.

Sloth-Nielsen, J. and Mezmur, B. D., "A dutiful child: the implications of article 31 of the African Children's Charter", *Journal of African Law* 2008 (52(2)), 159–189.

Sutherland, E. E., "Article 3 of the United Nations Convention on the Rights of the Child: The Challenges of Vagueness and Priorities", in E. E. Sutherland and L-A.B. Macfarlane (eds.), *Implementing Article 3 of the United Nations Convention on the Rights of the Child: Best Interests, Welfare and Well-being* (Cambridge: Cambridge University Press, 2016).

Tobin, J. "Introduction: The Foundation for Children's Rights" in J. Tobin (ed.), *The UN Convention on the Rights of the Child: A Commentary* (Oxford: Oxford University Press, 2019).

Tobin, J. and Varadan, S., "Article 5: The Right to Parental Direction and Guidance Consistent with a Child's Evolving Capacities" in J. Tobin (ed.), *The UN Convention on the Rights of the Child: A Commentary* (Oxford: Oxford University Press, 2019).

Office of the United Nations High Commissioner for Human Rights, *Legislative History of the Convention on the Rights of the Child* (New York: United Nations, 2007).

United Nations Committee on the Rights of the Child, *General Comment No. 5: General Measures of implementation of the Convention on the Rights of the Child* (2003), CRC/GC/2003/5.

United Nations Committee on the Rights of the Child, *General Comment No. 7: Implementing child rights in early childhood* (2005), CRC/C/GC/7/Rev.1.

United Nations Committee on the Rights of the Child, *General Comment No. 8: The right of the child to protection from corporal punishment and other cruel or degrading forms of punishment* (2006), CRC/C/GC/8.

United Nations Committee on the Rights of the Child, *General Comment No. 12: The Right of the Child to be Heard* (2009), CRC/C/GC/12.

United Nations Committee on the Rights of the Child, *General Comment No. 13: The right of the child to freedom from all forms of violence* (2011), CRC/C/GC/13.

United Nations Committee on the Rights of the Child, *General Comment No. 14 on the right of the child to have his or her best interests taken as a primary consideration (Art. 3, para. 1)* (2013), CRC/C/GC/14.

United Nations Committee on the Rights of the Child, *General Comment No. 20 on the implementation of the rights of the child during adolescence* (2016), CRC/C/GC/20.

United Nations Committee on the Rights of the Child, *General Comment No. 21 on children in street situations* (2017), CRC/C/GC/21.

United Nations Committee on the Rights of the Child, *Treaty-specific guidelines regarding the form and content of periodic reports to be submitted by States parties under article 44, paragraph 1 (b), of the Convention on the Rights of the Child*, CRC/C/58/Rev.3, 2015.

Varadan S., "The Principle of Evolving Capacities under the UN Convention on the Rights of the Child", *The International Journal of Children's Rights* 2019 (27(2)) 306–338.

CHAPTER 2

The Scope and Limitations of the Concept of Evolving Capacities within the CRC

Gerison Lansdown

1   **Introduction**

Article 5 is a unique provision in international human rights law, introducing for the first time a triangular relationship of rights, responsibilities and accountabilities between the child, the child's parents or caregivers and the state (Vuckovic Sahovic et al., 2012: 155–164). Its wording represents acknowledgement that although all the rights embodied in in the UN Convention on the Rights of the Child apply to all children, the nature of their realisation and the responsibility for their exercise will change in accordance with the growing maturity of the child. Its gradual evolution within the Convention text reflects the growing awareness of the implications of children as rights holders that took place over the 10 year drafting process. The original Polish draft contained no provision addressing the issues contained in Article 5 (Legislative History, Vol 1, 2007:357). Proposals were subsequently put forward to introduce a focus on the autonomy of the family and respect for their rights and responsibilities, reflecting existing provisions in other treaties (Legislative History, Vol 1, 2007:358).[1] However, further debate highlighted the imperative for a clearer focus on the rights of the child and led to the introduction of recognition that parents' rights and duties must address and be understood in accordance with the child's rights and their evolving capacities. In other words, the exercise of parental rights and duties must take account of the gradual capacity of the child to take increasing responsibilities for her or himself. The drafters were concerned to ensure that, while affirming the critical role of parents in providing direction and guidance to children, the rights of children should not rely exclusively on the parents without any role from the State (Legislative History, Vol 1:360). In this way, they acknowledged and sought to address the fundamental challenge in recognising the rights of a child through the transforma-

---

1   Articles 18 and 23, Covenant on Civil and Political Rights (CCPR); Article 10, Covenant on Economic, Social and Cultural Rights.

tion that takes place in the first 18 years of life, and the consequent differences in strategies and approaches to implementation.

2   CRC, Status of Childhood and other Comparable Treaties

In order to understand the significance of Article 5, it is useful to examine the nature of the CRC in its entirety as a human rights treaty in relation to other treaties that seek to address the human rights of a particular group, for example, the Conventions addressing the rights of women, people with disabilities or racial minorities.[2] These three Conventions address the social exclusion of, and consequent denial of human rights for the group of people they address. They are explicitly focused on challenging discrimination experienced by those groups, ensuring the full and equal enjoyment of all human rights and fundamental freedoms and imposing obligations on States to ensure they are able to enjoy those rights on an equal basis with others. In other words, women and people with disabilities, for example, must be recognised and afforded equal status and rights with, respectively, men and people without disabilities. The CRC, in common with these treaties, also recognises that children are subjects of rights, and emphasises that no child must be discriminated against. However, unlike the other group-focused treaties, it is not principally focused on achieving equality in relation to another constituency whose rights are recognized. Rather, it explicitly recognises that children do not have the same status as adults. Its aim is to establish recognition, and responsibility for implementation, of the human rights of every child, including both those rights that they share with adults and the additional rights to which they are entitled by virtue of their greater vulnerability (Lansdown, 2013). Its focus on discrimination is to emphasise that all the human rights it embodies must apply without discrimination to all children irrespective of circumstance, including disability, sex or age. Non-discrimination is a right, but it is also a core principle according to which the CRC must be implemented, rather than the inherent objective of the treaty as a whole, which is the case in respect of, for example, CEDAW, CERD and CRPD. Article 5, with its focus on the evolving capacities of the child, is at the core of this fundamental difference.

Most societies operate with a presumption of capacity once a person reaches adulthood, at whatever age the law determines that to take place. However, these presumptions of capacity are often denied for certain groups such as

---

[2] 1965 Convention on the Elimination of all Forms of Racial Discrimination (CERD); 1979 Convention on the Elimination of all Forms of Discrimination against Women (CEDAW); 2006 Convention on the Rights of Persons with Disabilities (CRPD).

women, hence the necessity for dedicated human rights treaties to remove all legal, social, economic and cultural barriers to equality. By contrast, a presumption of legal incapacity usually applies in respect of children's decision-making, whether expressed formally or informally within a country's legal frameworks. Additionally, different groups of children are often treated with differing levels of respect for their capacities. In many cultures, for example, girls are significantly discriminated against within families, and afforded fewer opportunities for exercising autonomy, or making decisions affecting their lives. Children with disabilities are 'commonly, over-protected, infantilized and denied opportunities for their emerging autonomy' (Lansdown, 2014:102–03). Interestingly, Article 3 of the CRPD includes a reference to respect for children's evolving capacities as one of its core principles. This provision was necessary in order to ensure that the treaty was interpreted in its entirety to extend to children with disabilities as well as adults. The first principle in Article 3 insists on 'individual autonomy including the freedom to make one's own choices'. This was a fundamentally important principle established to challenge the traditional paternalistic denial of autonomy for so many people with disabilities. However, it is clearly not a principle that can extend to children of all ages. Newborn babies with or without disabilities, for example, cannot exercise autonomy. The inclusion of the principle of evolving capacities was therefore included to achieve two key goals. First, it ensured an interpretation of the CRPD that took full account of children, aligning it with the provisions of the CRC and in so doing allowing for the gradual increase in the exercise of rights throughout childhood. Secondly, it explicitly affirms the importance of recognition the capacities of children with disabilities. In other words, as in the CRC, the principle of evolving capacities reflects the need for additional direction and guidance from parents during childhood, while acknowledging children with disabilities as subjects of rights with increasing entitlement and competence to exercise those rights for themselves as they acquire maturity.

Significantly, then, all the Conventions focusing on particular groups address this issue of legal capacity (see, for example, Article 12, CRPD, and Article 15, CEDAW). However, in the case of the CRC, the aim is not to recognise equity of capacity with adults. Rather, it adopts a more nuanced approach in recognition of the emerging nature of capacities throughout childhood, and in order to address discrimination in respect of recognition of capacity between different groups of children. The concept of evolving capacities needs to be understood as informing the implementation of all rights in the CRC. While affirming that many human rights extend equally to children, the CRC also recognizes that children don't have exactly the same rights as adults, and it does not afford them autonomy. In that regard, although some civil and political rights are broadly similar to those elaborated in other human rights treaties, for example, right to freedom of expression and rights to privacy (Articles 13 and 16), others introduce qualifications. The right to freedom of thought, conscience and religion references the rights and duties of parents to provide direction and guidance in accordance with the child's evolving capacities (Article 14). The right to freedom of association lacks the explicit provision afforded in the International Covenant on Civil and Political Rights to join a trade union (CCPR, Article 22.1). In addition, voting and marriage rights do not extend to children. Despite these differences, it is evident that the inclusion of civil and political rights affirm the understanding of the original drafters that respect for children's agency was a central dimension of human dignity, of equal importance to children as to adults. A number of the socio-economic rights in the CRC are also similar to those included in other treaties but, for example, the right to an adequate standard of living in the CRC (Article 27) focuses on its importance for the child's development and the right to play (Article 31) is included in recognition of this critical dimension of childhood. Unsurprisingly, too, the focus on protection in the CRC is far stronger than in other treaties, incorporating the concept of best interests, and additional rights relating to protection from violence, exploitation, child labour, to alternative care and adoption, non-separation from family, and in respect of child labour, youth justice and armed conflict.[3]

The CRC, throughout, seeks to balance recognition of the continuing development of the child and their emerging capacities to exercise rights, while simultaneously ensuring that appropriate additional protections, in light of greater vulnerability, are in place. It also establishes that all the rights embodied in the CRC apply to all children but the nature of their implementation must necessarily acknowledge evolving capacity of each child.

3   Agency of Children as Subjects of Rights: Articles 12 and 5

In order to understand the approach embodied in the CRC to children's emerging agency as subjects of rights, it is important to examine the relationship between Articles 5 and 12. Unlike Article 5, Article 12 has been the focus of considerable attention over the 30 years of the CRC's life, both by the Committee on the Rights of the Child (the Committee), the international monitoring body for the CRC, and by governments, NGOs, UN agencies, and human rights institutions for children across the globe. It recognizes that every child capable of forming a view has the right to express that view on all matters of concern to them and have it given due weight in accordance with age and maturity. At the time of drafting, this was a profoundly radical provision. It potentially transforms the

---

3   See, for example, CRC, Articles 3, 19, 20, 21, 25, 32- 40.

traditional relationship between children and adults who have power of decisions over their lives, demanding that children themselves are involved in those decision-making processes. The Committee has emphasised that the interpretation of capability of forming a view must be applied very broadly to include, for example, very young children and those with disabilities who may not communicate verbally (General Comment No. 12: para. 21). It has also argued that the scope of Article 12 with regard to matters of concern to children must be afforded a very wide definition, that it applies both to individual children as well as children as a constituency, and that it needs to be understood both as an instrumental right and a principle to be applied the implementation of all other rights. In other words, it has both substantive and procedural application (*ibid.*). The Committee affirms that the wording of Article 12 makes clear that age alone is insufficient to determine the significance of the child's views, highlighting that 'information, experience, environment, social and cultural expectations and levels of support' all contribute to the development of the child's capacities in this regard (*ibid.*: para. 29). Accordingly, while it does not afford children a right to autonomous decision-making, it does demand their active engagement in those processes. In this regard, Article 12 also differs from the right to freedom of expression that entitles children to articulate their views and opinions, but places no corresponding obligation on governments to ensure that those views are actively sought and taken seriously (Lundy *et al.*, 2019).

However, whereas Article 12 establishes recognition of entitlement of children to be involved in the decisions that adults make on their behalf, Article 5 implies a gradual transfer of that decision-making responsibility to children themselves. In so doing, it seeks to balance the potential tension between recognition of the integrity of the family and the necessity of boundaries on that integrity in order to guarantee the rights of the child. That balance comprises four critical elements.

The first is the re-affirmation of the widely held principle that States must respect the primacy of parents in the upbringing of their children.[4] In so doing, it recognises the 'responsibilities, rights and duties of parents' and the consequent boundaries on any arbitrary intervention of the State into family life (Legislative History:359). This focus is consistent with the emphasis in the CRC of the family as the fundamental group of society, the natural environment for growth and well being, and the need for necessary protection and assistance to enable families to assume their responsibilities.[5] Article 5 also extends responsibilities, rights and duties, where applicable, to other members of the

---

4 Covenant on Civil and Political Rights, Article 23; Human Rights Committee, General Comment No. 19.
5 CRC preamble; CRC Article 18; and General Comment No. 4.

extended family or community where they are recognised by local custom. In so doing, it acknowledges that children can be cared for in diverse family forms, including the nuclear family, extended family, and other traditional and modern community-based arrangements, all of which are valid provided they are consistent with children's rights and best interests (General Comment No. 7).

The second key element of Article 5 relates to the nature of direction and guidance that parents or caregivers can provide to children. Parental responsibilities, rights and duties are not defined in the CRC, and there has been very limited attention paid to any subsequent elaboration by the Committee (Tobin and Varadan, 2019). However, Article 5 makes clear that they are not absolute or inalienable. They derive from the obligation to act in the best interests of the child and to enable the exercise by the child of their rights (Hodgkin and Newell, 2007:76). Any direction or guidance must be 'appropriate' which necessitates that it is provided in a manner consistent with and in conformity with the rights embodied in the CRC. Parents do not have *carte blanche* with regard to their treatment of children (Lansdown, 2005). Accordingly, parents cannot discipline or treat a child in ways that violate or neglect their rights, nor justify such behaviours on grounds of traditional cultures.[6] The Committee has emphasised the importance of ensuring the balance between parental authority and the rights of the child (Committee on the Rights of the Child, 1994: Annex 5, 63). And in order to achieve that goal, the State must introduce a legislative and policy framework to ensure protection of the child from violations of their rights within the family.[7] In this way, Article 5 acknowledges that children are not the property of their parents, thus challenging the unqualified authority traditionally held by parents in many societies around the world. The Committee argues that as children acquire competence, parents must 'transform direction and guidance into reminders and gradually to an exchange on an equal footing' (General Comment No. 12: para. 84; General Comment No. 20: para. 18).

Thirdly, any direction and guidance must also be directed to the 'exercise *by* the child of [their] rights' (emphasis added). This provision highlights not only that the child is a subject of rights, but affirms that the primary rationale for parental rights is to protect and promote those rights. By emphasising the child both as the rights' holder and also as the person primarily entitled to exercise those rights, it implies clearly that the role of the parent is to oversee and support that process. Parental rights are therefore time limited and exist purely to ensure respect, protection and fulfilment of the child's rights.

---

6 See, for example, Committee on the Rights of the Child (1995: paras. 7 and 13); Hodgkin and Newell (2007: 78).

7 See, for example, General Comment No.13: paras 38–44; CRC General Comment No. 8: para. 22.

Finally Article 5 asserts that the process of the gradual transition in the exercise of rights must be determined with regard to the 'evolving capacities of the child.' In other words, parents have a duty to recognise and support the gradual acquisition of greater autonomy on the part of the child, involving respect for the child's increasing agency in beginning to claim and exercise rights for him or herself consistent with evolving capacities (General Comment No. 7: para. 14). This principle elaborates the process by which the transfer of rights takes place. For example, a parent of a newborn baby is, appropriately, afforded the right to give consent to any potential medical treatment or intervention. However, once the child has acquired the capacity to understand the need for and implications of such an intervention, then the decision to give or withhold consent should transfer to the child. This unique provision in international law thereby recognises that children aged between 0–18 years cannot all be treated exactly the same. It allows them the opportunity to progressively exercise their rights, protecting them from the burden of full responsibility until they have developed the necessary capacities (Zermatten, 2014). As they acquire competencies, they require less guidance and direction and are increasingly able to take responsibility for their own decisions.

Both Articles 5 and 12 place new obligations on the State in arenas traditionally controlled by the adults in children's lives. Article 12 requires States to introduce the necessary mechanisms through which to ensure that children's voices are heard and taken seriously – in the family, in schools, in health care, in the courts, in policy making and so on (General Comment No. 12). Article 5 establishes a role for the State in creating boundaries on the exercise of parental authority. It is important to affirm that the CRC is not anti-parent. Indeed, it also places explicit obligations on States to protect and promote the family.[8] However, it does demand that children are visible as subjects of rights with increasing levels of agency within the context of the family, and accordingly constructs a tri-partite relationship between the parent, child and State in creating the necessary framework for support, protection and emerging autonomy.

4   Unpacking the Concept of Evolving Capacities

Article 5 has not been formally identified by the CRC Committee as one of the general principles to be applied in the realisation of all other rights, although arguably it should be (Hanson and Lundy, 2017). Tobin and Varadan (2019), for example, view as curious the failure to have established it as a general principle,

---

[8]   See, for example, Articles 8, 9, 10, 11, and 18.

given that it was acknowledged during its drafting process as relevant to the implementation of all rights (Legislative History: 358; Commission on Human Rights 1987: para. 101). However, the concept of the evolving capacities of the child has subsequently been recognised by the Committee as 'an enabling principle that addresses the process of maturation and learning through which children progressively acquire competencies, understanding and increasing levels of agency to take responsibility and exercise their rights' (General Comment No. 20: para. 18). And although, beyond Article 5, the concept of evolving capacities is only referenced in Article 14, the drafting committee reinforced the view of its application in the realisation of all other rights when discussing, for example, Article 15.[9] It provides a lens through which to interpret the implementation of the CRC in its entirety, obliging States create an environment to ensure respect for, protection and fulfilment of children's evolving capacities (Lansdown, 2005:15). However, it is vital to recognise that children's capacities do not evolve according to rigid developmental stages and that development is a dynamic process requiring a more nuanced cultural, social and contextual understanding.[10] Children, too, play an active role in constructing, influencing and interpreting their own lives and are not, as has commonly been assumed, passive recipients of inexorable biological or developmental processes. The inclusion in the CRC, therefore, of a concept of evolving capacities rather than fixed age limits, is integral to the implementation of children's rights in a manner that reflects and respects their realities on the ground and within the environments in which they grow up. It avoids the imposition of rigid assumptions as to when children acquire the potential to exercise rights on their own behalf, but allows for the fact that capacities span a range of qualities – moral, social, cognitive, physical and emotional – that do not necessarily develop according to a uniform pattern but are highly contingent on context.

5   An Emancipatory Concept: Respect for Evolving Capacities

Article 5 demands respect for the child's evolving capacities, recognising the child as a subject of rights, with gradual and increasing agency in exercising those rights for her or himself. Too often, the capacities of children are significantly

---

9   During discussion on Article 15, the right to freedom of association and assembly, the Working Group drafting the CRC, argued against a reference to the evolving capacities of the child on the basis that a generic article would encompass the principle with application across all provisions of the CRC (Legislative History, volume 1: 467).
10 See, for example, Bronfenbrenner, 1979; James, and Prout, 1997: 7–34; Lansdown, 2005: 13.

under-estimated, with many of the day-to-day decisions children do take responsibility for unrecognised or disregarded. For example, they are often actively engaged in multiple decisions on a daily basis – choosing friends, mediating in parental conflict, negotiating rules of play, keeping safe, managing deadlines, balancing school and work life (Lansdown, 2005: 29). Article 5 places an obligation on the adults in children's lives to acknowledge and respect those capacities and create opportunities for children to take growing levels of responsibility for all those decisions they wish to take for themselves. Clearly, many of those decisions operate within the immediacy of the family, and therefore involve a gradual negotiation only between parents and children. They are not amenable to legal age limits, nor would such an approach be appropriate or helpful. However, where those decisions require some external intervention, the Committee has pressed States to uphold the principle of respect for evolving capacities by introducing age limits that allow children from given ages to take certain key decisions below the age of 18 years. Examples include consent to health care and treatment, adoption, change of name, and application to family courts (General Comment No. 20: para. 39). Furthermore, where children below that age limit are able to demonstrate capacity, the Committee argues that they should be entitled to give or refuse consent. And in all cases, it recommends the introduction of a legal presumption that children, of whatever age, are competent to seek sexual and reproductive health commodities and services. Interestingly, however, to date, there has been no real encouragement or recommendation on States to consider lowering the voting age to below 18 years.

Legal age limits can only play a limited role in creating significant change in the reality of most children's lives with regard to respect for evolving capacity. Significant transformation to powerful social norms, and cultural attitudes and practices that define the status and treatment of children is also necessary. To this end, the Committee has consistently encouraged States to provide comprehensive support and education programmes to promote an understanding of parenthood conducted through dialogue, negotiation and participation (General Comment No. 7: paras. 20–21; General Comment No. 20: paras. 18 and 50). For example, it has not suggested an age limit on exercising the right to freedom of religion, but has highlighted the need to recognise that this right must be exercised by the child not the parent, with the child taking an increasing role in exercising choice throughout adolescence (General Comment No. 20, para. 43). The Committee also insists that all professionals working with and for children must be provided with training in children's rights that enhances knowledge and active respect for all its provisions (General Comment No. 5). And of course, children cannot exercise rights unless they are aware that they have them and therefore systematic inclusion of the CRC within the school curriculum is also a vital component of the investment in making their rights a reality.

6 A Protective Concept: Protecting Children's Evolving Capacities

Children, by virtue of their youth, evolving capacities and consequent relative vulnerability, are entitled to special protection from exposure to risks or environments likely to cause them harm or place them at risk. Implicit in the text of Article 5 is the recognition, not only that parents must respect children's evolving capacities, but equally, that they must not place excessive demands on them beyond those capacities (Lansdown, 2005). The nature of such protections include the right to protection from physical and emotional harm, harmful social and economic factors, exploitation and abuse as well as in personal decision-making. Provisions within the CRC exist in respect of all four dimensions, all centrally premised on the fundamental principle that the best interests of the child must guide the determination of any intervention, support or decision. In this way, the concept of evolving capacities provides the framework for understanding the nature of protections to which children are entitled, and to guide parental direction towards an appropriate balance between the child's emerging autonomy and protection in the exercise of their rights.

Of course, the nature and extent of protection afforded to children differs widely in accordance with cultural and religious practices, economic development and assumptions made of children's capacities in different parts of the world. Awareness of these contextual factors has led to the Committee adopting a fairly cautious approach when making recommendations with regard to age limits necessary to ensure appropriate protection of children. However, there are some exceptions. For example, it stresses that in some areas of law, such as marriage, smoking and alcohol, and hazardous work, the minimum age of 18 years should be imposed (General Comment No. 20). Interestingly, the Committee had earlier argued that as a matter of respecting children's evolving capacities, in exceptional circumstances, a marriage of child of 16 years could be permitted (General Comment No. 18: para. 19). However, a consultation undertaken in respect of the General Comment being drafted on adolescence revealed 100% support from adolescents themselves for a minimum age of 18 years and this influenced the Committee in its consequent recommendation.[11] The issue of children and work, however, is a fiercely contested issue. Their

---

11 Unpublished report by Gerison Lansdown, consultant to the Committee on the Rights of the Child in the drafting of General Comment No. 20.

exposure to work environments in many parts of the Global South would be considered highly unacceptable in the richer nations of the world, where such activities would be viewed as contrary or harmful to the child in light of their evolving capacities (Lansdown, 2005:33–41). And children themselves perceive the role of work very differently according to their own direct experience. A recent global survey of working children identified a complex and nuanced picture of their working lives, demonstrating that while for many there were powerful material drivers underpinning their need to work, such as helping their families in situations of poverty, there were also many potential benefits including enjoyment, acquisition of skills, and being more independent (O'Kane *et al.*, 2018). For these children, many argue that blanket age prohibitions on work are neither helpful nor protective. Indeed, the Committee has argued that age appropriate work plays an important developmental role in the lives of children (General Comment No. 20: paras. 85–86). Nevertheless, the Committee recommends implementation of ILO Convention 138, which does introduce minimum ages for full time work. In general, it recommends protective age limits where the activities affected are considered to be unequivocally harmful for children regardless of culture or context. Significantly, it also consistently encourages States to raise the minimum age for recruitment to the armed forces, or participation in armed conflict to 18 years, despite the rather weaker levels of protection afforded in the CRC or the Optional Protocol.[12] It has also recently re-issued its General Comment on youth justice and raised the recommended minimum age of criminal responsibility to 14 years, drawing explicitly on recent neuroscientific evidence of the evolving nature of adolescent development (General Comment No. 24: para. 22). However, on other issues, it has preferred to recommend that a protective limit be introduced but without actually providing guidance on the specific age recommended – for example, in relation to the age of sexual consent, and school leaving age. A further key dimension of the child's right to protection is that demands are not placed on them in excess of their capacities or through inappropriate developmental expectations – for example, young children being punished for disobedience when engaging in behaviours that are exploratory or curious, or placing work burdens on them that allow no time for necessary rest and play.

Central to the creation of protective environments, of course, are children themselves. On the one hand, in circumstances where children feel a sense of safety and security, their scope for exploring and gaining experience to build knowledge and competencies will grow. On the other, it is often children

---

[12] CRC, Article 38; Optional Protocol to CRC on the involvement of children in armed conflict, 2000; see, also, for example, Committee on the Rights of the Child, 2017: para 48.

themselves who have the most direct experience of the nature and scale of risks they face, and insight into the solutions needed to provide adequate protection (General Comment No. 20: para.19). In other words, protecting children in accordance with their evolving capacities relies on equal recognition of their emerging capacities in the exercise of their rights, both dimensions being mutually reinforcing.

7 A Developmental Concept: Fulfilling Children's Evolving Capacities

All children have a common set of needs that must be fulfilled if they are to thrive – for love and security, new experiences, praise and recognition and for responsibility – although the way in which those experiences can and will be provided will inevitably vary across different cultures (Kellmer-Pringle, 1980; Woodhead, 2015). Clearly, people develop throughout their lives, but early childhood, in particular, is recognised as a unique period of rapid growth and change when their immediate environmental experiences have huge and enduring impact on their future life chances (Lagercrantz, 2016). And increasingly, there is a growing consensus that adolescence is a period of significant changes to the brain structure and functions, which offers a critical window of opportunity for positive development and future life chances if their rights are appropriately fulfilled (Steinberg, 2014). There is now considerable research evidence documenting the profound negative impact of material deprivation, toxic stress and adverse childhood experiences and their links with both poor physical and mental health (see, e.g., CSDH, 2008; McLauglin, 2017).

The CRC provides a framework of rights designed to guarantee children positive environments in which to grow up to ensure their present and future wellbeing and development – to fulfil their optimum capacities. Article 6 provides the overarching foundation for children's right to life and development, while multiple other social and economic rights address the conditions necessary to achieve that goal – the right to an adequate standard of living, to social security, education, health care, and play. Many forms of physical and intellectual disability, as well as mental illness are linked with material factors such a poor diet, environmental pollution, risk of accidents, and are compounded by lack of access to health care. Critically, poverty can be argued to be the most formidable enemy of healthy child development (Lansdown, 2005). In addition, children's capacities will be impeded if they experience abusive or neglectful environments in their childhood and are denied opportunities to participate and take increasing but appropriate levels of responsibility for decisions within their own lives. Indeed, children's development can be understood as a process arising from participation in the social and intellectual life around them. Like adults, they build competence and confidence through direct experience. Active participation affords children increasing levels of a sense of autonomy, independence, and heightened social competence and resilience, depending on the levels of engagement and responsibility afforded to children (Chawla and Heft, 2002).

8   Conclusion

The evolving capacities of the child, understood through these three closely inter-dependent concepts of emancipation, protection and development, provides the thread that holds the CRC together. From birth to 18 years, the child undergoes a period of rapid transformation from the total dependency of babyhood to an emerging capacity for autonomy when approaching adulthood. The concept of evolving capacities offers a 'road map' to navigate the challenging task of implementing such a comprehensive framework of rights for children at such hugely different stages of life. While every child is entitled to the best possible health, the vulnerabilities of newborns and their consequent health needs differ profoundly from those of teenagers facing puberty, potential exploration of sexual relationships, engagement in more risk-taking activities, exposure to alcohol and other drugs, and stresses associated with exams and potentially negotiating the worlds of school and work. And alongside those differences, the degree of children's agency in making choices and exercising control shifts profoundly. States can only give meaningful effect to every right in the CRC if they understand and engage with the importance and the complexities of respecting children's evolving capacities in the legal and policy frameworks they construct. At the same time, the means by which they achieve that goal is relevant, with a need to engage children increasingly in policy development in ways that acknowledge their evolving capacities. Finally, in doing so, they must recognise the role of parents and other caregivers, and transitional nature of their rights and responsibilities with regard to children's evolving capacities. Families are entitled to support to enable them to fulfil their obligations to children to achieve optimum development, for example through the provision of education, health care, child care and social security. They also need to be encouraged to understand and respond to children's developmental needs to allow both for sufficient space for a flourishing and protected childhood while also respecting the need to gradually step back to allow the child to exercise increasing autonomy. At the same time, the State must impose boundaries on the privacy of families to ensure that the child can be protected from harm where necessary.

Article 5 was a relatively late entrant into the drafting process of the CRC. However, it is to the great credit of the drafters that they understood the need for a mechanism through which to interpret childhood and the realisation of their rights. It is perhaps, the most transformatory principle in the CRC, offering a lens for interpretation without which it would be a less dynamic, less meaningful and less profound human rights treaty. That being so, it is all the more surprising that so little attention has been afforded to Article 5 – perhaps it is time for the Committee to develop a general comment to elaborate its understanding of the role it plays in challenging the status quo for children around the world.

References

Bronfenbrenner, U., *The Ecology of Human Development: Experiments by Nature and Design* (Cambridge, Mass.: Harvard University Press, 1979).

Chawla, L. and Heft, H., "Children's Competencies and the Ecology of Communities: A Functional Approach to the Evaluation of Participation", *Journal of Environmental Psychology* 2002(22(1-2)), 201-216. DOI: 10.1006/jevp.2002.0244.

Commission on Social Determinants of Health, *Closing the Gap in a Generation: Health Equity through Action on the Social Determinants of Health* (Geneva: World Health Organization, 2008).

Hanson, K. and Lundy L., "Does Exactly What it Says on the Tin? A Critical Analysis and Alternative Conceptualisation of the So-called 'General Principles' of the Convention on the Rights of the Child", *International Journal of Children's Rights* 2017 (25(2)), 285-306. DOI: 10.1163/15718182-02502011.

Hodgkin, R. and Newell P., *Implementation Handbook for the Convention on the Rights of the Child* (3rd edn., New York: Unicef, 2007).

James, A. and Prout, A., "A New Paradigm for the Sociology of Childhood? Provenance, Promise and Problems", in A. James and A. Prout (eds.), *Constructing and Reconstructing Childhood* (2nd edn., London: RoutledgeFalmer, 1997).

Kellmer-Pringle, M., *The Needs of Children* (London: Hutchinson, 1980).

Lagercrantz, H., *Infant brain development: Formation of the mind and the emergence of consciousness* (Switzerland: Springer International Publishing, 2016).

Lansdown, G., *The Evolving Capacities of the Child* (Florence: Unicef, 2005).

Lansdown, G., *Using the human rights framework to promote the rights of children with disabilities: Discussion Paper: An analysis of the synergies between CRC, CRPD and CEDAW* (New York: Unicef, 2013).

Lansdown, G., "Children with disabilities", in M. Sabatello and M. Schultze (eds.), *Human Rights and Disability Advocacy* (Philadelphia: Penn Press, 2014).

Lundy, L., Tobin, J., and Parkes, A., "The right to respect for the views of the child", in J. Tobin (ed.), *The UN Convention on the Rights of the Child: A Commentary* (Oxford: Oxford University Press, 2019).

McLaughlin, K., "The long shadow of adverse childhood experiences", *Psychological Science Agenda*, April 2017, American Psychological Association.

Office of the United Nations High Commissioner for Human Rights, *Legislative History of the Convention on the Rights of the Child: Volume 1*, (New York: United Nations, 2007).

O'Kane, C., Meslaoui, N. and Barros, O., *It's Time to Talk: Children's Views on Children's Work* (Terres des Hommes/Kindernothilfe, 2018).

Steinberg, L., "The Science of Adolescent Brain Development and its Implications for Adolescent Rights and responsibilities" in J. Bhaba (ed.), *Human Rights and Adolescence* (Philadelphia: University of Pennsylvania Press, 2014).

Tobin, J. and Varadan, S., "The right to parental guidance in accordance with the child's evolving capacities", in J. Tobin (ed.), *The UN Convention on the Rights of the Child: A Commentary* (Oxford: Oxford University Press, 2019).

UN Committee on the Rights of the Child, *Day of General Discussion: The Role of the Family*, Report on 5th Session, 1994, CRC/C/34.

UN Commission on Human Rights, *Report of the Working Group on a Draft Convention on the Rights of the Child*, E/CN/1987/25, 1987.

UN Committee on the Rights of the Child, *General Comment No. 4: Adolescent health and Development in the Context of the CRC*, CRC/GC/2003/4, 2003.

UN Committee on the Rights of the Child, *General Comment No. 5: General Measures of Implementation of the Convention on the Rights of the Child*, CRC.GC/2003/5, 2003.

UN Committee on the Rights of the Child, *General Comment No. 7: Implementing Child Rights in Early Childhood*, CRC/GC/C/7, 2005.

UN Committee on the Rights of the Child, *General Comment No. 8: The Right of the Child to Protection from Corporal Punishment and Other Cruel or Degrading Forms of Punishment*, CRC/C/GC/8, 2007.

UN Committee on the Rights of the Child, *General Comment No. 12: The Right of the Child to be Heard*, CRC/C/GC/12, 2009.

UN Committee on the Rights of the Child, *General Comment No. 13: The Right of the Child to Freedom from all Forms of Violence* CRC/C/GC/13, 2011.

UN Committee on the Rights of the Child, *General Comment No 18 on Harmful Practices*, CEDAW/C/GC/31-CRC/C/GC/18, 2014.

UN Committee on the Rights of the Child, *General Comment No. 20 on the implementation of the rights of the child during adolescence*, CRC/C/GC/20, 2016.

UN Committee on the Rights of the Child, *General Comment No. 24 on children's rights in the child justice system*, CRC/C/GC/24, 2019.

UN Committee on the Rights of the Child, *Concluding observations of the Committee on the Rights of the Child: Holy See*, CRC/C/15/Add.46, 1995.

UN Committee on the Rights of the Child, *Consideration of reports submitted by States parties under article 44 of the Convention: Combined third to fifth reports of States parties due in 2012: Democratic Republic of the Congo*, CRC/C/DRC/CO/3-5, 2017.

UN Human Rights Committee, CCPR *General comment No. 19: Article 23 (The family)*, Thirty-ninth session, 1990.

Vuckovic Sahovic, N., Doek, J.E. and Zermatten, J., *The Rights of the Child in International Law* (Bern: Stämpfli, 2012).

Woodhead, M., "Psychology and the Cultural Construction of Children's Needs", in A. James and A. Prout (eds.), *Constructing and Reconstructing Childhood* (3rd edn., London: RoutledgeFalmer, 2015).

Zermatten, J., "Protecting and Promoting Adolescent Rights", in J. Bhaba (ed.), *Human Rights and Adolescence* (Philadelphia: University of Pennsylvania Press, 2014).

CHAPTER 3

Assessing Children's Capacity

Reconceptualising our Understanding through the UN Convention on the Rights of the Child

Aoife Daly

1   Introduction

There are many areas of law and practice in which the capacity of children (that is, under-18s) comes into question. Capacity may be considered in an everyday context to establish that children understand a medical procedure or another process affecting them. Or it may concern a significant point of law and therefore come to court. Capacity issues can arise in relation to such matters as deprivation of liberty for children with mental health problems (see *In the matter of D (A Child)* [2019] UKSC 42); where a child wishes to instruct her own lawyer (*S v SBH (Appeal FPR 16.5: Sufficiency of Child's Understanding)* [2019] EWHC 634); or where a child's capacity to consent to medical treatment is in question (*An NHS Foundation Trust v A & Others* [2014] EWHC 920).

In the everyday context, professionals make the decisions necessary in order to work in children's interests. In England and Wales the '*Gillick* competence' standard ostensibly guides these processes. Yet it remains the case that what children's capacity actually entails is little understood – it has proven notoriously hard to define (Hein, *et al.*, 2015[a]; Lansdown, 2005; Alderson and Montgomery, 1996: 11). To a large extent, those working with children and/or relevant laws work around capacity – applying experience and instinct – acknowledging capacity without knowing much about relevant research or theory. This intuitive approach is generally satisfactory and, in most cases, adults make a judgment about a child's capacity and problems do not arise (in the medical context see further e.g. Hein *et al.*, 2015[a]; Cave and Stavrinides, 2013: 12).

Capacity is the point on which many of children's rights and responsibilities turn, however, as sometimes a definitive capacity/no capacity judgment is required on a given matter. One important consideration in this area is that approaches to understanding and assessing capacity should be guided by the primary international children's rights instrument, the UN Convention on the Rights of the Child (CRC). Article 5 states that parents and other responsible adults are to guide children in the exercise of their rights 'in a manner

© AOIFE DALY, 2020 | DOI:10.1163/9789004446854_005

consistent with the evolving capacities of the child'. Yet despite the influence of the CRC, and despite the everyday nature of children's capacity issues, little thought has been given by theorists, lawyers and others to understanding how and whether children's capacity can be assessed in a rights-based way via the CRC.

This chapter seeks to reconceptualise approaches to assessing children's capacity, particularly in light of Article 5 of the CRC. Law and practice in England and Wales, and particularly medical law, serve as a case study through which to examine what capacity means in relation to children. After considering some relevant points of law and practice in this area, it is argued that efforts by professionals, theorists and others to understand capacity should be done via a process which is explicitly rights-based. The CRC after all represents the 'hard-won consensus of the global community' (Lundy, 2007: 933) and should therefore be at the forefront of law and practice concerning children, particularly in areas as ill-understood, contested and fundamental to the exercise of rights as capacity. An approach to children's capacity is proposed through four concepts based on the CRC: Autonomy, Evidence, Support and Protection.

2 The Complex Terrain of Children's Capacity in Medical Law

Many commentators in the past decade have criticised the binary approach to capacity, that is, the idea that one has capacity or not (see e.g. Herring, 2016; Donnelly, 2010; Foster, 2009). There have also been critiques of the fact that efforts to understand children's capacity tend to position rational adulthood as the ultimate goal in child development (Cordero Arce, 2015). Nevertheless, in some cases a yes or no answer is required to determine, for example, whether or not a child can directly instruct a lawyer, or consent to treatment. Therefore sometimes children's capacity must be assessed, because their autonomy rights depend on it. Herring argues powerfully why an accurate assessment of capacity is important:

> First, you could be assessed to lack capacity when you do not … You lose control over your life. But second, you could be assessed to have capacity when you do not have it. You could suffer harms and injuries and you would be told that that was your choice … (Herring, 2016: 55).

Medical law has served as the main vehicle through which children's capacity has been examined because medical consent is treated with great seriousness

(Alderson, 1994: 46); it is linked to the right to bodily integrity – a 'powerful principle which states that, except in a few situations, one person cannot touch another person' (Herring, 2016: 45). This chapter centres around medical consent in England and Wales therefore, as children's capacity has been considered in this area by courts and commentators to an extent unseen in other areas such as family law (Daly, 2018: 310).

The term "capacity" (sometimes used interchangeably with "competence"[1]) is used colloquially to refer to one's cognitive abilities, i.e. mental processes such as knowing, judging and evaluating. This will be the definition of capacity for the purpose of this chapter unless otherwise indicated. However, it is important to note that there are two elements of capacity – 1) *legal capacity*, referring to the standard for someone to make legally effective decisions; and 2) *mental capacity*, which refers to judgments about decision-making skills (Ruck-Keene et al., 2019: 58), denoting more of a sliding scale than a legal standard.

"Legal capacity" is used in the legal sphere to denote the standard for someone to make legally effective decisions, for example under the Mental Capacity Act (MCA) 2005 – the statutory framework in England and Wales for adults whose capacity to make specific decisions is in doubt – or "*Gillick* competence" for children under 16 years where they understand fully the matter at hand. Childhood in England and Wales has been defined as those under 18 years (General Medical Council, 2015). Adults are assumed to *have* capacity, and under-18s are generally legally assumed to *lack* it, on the basis that they ostensibly do not have the cognitive abilities to make decisions.

There are exceptions to this, of course. In the medical arena alone, obvious exceptions are evident – the age of consent to medical treatment in England and Wales is 16 (Family Law Reform Act 1969, s. 8), and the MCA applies to 16- and 17-year olds. However, in reality under-16s also need medical treatment, and they may need it independent of parental guidance. To deal with this reality, *Gillick* competence is relied upon to determine whether under-16s can themselves consent to treatment. *Gillick* has also become the standard for questions of children's capacity in other areas of the law such as decision making in the context of public and private family proceedings (*S v.* SBH, para. 51); and has had significant influence in other common law jurisdictions (Cave, 2014: 114).

It is not always easy to define exactly what "capacity" entails in practice, however. To turn to the MCA, it requires that an individual understands

---

1 The term "competence" to denote the legal standard has decreased in use in recent years, presumably because of the introduction of the Mental Capacity Act 2005 which uses the term "capacity". Confusingly regarding the legal standard in the case of children, the term "*Gillick* competence" is still used, although not exclusively. In *X. (A Child)* [2014] EWHC 1871: para. 12, for example, it was referred to as "*Gillick* capacity".

information but also retains, uses, weighs it; and communicates a decision (section 3[1]). Many theorists have written about the MCA and the challenges of pinning down exactly what capacity (in the case of adults) might be and how to assess it (see, e.g. Banner, 2013: 74–76; Donnelly, 2010: 142; Foster, 2009). Of ascertaining what capacity entails, Herring notes: 'This is clearly not a straightforward issue. The courts have avoided issuing general guidance' (2016: 46).

Similarly, there is a lack of elaboration beyond *Gillick* as to what *children's* capacity involves (Lansdown, 2005: xi). In the *Gillick* case (*Gillick v. West Norfolk and Wisbech Area Health Authority* [1986] AC 112) it was determined in England and Wales that doctors could provide contraceptive treatment to girls where they were deemed by the doctor to have 'sufficient understanding and intelligence' to 'understand fully what is proposed' (at 253). In *An* NHS *Foundation Trust Hospital v. P*, the court described *Gillick* competence as 'having a state of maturity, intelligence and understanding sufficient to enable her to take a decision as to medical treatment for herself' ([2014] EWHC 1650 (Fam): para. 12).

This appears to require a high level of understanding of what is involved in the matter in question. In *Gillick* the court elaborated that many factors beyond the medical advice would have to be understood for a child to have legal capacity to consent to such treatment. She would have to understand 'moral and family questions, especially her relationship with her parents, long-term problems associated with the emotional impact of pregnancy and its termination.' In *Re H (A Minor) (Role of Official Solicitor)* the court pointed to a similarly high level of understanding to instruct a lawyer: a child must have sufficient understanding to participate as a party in the proceedings which means much more than instructing a solicitor. It may also mean giving evidence and being cross-examined ([1993] 2 FLR 552: 554H).

There persists a lack of clarity surrounding the application of *Gillick* in practice, however. It seems that professionals are not always clear as to what exactly capacity for children entails, whether it be in the area of medicine (Cave, 2014; Cave and Stavrinedes, 2014: 16; Ashteka *et al.*, 2007: 632); in family law (Cashmore and Parkinson, 2009: 20–21); or social work (Thomas and O'Kane, 1998: 151). Yet for the most part the ability of children to consent to medical treatment is determined implicitly (Hein *et al.*, 2015[a]); 'day in and day out ... as part of routine' (Appendix to *A (A Child)* [2014] EWFHC 1445 (Fam.)). Indeed, *Gillick* refers to the discretion of the clinician to treat children and to refrain from contacting parents (174B-D) – so it is ultimately about enabling professional discretion rather than offering a clear means for assessing capacity.

Although implicit assessment generally suffices, the lack of clarity about what capacity entails can sometimes pose a problem. Disagreements can arise between patients and doctors about treatment, though this may not reach the public eye (Cave and Stavrinides, 2013: 5). There can then be differences of opinions between professionals as to whether the child in question actually *has* capacity (note disagreements between clinicians in *An* NHS *Foundation Trust Hospital v P*: para. 9; and *A (A Child)* [2014]: para. 8; and between lawyers in *S v.* SBH).

3 Considering What Capacity Entails

It seems that there is no quick-fix definition for professionals, then, of what capacity is, whether in the mental capacity or the legal capacity sense. Yet one can look to guidance from various quarters. In Ontario, Canada, a presumption of capacity applies to adults *and* children. A single test for capacity exists under the Health Care Consent Act 1996, section 4(1), that is, whether:

> the person is able to understand the information that is relevant to making a decision about the treatment, admission or personal assistance service, as the case may be, and able to appreciate the reasonably foreseeable consequences of a decision or lack of decision.

The key points seem to be about understanding information and consequences. Practice guidance advises nurses to use 'professional judgment and common sense to determine whether the client is able to understand the information' (College of Nurses of Ontario, 2017: 9).

In England and Wales, the MCA (section 3[1]), as noted above, reflects the test involving four elements which is often relied upon when the question arises as to whether an adult's capacity is in doubt (see Hein *et al.*, 2015[a] and Grisso *et al.*, 1997). It requires that an individual understands information but also retains, uses, weighs it and communicates a decision. Even when it comes to clarifying what the standards are for adults, 'there is surprisingly little discussion in the theoretical and empirical literature' on what a procedurally rational decision-making process would look like (Banner, 2013: 74–76). The courts set out what the *inability*, rather than the *ability* entails (see consideration of the case law in Donnelly, 2010: 142). The case law is strikingly focused on impairment, as this must be present for incapacity to be determined under the MCA (section 2). Therefore, MCA case law is not well suited for a more constructive consideration of children's capacity outside of the impairment context. The MCA is noted by the court to be 'hardly of direct relevance' in relation to a child instructing a lawyer in *S v.* SBH (para. 62), although the section 3(1) factors are briefly considered. (see also the comparison in *S (Child as Parent - Adoption - Consent)* [2017] EWHC 2729 (Fam)).

An increasing number of tools have been developed to bring greater objectivity to assessments of decision-making abilities for consent to treatment and clinical research in adults, such as the MacArthur Competence Assessment Tool for Treatment (MacCAT, see Dunne *et al.*, 2006). The research of Hein *et al.* (2015[a] and [b]) sought to determine whether a tool for assessing "competence to consent" to medical treatment could be used with children. The tool requires that the assessor assign numerical scores when examining the four elements of capacity: (1) understanding information; (2) reasoning about choices; (3) appreciation of consequences; and (4) expressing a choice. There is little empirical research data on their efficacy, however. One study determined that the MacCAT, modified for children, was feasible (Koelch *et al.*, 2010) but also that clinicians were more likely to determine capacity without reference to the tool than if they applied it. This points to the tool failing to capture something which a less clinical (and more personal, holistic) interaction does (Hein *et al.*, 2014). These tools do not seem to provide much clarity, therefore, on what capacity entails in practice, and perhaps the tools facilitate assessments of capacity on paper, but reduce conclusions that children have capacity.

Recent jurisprudence is another source of guidance on children's capacity. In *S v.* SBH [2019] the court outlined (at para. 64) the main factors relevant to the assessment of whether a child can directly instruct a lawyer in a family law case, rather than being assigned a guardian to instruct the lawyer on the child's interests: i) intelligence; ii) emotional maturity; iii) factors which might undermine their understanding such as their emotional state; iv) their reasons for wishing to instruct a solicitor directly; v) potential undue influence; vi) their understanding of the process of litigation; vii) the risk of harm to the child from participation. These points are, of course, quite specific to instructing a lawyer. They are also, perhaps, demanding much from a child (and certainly more than is required from an adult wishing to instruct a solicitor) in order to reach the requisite standard of capacity.

An NHS *Foundation Trust v. A & Others* [2014] highlights the court's *ad hoc* approach to capacity in a medical law context. It concerned the medical treatment of a 16-year old girl ("A") whose life was in immediate danger because of her disordered relationship with food. Two psychiatric reports established that the girl lacked capacity to make decisions about medical treatment and the court relayed the evidence as follows:

It was concluded that A struggled to make decisions about her own care and presently suffered from a disorder of mind or brain ... In Dr G's analysis there was no evidence that any further time would alleviate the problem or effectively assist in aiding A's understanding (paras. 14–15) ... [She] had shown no capacity to focus on her emotional feelings or the 'powerless nature of her own situation'. Dr G told me that A presented as a much younger girl, sometimes petulant and child like ... she lacks a real appreciation that unless immediate action is taken that she will die (para. 41).

The court did not consider *Gillick* competence,[2] it instead expressed that A's wishes were important (para. 12), particularly since use of force was being sanctioned by the court. The court referenced the MCA although acknowledged it would not be applied in her case, presumably because she was under 18, although the fact that the MCA applies to 16- and 17-year olds was not mentioned in the judgment (bearing in mind A was 16 years old).[3] The elaboration of why she does not have capacity is somewhat vague and subjective, referring, for example, to perceived immaturity ('petulan[ce]').

In another 2014 case, *A (A Child)* [2014] EWFHC 1445 (Fam), the question was whether a 13-year old had the capacity to consent to a termination. This time *Gillick* competence *was* explicitly considered. A psychiatrist again provided evidence and, on this occasion, convinced the court that the girl had capacity to consent, although other doctors involved were in doubt (para. 8). She was deemed by him to have capacity as:

[S]he fully understood the implications of the options; the risks ... she was able to explain to him that her wish was to terminate the pregnancy as she felt that she could not cope with its continuance ... the decision that was reached by A was hers alone and was not the product of influence by adults in her family (paras. 13–14).

In *An NHS Foundation Trust v. A & Others*, it is outlined that the 16-year old does not understand the consequences of refusing treatment. In *A (A Child)* it

---

2 Neither did the court refer to *Gillick* when making an order for treatment on a 12-year old in *X Health Authority v. D* [2019] EWHC 2311 (Fam.). In *F (Mother) v. F (Father)* [2013] EWHC 2683 (Fam.) in which the court made an order to inoculate adolescent girls against their wishes, neither the words "competence" nor "capacity" were even explicitly referenced. Nor is *Gillick*.

3 In *An NHS Foundation Trust Hospital v. P* [2014] EWHC 1650, however, the court *did* apply the MCA when making an order for treatment on a 17-year old.

is outlined that the 13-year old does understand. Some convincing reasons are provided for these conclusions. Nevertheless, a somewhat *ad hoc* approach to considering capacity is evident in such judgments, in that the court does not have a standard approach. It does not rely upon any kind of checklist, for example. *Gillick* competence may or may not be explicitly mentioned. Elements of the MCA 2005 may or may not feature.

It seems very difficult, therefore, to ascertain how a professional is to apply an objective and standardised approach in an informal assessment of a child's capacity. This is particularly the case when we bear in mind that in both of these cases – *An NHS Foundation Trust v. A & Others* and *A (A Child)*) – expert psychiatrists were introduced and therefore the assessments could be described as formal,[4] and yet a fairly *ad hoc* approach to assessing capacity is evident in the judgments. Some such cases show that experts may even be in disagreement with each other as to whether a child has capacity (see *An NHS Foundation Trust Hospital v. P; A (A Child)*; and *S v. SBH*), demonstrating all the more how difficult it may be for a non-psychology/psychiatry expert to make such a determination.

Consider also the difficulties in defining capacity for adults, as well as the fact that standardised tests such as the MacCAT do not provide a definitive objective measure of capacity. It is telling that the courts in *S v. SBH*, after outlining elements to consider when determining a child's capacity to instruct a lawyer, stated that '[i]nevitably the evaluation is more an art than a science and the weight to be given to each component cannot be arithmetically totted up' (para. 80). It seems that perhaps an intuitive assessment of a child's capacity (based on experience and impressions) is inevitable in some practice contexts, and that attempting to quantify or to be overly rigid in defining capacity is unhelpful. Or perhaps it is possible to apply a solid definition but one has not yet been established to a satisfactory degree. In any case, professionals would benefit from a framework in which to work when assessing or understanding a child's capacity, and it is important that this framework is based in children's rights.

4   Considering Children's Capacity Rights

One important source for better understanding capacity is the CRC. The term "evolving capacities" in Article 5 implies the CRC's recognition and appreciation

---

[4] This reliance on experts appears to generally occur in only the most serious of medical law cases (although in the most acrimonious family law cases, psychologist and other expert evidence is very occasionally introduced, see Daly, 2018: 299).

of the sliding scale of capacities that children move through as they grow to adulthood. Although 'the evolving capacities of the child' is not defined in the Convention, the Committee on the Rights of the Child ("the Committee") opines that it refers to 'processes of maturation and learning whereby children progressively acquire knowledge, competencies and understanding, including acquiring understanding about their rights and about how they can best be realized' (General Comment No. 7: para. 17).

Article 5 is a ground breaking provision of the CRC. Lansdown points out that traditionally, it was assumed that adults were the primary agents for protecting children, and that children were seen as mere recipients; but that 'the reality is more complex, involving a dynamic process that recognises children's capacities to contribute towards their own protection and allows them to build on their strengths' (Lansdown, 2005: 41). It is highly significant then that Article 5 positions parents not as owners or even solely protectors of their children but, similar to the *Gillick* case, as holders in trust of children's rights. The parental role will change as the child matures and develops abilities and desires to exercise rights on her own behalf. Article 5 then 'transforms the role of the parent from primary rights-holder over their child, to duty-bearer to their child in the child's exercise of her rights under the UNCRC' (Varadan, 2019: 320).

Article 5 may place emphasis on the position of parents but it envisages a balancing of children's autonomy and protection rights in accordance with their capacities (Lansdown 2005). We can infer from this that children themselves have "capacity rights" under Article 5 in that, on relevant matters, the extent of their capacity must be considered and they should be given the freedom to make their own decisions to the extent possible.

Whilst acknowledging that what constitutes capacity is a contested matter, and that there are no quick-fix definitions of capacity, it can be said that efforts to understand it should be grounded in the CRC. With the intuitive, informal approach to assessing children's capacity in mind, I am therefore proposing a rights-based model, based on the CRC, to guide assessment or understanding of a child's or children's capacity in a rights framework.

The model below proposes that in order for professionals to take a rights-based approach to assessing or understanding the capacity of a child or of children generally, they should consider the following concepts:

1. Autonomy (Article 12): Children have autonomy rights, and to deny them their wishes should be considered a matter of seriousness.
2. Evidence (Article 2): Decision-makers should have basic knowledge about childhood including psychology and other relevant theories.
3. Support (Article 5): Capacity can be increased through appropriate support, guidance and information.

4. Protection (Article 3): Children are a group who are in a unique position of relative vulnerability and adults are obliged to offer them protection from harm.

All of these concepts have been specifically situated in this model via various 'cross-cutting standards' (Hanson and Lundy, 2017: 301) or provisions of the CRC. It must be borne in mind that CRC rights are indivisible and interdependent, however, so there will be overlapping elements to these points. Some further sub-headings have been included to assist assessment – under concept 1. *Autonomy*, 'accord due weight to views' is instructed, for example. These points are not intended to be exhaustive however, as each capacity assessment will need to be tailored to the specific context, such as a determination of capacity to consent to medical treatment, to participate in legal proceedings, and so on.

4.1 *Autonomy (Article 12 Right to be Heard)*

4.1.1 Understand Autonomy Rights

When assessing or understanding a child's capacity, it is important to be aware of the importance of autonomy to all individuals, including children (see *X Health Authority v. D*: para. 12 and *S v. SBH*: para. 63). Autonomy – the ideal that we should decide our own destiny to the extent possible – is the most valued characteristic for the individual in a liberal democracy (see Daly, 2018). Evidence indicates that it is inherently good for wellbeing. Greater autonomy has been found to be correlated positively with a variety of outcomes for children, particularly where they make decisions together with adults (Bindman, Pomerantz and Roisman, 2015: 775). There are laws upholding autonomy and social policies based around it.

Capacity is often the gateway to autonomy. For example, being determined *Gillick* competent may permit you to access the treatment you wish to have. Assessing capacity therefore requires an understanding that denying children autonomy should be taken seriously, as it is for adults (Daly, 2018). This requires that capacity assessment contains an understanding that a child is supported to understand the matter at hand before they are deemed to lack capacity (see further 4.3 below). It also requires that the *nature* of the decision is considered – less serious issues will likely require lower levels of understanding for children to be deemed capable of making decisions (see further 4.4.2 below).

There has been resistance to an overly-individualistic liberal notion of the autonomous individual in medical law (see e.g. Donnelly, 2016: 322; Herring, 2016; Foster, 2009). Yet a relational approach can be taken to autonomy which can provide a more holistic and less individualistic approach to it. There are

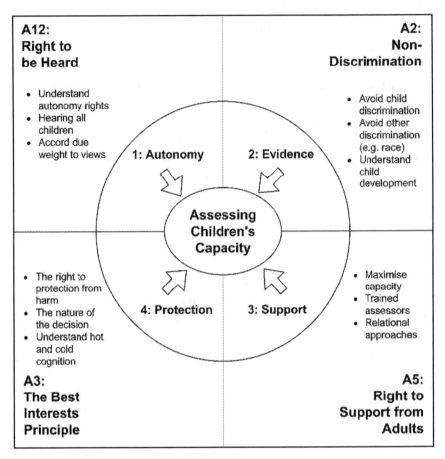

FIGURE 1   Children's Capacity Rights

various accounts of relational autonomy. Donnelly (2016: 322) opines that a useful unifying concept is that advanced by Christman (2004: 147): a conception of autonomy is uniquely relational when 'among its defining conditions are requirements concerning the interpersonal or social environment of the agent'. Understandings of children's autonomy and capacity, therefore, requires acceptance that we are all defined through our relationships with others and through the environments in which we are operating (see further 3.3 below).

4.1.2   Hearing All Children

Article 12 of the CRC requires that states 'shall assure' to children the right to be heard (Article 12[1]), and in particular children should be 'provided the opportunity' in proceedings affecting them (Article 12[2]). Although autonomy is not explicitly mentioned in the CRC, Article 12, taken together with Article 5, can be interpreted as meaning that children should have autonomy to the extent possible. When assessing a child's capacity, hearing what they have to say will be crucial. This will provide information about whether a child has made a decision, what their wishes are, and of course give indications as to their mental capacity. The Committee also makes the point that states should not just ensure children are heard, but also positively *encourage* children to provide views (General Comment No. 12: para. 11). Communication for the purpose of assessing capacity should therefore be encouraged.

There are different opinions on the age at which it is appropriate to hear children's views, but even young children can form views and express wishes. There is no age limit set by Article 12 for extending to a child the right to be heard; the text refers solely to the child 'capable of forming his or her own views' without designating a specific cut-off point. Therefore children must be assumed capable of forming views (this is not the same as assuming that a child has legal capacity), and children must be informed about the fact that they are in possession of this right to be heard (*ibid.*, para. 20). The Committee defines 'young children' as those up to eight years of age, and states that their participation rights mean that adults must 'show patience and creativity by adapting their expectations to a young child's interests, level of understanding and preferred ways of communicating' (General Comment No. 5: para. 11[c]). Even children who clearly do not have capacity can potentially provide views through communication such as play or art (see General Comment No. 12: para 21; and Daly, 2018: 49).

In order to assess children's capacity, professionals must engage in communication in 'a child friendly manner' (Day of General Discussion on the Right to be Heard, para. 40). There are now guidelines in many areas of practice as to how to communicate with children, for example in legal proceedings (see e.g. the Council of Europe Guidelines on child-friendly justice, 2010).

4.1.3 According Due Weight to Views: Participation Without Full Capacity

Part of facilitating children's autonomy rights is to ensure not just that children are heard, but that what they say is given due weight. The Committee states that 'simply listening to the child is insufficient', but that the views of the child have to be seriously considered (General Comment No. 12: para. 28). There are also obligations to provide children with feedback and information on the position of their views in the outcome of decisions (*ibid.*, para. 45). There must therefore *always* be some level of weight accorded to their views (Daly, 2018). Even if hearing a child indicates that she is not *Gillick* competent, her views should still be given due weight in accordance with Article 12.

Participation has become a key notion associated with Article 12 – the right to be heard means that children should enjoy participation in an all matters affecting them (General Comment No. 12: 86). The notion of participation is highly relevant to children's capacity, as the principle of the evolving capacities of the child means that children have a right to participate to the extent possible – the level of their of involvement will accord with their mental capacity. Children should not simply be "assessed", however, they should be supported to participate, as is outlined in section 4.3 below. This should be the case for even young children who can have sophisticated knowledge of their medical condition, particularly if they have had a serious illness for some time. In these circumstances they may develop decision-making capacities that far exceed expectations of children of their age group (Alderson and Montgomery, 1996).

4.2 Evidence (*Article 2 Non-Discrimination*)

4.2.1 Refraining from Discriminating against Children as a Group

Article 2 of the CRC requires states to ensure that rights are secured: 'to each child within their jurisdiction without discrimination of any kind', noting characteristics such as race, colour, sex, 'or other status'. The emphasis here is often on characteristics such as race but 'other status' can also be interpreted to include age, that is, the status of the child as a child.

There are strong non-discrimination movements in the areas of disability rights, gender and race, but the unfair treatment of children on the basis that they are under 18 years is little examined, considered or discussed in the sphere of children's rights (Daly, 2018), though the Committee has on occasion emphasised discriminatory attitudes against adolescents (General Comment No. 20, para. 21). In efforts to understand capacity, greater attention must be given to the part played by adult attitudes to children and how this affects perceptions of the capacity of individual children, as well as children generally.

Contemporary scholarship provides evidence that children are not undeveloped adults. They are complete entities who are deserving of respect. Childhood, of course, has a biological component. Yet it is now accepted, due to scholarship rooted in childhood studies, that childhood is to some extent constructed. Such constructions have tended to underestimate children's capacity and ability to exercise agency in their own lives (Prout and James, 1990: 7–33). Alderson and Montgomery state that the greatest obstacles to children's capacity likely arise from prejudices about children, and beliefs that it is unwise to listen to children (1996: 58). Children's relative inexperience does render them vulnerable and they require special protections. However, they are frequently denied opportunities for decision making in accordance with their evolving capacities (Lansdown, 2005: 31).

Non-discrimination in capacity assessment will therefore involve awareness of and resistance to discriminatory attitudes against children as a group. Koh-Peters (2018), in her work representing children in child protection proceedings, poses questions "to keep us honest" such as: if one is treating this client or patient differently because she is a child, then why is that? Is it justifiable? A positive example of non-discrimination in the specific context of consideration of children's evolving capacities is noted in New Zealand by Lansdown (2005: 53). There the Ministry for Youth Affairs developed guidelines for government departments and public bodies when considering age-limits in law and policy. Various prompting questions are encouraged, including: 'Does the age-limit discriminate against young people?' noting that '[i]t is not acceptable to treat young people differently just because of their age.'

Applying the principle of non-discrimination when considering a child's capacity also means refraining from an overly conservative application of *Gillick* and other standards of assessment of capacity. Being 'fully' informed, as *Gillick* requires, is beyond the requirements for an adult, who simply needs to be aware in broad terms of the nature of the treatment (*Rogers v. Whitaker* [1992] 175 CLR 479, 489 see also *S (Child as Parent - Adoption - Consent)* [2017], para. 60). The court in *S v.* SBH advocates 'a shift away from a paternalistic approach in favour of an approach which gives significantly more weight to the autonomy of the child in the evaluation of whether they have sufficient understanding' (para. 63). Careful consideration should be given to a child's capacity in circumstances such as obtaining consent for medical treatment. Yet one should avoid an overly stringent interpretation of what a child's understanding entails.

4.2.2 Supporting Marginalised Children

Lundy (2007: 934–935) emphasises that participation rights should not be afforded only to articulate and literate children. The Committee provides evidence of the particular need to guarantee the participation of children with disabilities. This is important when it comes to assessing capacity, as adults may have difficulty accepting that a child with disabilities might have capacity (1997, para. 334). It is also the case that children with language barriers: 'minority, indigenous and migrant children and other children who do not speak the majority language' (General Comment No 12: para. 21) may struggle to have their capacity taken seriously, for example in the context of immigration cases.

It is not simply the case that the capacities of children may be underestimated; there may also be less sense of a duty to support and maximise the capacity of these groups. Lansdown points to the fact that children from minority groups may experience negative assumptions about their capacity and their ability to learn (2005: 30). Yet there are particular obligations to ensure that groups are supported to have their views and understandings made clear. The Committee states that children with disabilities have a right to 'any mode of communication necessary to facilitate the expression of their views' and also that particular efforts must also be made to support children with language issues (General Comment No 12: para. 21).

4.2.3   Understand Child Development: Theory and Unknowns

It is important to remain critical of the notion that children's capacity can be measured in a straightforward way considering the fraught and contested nature of the concept of capacity in the case law and literature outlined above. Yet the Committee states that professionals working with children should have the relevant training, including on children's capacities (General Comment No. 20: para 37[e]). It is therefore useful to consider briefly what claims are made within developmental psychology and in empirical research about children's evolving capacities, in order to determine the relevance of those claims and findings for how the law approaches and treats children. This section does not aim to provide a comprehensive analysis of what psychology and neuroscience can tell us about capacity, but rather serves to provide an overview of relevant evidence from these fields of study.

It is important to emphasise, as the Committee does, that 'age alone cannot determine the significance of a child's views' and that other factors such as experience will also be significant (General Comment No. 12: para. 29). Much of the thinking around children's decision-making abilities, however, revolves around what children should be expected to do within their particular age range. Piaget's "stage theory" (see e.g. Piaget and Inhelder, 1969) is prevalent within developmental psychology. Piaget worked on developing early IQ testing with Alfred Binet (an intelligence quotient [IQ] is a score based on standardised tests to assess human intelligence). Piaget noticed that children of approximately the same age have a tendency to engage in similar behaviours. Piaget's work was novel, and increased perceptions that children's cognition was worth understanding. However, he has been criticised as underestimating children's abilities, and later theorists such as Vygotsky (1978) and Bronfenbrenner (1979) have placed greater emphasis on the importance of the environment of the child as opposed to particular stages of development. There is continued acknowledgement, nevertheless, that ages and stages are important in understanding the cognitive development of children (Gay Hartman, 2000: 1285). Rutter and Rutter (1993: 195) make the point that no amount of training or environmental fine-tuning will enable a four-month old baby to walk.

Since Piaget, many researchers have further examined what children can generally do at certain ages. Empirical research and advances in neurobiology have added to the body of evidence (see also Kilkelly in this volume). In general, the evidence paints a complex picture and it is important to remember that developmental psychology is theory rather than fact. However, there are some trends in the findings that we can point to. It is also important to acknowledge that the question, 'what can children be expected to know/decide at a particular age?' is very common, as we tend to have a preoccupation with age. This inescapable question therefore requires a response, and the response should involve both available evidence, and an appeal for balance, in that factors besides age must also be considered.

From birth to age two, Piaget stated that children are in the "sensorimotor stage" whereby they experience the world through movement and their senses. Babies are conscious and active agents who alter environments, families, relationships (Alderson and Montgomery, 1996). Their experiences are to be taken seriously but they are not going to have capacity to consent to medical treatment, for example. The "preoperational" stage continues from age two to seven whereby there is an increasing ability to use and represent objects through words and images ("symbolic thinking"). Mental reasoning (that is, solving problems and making decisions) is developing. It is thought, however, that children are expected to think in "egocentric" terms, that is, to have difficulty in considering the viewpoints of others, although they are increasingly gaining these skills. "Cognitive control" – that is, controlling your behaviour in line with your goals – is thought to be weak in children of this age (Kidd *et al.*, 2013) although more recent research (e.g. Murray *et al.*, 2016; Blakemore, 2019: 149–154), points to the influence which environment, assistance and support has on the ability of children (and all individuals) to make more objectively "good" decisions.

Seven years appears to be a developmental turning point, and children from this age are considered, for example, capable of assenting (i.e. actively agreeing) to medical research (see e.g. Hein *et al.*, 2015[b] and Varadan, this volume). Children are developing metacognitive skills, that is, a more abstract and complex idea of identity and interests. Piaget, identifying a "concrete operational stage" from 7 to 11 years, pointed to the ability to think logically about concrete events from age 7, though he argued that children may still be unable logically to consider all outcomes.

The research indicates another leap in development *within* this stage, at age nine. The research of Hein *et al.* indicates that those between 9.6 and 11.2 years are in a period of transition; they are developing important abilities but their maturity is not yet "effective" (2015[a] and [b]). Their research estimates that children of 11.2 years and above generally seemed to have the mental capacity necessary to consent to medical treatment, while children of 9.6 years and younger generally did not. Other research has been even more positive about abilities at this age. In Greenberg Garrison's research examining children's decisions in hypothetical scenarios concerning arrangements for children on family breakdown, it was found that nine-year olds were as rational as adults in their reasons for decision-making (1991: 78).

"Adolescence", then, is usually defined as puberty (around age 12) to age 18, which is the age of majority for most purposes. At some time around age 12, Piaget argued, children enter the "formal operational stage", and abstract thought starts to become sophisticated. Individuals reason logically, draw conclusions from available information and apply to hypothetical situations all of these processes. Neuroscience likewise indicates that the thickening of the part of the brain involved in judgment and planning peaks at approximately age 11 in girls and age 12 in boys (Giedd, 2004). There is a consequent development of cognitive skills facilitating greater ability to develop hypothetical solutions, and the development of the means to choose the best one (Broome, 1999). Within this stage, 14 years appears to be a significant turning point for decision-making abilities (see e.g. Bosisio, 2008: 290). Some research indicates that 14-year olds' ability to make decisions is as advanced as that of adults, when considering their understanding of the facts, their processes of decision making and their understanding of potential outcomes of choice (see e.g. Greenberg Garrison, 1991: 78).

Other research points, however, to cognitive limitations which persist in adolescence. It indicates that the frontal lobes, which govern executive functions (cognitive processes in the brain responsible for reasoning and problem solving, helping us to prioritise, think ahead and regulate emotion), matures in our early to mid-twenties (Lipstein *et al.*, 2013). This has led to a new developmental period explored by researchers: "emerging adulthood". Evidence points to an important transition between 15 and 19 years (Scott *et al.*, 1995). Weijers and Grisso (2009: 64) argue that the 'lesser maturity of adolescents' decision-making capacities may be linked to brain structures that also have not yet reached adult maturity'. This has led to theories that adolescents make riskier decisions than adults, even in medical treatment (see e.g. Lipstein *et al.*, 2013). It is important to remember, however, that this does not write off all under-18s in terms of reasoning tasks: 'It is not that these tasks cannot be done before young adulthood, but rather that [in adulthood] it takes less effort, and hence is more likely to happen.'[5] Individual differences will dictate a lot – some individuals are risk-takers, whilst others are not (Blakemore, 2019: 134).

Even when considered through the lens of developmental psychology then, the difficulties with measuring and defining capacity have to be acknowledged. Commentators question whether developmental psychology is objective and neutral, and the legitimacy of focusing on children reaching particular stages at particular times (Cordero Arce, 2015). Furthermore, it must be emphasised that capacity cannot be understood as located solely in the individual; it is highly dependent on the environment in which an individual is operating, and particularly whether they are receiving support to maximise capacity.

4.3 Support (*Article 5, The Evolving Capacities of the Child*)

4.3.1 Maximising Capacity

Providing children with support and information will boost capacity. The level of assistance and support which children receive will likely be far more important than their decision-making abilities *per se*: 'Children's capacities are very much an interactive and relational process of dialogue, determined as much by the "hearing" and "scaffolding" capacities of the adults they engage with as their own expressive capacities' (Cashmore, 2011: 520).

The Committee stipulates that states must ensure that a child receives all necessary information and advice to make a decision in favour of her or his best interests (General Comment No. 12: para. 16). Adults have duties to maximise children's capacities, specifically because of the relative lack of experience of children: the Committee states that 'the child has a right to direction and guidance, which have to compensate for the lack of knowledge, experience and understanding of the child and are restricted by his or her evolving capacities' (*ibid.*, para. 84), although the meaning of 'parental direction and guidance' under Article 5 has remained largely without definition (Varadan, 2019). The Committee points to duties on adults to support capacity: the more the child knows, has experienced and understands, the more adults must move from 'direction and guidance into reminders and advice' and later to an approach to important issues as equals. This will 'steadily increase' over time (General Comment No. 12: para. 84).

---

5 Massachusetts Institute of Technology, *Young Adult Development Project*. Available at http://hrweb.mit.edu/worklife/youngadult/changes.html (last accessed 2 Jul. 2020).

In cases where adult capacity is at issue, there is an MCA duty to support capacity (in section 1[3]), although Ruck-Keene *et al.* (2019) found that there is much more work to be done in achieving this. There is no comparable obligation in England and Wales in cases concerning children. In *F (Mother) v. F (Father)* [2013] EWHC 2683 (Fam.), for example, two adolescent sisters and their mother were resisting vaccinations sought by the father for the girls. The court noted that the girls did not have 'a rounded appreciation of the pros and cons of the vaccine'. Cave makes the points that the girls could have been given this information, and their capacity then considered (2014b: 639 see also *S (Child as Parent - Adoption - Consent)* [2017], para. 57 where information was to be provided to the 'child parent' about adoption).

4.3.2 Trained Assessors

Professionals should have some basic knowledge of theories around children, developmental psychology and capacity when working with children. The Committee states that when there are proceedings in relation to children, the capacity to form views has to be assessed (2009: para. 28) and that all personnel involved in proceedings regarding decision-making are to be trained in this regard (Day of General Discussion on the Right to be Heard: para. 41). Alderson suggests that a test should be required to determine whether *practitioners* understand children's competence and how to enhance it. She suggests that the test should enquire as to whether a professional is able: 'to understand all the relevant information; to retain and explain all the issues clearly and resolve misunderstandings; to assist children and parents in their reasoned choice-making; and to respect their decisions, putting no undue pressures on them?' (1994: 53).

I consider elsewhere how "autonomy support" can be used to assist children in decision-making – that they should be provided with non-controlling, impartial information and support to form and/or express views and decisions (Daly, 2018: 418). There are a wealth of resources on maximising capacity and providing support which could be adapted for maximising children's capacity. The UN Convention on the Rights of Persons with Disabilities enshrines an obligation to support exercise of capacity (Article 12) rather than assuming abilities can be measured. Consequently, decision-making support for those with cognitive disability has been incorporated into policy and legislation around the world.

Guidance is available, for example, for implementing support under the MCA 2005. The Office of the Public Guardian (2013) states that, to support someone to make a decision for themselves, one must ask, does the person have all the relevant information they need? Do they understand alternatives?

And has communication of the information been conducted well? In medical practice research has been conducted on supporting decision-making by ensuring quality of communication (Hein, I. *et al.*, 2015[a]) and enhancing competence through various techniques such as breaking the process down into smaller but linked choices, and making the child feel valued (Larcher and Hutchinson, 2010: 309). Given the clear obligation under Article 5 of the CRC to support children's decision-making (Varadan, 2019: 329), it is crucial that professionals engage in supportive, capacity-maximising of this nature where capacity is being assessed.

A basic understanding of child development is not only necessary to understand how to assess children's capacity, it will also be important for understanding how to maximise the capacity of children of various ages through autonomy support. The Committee points out that '[c]onsideration needs to be given to the fact that children will need differing levels of support and forms of involvement according to their age and evolving capacities' (2009: para. 184) and assessors will have to have training in these points. This means that states have obligations to ensure training similar to that which is now common in the area of capacity support for people with cognitive disability.

4.3.3 Relational Approaches

Available research on children's views indicates that they wish jointly to make decisions with parents and others rather than be the sole decision-maker (Alderson and Montgomery, 1996: 2). It is considered good practice to involve the child's family in the decision-making process, if the child consents to this (Department of Health, 2009: 33). Of course, children are particularly dependent on those close to them, socially, emotionally, financially and legally. It is important to ascertain that children are not under undue influence in the decision that they have made. This is complex, as choosing an option because it aligns with the interests of those close to you can still be "your own" choice. Helpfully, courts make a distinction between this and "parroting" the views of parents (see e.g. *S v.* SBH: para. 64).

Because of the relational nature of decision-making, there may legitimately be an element of "persuasion" to do the right thing. One can imagine scenarios in which this would be entirely appropriate. Consider, for example, where needle fear is preventing a child from accepting life-saving treatment which requires an injection (see e.g. *Re M. B. (An Adult: Medical Treatment)* ([1997] EWCA Civ. 1361 where the patient was an adult). A child may need to be persuaded to endure the discomfort of an injection in order to avoid much greater harm. Research indicates that children's attitudes to compulsion is more dependent on their relationship with parents and clinicians than the degree of compulsion (Tan *et al.*, 2010), highlighting the importance of communication, and the intimate connection of capacity to factors such as trust and positive relationships. There is a difference between providing information and persuading on the one hand and coercing on the other however, and professionals should be aware of the power dynamics between adults and children.

An assessment of capacity should include consideration of factors relating to the child's relationships, cultural context and his/her particular perspectives and experiences (Alderson 1993: 123). Having experienced a chronic illness for a number of years, for example, would clearly be relevant to a child's capacity for making decisions in relation to that illness. There is evidence that such experience is a more indicative factor than age in assessing capacity (Chico and Hagger, 2011: 161).

4.4 *Protection (Article 3: The Best Interest of the Child)*
4.4.1 The Right to Protection from Harm

The principle of the best interest as enshrined in Article 3 is many-faceted. It is, for example, a legal device for courts to ensure that children's interests are given due consideration in proceedings affecting them. It also has a protective function: Cave and Stavrinides make the point that, 'Article 3 places great responsibility on parents and public officials to protect the health and welfare interests of children' (2013: 13). This is reflected in domestic law in systems all over the world. The Children Act 1989 stipulates that, 'the child's welfare shall be the court's paramount consideration', although a child's wishes will form part of that consideration.

The basis for this paternalism is a recognition that children's capacities are still evolving and, therefore, they are owed a duty of protection from activities likely to cause them harm, although this paternalism should diminish over time (Lansdown, 2005: x). States have obligations to all citizens to engage in a balancing act between autonomy and protection. Where children are making a decision which is disastrous to their health, such as resisting life-saving treatment for religious reasons (see e.g. *Re E.* [1993] 1 FLR 386), then the state has an obligation to override their immediate decision as failure to do so would prevent children from developing into autonomous agents (Cave, 2014: 111). This can be argued to be the case even for those who are *Gillick* competent, on the basis that special protection is owed to under-18s. The reason why controversy has arisen in terms of the inability of children to refuse consent is because treatment will not be offered unless it is in the child's best interests (Cave and Stavrinides, 2013: 19). Therefore refusing is sometimes significantly different in outcome to consenting. It seems logical then that a difference is drawn between the two, and that autonomy must sometimes be overridden in favour of protection.

4.4.2   The Nature of the Decision

Many commentators emphasise that the same thresholds of capacity are not necessary for all decisions. The MCA's approach is that capacity is 'issue specific': the question is whether a person has capacity to decide *this* particular question (Herring, 2016: 45), not all questions. Moreover, capacity is not a single, one-off event (British Medical Association, 2010: 4) or definitive. Ruck-Keene *et al.*, for example, found that in 12.5 per cent of MCA cases, the individual in question was found to have capacity in relation to some issues but lacking capacity in relation to others. In one case referred to, for example, the person was found to have capacity for sexual relations and marriage, but not to litigate these issues (2019: 66 see also *S (Child as Parent - Adoption - Consent)* [2017], para. 17).

Likewise, in *D Borough Council v AB*, the court stated that: 'The terms of [*Gillick*] show clearly that the capacity in question is act and not person specific' ([2011] EWHC 101 (COP): para. 18). Cave opines that this means that a child's ability to understand will depend on the complexities of a particular decision (2014: 106). The Committee notes that the importance of the matter may mean that assessing maturity accurately becomes more important (2009: para. 30). This is reflected in the fact that in the cases where serious medical issues are at play, courts may engage the expert evidence of a psychiatrist (and in family law cases there is sometimes reliance on psychologists' evidence, see section 2 above).

The nature of the decision may also be significant not just for capacity, but to determine how much weight children's wishes should have. Lansdown suggests a principle of proportionality with a sliding scale of capacity in accordance with the seriousness of the decision. Low-risk decisions would mean that children could take responsibility without demonstrating high capacity levels. For a child's wishes to be overruled, one would have to demonstrate that the child does not understand the implications of the choice and the risk it poses to his/her best interests (Lansdown, 2005: x).

4.4.3   Understand Hot and Cold Cognition: The Consequences for Criminal Behaviour

The context of the decision will also be very relevant to considerations of capacity. This becomes particularly important in the context of children's criminal behaviour. The United Nations Standard Minimum Rules for the

Administration of Juvenile Justice requires 'a close relationship' between children's responsibility for criminal behaviour and 'other social rights and responsibilities' (Official commentary on Article 4(1)). Yet this is rarely achieved – in England and Wales, for example, the age of criminal responsibility for serious crimes is 10 years (Children and Young Persons Act 1963, Section 16), yet the courts can overrule a child's refusal to consent to medical treatment up to the age of 18 years (*Re W* (*A Minor*) (*Medical Treatment: Court's Jurisdiction*) [1993] Fam. 64, [1993] 1 FLR 1). This is 'a dichotomy that appears not to have been subjected to detailed analysis' (Lyons, 2010: 258). Lyons argues that if children are to be denied responsibility for their healthcare decisions, then when they commit crimes, 'they should be dealt with ... by agencies outside of the criminal law' (2010: 277).

Available research on children's capacities indicates that the context of the decision is crucial to whether adult-child differences will emerge for under-18s in their reasoning: '[i]n the heat of passion, in the presence of peers, on the spur of the moment, in unfamiliar situations' adolescents may not reason as well as an adults might (Reyna and Farley, 2006: 1). This is because the prefrontal cortex, which prevents us from acting on impulse, is not yet fully developed (Blakemore, 2019: 135). Where adolescents can consult others, however, and consider their options at a measured pace, their decision-making abilities can match maturity attained in adulthood (Steinberg, 2005). Children become more adept at problem-solving when they have practised solving problems with parents or older children (Gay Hartman, 2000: 1285; Vygotsky, 1978; Bronfenbrenner 1979). The difference in contexts has been described as "hot" cognition – making decisions in a heightened emotional state; and "cold" cognition – a more deliberative type of decision-making process in less stressful environments (Blakemore, 2019: 143–148; Albert and Steinberg, 2011).

This points clearly, therefore, to why children's capacity in different contexts should be treated distinctly; and why children should be considered to have greater potential for good decision-making in the medical law context as opposed to the criminal law context. The Committee astutely emphasises the need for 'recognition that competence and understanding do not necessarily develop equally across all fields at the same pace and recognition of individual experience and capacity' (General Comment No. 20: para. 20). The same child may have different abilities for decision-making in relation to a criminal matter and a medical law matter. Two children of the same age could have entirely different decision-making abilities in relation to the same matter because of individual differences. The context in which the decision is made, therefore, will likely have a major effect on how capacious a child will be.

5 Conclusion

It is important to remain critical of the notion that children's capacity can be measured in a straightforward way. However, law is often dichotomous in nature: guilty/not guilty; liable/not liable; rational/not rational (Lyons, 2010: 277), and judgment calls must sometimes be made about a child's capacity. In such a binary context it is difficult to operationalise the principle of the evolving capacities of the child. It is significant, however, that Article 5 emphasises the sliding scale of capacities that children move through as they grow to adulthood. Children's "capacity rights" therefore mean that, on relevant matters, children's capacity must be assessed, and this should be done in accordance with children's rights.

Although "*Gillick* competence" is supposed to be the standard for under-16s in England and Wales, the approach of the courts to assessing capacity can be vague and inconsistent. It is clear that children need a high level of understanding to be considered to have legal capacity in a certain area, and that they will have to demonstrate awareness of various risks and consequences (see e.g. *An* NHS *Foundation Trust v. A & Others*). It remains challenging, however, for professionals to understand how to assess capacity and what "*Gillick* competence" means in practice. The intuitive approach is generally satisfactory, but it is important that it is informed by the CRC. This, it has been argued here, should specifically require: an appreciation of autonomy, because this is so valued in the liberal democracy; evidence, because this will ensure that childhood is properly understood; support, because capacity is not static but can be maximised; and protection, because it must be emphasised that with childhood comes relative vulnerability.

In order to ensure that children's capacity rights are met, and particularly to ensure that adults have a rounded understanding of capacity, there will have to be significant efforts made by states to ensure that medical professionals, lawyers and others working with children are trained in children's rights and child development. This is going to require significant investment, but it is an obligation that states undertake when they ratify the CRC, which requires that the provisions of the treaty are made widely known and that relevant professionals are trained accordingly (General Comment No. 12: para. 135).

Although it may not necessarily be possible objectively and precisely to assess children's capacity, insisting on understanding capacity through a children's rights lens will at least prompt challenging questions which get to the heart of what it is to respect children as equals.

Acknowledgements

This research was generously funded by the Independent Social Research Foundation. I owe great thanks to the staff of the School of Law, University of Liverpool, as well as the staff of the Law School at University College Cork (particularly Conor O'Mahony), for invaluable feedback at seminars. Many thanks to Alan Connolly, Helen Stalford, Brian Sloan, Beverley Clough and Craig Jones for their very helpful feedback on drafts of this chapter.

References

Albert, D. and Steinberg, L. (2011), "Judgment and Decision Making in Adolescence", *Journal of Research in Adolescence* 21(1), 211–224.

Alderson, P. (1994), "Researching Children's Rights to Integrity" in Mayall, B. (ed.), *Children's Childhoods: Observed and Experienced*, London: The Falmer Press, 45–62.

Alderson, P. and Montgomery J. (1996), *Healthcare Choices: Making Decisions with Children Vol. 2*, London: Institute for Public Policy Research.

Ashteka, C. et al. (2007), "How Much do Junior Staff Know about Common Legal Situations in Paediatrics?", *Child Care Health Development* 33(5), 631–634.

Banner, N. (2013), "Can Procedural and Substantive Elements of Decision Making be Reconciled with Assessments of Mental Capacity?", *The International Journal of Law in Context* 9(1), 71–86.

Blakemore, S. (2019), *Inventing Ourselves: The Secret Life of the Teenage Brain*, London: Black Swan.

Bosisio, R. (2008), "'Right' and 'Not Right': Representations of Justice in Young People", *Childhood* 15(2), 276–294.

British Medical Association (2010), *Best Interests Decision Making for Adults who Lack Capacity: A Toolkit for Doctors Working in England and Wales*, London: British Medical Association.

Bronfenbrenner, U. (1979), *The Ecology of Human Development: Experiments by Nature and Design*, Harvard: Harvard University Press.

Broome, M. (1999), "Consent (Assent) for Research with P[a]ediatric Patients", *Seminars in Oncology Nursing* 15(2), 96–103.

Cashmore, J. (2011), "Children's Participation in Family Law Decision-Making: Theoretical Approaches to Understanding Children's Views", *Child Inclusive Research, Policy and Practice, Children and Youth Services Review*, 33(4), 515–520.

Cashmore, J. and Parkinson, P. (2009), "Children's Participation in Family Law Disputes: The Views of Children, Parents, Lawyers, Counsellors", *Family Matters*, 82(1), 15–21.

Cave, E. (2014), "Goodbye Gillick? Identifying and Resolving Problems with the Concept of Child Competence", *Legal Studies* 34(1) 103–122.

Cave, E. (2014b), "Adolescent Refusal of MMR Inoculation: F (Mother) v F (Father)", *The Modern Law Review* 2014 77(4) 619–640.

Cave, E. and Stavrinides, Z. (2013), *Medical Practitioners, Adolescents and Informed Consent: Final Report*.

Chico, V. and Hagger, L. (2011), "The Mental Capacity Act 2005 and Mature Minors: A Missed Opportunity?", *Journal of Social Welfare and Family Law*, 33(2), 157–168.

Christman, J. (2004), "Relational Autonomy, Liberal Individualism and the Social Construction of Selves" *Philosophical Studies*, 117(2), 143–164.

College of Nurses of Ontario, *Practice Guideline: Consent* (College of Nurses of Ontario, 2017).

Cordero Arce, M. (2015), "Maturing Children's Rights Theory", *The International Journal of Children's Rights*, 23(2), 283–331.

Committee on the Rights of the Child (2016), *General Comment No. 20: The Implementation of the Rights of the Child during Adolescence*, CRC/C/GC/20, Geneva: United Nations.

Committee on the Rights of the Child (2009), *General Comment No. 12: The Right to be Heard*, CRC/C/GC/12, Geneva: United Nations.

Committee on the Rights of the Child, (2006), *Day of General Discussion on the Right to be Heard*, Forty-third session, Geneva: United Nations.

Committee on the Rights of the Child (2005) *General Comment No. 7: Implementing Child Rights in Early Childhood*, UN/CRC/GC/7, Geneva: United Nations.

Committee on the Rights of the Child (1997) *General Discussion on the Rights of Children with Disabilities*, UN/CRC/C/66, Annex V, Geneva: United Nations.

Daly, A. (2018), *Children, Autonomy and the Courts: Beyond the Right to be Heard*, Leiden: Brill/Nijhoff.

Department of Health, (2009), *Reference Guide to Consent for Examination or Treatment*.

Donnelly, M. (2016), "Best Interests in the Mental Capacity Act: Time to Say Goodbye?", *Medical Law Review*, 24(3), 318–332.

Donnelly, M. (2010), *Autonomy, Capacity and the Limitations of Liberalism: An Exploration of the Law Relating to Treatment Refusal*, Cambridge University Press: Cambridge.

Dunn, L. et al. (2006), "Assessing Decisional Capacity for Clinical Research or Treatment: A Review of Instruments", *American Journal Psychiatry*, 163(8), 1323–1334.

Foster, C. (2009), *Choosing Life, Choosing Death: The Tyranny of Autonomy in Medical Ethics and Law*, Oxford: Hart.

Gay Hartman, R. (2000), "Adolescent Autonomy: Clarifying an Ageless Conundrum", *Hastings Law Journal*, 5(1), 1265–1362.

General Medical Council (2015), *Definitions of Children, Young People and Parents*, London: General Medical Council.

Giedd, J. (2004), "Structural Magnetic Resonance Imaging of the Adolescent Brain", *Annals of the New York Academy of Sciences*, 1021(1), 77–85.

Greenberg Garrison, E. (1991), "Children's Competence to Participate in Divorce Custody Decisionmaking", *Journal of Clinical Child Psychology*, 20(1), 78–87.

Grisso, T. et al. (1997), "The MacCAT-T: A Clinical Tool to Assess Patients' Capacities to Make Treatment Decisions", *Psychiatric Services*, 75(11), 1415–1419.

Hanson, K. and Lundy, L. (2017), "Does Exactly What it Says on the Tin? A Critical Analysis and Alternative Conceptualisation of the So-called 'General Principles' of the Convention on the Rights of the Child", *The International Journal of Children's Rights* 25(2), 285–306.

Hein, I. et al. (2015a[a]), "Feasibility of an Assessment Tool for Children's Competence to Consent to Predictive Genetic Testing: a Pilot Study?", *Journal of Genetic Counselling*, 24(6), 971–7.

Hein, I. et al. (2015b [b]), "Informed Consent Instead of Assent is Appropriate in Children from the Age of Twelve: Policy Implications of New Findings on Children's Competence to Consent to Clinical Research", BMC *Medical Ethics*, 16(1), 1–7.

Hein, I. et al. (2014), "Accuracy of the MacArthur Competence Assessment Tool for Clinical Research (MacCAT-CR) for Measuring Children's Competence to Consent to Clinical Research", *P[a]ediatrics*, 168(12), 1147–53.

Herring, J. (2016), *Vulnerable Adults and the Law*, Oxford: Oxford University Press.

Kidd, C. et al. (2013), "Rational Snacking: Young Children's Decision-Making on the Marshmallow Task is Moderated by Beliefs about Environmental Reliability", *Cognition*, 126(1), 109–14.

Koelch, M. et al. (2010), "Report of an Initial Pilot Study on the Feasibility of using the MacArthur Competence Assessment Tool for Clinical Research in Children and Adolescents with Attention-Deficit/Hyperactivity Disorder", *Journal of Child and Adolescent Psychopharmacology*, 20(1), 63–7.

Koh Peters, J. (2018), "Seeking Dignity, Voice and Story for Children in Our Child Protective Systems", *The International Journal of Children's Rights*, 26(1), 5–15.

Lansdown, G. (2006), *The Evolving Capacities of the Child*, Florence: UNICEF Innocenti Research Centre.

Larcher, V. and Hutchinson, A., (2010), "How Should Paediatricians Assess Gillick Competence?", *Archives of Disease in Childhood*, 95(4), 307–311.

Lipstein, E. et al. (2013), "Making Decisions about Chronic Disease Treatment: A Comparison of Parents and their Adolescent Children", *Health Expectations*, 19(3), 716–726.

Lundy, L. (2007) "'Voice' Is Not Enough: Conceptualising Article 12 of the United Nations Convention on the Rights of the Child", *British Educational Research Journal*, 33(6), 927–942.

Lyons, B. (2010), "Dying to be Responsible: Adolescence, Autonomy and Responsibility", *Legal Studies*, 30(2), 257–278.

Murray, J. et al. (2016), "Can the Attention Training Technique Turn One Marshmallow into Two? Improving Children's Ability to Delay Gratification", *Behaviour Research and Therapy*, 77(1), 34–39.

Office of the Public Guardian, *Mental Capacity Act Code of Practice* (Office of the Public Guardian, 2013).

Piaget, J. and Inhelder, B. (1969), *The Psychology of the Child*, London and New York: Routledge and Keegan Paul.

Prout, J. and James, A. (1990), "A New Paradigm for the Sociology of Childhood?" in Prout, J. and James, A. (eds.), *Constructing and Reconstructing Childhood: Contemporary Issues in the Sociological Study of Childhood*, London: Routledge/Falmer.

Reyna, V. and Farley, F. (2006), "Risk and Rationality in Adolescent Decision Making: Implications for Theory, Practice, and Public Policy", *Psychological Science in the Public Interest*, 7(1), 1–44.

Ruck-Keene, A. et al. (2019), "Taking Capacity Seriously? Ten Years of Mental Capacity Disputes before England's Court of Protection", *International Journal of Law and Psychiatry*, 62(1), 56–76.

Rutter, M. and Rutter, M. (1993), *Developing Minds: Challenge and Continuity Across the Lifespan*, London: Penguin.

Scott, E. *et al.* (1995), "Evaluating Adolescent Decision Making in Legal Contexts", *Law and Human Behaviour* 19(3), 221–244.

Steinberg, L. (2005), "Cognitive and Affective Development in Adolescents", *Trends in Cognitive Science*, 9(2), 69–74.

Tan, J. et al., (2010), "Attitudes of Patients with Anorexia Nervosa to Compulsory Treatment and Coercion", *International Journal of Law and Psychiatry* 33(1), 13–19.

Thomas, N. and O'Kane, C. (1998), "When Children's Wishes and Feelings Clash with their 'Best Interests'", *The International Journal of Children's Rights*, 6(2), 137–154.

Varadan, S. (2019), "The Principle of Evolving Capacities under the UN Convention on the Rights of the Child", *The International Journal of Children's Rights* 27(2), 306–338.

Vygotsky, L. (1978), "The Role of Play in Development" in Cole, M. *et al.* (eds.), *Mind in Society: The Development of Higher Processes*, Harvard: Harvard University Press.

PART 2

Article 5 and Domestic Legal Systems

CHAPTER 4

"Evolving Capacities" and "Parental Guidance" in The Context of Youth Justice

Testing the Application of Article 5 of the Convention on the Rights of the Child

Ursula Kilkelly

1   Introduction

Article 5 of the United Nations Convention on the Rights of the Child (UNCRC) is a pivotal children's rights provision, which recognises the 'responsibilities, rights and duties of parents' to provide 'appropriate direction and guidance' to the child in the exercise of his/her rights, in a manner consistent with 'the evolving capacities of the child'. Underpinning children as holders of rights, Article 5 bridges the gap between children who require parental support to exercise their rights and those who are capable of exercising them on their own behalf. Although often neglected, the relevance of the principle of evolving capacities to all Convention provisions has been recognised by the UN Committee on the Rights of the Child ('the Committee') although it is not included among the four general principles (General Comment No. 5; Hanson and Lundy, 2017). What limited consideration there has been of Article 5 to date has been general in nature, analysing the meaning and application of "evolving capacity" in the context of the general exercise of children's rights (see Tobin and Varadan, 2019; Varadan, 2019). Analysis has so far been light on the meaning and scope of 'parental responsibility to provide guidance'.

The UNCRC has particular relevance to children in conflict with the law and Articles 37 and 40 are especially important to the rights of the child in youth justice (General Comment No. 24). A child may have criminal responsibility under Article 37(c) of the Convention and will, if the subject of criminal proceedings, be entitled to the due process protections set out in Article 40. Given the relevance of the concept of "capacity" to the criminal process, and the important role played by parents who have the primary responsibility for the child's upbringing and development under Article 18, it is surprising that there has been little, if any, analysis of how Article 5 might apply in this context. What does capacity mean when a child is held to be criminally responsible and what is the role of parental guidance when the child is party to a criminal legal process?

It is the aim of this chapter to explore the application of Article 5 in the context of youth justice. It aims to query the relevance of the principle of "evolving capacities" to children in conflict with the law and to the exercise of children's rights in the criminal justice system. It considers what role, if any, 'the responsibilities, rights and duties' of parents have in such proceedings[1] while addressing, more generally, whether Article 5 adds value to the child's rights approach to youth justice. It begins with an introduction to Article 5, goes on to consider the two issues of "evolving capacity" and "parental responsibility" and then concludes with a final analysis.

2   Article 5: An Introduction

Article 5 requires states parties to 'respect the responsibilities, rights and duties of parents … to provide in a manner consistent with the evolving capacities of the child, appropriate direction and guidance in the exercise by the child of the rights recognised in the present Convention'. Article 5 is a provision unique to the UNCRC – there is no equivalent provision in any of the general human rights treaties (Tobin and Varadan, 2019: 159). From a children's rights perspective, it is a both a creative provision that recognises the 'responsibilities, rights and duties of parents' in a children's rights context, and an enabling provision that reflects the important role that parents play in guiding children in the exercise of their rights (Lansdown, 2005). As Sutherland explains, Article 5 addressed two aims – first, it recognised the significance of the child's evolving capacity and second, it highlighted the role of parents to guide the child in the exercise of his/her rights, thus reaffirming the importance of the role of parents in the child's life (Sutherland, this volume).[2] In this way, Article 5 offers an important mechanism to support children to navigate their rights from the point where they have no or limited capacity and require assistance in the exercise of those rights, to the point where they are capable of exercising their

---

[1] Note, for brevity that although Article 5 refers to, 'parents or, where applicable, the members of the extended family or community as provided for by local custom, legal guardians or other persons legally responsible for the child', the shorthand term "parents" will be used throughout.

[2] This is also articulated clearly in Article 18 of the UNCRC which recognises that parents have the primary responsibility for the child's upbringing and development.

rights autonomously (General Comment No. 12, para. 84). In this context, underpinned by the principle of children as rights holders, Article 5 can be said to offer a flexible solution to the dilemma of capacity in children's rights, recognising that children's parents and guardians play a crucial role in acting as a bridge between "no" and "full" capacity helping to guide the child across that bridge, with appropriate direction and guidance (General Comment No. 12, para. 84) (Lansdown, 2005).

The purpose of Article 5 is thus clear in the broad context of the Convention. As Tobin and Varadan observe, however, the absence from the other human rights treaties of a similar or comparable provision has "robbed" Article 5 of the interpretative guidance that this might have generated (Tobin and Varadan, 2019: 162). Despite proposals made during the Convention's drafting process that Article 5 should be highlighted as an interpretive principle,[3] it was not included among the four general principles identified by the Committee on the Rights of the Child (Articles 2, 3, 6 and 12) (Committee on the Rights of the Child, 1996) as 'underlying and fundamental values that are relevant to the realization of all children's rights' (Marta Santos Pais in Hanson and Lundy, 2017: 292). This has ultimately resulted in the provision enjoying less attention if not, in effect, a lower status than the general principles. At the same time, Article 5 has genuine supportive and interpretive value across the entire Convention and for this reason, drawing on emerging practice from the UN Committee on the Rights of the Child, Hanson and Lundy have proposed its inclusion as a cross-cutting provision alongside Articles 2, 3 and 12 in their recast of the Convention's general principles (Hanson and Lundy, 2017: 301).

The concept of "evolving capacity" is not defined in the Convention. According to the Committee on the Rights of the Child, Article 5 draws on the concept of "evolving capacities" to refer to 'processes of maturation and learning whereby children progressively acquire knowledge, competencies and understanding, including acquiring understanding about their rights and about how they can best be realized' (General Comment No. 7, para. 17). The Committee has both highlighted its significance to early years because of children's rapid development during that time (General Comment No. 7, para. 17), while equally underscoring the importance of the concept to the agency and participation rights of older children (General Comment No. 12, para. 84). This is clearly reflective of the broad-based application of the concept to the exercise of children's rights under the Convention.

Interestingly, most of the academic analysis of Article 5 has focused on "evolving capacity(ies)", as a somewhat autonomous concept, rather than on

---

[3] Proposals were made both by UNICEF and the Secretariat. See Hanson and Lundy, 2017: 291.

evolving capacity in the context of parental rights, responsibilities and duties to provide guidance to the child, i.e. how it is framed in Article 5. This is despite the fact that records of the drafting process show that the concepts were intended to be inextricably linked (Tobin and Varadan, 2019: 159–160). Reinforcing the earlier point, there is a ubiquity of references to "evolving capacities" in the Committee's General Comments and Days of Discussion where use of the term has become relatively commonplace (Varadan, 2019: 307–308). Varadan's analysis of the Committee's use of Article 5 suggests the provision has a role and function that can be classified as an enabling principle, an interpretive principle and a policy principle, where it guides states in their policy-making and programming activity (*ibid.*: 309). But, as she notes, the Committee's use of "evolving capacities" has:

> introduced a role and function for the term that go well beyond the scope of Article 5 of the UNCRC; and, in so doing, it has recognised a broader principle of evolving capacities under the UNCRC that not only informs the framework of parental direction and guidance, but the interpretation and implementation of the whole of the Convention (*ibid.*).

As a result of the Committee's approach, the concept of evolving capacity 'appears to have taken on a broader role and function outside of the framework of parental guidance and direction' (*ibid.*: 316). At the same time, there has been a neglect of the scope and meaning of 'parental direction and guidance' under Article 5, and such terms remain largely without definition or classification, with neither the Convention nor the Committee expanding on its precise meaning (Tobin and Varadan, 2019: 171). The Committee has articulated that parental guidance is to be exercised in the context of the Convention, to reinforce the child's exercise of their rights and not to diminish the child's status as a rights holder (General Comment No. 7, para. 17). Evidently, parental direction and guidance must be exercised in a manner consistent with all the provisions of the Convention and it must be directed towards enhancing the ability of the child to enjoy his/her rights (Tobin and Varadan, 2019: 172). Taking Article 5 as a whole, then, "evolving capacity" is a mechanism that 'transforms the role of the parent from primary rights-holder over their child, to duty-bearer to their child in the child's exercise of her rights under the UNCRC' (Varadan, 2019: 320). Reflecting the triangular relationship between the child, his/her parents and the state (Lansdown, 2005: ix-x), Article 5 casts the parents in the role of enabler of children's rights, positioned between the state as duty-bearer and the child as rights holder. As this analysis suggests, the role played by parents must change as the child matures and develops the capacity to exercise rights on his/her own behalf. Reflective of its general application, then, the provision has clear relevance to all children and to all areas of the child's life, even if it appears to be particularly important in some areas – like medical decision-making – over others (*ibid.*: xi).

The application to youth justice of the Article 5 concepts of "evolving capacity" and "parental guidance" has not been explored to date and although they have many strengths and possibilities, they come with both conceptual and practical challenges when applied to this area. It is these challenges that this chapter now seeks to explore, before concluding with some ways in which its potential can nonetheless be maximised. The next section introduces the Convention's youth justice provisions before returning to the application of Article 5 to this area.

3   Youth Justice under the UNCRC

The specific rights of children in conflict with the law are recognised in Articles 37 and 40 of the Convention. Article 37 deals mainly with the deprivation of liberty, prohibiting torture and ill-treatment, capital punishment and life imprisonment under Article 37(a) (Nowak, 2019). It protects against arbitrary and illegal use of detention, requiring that any deprivation of liberty is a measure of last resort and for the shortest appropriate period of time (Article 37(b)). It also recognises the child's right to prompt access to legal and other assistance as well as the right to challenge the legality of their detention before a court (Article 37(d)). Article 37(c) recognises the special vulnerability of children deprived of liberty and sets out the specific rights of such children, making particular reference to the importance of family contact. According to the provision:

> Every child deprived of liberty shall be treated with humanity and respect for the inherent dignity of the human person, and in a manner which takes into account the needs of persons of his or her age. In particular, every child deprived of liberty shall be separated from adults unless it is considered in the child's best interest not to do so and shall have the right to maintain contact with his or her family through correspondence and visits, save in exceptional circumstances;

The more general rights of children in conflict with the law are set out in Article 40 of the Convention. Article 40(1) recognises the right of every child alleged as, accused of, or recognized as having infringed the penal law to be treated in a manner consistent with the promotion of the child's sense of dignity and worth, which reinforces the child's respect for the human rights and fundamental freedoms of others and which takes into account the child's age and the desirability of promoting the child's reintegration and the child's assuming a constructive role in society.

This general principle is supplemented by more detailed rights in Article 40(2) which includes a set of minimum due process guarantees such as the presumption of innocence (Article 40(2)(b)(i)), the right to be promptly informed of the charges against him/her (Article 40(2)(b)(ii)), the right to have the matter determined without delay by an independent and fair tribunal (Article 40(2)(b)(iii)), the right to an appeal (Article 40(2)(b)(v)), the right to the assistance of an interpreter (Article 40(2)(b)(vi)), and the right to have privacy full respected throughout the proceedings (Article 40(2)(b)(vii)). Article 40(3) effectively requires states to establish a youth justice system, with specifically applicable law, policies and institutions and in this regard it requires first, the establishment of a minimum age below which children shall be presumed not to have the capacity to infringe the penal law (Article 40(3)(a)) and second, recourse to diversion mechanisms that respect the child's rights and legal safeguards. Finally, then, Article 40(4) requires states to make available a variety of mechanisms, measures and interventions that ensure children are dealt with 'in a manner appropriate to their well-being and proportionate both to their circumstances and the offence'.

These Convention provisions are supplemented by the interpretive guidance of the Committee on the Rights of the Child in its General Comment No. 24, strengthened by several recommendations of the United Nations[4] and the Council of Europe[5] that seek to guide states parties to comply with the standards of children's rights in youth justice. While several children's rights scholars have considered the application of the Convention's youth justice provisions,[6] there has so far been no analysis of Article 5 in this context. This chapter will now seek to address this deficit by dealing first with the concept of evolving capacity, predominantly in the context of "criminal

---

4   See, in particular, the UN Rules on the Administration of Juvenile Justice ("the Beijing Rules"). Adopted by General Assembly resolution 40/33 of 29 November 1985.
5   See the Guidelines of the Committee of Ministers of the Council of Europe on child-friendly justice ("the Guidelines on Child-friendly Justice") adopted by the Committee of Ministers of the Council of Europe on 17 November 2010.
6   See, for example, the special issue of *Youth Justice* in 2008, with the following editorial: Kilkelly, 2008. See also Hollingsworth, 2013.

responsibility", and then, by extension, considering the role of parental guidance and direction in the exercise of children's rights in youth justice proceedings.

4 Evolving Capacity and Criminal Responsibility

As we have learned, Article 5 recognises the right of the child to guidance and direction from parents in the exercise of their rights, in line with their evolving capacity. As Lansdown explains, the provision reflects the reality that when children are young most of the decisions made for their protection are taken by the adults with responsibility for them, with the rationale that such children 'lack the competence to exercise judgement in their own best interests' (Lansdown, 2005: 34). As the child matures into adolescence, matters that affect them personally – choice of school, health-care decision-making – come into view and depending on the cultural context, the 'transfer of control over decision-making' takes place within the family (*ibid.*). However, many decisions are in fact subject to legal boundaries 'that demarcate the age at which the law considers children competent to take responsibility to exercise choice' (*Ibid.*: 35). The purpose of such ages is, in the main, to protect the child from harm or exploitation – this is the case for the legal age of marriage, consenting to medical treatment, sexual consent for instance – and reaching the age in question denotes achievement of a level of capacity commensurate with taking on the relevant responsibility. The age of criminal responsibility is another example, although significantly it is the only area where an age-based approach is mandated by the Convention. As noted above, Article 40(2)(b) of the Convention requires states parties to establish a 'minimum age below which children shall be presumed not to have the capacity to infringe the penal law'. No particular age is mandated by the Convention, but the Committee has recommended the age of 14 years as the minimum that is internationally acceptable (General Comment No. 24, para. 21), taking account of the latest evidence highlighting that adolescence is a unique stage of development characterised by risk-taking, poor impulse control and impaired judgement (General Comment No. 24, para. 22).

The Committee commends those states that have set the age of criminal responsibility at 15 or 16 years in light of the evidence that the adolescent brain continues to mature well beyond the teenage years (General Comment No. 24, para. 22). At the same time, states parties that set the age of criminal responsibility at a low level have been criticised by the Committee (General Comment No. 24, para. 21) and arguments have been put forward to contest what is seen as an unfair and unreasonable approach to holding children responsible in the penal context. For instance, Goldson has argued that there should be coherence between the age of criminal responsibility and age limits in the civil sphere like consenting to medical treatment (Goldson, 2009). As Hollingsworth points out, however, there is a clear, if legal distinction, between legal liability (in the civil sense) and criminal responsibility. The latter, she argues, is distinct from capacity or actual competence, in that it is possible in some legal systems at least, for a child to be held criminally responsible without having capacity (Hollingsworth, 2007). In reality, the age at which the minimum age of criminal responsibility is set is often a political decision, rather than one that is determined by children's capacity to form mens rea: If this were the case there would be no split ages (much criticised by the Committee on the Rights of the Child) where children are deemed to have capacity at one age for certain types of offences and at others for more serious crimes (General Comment No. 24, para. 26). The same applies in jurisdictions where there is no minimum age of criminal responsibility at all or where criminal responsibility is determined with reference to the seriousness of the crime as much as the capacity of the child to understand right from wrong (Cipriani, 2009). McDiarmid has argued that the setting of the age must take account of its underlying complexity and the acquisition of autonomy, reflecting on factors like the child's knowledge of wrongfulness, their understanding of criminality and its consequences, together with his/her psychological development and lived experience (McDiarmid, 2013). Separate again, Elliot argues that until the striking correlation between poor parenting, poverty, abuse and youth offending fades, young people cannot genuinely be considered autonomous individuals who have 'made a choice to commit crime and can be subjected to criminal responsibility' (Elliot, 2011: 297).

While the Committee on the Rights of the Child has not gone so far as to suggest that children who suffer disadvantage and adversity should never be subject to criminal responsibility, it has highlighted the fundamental role that families play in preventing children becoming involved in criminal activity (General Comment No. 24, para. 9). To address this, it has recommended investment to support family capacity and parenting, including programmes that expressly strengthen the family environment (General Comment No. 24, paras. 9–10). The reference to Article 5 in this context makes clear that securing these rights to the child is both a parental responsibility and a measure essential to prevent the child's involvement with criminal activity. It is striking that the guidance of the Committee on the Rights of the Child and international instruments like the UN Guidelines for the Prevention of Juvenile

Delinquency (Riyadh Guidelines) rely heavily on the role of parents to prevent children from coming into conflict with the law. In line with the recognition in Article 18 of the Convention of both parental responsibility to rear their children and the duty of states parties to support parents in this process, the Committee has recommended 'strong involvement' of parents in programmes that prevent children getting into trouble (General Comment No. 24, para. 9).

It is arguable that the concept of "criminal responsibility" is not concerned with whether the child had the autonomy to become involved in criminal activity, but rather whether, in all the circumstances, the child is judged to have the necessary maturity to accept responsibility for those criminal acts. Others have argued that viewed from a children's rights perspective, imposing responsibility in such cases is a coherent children's rights approach. As Cipriani, explains:

> Children's criminal responsibility is indeed an integral and necessary part of children's rights – a logical extension of the concept of children's evolving capacities insofar as it is an appropriate step in respecting children's progression from lesser to greater competence, which gradually prepares them for adult rights and responsibilities in society (Cipriani, 2009: 34).

This viewpoint reinforces the link between a child's autonomy and criminal responsibility, suggesting too that it is difficult to argue that a child with capacity should be protected from being held criminally responsible. Reflecting the complexity here, Hollingsworth considers that imposing criminal responsibility is consistent with respecting a child's autonomy rights (Hollingsworth, 2007), although she accepts it may undermine their protection rights (Eekelaar, 1986).

According to the Committee in General Comment No. 20, Article 5 is 'an enabling principle that addresses the process of maturation and learning through which children progressively acquire competencies, understanding and increasing level of agency to take responsibility and exercise their rights' (General Comment No. 20, para. 18). Tobin and Varadan argue, in line with this, that the concept of "evolving capacities of the child" is:

> an affirmation that all children have a right to exercise their rights irrespective of their age, and as they grow and mature, they become entitled to an increasing level of responsibility, agency and autonomy in the exercise of those rights (Tobin and Varadan, 2019: 178).

It can be argued, therefore, that the downside of evolving capacity is that a child will not always be protected from full responsibility and indeed, as capacity evolves, will be required to take on full responsibility for the exercise of their rights. The question is whether this approach can be considered compatible with the fundamental tenet of children's rights which views children as rights holders, while at the same time assuring to them greater protection than adults on account of their special status and vulnerability. Relevant here is Article 1 of the Convention, which effectively entitles states parties to limit the protection of the Convention through national law. Under Article 1, 'a child means every human being below the age of eighteen years unless under the law applicable to the child, majority is attained earlier'. Although the Committee on the Rights of the Child has been critical of states parties using this provision to avoid their international obligations to children, it is evident nonetheless that Article 1 provides states parties with a mechanism to limit the Convention's protection.

This reflects some of the tensions inherent in recent research that indicates that full maturity of the brain – in areas of decision-making relevant to youth justice – does not occur until early adulthood (Steinberg, 2008). This supports the view that a young person's capacity to make rational decisions depends on his/her maturity, recognising that a distinction can be drawn between "hot" decision-making where the young person is in an aroused state – and "cold" – where more considered judgement can be exercised – to explain why different standards should apply to a young person's decision-making depending on its context (Albert and Steinberg, 2011). It also justifies why young people whose capacity to make rational decisions is not yet fully developed should be spared the full force of the criminal law, or at least full culpability (Scott, 2006). A further reason for distinguishing between criminal capacity and capacity in other areas relates to the fact that there is, as McDiarmid highlights, a public interest at play in pinpointing the age at which criminal responsibility should be imposed on a child that is not evident – at least not as pressing – in age-related decisions in other spheres of a child's life, such as the right to vote, to smoke or to get married (McDiarmid, 2013: 156). At the same time, it is inescapable that, as Lansdown explains,

> ...the potential harm that can accrue from early involvement in the criminal justice system cannot possibly be justified in terms of any perceived benefits to children or the wider society. Children are entitled to have their moral, cognitive, and social capacities respected while simultaneously recognising their entitlement, as children, to protection

from environments and experiences that will damage their immediate and long-term well-being (Lansdown, 2005: 37).

But, in these terms, can it really be said that the concept of evolving capacity does not offer the child protection from the harmful effects of criminal responsibility, especially where the child is not considered to have the capacity for autonomous decision-making in other areas? Taking account of the scientific consensus that exists around the developmental differences between children and adults, certain jurisdictions have accepted the reduced culpability of children (Scott *et al.*, 2016). While the brain science has also been used to raise questions, pertinent to legal capacity, about whether children can in certain circumstances be said to lack developmental competence to stand trial (O'Donnell and Gross, 2012), criminal responsibility does not always mean full culpability.[7] Just because a child is considered competent to stand trial does not mean that no account is taken of his/her particular circumstances either by adapted proceedings or in sentencing (see Bernuz Beneitez and Dumortier, 2018). The European Guidelines on Child-friendly Justice, which go beyond the Article 40 due process guarantees to require a specially-adapted criminal process, are arguably based on this precise premise (Liefaard, 2015; General Comment No. 24, para. 46). Returning to the terms of Article 5, it is important to remember that under this provision, evolving capacity is not an autonomous concept, but rather one that must be viewed in light of the exercise of the parental responsibility of guidance and direction provided to the child in the exercise of his/her rights. Where and how then does parental guidance and direction come into play in youth justice? The paper now turns to address this question.

5 Parental Guidance and Direction

Before considering how Article 5 applies to those parts of Article 40 which make express reference to the role of parents, this chapter will first address the residual question of whether the provision continues to apply to the child who has reached the age of criminal responsibility. If a child is deemed also to have full capacity in line with Article 5, what does this mean for the level of support and guidance that a parent must give to the child in the exercise of his/her

---

[7] See the jurisprudence of the US Supreme Court on this matter in Scott, *et al.*, above. See also the discussion in Kilkelly, U., 'Advancing the rights of Young people in Juvenile Justice: the Impact of Juvenile Law Centre' 88(4) *Temple Law Review* (2016) 629–652.

rights? According to the Committee, parents have a responsibility to 'continually adjust the levels of support and guidance they offer to a child'… taking account of 'a child's interests and wishes as well as the child's capacities for autonomous decision-making and comprehension of his/her best interests' (General Comment No. 7, para. 17). Under Article 18, parents are recognised to have ultimate responsibility for the child's upbringing and development, with the child's best interests as their basic concern. While it is well understood that the exercise of parental responsibility to provide direction and guidance to the child is a dynamic process that depends on the child's capacity, Tobin and Varadan query at what point the threshold of full capacity – where presumably parents no longer play a role – will be met (Tobin and Varadan, 2019: 174). In its General Comment on Adolescent Rights, the Committee explained that in reaching this balance, consideration should be given to a range of factors including, *inter alia*, 'the level of risk involved' and 'the potential for exploitation' (General Comment No. 20, para. 20). At the same time, if a child has reached the level of capacity that, if demonstrated by an adult, would lead to full autonomy, it can be argued that the parent has a residual role to provide continued guidance to the child, where that is in the child's best interests under Article 3. This is also supported by Article 18. Alternatively, it could be said that full capacity permits the child to self-determine whether continued parental involvement is in his/her best interests (Tobin and Varadan, 2019: 175–6). Indeed, as Cipriani suggests above, this may be an inevitable outcome of the application of Article 5 here. An intermediate position may be that even where the child has reached the age of criminal responsibility under Article 40(3) and has achieved full capacity within the meaning of Article 5, the role of a parent to provide direction and guidance may only be extinguished to the extent compatible with full protection of the rights of the child under the Convention. At the same time, it is clearly arguable that where a child has reached capacity equivalent to an adult, meaning that the child has a right autonomously to determine what is in his/her best interests, the parents' role subsides if not disappears altogether (General Comment No. 14, para. 44; see also Tobin and Varadan, 2019: 176). In this scenario, it could be said, the Convention's protections no longer need apply. But autonomy and protection are not a zero sum game and by the same token, incapacity (or indeed capacity) does not have to be 'all or nothing' (Eade, 2001: 168). As Freeman notes, dependency, and thus the need for protection, need not be precluded by autonomy (Freeman, 2008). By extension, the vulnerability of a child entering the criminal justice system – having reached the age of criminal responsibility – should not preclude the application of Article 5, where the responsibility of parents is exercised to effect substantive rights protection. Admittedly, much of the analysis of the inter-play between Articles 3, 5 and 12 focuses on medical decision-making; things may play out differently where criminal responsibility is invoked, not least given the consequences for the child of criminal prosecution. While it could be argued that the case is strengthened even further when the child is to be treated as an adult under the criminal law (as opposed, for example, to being adjudicated in a specially adapted juvenile system), it is arguably irrelevant whether or not the child is treated as a child or an adult once criminal responsibility applies.[8] Tobin and Varadan submit that children should not be 'abandoned to their autonomy' and consider that Article 5 anticipates that parents 'must play an intimate and ongoing role in enabling children to enjoy their rights' (Tobin and Varadan, 2019: 176). Article 12, which recognises the child's right to participate in decisions that affect him/her is relevant here too, along with Article 3 (General Comment No. 12, paras. 57–64; General Comment No. 24, para. 22). How all of these rights are exercised will depend on the context and the circumstances, informed most importantly by the views and needs of the child.

Various Convention provisions recognise the important role that parents play in the lives of children (e.g. Article 9) and in the context of children in conflict with the law, this is specifically reflected in Article 37(c), which recognises the right of children deprived of liberty to maintain contact with family. Although there are clearly circumstances in youth justice where parental involvement is to the child's detriment, if a child can benefit, then the Convention arguably requires that he/she retains the right to guidance and direction from his/her parents with respect to the exercise of his/her rights under Article 40. It is important that the role of parents is explicitly recognised at multiple points in this provision where they play an important supportive role in the exercise of a child's due process rights. Indeed, there are several references to parents in Article 40 of the Convention, some, but not all of which echo the clarity of purpose in Article 5. The first such reference appears in Article 40(2)(ii) which concerns the guarantee that the child will be informed 'promptly and directly of the charges' against his/her, 'if appropriate, through his or her parents or legal guardians'. It is not clear what 'appropriate' means in this context although it is most likely a reference to circumstances where the child needs support to ensure that the charges against him are communicated and, more importantly, understood. Depending on their circumstances, children can often face a challenge understanding the legal and technical jargon

---

[8] Capacity is viewed differently in the civil legal context. See, for example, Liefaard, T., "Access to Justice for Children: Towards a Specific Research and Implementation Agenda" (2019) 27(2) *International Journal of Children's Rights* 195–227.

associated with criminal charges (La Vigne and Miles, 2019). For this reason, the European Guidelines on Child-friendly Justice advocate the importance of the police communicating with children in language that is accessible and easily understood (Guidelines on Child-friendly Justice, 2010, Section C). Equally important is the reliance placed in the Guidelines on the role of parents as a means of supporting children to navigate the criminal justice system (Liefaard, 2015). Article 40(2)(ii) of the UNCRC reflects the Article 5 principle of ensuring parental support in the protection of children's rights. At the same time, the Committee on the Rights of the Child has made it clear that communicating to parents is not 'an alternative to communicating this information to the child' and that rather than leaving it to parents to ensure that the child understands the charge(s) against him/her, it is the responsibility of the authorities to ensure that both the child and his/her parents receive this information in a manner that is easily understood (General Comment No. 24, para. 48).

A more detailed, but similar reference to the supportive parental role is found in Article 40(2)(iii) of the Convention. This provision recognises the child's right to a fair hearing according to law 'in the presence' of the child's parents or legal guardians 'unless it is considered not to be in the best interest of the child, in particular, taking into account his or her age or situation.' Fully in line with the sentiment of Article 5, this provision recognises that there is value to the child of having his/her parents in attendance at their criminal trial insofar as it offers protection to the child in the exercise of his/her rights (Peterson-Badali and Broeking, 2010). According to the Committee on the Rights of the Child, the attendance of parents during trial 'can provide general psychological and emotional assistance to the child' (General Comment No. 24, para. 57). Despite these benefits, however, Article 40 recognises there may be circumstances where a parent's attendance at trial is not in the child's interests. In this regard, the Committee has recommended that it should be up to the competent authority – either at the request of the child and/or his legal or other appropriate assistance – to limit, restrict or exclude the presence of the child's parents from the proceedings in line with Article 3 (General Comment No. 24, para. 56).

Even though research shows that there may indeed be difficulties making parental participation meaningful, mandating parental attendance as a default should in most circumstances offer the child an important base-line of protection during the trial process (Varma, 2007). The importance of family support to children came through the consultation with children on child-friendly justice undertaken by the Council of Europe as part of its development of the European Guidelines on Child-friendly Justice in 2010 (see Liefaard and Kilkelly, 2018). This gave rise to a strengthening of the provision in the

Guidelines for the supportive role that parents can play.[9] At the same time, such participation must be effective – simply compelling participation will not ensure the child's protection of his/her fair trial rights especially in the absence of expert legal representation (Peterson-Badali and Broeking, 2010).

The remainder of Article 40(2)(b) makes no reference to the role of parents, focusing squarely on the due process rights that apply to child defendants in criminal proceedings. Viewing these provisions through the prism of Article 5 raises important questions about the role of parents in the criminal process however. In particular, the question arises as to what guidance and direction is a parent expected to offer with respect, for instance, to the child's right to be presumed innocent or to cross examine witnesses under Article 40(2)(b)(iv) (General Comment No. 24, paras. 54–57)? Similarly, how would parents be expected to guide a child as to his/her right to appeal under Article 40(2)(b)(v)? Evidently, these are technical matters on which the child's legal representative is best placed to provide guidance and direction.[10] It is notable, however, that under Article 40(2)(b)(ii) the child is guaranteed 'legal or other appropriate assistance in the preparation of his or her defence' although the Committee on the Rights of the Child has now recommended that every child accused of a criminal offence receive effective legal representation (General Comment No. 24, para. 51). Nonetheless, the Convention provision contrasts with the European Guidelines on Child-friendly Justice which recognise that a child should be 'provided with access to a lawyer *and* be given the opportunity to contact their parents or a person whom they trust [emphasis added] (Guidelines on Child-friendly Justice, 2010, para. 28). This approach better reflects the distinct roles played by legal representatives and parents in ensuring effective protection of children's rights in the legal system (see Liefaard and Kilkelly, 2018).

Article 40(3) of the UNCRC provides that 'whenever appropriate and desirable, measures are in place for dealing with such children without resorting to judicial proceedings, providing that human rights and legal safeguards are fully respected'. Although there is no reference to parents in this provision, it is important, when read with Article 5, that parents offer direction and guidance in ensuring that the child's rights are protected during diversion. The Committee on the Rights of the Child has highlighted the importance of ensuring that the child's consent to the use of diversion is free and voluntarily given and it

---

9   See the report of the consultation with children and its impact on the drafting process in the published edition of the Guidelines, p. 41.
10 Even this is not simple – see Marrus, E., "Can I Talk Now: Why Miranda Does Not Offer Adolescents Adequate Protections" 79 *Temple Law Review* (2006) 515–534.

has recommended that the child's parents be involved in this process (General Comment No. 24, para. 18). Interestingly, the Committee had, in its General Comment No. 10, specifically recommended that states parties consider requiring the consent of parents to such processes where the child is below the age of 16 years, in order to 'strengthen parental involvement' (General Comment No. 10, para. 27), but this provision was removed when the General Comment was revised. Removal of this provision is welcome given that it was not clear why parental consent was recommended to be mandatory in such situations. Effectively giving parents a veto on whether or not a child can submit to a process designed to divert him/her from the court process could be problematic in light of the fact that not all parents will have the knowledge or understanding to identify the risks associated with submitting to or rejecting a diversionary process (Karp *et al.*, 2004). Poor relationships and/or communication between adolescents and their parents is not uncommon (Steinberg, 2001) and so even though parental guidance will often be conducive to the child's realisation of their rights in such processes, it cannot always be assumed that this will be well received by the child in every case (Peterson-Badali and Broeking, 2010). Although it is beyond the scope of this chapter to discuss the responsibilisation of parents which can occur, including through restorative processes, it is an important reminder of the fine line between parental support for the exercise of the child's rights and a more negative form of parental influence (Richards, 2017). Indeed, it is these precise circumstances that reflect the importance of Article 5.

6 Concluding Analysis

The application of Article 5 in the context of youth justice is complex and as this chapter shows, there is no great clarity between the concepts of autonomy, capacity and responsibility from a children's rights perspective. Although youth justice systems vary, many are either weak or silent on the role of parents while imposing responsibility – sometimes with reduced culpability – on children themselves. This approach is arguably reinforced by Article 40(3)(a) which requires states to identify a minimum age of criminal responsibility, even if the meaning of this status from the perspective of a child's evolving capacity is far from certain. The situation is compounded by a number of other Convention provisions and factors – first, Article 1 of the Convention sets out that all children under 18 years are entitled to enjoy Convention rights unless under applicable national law majority is attained earlier. This suggests

18 as an age of majority – of full capacity – which is contested in the criminal context. Related to this, as noted above, Article 40(3)(a) requires the establishment of a minimum age below which children shall be presumed not to have the capacity to infringe the penal law. Defining what the Convention means by 'the age of criminal responsibility' is not straightforward. Clearly it has a technical meaning in the criminal law in that it reflects the judgement that children above the age have the necessary capacity to form mens rea – but there are also other variables at play, from developmental to political factors, as to whether states parties set an age and, if so, what age they choose. Rarely considered as part of this analysis is the question of what the consequences are for the child who reaches the age of criminal responsibility. For some, these can be very harsh indeed – with long sentences of detention – whereas for others, diversionary schemes or more progressive interventions are possible. It is important that the Convention contemplates that some children or at least children below a certain age, do not have criminal capacity or competence to stand trial, although it is problematic that the Convention does not specify a minimum age given that states can and do pick ages that are extremely low. In this regard, it is welcome that the Committee on the Rights of the Child has now identified 14 as the minimum age that is internationally acceptable. At the same time, the latest research on developmental psychology and neuroscience raises serious questions about the unfairness (if not illegitimacy) of imposing responsibility on children whose blameworthiness is evidently diluted by their developmental stage, including their inability to assess consequences and likely engagement in reckless and impulsive risk taking. While this body of evidence provides important guidance – on the question of culpability if not also capacity – it does not answer the fundamental question of the age at which it is Convention compliant to impose full criminal responsibility on children, to subject them to the rigours of a full criminal trial and to impose on them penalties that pay no attention to a child's susceptibility to develop and change. It is arguably time to develop a more robust argument, based on these factors, for never imposing full criminal responsibility on children whose choices and decision-making may well be fundamentally impaired by their reduced capacity. Article 5 should be used in the articulation of such arguments.

Turning to the other aspect of Article 5, it is important that this provision, combined with Article 18, requires parental responsibility to be directed to the child's positive and constructive development, even if the Convention and its guidance says little about what role it should play in decision-making around criminal responsibility. A child with fully evolved capacity can decline parental guidance and direction in the exercise of his/her rights under Article 5. However, it does not follow that reaching the age of criminal responsibility, however harsh the consequences for the child, deprives a child of the Convention's vital protections. Indeed, it is arguable that reaching the age of criminal responsibility strengthens rather than undermines the importance of ensuring that the child receives the requisite support to enable his/her enjoyment of the fair trial rights set out in Article 40 wherein the supportive role of the parent is re-enforced. The participation of parents is mandated at key points in the criminal process even if the limits of their role – and the possibility that it may at times undermine the child's rights – are recognised. The bulk of Article 40, with some exceptional references to parents, sets out the procedural guarantees of due process to which every child is entitled and which are fundamental to the fairness of the child's criminal proceedings. This provision directs itself almost exclusively to the child as rights holder and the framing of the provision leaves no doubt that the child is the person who not only holds (as with other Convention provisions) but also must exercise those rights. In addition, Article 40 rights demand active participation in the trial process (Rap, 2016). For example, the rights set out under 40(2)(b) must be exercised by the child as the subject of the trial process, as the child decides whether to cross-examine witnesses, appeal or seek the assistance of an interpreter. Given what is at stake for the child in such proceedings, it is submitted that Article 5 must have a very different application here, if indeed it applies at all. The difference between the emotional support provided by parents in supporting the child to exercise his/her rights and the professional, independent representation of a lawyer is clear, even if the absence of the legal representative, this most important enabler of the child's rights, is not of itself contrary to the Convention. By contrast, the Guidelines on Child-friendly Justice do more to recognise the vulnerability of the child as a subject of the criminal process, setting out the advocacy, representation and support requirements that are essential to enable legal safeguards to be effective (Liefaard, 2015). If parental responsibility could be exercised to promote mandatory independent representation for children in criminal proceedings, that would truly enable the exercise of the child's rights in youth justice in line with Article 5.

Acknowledgement

Thanks to the editors, Dr Claire Fenton-Glynn and Dr Brian Sloan, for their support and to the anonymous reviewer for their very helpful comments.

References

Albert, D. and Steinberg, L., "Judgment and Decision-making in Adolescence", *Journal of Research on Adolescence* 2011 (21(1), 211–224.

Bernuz Beneitez, M. J. and Dumortier, E., "Why Children Obey the Law: Rethinking Juvenile Justice and Children's Rights in Europe through Procedural Justice", *Youth Justice* 2018 (18(1)), 34–51.

Cipriani, D., *Children's Rights and the Minimum Age of Criminal Responsibility: A Global Perspective* (Abingdon: Ashgate, 2009).

Eade, S., "Legal Incapacity, Autonomy and Children's Rights", *Newcastle Law Review* 2001 (5), 157.

Eekelaar, J., "The emergence of children's rights", *Oxford Journal of Legal Studies* 1986 (6), 161–182.

Elliot, C., 'Criminal responsibility and children: A new defence required to acknowledge the absence of capacity and choice', *Journal of Criminal Law* 2011 (75(4)), 289–308.

Freeman, M. "The Sociology of Childhood and Children's Rights", *The International Journal of Children's Rights* 1998 (6), 433–444.

Goldson, B., "Counterblast: 'Difficult to Understand or to Defend': A Reasoned Case for Raising the Age of Criminal Responsibility", *The Howard Journal of Criminal Justice* 2009 (48), 514–521.

Hanson, K. and Lundy, L., "Does Exactly What it Says on the Tin? A Critical Analysis and Alternative Conceptualisation of the So-called 'General Principles' of the Convention on the Rights of the Child", *The International Journal of Children's Rights* 2017 (25), 285–306.

Hollingsworth, K., "Responsibility and Rights: Children and Their Parents in the Youth Justice System", *International Journal of Law, Policy and the Family* 2007 (21(2)), 190–219.

Hollingsworth, K., "Theorising Children's Rights in Youth Justice: the Significance of Autonomy and Foundational Rights", *Modern Law Review* 2013 (76(6)), 1046–1069.

Karp, D., Sweet, M., Kirshenbaum, A. and Bazemore, G., "Reluctant Participants in Restorative Justice? Youthful Offenders and Their Parents", *Contemporary Justice Review* 2004 (7(2)), 199–216.

Kilkelly, U., "Youth Justice and Children's Rights: Measuring Compliance with International Standards", *Youth Justice* 2008 (8(3)), 187–192.

La Vigne, M. and Miles, S., "Under the Hood: Brendan Dassey, Language Impairments and Judicial Ignorance", *Albany Law Review* 2019 (82(3)), 873–974.

Lansdown, G., *The evolving capacities of the child* (Florence: UNICEF Innocenti Research Centre, 2005).

Liefaard, T., "Child-friendly Justice: Protection and Participation of Children in the Justice System", *Temple Law Review* 2015 (88), 905–928.

Liefaard, T. and Kilkelly, U., "Child-friendly Justice: Past, Present and Future" in Goldson, B. (ed.), *Juvenile Justice in Europe: Past, Present and Future* (Abingdon: Routledge, 2018).

McDiarmid, C., "An Age of Complexity: Children and Criminal Responsibility in Law", *Youth Justice* 2013 (13(2)), 145–160.

Nowak, M., *UN Global Study on Children deprived of Liberty* (Geneva: United Nations, 2019).

O'Donnell, P. and Gross, B., "Developmental Incompetence to Stand Trial in Juvenile Courts", *Journal of Forensic Sciences* 2012 (57(4)) 989–996.

Peterson-Badali, M. and Broeking, J., "Parents' Involvement in the Youth Justice System: Rhetoric and Reality", *Canadian Journal of Criminology and Criminal Justice* 2010 (52(1)), 1–27.

Rap, S., "A children's rights perspective on the participation of juvenile defendants in the youth court", *The International Journal of Children's Rights* 2016 (24(1)), 94–112.

Richards, K., 'Responsibilising the parents of young offenders through restorative justice: a genealogical account', *Restorative Justice* 2017 (5(1)), 93–115.

Scott, E., "Adolescence and the Regulation of Youth Crime", *Temple Law Review* 2006 (79), 337–356.

Scott, E., Grisso, T., Levick, M. and Steinberg, L., "Juvenile Sentencing Reform in a Constitutional Framework", *Temple Law Review* 2016 (88), 675–716.

Steinberg, L., "A Social Neuroscience Perspective on Adolescent Risk-Taking", *Developmental Review* 2008 (28(1)) 78–106.

Steinberg, L., 'We Know Some Things: Parent–Adolescent Relationships in Retrospect and Prospect', *Journal of Research and Adolescence* 2001 (11(1)), 1–19.

Sutherland, E.E., "The Enigma of Article 5 of the United Nations Convention on the Rights of The Child: Central or Peripheral?", *The International Journal of Children's Rights* 2020 (28(3), 447–470.

Tobin, J. and Varadan, S., "Article 5: The Right to Parental Direction and Guidance Consistent with a Child's Evolving Capacities" in Tobin, J. (ed.), *The UN Convention on the Rights of the Child* (New York: OUP, 2019).

UN Committee on the Rights of the Child (1996), General guidelines regarding the form and contents of periodic reports to be submitted by States Parties under Article 44, para. 1 (b), of the Convention, adopted by the Committee.

UN Committee on the Rights of the Child, General Comment No. 10 (2007), Children's rights in juvenile justice, 25 April 2007, CRC/C/GC/10.

UN Committee on the Rights of the Child, General Comment No. 12, the right of the child to be heard (2009), 20 July 2009, CRC/C/GC/12.

UN Committee on the Rights of the Child, General Comment No. 14 (2013) on the right of the child to have his or her best interests taken as a primary consideration (art. 3, para. 1), 29 May 2013, CRC/C/GC/14.

UN Committee on the Rights of the Child, General Comment No. 20 (2016) on the implementation of the rights of the child during adolescence, 6 December 2016, CRC/C/GC/20.

UN Committee on the Rights of the Child, General Comment No. 24 (2019), Children's Rights in the Child Justice System, 18 September 2019, CRC/C/GC/24.

UN Committee on the Rights of the Child, General Comment No. 5 (2003), General measures of implementation of the Convention on the Rights of the Child, 27 November 2003, CRC/GC/2003/5.

UN Committee on the Rights of the Child, General Comment No. 7 (2005), Implementing child rights in early childhood, 20 September 2006, CRCC/GC/7/Rev.1.

Varadan, S., "The Principle of Evolving Capacities under the UN Convention on the Rights of the Child", *The International Journal of Children's Rights* 2019 (27), 306–338.

Varma, K., "Parental Involvement in Youth Court", *Canadian Journal of Criminology and Criminal Justice* 2007 49(2), 231–260.

CHAPTER 5

Parental Guidance in Support of Children's Participation Rights

The Interplay Between Articles 5 and 12 in the Family Justice System

Nicola Taylor

1   Introduction

Articles 5 and 12 are each acclaimed for their significance within the United Nations Convention on the Rights of the Child (UNCRC) 1989 but, in the context of post-separation parenting arrangements, there is benefit in considering them in relation to each other. Article 5 states that parents have responsibilities, rights and duties, in a manner consistent with their child's evolving capacities, to provide direction and guidance to their child in the exercise of their rights under the UNCRC. Article 12, the child's right to express their views, is therefore one of the rights in the Convention that Article 5 behoves parents to assist their child in exercising. This can be particularly important when decisions are needing to be made about a child's care and contact arrangements in the aftermath of parental separation. The focus of the family justice system to date has, however, primarily been on the role that a range of professionals play in ascertaining children's views and giving effect to their right to participate in the decision-making processes affecting them. There has been much less emphasis on parents' responsibilities, rights and duties in helping children achieve their Article 12 rights. Even where this is evident, it is often framed from a professional perspective of concern about parental manipulation, coaching or undue influence on the child's views in high conflict interparental disputes and litigation.

This chapter begins by considering Article 12 and Article 5 and then the interplay between them. Sociocultural considerations are discussed, and the concept of scaffolding used to illustrate the collaborative endeavour envisaged by the nexus between Articles 5 and 12 when parents support, guide and assist a child to express their views and be heard. To ascertain how the expression of children's thoughts, feelings and views contributes to the making of post-separation parenting arrangements the key findings of a nationwide empirical study (2016–2020) with 655 separated parents and 364 family justice professionals, following the

2014 reform of New Zealand's family justice system, are explored. These data confirm the significance of parental engagement with children when post-separation issues arise and provide encouraging evidence of the scope and impact of such child consultation in intrafamilial decision-making contexts.

2 Article 12

Article 12 of the UNCRC is well recognised as the foundation for the child's right to express their views. However, child participation is not just a right in itself, it is also one of the four General Principles for interpreting and implementing all other provisions within the Convention (UN Committee, 2009). The elevated status that Article 12 thus enjoys is reflected in contemporary family law contexts where national law emphasises the need to provide opportunities to hear children, either directly or through a representative, in judicial and administrative proceedings that affect them. Internationally, this has given rise to a myriad of procedural mechanisms and a diverse range of legal, judicial and social science professionals seeking to give effect to domestic obligations to comply with the UNCRC and afford children their Article 12 rights. This focus has, to date, been strongly directed to the more formalised means by which children can express their views in family law proceedings – for example, through the appointment of children's legal representatives, by the judge meeting directly with the child, through the child's engagement with counsellors, mediators, social workers or psychologists, or by the child being able to initiate proceedings, or appeal a decision, in their own right (Birnbaum, 2009; Goldson and Taylor, 2009; Morrison et al., 2020; Schrama et al., 2021; Taylor, 2017; Taylor et al., 2007, 2012; Tisdall, 2016).

Research in this field has also flourished over the past 25 years (Birnbaum and Saini, 2012; Gal and Duramy, 2015) and confirmed children's desire for opportunities to be heard within the family justice system when decisions about their post-separation parenting arrangements are being made (Beckhouse, 2016; Cashmore, 2011; Clarke, 2013; Gollop et al., 2000; Taylor and Gollop, 2015; Yasenik and Graham, 2016). Much of this research has explored children's perspectives on their experiences of expressing their views to professionals within mediation and court contexts (Bala and Birnbaum, 2018; Bala et al., 2013; Bell, 2016a; Bell et al., 2013; Birnbaum and Bala, 2009, 2010; Birnbaum et al., 2011; Carson et al., 2018; Cashmore and Parkinson, 2008, 2009; Gollop and Taylor, 2012; Hayes and Birnbaum, 2019; Holt, 2018; Lodge and Alexander, 2010; McIntosh et al., 2009; Morag et al., 2012; Quigl and Cyr, 2018; Turoy-Smith and Powell, 2016; Turoy-Smith et al., 2018; Walker, 2013). This has revealed the importance of adults' ability to engage effectively with children, provide information, aid understanding of their family situation and/or parents' dispute, scaffold the expression of their views, and explain the implications of the decision ultimately made. Major barriers thwarting child participation have been found to include professionals' lack of skills, time and commitment to participatory practice, children's loyalty conflicts and related fears (especially in the context of heightened interparental conflict and hostility), parental influence or manipulation, and adults' beliefs about children's cognitive capabilities and the burden of responsibility they may bear from becoming involved in the decision-making process (Bell, 2016b; McMellon and Tisdall, 2020; Morrison et al., 2020; Parkinson and Cashmore, 2008; Turoy-Smith et al., 2018).

Despite the prominent role of professionals in ascertaining children's views in family law proceedings, parents have, of course, long shared their children's thoughts, views and feelings with professionals and courts. This was – and still is – a key way that courts come to know what may be important to the child, particularly when there is no direct or indirect engagement by professionals with the child. However, there can be concern about the objectivity of this parent-provided information when it is cited to support each parent's own position rather than their child's best interests. Having children express their own views directly to a judge or to another professional who relays them to the court can therefore assist in avoiding the partisanship that parents may employ in their applications, affidavits and evidence. However, it should not negate the onus placed on parents to co-parent effectively, which includes engaging positively with their children during times of family transition. Nor should it displace the onus on family justice professionals to better encourage and support parents to consult with their children.

3 Article 5

Article 5 of the UNCRC requires States Parties to 'respect the responsibilities, rights and duties of parents ... to provide, in a manner consistent with the evolving capacities of the child, appropriate direction and guidance in the exercise by the child of the rights recognized in the present Convention'. The interplay between Articles 5 and 12 of the UNCRC in the context of decisions about post-separation parenting arrangements is a previously under-considered, yet promising, avenue in family dispute resolution in that it focuses on how best to enhance parental responsibilities, rights and duties in support of child-inclusive practice. Shifting the emphasis to incorporate familial aspects has the benefit of widening the family justice frame of reference for child participation beyond the existing statutory provisions, professionals' roles and court processes that already feature so prominently.

4 The Interplay between Articles 5 and 12 and Sociocultural Considerations

The United Nations Committee on the Rights of the Child (2009) explicitly discusses both Articles 12 and 5 in General Comment Number 12: The Right of the Child to be Heard (paras 84–85). The Committee first emphasises the child's 'right to direction and guidance' by parents, legal guardians or members of the extended family or community and notes that this has 'to compensate for' the child's 'lack of knowledge, experience or understanding' which 'are restricted by his or her evolving capacities' (para 84). The Committee then states:

> The more the child himself or herself knows, has experienced and understands, the more the parent, legal guardian or other persons legally responsible for the child have to transform direction and guidance into reminders and advice and later to an exchange on an equal footing. This transformation will not take place at a fixed point in a child's development, but will steadily increase as the child is encouraged to contribute her or his views. (2009, para 84)

It is in paragraph 85 that the UN Committee (2009) makes an explicit link between Articles 5 and 12:

> This [article 5] requirement is stimulated by article 12 of the Convention, which stipulates that the child's views must be given due weight, whenever the child is capable of forming her or his own views. In other words, as children acquire capacities, so they are entitled to an increasing level of responsibility for the regulation of matters affecting them.

It is evident that the Committee's link between the two Articles is focused upon the 'evolving capacities' aspect of Article 5 and the requirement in Article 12(1) for a child 'capable of forming his or her views' to have those views 'given due weight'. Interestingly, the Article 12(1) qualification 'in accordance with the age and maturity of the child' is absent from paragraph 85. The Committee's emphasis is thus on the child's capacities and capabilities in forming and expressing their views and on their evolving sophistication in this regard as they steadily advance towards being able to 'exchange on an equal footing' and become 'entitled to an increasing level of responsibility for the regulation of matters affecting them'. The Committee appropriately noted that a 'parent, legal guardian or other persons legally responsible for the child' must 'transform [their] direction and guidance' to match the child's emerging ability to contribute their views (2009, para 84).

This transformative role for parents is consistent with the sociocultural approach to child development in which Vygotsky invented the concept of a "zone of proximal development" to indicate the difference between aided performance and independent solving of a task by a child (Smith, 1998).

> Vygotsky argued that instruction should be more closely linked with the child's level of potential development, rather than be tied to their level of actual development as measured by their independent performance, because the skilled help of an adult (or more competent peer) working jointly with the child could greatly extend the child's competencies. (Taylor, 2006, p. 160)

Instead of waiting for children's cognitive readiness to emerge at a particular age or stage of development (as Piaget espoused), adults can stimulate a child's development through the relationships and interactions in social contexts in which they have participated (Smith, 1998). The guidance and interactional support given to the child by a more competent other in the zone of proximal development gradually builds the child's understanding and competency. "Scaffolding", a sociocultural concept coined by Bruner, explains the role of the adult in enabling children to do as much as they can by themselves, while supporting and guiding them in what they cannot yet achieve (Wood et al., 1976).

> The child moves from being a spectator to a participant and, with the support of the more competent other, gradually acquires mastery over the task. This is not just a one-way process from adult to child. Instead children take an active inventive role as they reconstruct a task through their own understanding. (Taylor, 2006, p. 160)

Family justice professionals have embraced this concept of scaffolding by adopting more child-inclusive modes of practice to enhance children's meaningful participation within family, legal and judicial decision-making processes (Taylor, 2005, 2006). Instead of the longstanding preoccupation with children's cognitive capacity, age and maturity, sociocultural principles have shifted the onus onto adults to understand, support, guide and assist the child to build their competence.

> The job of taking children seriously is the responsibility of adults and requires the development of a mindset and skills to translate the principles into practice. It means that parents and professionals need to be accepting of children's involvement and not dismissive of children's capacity to formulate and express a view simply by reason of age. Children's capaci-

> ties are very much an interactive and relational process of dialogue, determined as much by the "hearing" and "scaffolding" capacities of the adults they engage with as their own expressive capacities. At the same time, it means providing a space and the means for children to be involved, or not as they wish, and importantly recognising both children's need and right to protection and their right to participate. (Cashmore, 2011, p. 520)

This sociocultural focus on the child's evolving mastery over tasks can be extrapolated to the ascertainment and expression of children's thoughts, feelings and views (Smith, 2002; Smith et al., 2003) and to the key role that parents play in their children's lives. As Article 5 states, parents have responsibilities, rights and duties to provide appropriate direction and guidance to their children in the exercise of their rights. Together with Article 12, this means that in post-separation family justice contexts when parenting arrangements are being decided, how parents fulfil their role in scaffolding their children's understanding and expression of views is as important, if not often more important, than the role undertaken by the counsellors, mediators, psychologists, social workers, lawyers or judges involved in negotiating or judicially determining the children's residence and contact arrangements. Parents (usually) enjoy an enduring relationship with their children, while family justice professionals have a singular or intermittent, rather than continuous, relationship. This means it is particularly important to turn our attention to the collaborative endeavour envisaged by the nexus between Articles 5 and 12 to better respect the responsibilities, rights and duties of parents to scaffold their children's understanding and free expression of their views in all relevant matters. The findings from a large-scale nationwide study undertaken in New Zealand on post-separation parenting arrangements provide promising support for this. To set this research in context, the 2014 reforms to New Zealand's family law system are first outlined, together with an explanation of the law relating to the ascertainment of children's views and parents' duties, powers, rights, and responsibilities as guardians.

5   The 2014 Reforms of New Zealand's Family Law System

The family law reforms that took effect in New Zealand on 31 March 2014 were based on a review undertaken by the Ministry of Justice from 2011–2014 and marked the most significant changes to the family justice system since the Family Court's establishment in 1981 (Taylor, 2017). The review had identified that the Court's processes were complex, uncertain and too slow; there was a lack of focus on children and vulnerable people; and insufficient support for resolving parenting issues out-of-court (Office of the Minister of Justice, 2012). The reforms were intended 'to ensure a modern, accessible family justice system that is responsive to children and vulnerable people, and is efficient and effective' (Family Court Proceedings Reform Bill 2012, Explanatory Note: General Policy Statement).

They largely focused on Care of Children Act 2004 matters, which include issues relating to children's post-separation care arrangements such as guardianship, day-to-day care and contact, and aimed to shift the emphasis away from resolving such parenting disputes within the Family Court to encouraging and supporting parents to reach agreement themselves.

Amongst other things, the reforms involved an update to the Ministry of Justice website, introduced a phoneline for parents to call for advice and made the free information programme, Parenting Through Separation, mandatory for many applicants before they proceed to the Family Court. A new mediation service, Family Dispute Resolution (FDR), was also established for parents to resolve parenting and guardianship matters out-of-court. An approved FDR provider (a mediator) assists parents and guardians to identify the issues in dispute, facilitates discussion, and helps them to reach agreements that focus on the needs of their children. FDR is mandatory for most parties prior to commencing Care of Children Act 2004 proceedings, unless an exemption is granted (such as when the matter is urgent, there are safety risks or a significant power imbalance exists, or parties consent to orders). Access to the Family Court is still available if FDR is unsuccessful. The cost of FDR is fully subsidised for parties who meet an eligibility test for out-of-court support. For those not eligible, the cost is $897.00. In December 2016, a new 12-hour mediation model was introduced which finally placed greater emphasis on child participation in FDR and extended Preparation for Mediation (PFM, initially called Preparatory Counselling) to better prepare parents for the mediation process (Taylor, 2017).

Within the Family Court, the reforms introduced a new three-track system, excluded lawyers from the initial stages of non-urgent on-notice court processes, promoted self-representation, and limited the appointment criteria for lawyers representing children to situations where there are 'concerns for the safety or well-being of the child' and such an appointment is 'necessary' (s 7, Care of Children Act 2004).

6   Care of Children Act 2004

6.1   *Ascertaining Children's Views*

The Care of Children Act 2004 includes an expansive provision for children's participation (s 6), which requires a child to 'be given reasonable opportunities' to express their views on matters affecting them and to have their views taken into account whether expressed directly (for example, at a judicial meeting) or through a representative (for example, a lawyer appointed by the Family Court to represent them). Section 6 does not mention any constraints on this requirement such as the child's 'age and maturity' qualification in Article 12(1), nor the child's 'evolving capacities' in Article 5. However, despite New Zealand's progressive statutory provision, judges still tend to attach greater significance to the views of children aged 11 or older, who express strongly and consistently held views, rather than younger children aged under seven or any child considered to have been influenced, coached or aligned by a parent (Robinson and Henaghan, 2011).

Section 6 only applies in proceedings involving the guardianship of, or the role of providing day-to-day care for, or contact with, a child (s 6(1)(a)). It is interpreted as being primarily directed to the ascertainment of children's views by professionals (mainly lawyer for the child and/or judges in the New Zealand context) rather than parents, although its wording could perhaps allow for this if a parent was considered to be a 'representative' of the child.

6.2   Guardianship

Article 5 is reflected in New Zealand's law governing the definition and exercise of guardianship. Guardianship of a child means having, in relation to the child, 'all duties, powers, rights, and responsibilities that a parent of the child has in relation to the upbringing of the child' (s 15(a) Care of Children Act 2004). In exercising these duties, powers, rights, and responsibilities, 'a guardian of the child must act jointly (in particular, by consulting wherever practicable with the aim of securing agreement) with any other guardians of the child' (s 16(5) Care of Children Act 2004). Furthermore, the guardian(s) duties, powers, rights, and responsibilities include 'determining for or with the child, or helping the child to determine, questions about important matters affecting the child' (s 16(1)(c) Care of Children Act 2004). These important matters are further defined in s 16(2) as including the child's name, place of residence, medical treatment, education, culture, language and religion – all of which can become very important when post-separation disputes arise over where, for example, a child will live or attend school.

The duties, powers, rights, and responsibilities of guardians, who will most often also be the child's parents, in New Zealand are consistent with the duties, rights and responsibilities of parents articulated in Article 5. The statutory imperative for guardians to consult together and to help the child determine important matters affecting the child is reflected in the Article 5 wording about the role of parents in providing 'appropriate direction and guidance' to their child in the exercise of the child's rights. This synergy between New Zealand's domestic law and the UNCRC is, of course, welcome but most parents/guardians are unlikely to be aware of it. Explaining the significance of guardianship can be an important tool in reassuring recently separated parents of the nature of their enduring role in their children's lives – their duties, powers, rights, and responsibilities remain intact even though their household arrangements are now divided. The emphasis in lawyers' offices and the courts, however, is usually on the requirement for guardians to act jointly by consulting each other and, ideally, securing agreement (s 16(5)). Less emphasis seems to be placed on encouraging parents to engage with their child to help determine important matters affecting the child (s 16(1)(c)). There is thus much scope for this to be addressed in the context of the interplay between Articles 5 and 12. The recent findings of a New Zealand study are now considered to see whether talking with children is something that is important or helpful to separated parents when determining the future care and contact arrangements.

7 New Zealand Parenting Arrangements After Separation Study

7.1 *Methodology and Sample*

A nationwide study was undertaken from 2014–2020 to evaluate New Zealand's 2014 family law reforms and to better understand the range of pathways that families use to resolve decisions about their children's post-separation care. Phase One (2014–2015) involved consultation with the family justice sector and the initial scoping and planning for an empirical project (Gollop *et al.*, 2015). In Phase Two (2016–2020), a large-scale mixed-methods study examined 364 family justice professionals' and 655 separated parents' perceptions and experiences of dispute resolution processes regarding decisions about children's care arrangements since the reforms took effect (Gollop *et al.*, 2019, 2020; Taylor *et al.*, 2019).

Separated parents who had made or changed their parenting arrangements since 31 March 2014 completed an online survey on the study website that was open for nine months from July 2017 to April 2018. The majority of the 655 parents were female (80%) and mothers (78%). Most identified as New Zealand European (87%) and/or Māori, Pasifika, Asian or other (Gollop *et al.*, 2019). They lived across all 16 regions of New Zealand, reflecting comparable regional population estimates. Family violence, mental health issues and Police involvement were present in around a third or more of the participants' situations and a third (33%) held safety concerns for themselves. An even higher proportion (42%) were concerned for their children's safety. Over a third reported that mental health (39%) or family violence (37%) was an issue at the time they were making the parenting arrangements. In nearly a quarter of cases there were addiction issues and supervised contact. Just under a fifth (18%) reported involvement with the statutory child protection department or the existence of a protection order. Most (70%) reported a 'poor' or 'very poor' relationship with their former partner at the time they were making or changing parenting arrangements, with nearly half (47%) describing the relationship as 'very poor'. Only 13% reported a 'good' or 'very good' relationship.

At the end of the online survey, respondents were invited to express their interest in taking part in an interview to share, in greater depth, their experiences and perspectives. One hundred and eighty of these parents and caregivers participated in an interview with a member of the research team, mostly by telephone. The majority of the interviewees were female (77%), mothers (75%) and the resident or shared care parent (70%) (Gollop et al., 2020). Most identified as New Zealand European (84%) and/or Māori (11%) and they lived across most regions of New Zealand. The interviewee sub-sample was therefore very similar to the survey sample. Their semi-structured interview schedule asked about the dispute resolution pathway and steps they had taken to make or change their parenting arrangements, their use of family justice services, what had helped or hindered them, the outcome they achieved, and their advice to family justice professionals and other separated parents.

7.2   Children's Thoughts, Feelings and Views

The survey asked parents which steps (out of a possible 33) they had taken to make or change their parenting arrangements (Gollop et al., 2019). Most had taken informal steps (97%), with around two-thirds (67%) using family justice services funded by the government, lawyers (66%), and community or private services (57%).[1] Sixteen steps were the ones most commonly taken by at least 20% of the participants (see Table 5.1).

With the exception of seeking legal advice (59.2%), the most frequently taken steps were informal ones, with parents discussing the arrangements with their former partner (74.6%) being their most common step. Talking with their children and seeking their thoughts, feelings and views was reported by 66% of the parents and was the second most common step taken. Discussing matters with family members (57.8%) and friends/acquaintances (55.9%) was also frequently reported, as was reading books, articles or pamphlets (42.9%),

---

1   Only data from the 417 parents who had completed making or changing their parenting arrangements was included in this particular analysis; those still in the process were excluded.

TABLE 5.1 Most common steps taken to make or change parenting arrangements

Step Taken	n	Percent
Discussed them with the other parent/party	311	74.6
Talked with the children and sought their thoughts, feelings and views	275	66.0
Sought legal advice	247	59.2
Discussed them with family members/whānau (extended family)	241	57.8
Discussed them with friends/acquaintances	233	55.9
Read books, articles or pamphlets	179	42.9
Used the Internet and/or social media	173	41.5
Used the Ministry of Justice website	166	39.8
Went to the Family Court	154	36.9
Negotiated with ex-partner/the other party through lawyers	154	36.9
Attended a Parenting through Separation (PTS) course	138	33.1
Sought advice from a health, social service or education professional	119	28.5
Accessed support groups (including online)	114	27.3
Attended privately-paid counselling	103	24.7
Used the Ministry of Justice 'Making a Parenting Plan' workbook	101	24.2
Went to Family Dispute Resolution/Family mediation	100	24.0

Note: Multiple selection was possible. Hence, percentages do not sum to 100.

using the Internet or social media (41.5%) or accessing the Ministry of Justice website (39.8%).

Once the parents had selected all the steps they had taken, they were asked to indicate which ones they found most helpful in making or changing their parenting arrangements by ranking the top three – see Table 5.2.

Talking with the children and seeking their thoughts, feelings and views was the step that the greatest percentage of separated parents (58.2%) rated as one of the top three most helpful steps. Discussions with their former partner (48.6%) and seeking legal advice (48.2%) were reported to be the second and third most helpful steps taken.

> We've always been really open with the kids about all of our discussions. Any decisions that we make as a family, we've always sat down together. Firstly, my ex and I sat down, and we talked about what each of us wanted and what we thought would be best for the kids. Then we sat down as a family and discussed it with the kids and gave them an opportunity to tell us how they felt. We're always mindful that the kids may feel a little bit of

TABLE 5.2 Most helpful steps taken to make or change parenting arrangements

Step Taken	n	Percent
Talked with children and sought their thoughts, feelings and views	160	58.2%
Discussed with the other parent/party	151	48.6%
Sought legal advice	119	48.2%
Went to the Family Court	64	41.6%
Attended private counselling	41	39.8%
Attended community counselling	23	35.4%
Discussed with family members/whānau (extended family)	82	34.0%
Went to Family Dispute Resolution/Family mediation	32	32.0%
Attended a Parenting Through Separation course	43	31.2%
Discussed with friends	69	29.6%
Negotiated with ex-partner/the other party through lawyers	43	27.9%

> pressure to agree with one parent or not, or didn't want to hurt another parent's feelings. We put it to them as, 'Mum and Dad have talked about it and this is what we think would be best, but we want to hear what your opinions are'. (1501, Mother; Interview – Gollop et al., 2020, p. 53)

The parents were next asked to indicate how their parenting arrangements were ultimately decided and by whom. Three per cent said the parenting arrangements 'just happened' and no-one decided. Mostly, though, the parents decided together (44%) or a unilateral decision was made by the survey respondent (12% - 'I decided') or by their former partner (8%). Interestingly, in 7% of cases the children were said to have decided the parenting arrangements. A third (34%) had resolved the arrangements through the Family Court, but only 23% of them reported that a judge had determined the arrangements – the remaining 11% of cases involved the parties reaching an agreement at some point during the court process before a judicial decision was needed.

> Our daughter expressed an interest in making the change so we all talked about it, gave her options that worked for all of us, and she decided which she wanted to try. (1001, Mother; Survey – Gollop et al., 2019, p. 36)

Parents reported that consulting together (as guardians) to agree on important aspects of their children's lives, as well as talking with their children and taking their views and feelings into account, were among the most helpful strategies they had used to reach agreement on their children's day-to-day care and contact. Children became better informed about their family situation and could contribute, where appropriate, to the arrangements being made. Some parents had felt encouraged in this approach by the family justice professionals they encountered (for example, lawyers, mediators, counsellors, judges) and the services (like Parenting Through Separation) they had utilised.

> The judge showed me how getting input out of the child was good and the seminars we went to talked about it as well. I have to admit that played a big part in how I was talking to my family about these changes. ... So, I guess I have used a lot from what I have learned and what was suggested to me. (1076, Mother; Interview – Gollop et al., 2020, p. 53)

> Our eldest has been very pragmatic about this. She straight away wanted to be shown the Google calendar that we have the kids' schedule in and that we base the rules around, in terms of notice, if we need to make any changes. She wanted to be able to see that so she could visualise it and work it out in her mind. When we made this most recent change, we both agreed that it made sense to ask her what she thought – we both agreed that she was old enough. So, it was good to get her feedback. (1004, Mother; Interview – Gollop et al., 2020, p. 53)

7.3   *Parenting Through Separation*

Parenting Through Separation (PTS) is a nationwide four-hour programme that provides information for parents on the effect of separation on their children and how to make a parenting plan. The two sessions, which are free, have to be attended by former partners separately. Since the 2014 reforms, PTS has been compulsory for separated parents wanting to make an application to the Family Court for a parenting order or to resolve a disagreement about their children's care arrangements. PTS is thus the key service in New Zealand's family justice system that helps parents/guardians better understand the impact of separation on children, how to communicate with children, and how to co-parent effectively. The majority (85%) of the survey respondents were aware of PTS and 40% ($n = 260$) had attended a course since the reforms took effect (Gollop et al., 2019). This meant that PTS was the third most commonly used service (after the Ministry of Justice website and the Family Court). When asked how helpful the parents had found the PTS content, two-thirds (66%) rated 'how separation affects children, what children need, and how to talk to them about it' as the most helpful information shared with them by the facilitators.

> You are being helped to see through the children's eyes rather than what you think is best for the child. It gives you the forum to ask questions so

that you are able to make better decisions down the road. I think Parenting Through Separation does help to open people's eyes to the views of the children. (1123, Step-mother; Interview – Gollop et al., 2019, p. 118)

I got confirmation that the way I was communicating to my children was correct. (1367, Mother; Survey – Gollop et al., 2019, p. 124)

They did reinforce to try and keep the kids out of the whole process and the angst. One of the things that stuck in my mind from that was they said, 'Think about this – when the kids look back on it, do they want to be seeing you as the parent that tried to make things happen, or the parent who was trying to stop things from happening?' So, there were a few things like that that helped. (1585, Father; Interview – Gollop et al., 2019, p. 119)

This encouragement to place children at the centre of the process was confirmed by family justice professionals as one of the reasons they referred parents to PTS.

It works well in that it gets parents out of their own heads and into their children's headspace and what it might be like for the kids. (2166, Mediator, Counsellor; Survey – Taylor et al., 2019, p. 41)

It is effective in reminding people to be child focused through the family dispute process. (2564, Lawyer, Lawyer for the Child; Survey – Taylor et al., 2019, p. 42)

A PTS facilitator also discussed how the course provides practical tips to help parents talk with their children, but noted that the reality of doing this at home can be 'vastly different'.

An issue that often comes up for parents is how to elicit their children's views – like how to do that in a way that's actually okay, because you don't want children to feel like they're being pressured into having to choose between their parents. ... Parents are often really scared that they'll say the wrong thing or that they'll create more stress and harm for their children if they don't ask them the right way. ... We do talk about how you should let your child comment, and that you need to take that into account, but that ultimately you are the decision maker. It's important children feel they have been heard, but not that they are being required to choose. But talking about it at a two-hour session with a bunch of parents is vastly different from actually trying to do that with a 7-year-old [at home]. (2339, PTS Facilitator; Interview – Taylor *et al.*, 2019, p. 61)

7.4 *Advice to Other Separated Parents*

The parents provided a wealth of advice for other parents making parenting arrangements (Gollop *et al.*, 2020). The most common advice offered was maintaining a focus on the children and their needs. Parents urged separated parents to put their other issues aside, particularly those involving emotional angst or animosity towards their former partner, and to prioritise their children. They encouraged parents to try and see the situation from their children's perspectives, to listen to their views and to acknowledge the importance of both parents and wider family to children.

> Look out for your child. I mean, be really centred around your child. You have to forget yourself and get over a lot of stuff and move forward for them. (1086, Father; Interview – Gollop *et al.*, 2020, p. 162)

> At the end of the day, they come first, not whatever issues you may or may not have with your ex-partner. The children always have to be at the front of every decision that you make. So, just think about the kids and what you want for them going forward. If you can get it right early on, then you'll set yourself up fine for the years going forward. (1146, Mother; Interview – Gollop *et al.*, 2020, p. 162)

7.5 *Children's Perspectives*

Unfortunately, the online survey and telephone interview research design did not allow for the inclusion of a sub-sample of children of the parents participating in the Parenting Arrangements After Separation Study. I readily acknowledge that children's views on the making or changing of their post-separation care arrangements would better honour the very arguments I have made about the significance of Articles 5 and 12 and add an important dimension to those reported by their parents. I have, however, been involved in undertaking much earlier qualitative studies in New Zealand with children and young people aged 5–18 years on:

– Access (contact) arrangements following parental separation (1997–1999) involving 107 children and young people from 73 families (Gollop *et al.*, 2000);

- The role of children's legal representatives (1998) involving 20 children and 12 lawyers in two Family Court districts (Taylor et al., 2000);
- Relocation after parental separation (2007–2009) involving 114 parents from 100 families (73 mothers and 41 fathers; in 14 families both parents took part) and 44 children and young people from 30 of the 100 families who had experienced a relocation dispute (Gollop and Taylor, 2012).

Key themes to emerge across all three studies related to children and young people's desire to have their views heard, to be consulted by their parents, to have better knowledge and understanding of family and legal processes, and to enjoy quality relationships with family law professionals (Taylor and Gollop, 2013, 2015). For example, when the children in the study on post-separation access arrangements were asked what advice they would give to parents who were separating the most common response (mentioned by half of the 107 children and young people) related to the importance of consulting children (Gollop et al., 2000). This included listening to children, asking children for their views and letting them have a say, giving children a choice and respecting those choices. They thought that parents should not assume they knew what their children were thinking or feeling.

The children varied in how much they were consulted and their role in decisions about their living arrangements and contact with their non-resident parent. Very few children (19%) reported being consulted about their initial custody arrangements, while 37% said they had been consulted about their initial contact arrangements (Gollop et al., 2000). The post-separation arrangements were mostly determined by their parents. Generally, those who were given a say, valued and appreciated this opportunity, whereas those who had little input into the decision-making process, despite wanting to, evidenced the most dissatisfaction. This was particularly so when children endured arrangements they did not like and could not change, such as being forced to have contact with a parent they did not want to spend time with or, conversely, a parent reduced or ceased contact altogether when the children wanted to have more time and a meaningful relationship with them.

Across the studies, children and young people emphasised the importance of professionals establishing positive relationships with them (Taylor and Gollop, 2013, 2015). For example, they liked lawyers who were friendly, trustworthy, respectful and child-centred (Taylor et al., 2000). Those children who spoke negatively about their lawyer often described having a distant or minimal relationship with them, did not like talking with strangers about family matters, did not like or trust their lawyer, or found the encounter boring.

There is thus evidence in New Zealand, from two decades ago, that children and young people had limited involvement in post-separation care, contact and/or relocation decisions, yet strongly desired greater opportunities to have a say and be heard by their parents and, where applicable, family justice professionals. This mirrors overseas research trends in the child participation field (Birnbaum and Saini, 2012; Gal and Duramy, 2015). The findings in the more recent Parenting Arrangements After Separation Study (Gollop et al., 2019, 2020; Taylor et al., 2019) indicating that New Zealand parents have embraced the importance of talking with their children about post-separation arrangements likely reflect the changes encouraged over the past 20 years by ratification of the UNCRC, introduction of the Care of Children Act 2004, the regular undertaking of large-scale child consultations in social policy contexts (Office of the Children's Commissioner, 2019) and wider shifts in societal attitudes and professional practices relating to children's rights, especially those influenced by Article 12. Since these research findings are based on parents' and professionals' perceptions, but not children's views and experiences, some caution must be exercised in determining whether the gulf between child and parent input, as reported in the earlier studies, has been bridged in more contemporary times. It is to be hoped that future research ascertaining New Zealand children's perspectives on their role in post-separation care and contact decision-making might be more reflective of the confidence reported by parents in the Parenting Arrangements After Separation Study regarding engagement with their children in intrafamilial and family justice post-separation decision-making contexts.

8 Independent Panel's Review of the 2014 Reforms and the Government's Response

In 2018, the Minister of Justice appointed a three-member Independent Panel to examine New Zealand's 2014 reforms. Their 2019 report noted that 'children's participation in decisions that affect them is a fundamental right in the United Nations Convention on the Rights of the Child (CRC) but is still not widely recognised or valued' (Independent Panel, 2019, p. 33). Child-inclusive practice has been developing 'in an ad hoc way' in New Zealand, and there has been 'no resolution of critical issues relating to children's participation' (p. 34). Decisions about children's care arrangements were said to be 'decisions made about children, not decisions involving children' and 'there is no requirement for parents to consult children on decisions about their care' (p. 34). The Independent Panel recommended that the Ministry of Justice, together with relevant experts and key stakeholders, be directed 'to undertake a stocktake of appropriate models of child participation, including at FDR, as a priority' (p. 35). As well, it was recommended that children be allowed to attend court-directed counselling with one or both parents, the role and remuneration of a lawyer for the child be strengthened, and a children's advisory group be established to provide advice and insight into children's experiences of Care of Children Act 2004 matters to inform policy and practice. While section 6 of the Care of Children Act 2004 was said by the Independent Panel (2019) to adopt 'the language of the CRC' and to 'give effect to article 12 of the CRC' it was thought that more could 'be done to provide clarity about what this means for children in Care of Children Act proceedings' (p. 35).

The Government's response to the Independent Panel's child participatory recommendations has been limited. It recently introduced the Family Court (Supporting Children in Court) Legislation Bill 2020 proposing to amend s 6 to explicitly state that its purpose is to implement Article 12 of the UNCRC (clause 6). This is somewhat puzzling given the Panel's statement that, in their view, s 6 already gives effect to Article 12. However, setting this out explicitly will do no harm. The Government is also proposing to amend s 5 of the Care of Children Act 2004 to insert a new principle relating to a child's welfare and best interests:

> A child who is capable of forming their own views about any matter affecting their care and welfare should be given reasonable opportunities to participate in any decision affecting them and that, commensurate with their age and maturity, their views should be taken into account. (Family Court (Supporting Children in Court) Legislation Bill 2020, clause 4)

This, again, is rather perplexing since the Bill, if passed by Parliament, will require the child's 'age and maturity' to be taken into account when considering the child's welfare and best interests in s 5, while this continues to remain absent from s 6 when reasonable opportunities are provided for a child to express their views. It would be preferable for the proposed new principle in s 5 to be consistent with the current wording of s 6. As well, the Bill proposes amending the Family Dispute Resolution Act 2013 to require a FDR provider to make every endeavour to facilitate participation by children who are the subject of a family dispute in the discussions between the parties during a FDR process (clause 11). This, too, is effectively a restatement of current practice. The Bill therefore unfortunately represents a missed opportunity to push further forward on child participation in New Zealand. More explicit implementation of the Independent Panel's excellent recommendations would ensure that the benefits of child participation, so well documented in the research literature (Birnbaum and Saini, 2012; Gal and Duramy, 2015), become better reflected in the practices of both parents and family justice professionals.

9 Conclusion

To date, the New Zealand family justice system has primarily concerned itself with the roles of the professionals involved in ascertaining children's views in FDR mediation processes and/or Family Court proceedings. Little emphasis has been placed on the role of parents, yet the Care of Children Act 2004 requires guardians to determine for or with the child, or to help the child to determine, questions about important matters affecting them (s 16(1)(c)). The Independent Panel (2019) reviewing New Zealand's 2014 reforms lamented the lack of focus on parents' consultations with their children regarding decisions about their post-separation care and the Government's disappointing response to their recommendations is really little more than window dressing.

There is thus considerable scope to harness the interplay between Articles 5 and 12 of the UNCRC to broaden our thinking on child participation in the family justice system to enhance parental responsibilities, rights and duties in support of child-inclusive practice and to provide parents with strategies for this. The Parenting Arrangements After Separation Study found that New Zealand parents rated talking with their children and seeking their thoughts, feelings and views highly – it was the second most common step they took (after discussing the arrangements with their former partner) and was the step that the greatest percentage of parents (58%) rated as one of their top three most helpful steps. In 7% of cases the children were said to have decided the parenting arrangements. The majority (85%) of separated parents knew about the PTS programme and it was their third most commonly used service when making or changing parenting arrangements. Two-thirds (66%) of the 260 parents in the study who had attended PTS rated 'how separation affects children, what children need, and how to talk to them about it' as the most helpful information they had learnt at PTS. Professionals were also enthusiastic about PTS for encouraging parents to place their children at the centre of the dispute resolution process. The most common advice the parents in the study gave to other separated parents making parenting arrangements involved putting their children first, keeping the focus on children and their needs, seeing the situation from their children's perspective, listening to their views and acknowledging the importance of both parents and wider family to children. These findings confirm the significance of parental engagement with children when post-separation issues arise and provide encouraging evidence of the scope and impact of child participation in intrafamilial decision-making contexts. Articles 5 and 12, when coupled with a sociocultural tool like scaffolding, can help provide the practical means by which statutory imperatives can be given greater effect in the quest to support children to express their views on important matters affecting their post-separation care.

References

Bala, N., and Birnbaum, R., "Preferences and Perspectives of Children in Family Cases: Rethinking the Role of Children's Lawyers" *Les Cahiers de droit* 2018 (59(4)), 787–829.

Bala, N., Birnbaum, R., Cyr, F., and McColley, D., "Children's Voices in Family Court: Guidelines for Judges Meeting Children", *Family Law Quarterly* 2013 (47(3)), 379–408.

Beckhouse, K., "Laying the Guideposts for Participatory Practice: Children's Participation in Family Law Matters", *Family Matters* 2016 (98), 26–33.

Bell, F., "Meetings Between Children's Lawyers and Children Involved in Private Family Law Disputes", *Child & Family Law Quarterly* 2016a (28(1)), 5–24.

Bell, F., "Barriers to Empowering Children in Private Family Law Proceedings", *International Journal of Law, Policy and the Family* 2016b (30), 225–247.

Bell, F., Cashmore, J., Parkinson, P., and Single, J., "Outcomes of Child-Inclusive Mediation", *International Journal of Law, Policy and the Family* 2013 (27(1)), 116–142.

Birnbaum, R., *The Voice of the Child in Separation/Divorce Mediation and Other Alternative Dispute Resolution Processes: A Literature Review* (Canada: Family, Children and Youth Section, Department of Justice, 2009).

Birnbaum, R., and Bala, N., "The Child's Perspective on Legal Representation: Young People Report on Their Experiences with Child Lawyers", *Canadian Journal of Family Law* 2009 (25(1)), 11–71.

Birnbaum, R., and Bala, N., "Judicial Interviewing with Children in Custody and Access Cases: Comparing Experiences in Ontario and Ohio", *International Journal of Law, Policy and the Family* 2010 (24(3)), 300–337.

Birnbaum, R., Bala, N., and Cyr, F., "Children's Experiences with Family Justice Professionals and Judges in Ontario and Ohio", *International Journal of Law, Policy and the Family* 2011 (25(3)), 398–422.

Birnbaum, R., and Saini, M., "A Qualitative Synthesis of Children's Participation in Custody Disputes", *Research on Social Work Practice* 2012 (22(4)), 400–409.

Cashmore, J., "Children's Participation in Family Law Decision-making: Theoretical Approaches to Understanding Children's Views", *Children and Youth Services Review* 2011 (33(4)), 515–520.

Cashmore, J., and Parkinson, P., "Children's and Parents' Perceptions on Children's Participation in Decision Making after Parental Separation and Divorce", *Family Court Review* 2008 (46(1)), 91–104.

Cashmore, J., and Parkinson, P., "Children's Participation in Family Law Disputes: The Views of Children, Parents, Lawyers and Counsellors", *Family Matters* 2009 (82), 15–21.

Carson, R., Dunstan, E., Dunstan, J., and Roopani, D., *Children and Young People in Separated Families: Family Law System Experiences and Needs* (Melbourne: Australian Institute of Family Studies, 2018).

Clarke, J., "Do I Have A Voice? An Empirical Analysis of Children's Voices in Michigan Custody Litigation", *Family Law Quarterly* 2013 (47(3)), 457–473.

Gal, T., and Duramy, B.F., (eds.), *International Perspectives and Empirical Findings on Child Participation* (Oxford: Oxford University Press, 2015).

Goldson, J., and Taylor, N.J., "Child-inclusion in Dispute Resolution in the New Zealand Family Court" *New Zealand Family Law Journal* 2009 (6(7)), 201–209.

Gollop, M.M., Smith, A.B., and Taylor, N.J., "Children's Involvement in Custody and Access Arrangements After Parental Separation", *Child & Family Law Quarterly* 2000 (12), 383–399.

Gollop, M., and Taylor, N.J., "New Zealand Children and Young People's Perspectives on Relocation Following Parental Separation", in M. Freeman (ed.), *Law and Childhood Studies: Current Legal Issues Vol. 14* (London: Oxford University Press, 2012).

Gollop, M., Taylor, N., Cameron, C., and Liebergreen, N., *Parenting Arrangements after Separation Study: Evaluating the 2014 Family Law Reforms – Parents' and Caregivers' Perspectives – Part 1* (Dunedin, New Zealand: Children's Issues Centre, University of Otago, 2019).

Gollop, M.M., Taylor, N.J., and Henaghan, R.M., *Evaluation of the 2014 Family Law Reforms: Phase One* (Dunedin, New Zealand: Children's Issues Centre, University of Otago, 2015).

Gollop, M., Taylor, N.J., and Liebergreen, N., *Parenting Arrangements after Separation Study: Evaluating the 2014 Family Law Reforms – Parents' and Caregivers' Perspectives – Part 2* (Dunedin, New Zealand: Children's Issues Centre, University of Otago, 2020).

Hayes, M., and Birnbaum, R., "Voice of the Child Reports in Ontario: A Content Analysis of Interviews with Children", *Journal of Divorce & Remarriage* 2019 (60), 1–19.

Holt, S., "A voice or a Choice? Children's Views on Participating in Decisions about Post-separation Contact with Domestically Abusive Fathers" *Journal of Social Welfare and Family Law* 2018 (40(4)), 459–476.

Independent Panel, *Te Korowai Ture ā-Whānau: The Final Report of the Independent Panel Examining the 2014 Family Justice Reforms* (Wellington, New Zealand: Ministry of Justice, May 2019).

Lodge, J., and Alexander, M., *Views of Adolescents in Separated Families: A Study of Adolescents' Experiences after the 2006 Reforms to the Family Law System* (Melbourne, Australian Institute of Family Studies, 2010).

McIntosh, J., Long, C. and Wells, Y., *Children Beyond Dispute: A Four Year Follow Up Study of Outcomes From Child Focused and Child Inclusive Post-separation Family Dispute Resolution* (Canberra: Attorney General's Department, 2009).

McMellon, C., and Tisdall, E.K.M., "Children and Young People's Participation Rights: Looking Backwards and Moving Forwards", *International Journal of Children's Rights* 2020 (28(1)), 157–182.

Morag, T., Rivkin, D., and Sorek, Y., "Child Participation in the Family Courts - Lessons from the Israeli Pilot Project", *International Journal of Law, Policy and the Family* 2012 (26(1)), 1–30.

Morrison, F., Tisdall, E.K.M., and Callaghan, J.E.M., "Manipulation and Domestic Abuse in Contested Contact – Threats to Children's Participation Rights", *Family Court Review* 2020 (58(2)), 403–416.

Morrison, F., Tisdall, E.K.M., Warburton, J., Reid, A., and Jones, F., *Children's Participation in Family Actions - Probing Compliance with Children's Rights: Research Report* (Scotland: University of Stirling, University of Edinburgh and Clan ChildLaw, 2020).

Office of the Children's Commissioner and Oranga Tamariki – Ministry for Children, *What Makes a Good Life? Children and Young People's Views on Wellbeing* (Wellington, New Zealand: Office of the Children's Commissioner and Oranga Tamariki – Ministry for Children, 2019).

Office of the Minister of Justice, *Family Court Review Cabinet Paper – Proposals for Reform* (Wellington, New Zealand: Minister of Justice and Cabinet Social Policy Committee, 2012).

Parkinson, P., and Cashmore, J., *The Voice of a Child in Family Law Disputes* (Oxford: Oxford University Press, 2008).

Quigl, C., and Cyr, F., "The Voice of the Child in Parenting Coordination: Views of Children, Parents, and Parenting Coordinators", *Journal of Divorce & Remarriage* 2018 (59(6)), 501–527.

Robinson, A., and Henaghan, R.M., (2011). "Children: Heard But Not Listened To? An Analysis of Children's Views Under s 6 of the Care of Children Act 2004", *New Zealand Family Law Journal* 2011 (7(2)), 39–52.

Schrama, W., Freeman, M., Taylor, N.J., and Bruning, M., (eds.), *International Handbook on Child Participation in Family Law* (Cambridge: Intersentia, 2021)

Smith, A.B., *Understanding Children's Development: A New Zealand Perspective* (4th ed.) (Wellington, New Zealand: Bridget Williams Books, 1998).

Smith, A.B., "Interpreting and Supporting Participation Rights: Contributions from Sociocultural Theory", *International Journal of Children's Rights* 2002 (10(1)), 73–88.

Smith, A.B., Taylor, N.J., and Tapp, P., "Rethinking Children's Involvement in Decision-making After Parental Separation", *Childhood* 2003 (10(2)), 201–216.

Taylor, N.J., *Care of Children: Families, Dispute Resolution and the Family Court* (Dunedin, New Zealand: University of Otago PhD thesis, 2005).

Taylor, N.J., "What Do We Know About Involving Children and Young People in Family Law Decision Making? A Research Update", *Australian Journal of Family Law* 2006 (20(2)), 154–178.

Taylor, N.J., "Child Participation: Overcoming Disparity Between New Zealand's Family Court and Out-of-court Dispute Resolution Processes", *International Journal of Children's Rights* 2017 (25), 658–671.

Taylor, N.J., Fitzgerald, R., Morag, T., Bajpai, A., & Graham, A., "International Models of Child Participation in Family Law Proceedings Following Parental Separation / Divorce", *International Journal of Children's Rights* 2012 (20(4)), 645–673.

Taylor, N.J., and Gollop, M., "Children and Young People's Participation in Family Law Decision-making", in N. Higgins and C. Freeman (eds.), *Childhoods: Growing up in Aotearoa New Zealand* (Dunedin, New Zealand: Otago University Press, 2013).

Taylor, N.J., and Gollop, M., "Children's Views and Participation in Family Dispute Resolution in New Zealand", in A.B. Smith (ed.), *Enhancing Children's Rights: Connecting Research, Policy and Practice* (England: Palgrave MacMillan, 2015).

Taylor, N.J., Gollop, M.M., and Liebergreen, N., *Parenting Arrangements after Separation Study: Evaluating the 2014 Family Law Reforms – Family Justice Professionals' Perspectives* (Dunedin, New Zealand: Children's Issues Centre, University of Otago, 2019).

Taylor, N.J., Gollop, M., and Smith, A.B., "Children and Young People's Perspectives on the Role of Counsel for the Child", *Butterworths Family Law Journal* 2000 (3(6)), 146–154.

Taylor, N.J., Tapp, P., and Henaghan, R.M., "Respecting Children's Participation in Family Law Proceedings", *International Journal of Children's Rights* 2007 (15(1)), 61–82.

Tisdall, E.K.M., "Subjects with Agency: Children's Participation in Family Law Proceedings", *Journal of Social Welfare and Family Law* 2016 (38(4)), 362–379.

Turoy-Smith, K.M., and Powell, M.B., "Interviewing of Children for Family Law Matters: A Review", *Australian Psychologist* 2016, 1–9.

Turoy-Smith, K.M., Powell, M.B., and Brubacher, S.P., "Professionals' Views about Child Interviews for Family Law Assessments", *Family Court Review* 2018 (56(4)), 607–622.

United Nations Committee on the Rights of the Child, *General Comment Number 12: The Right of the Child to be Heard* (Geneva: CRC/C/GC/12, 2009).

Walker, J., "How Can We Ensure That Children's Voices are Heard in Mediation?", *Family Law* 2013, 191–195.

Wood, D., Bruner, J., and Ross, G., "The Role of Tutoring in Problem Solving", *Journal of Child Psychology and Psychiatry* 1976 (17), 89–100.

Yasenik, L.A., and Graham, J.M., "The Continuum of Including Children in ADR Processes: A Child-centered Continuum Model", *Family Court Review* 2016 (54(2)), 186–202.

New Zealand Statutes and Bills

Care of Children Act 2004
Family Court Proceedings Reform Bill 2012
Family Court (Supporting Children in Court) Legislation Bill 2020
Family Dispute Resolution Act 2013

PART 3

Parental Responsibility and Evolving Capacities

CHAPTER 6

Do Parents Know Best?

John Eekelaar

1   Introduction

While there is legitimate discussion about what direction and guidance which parents and some others are responsible to provide their children is 'appropriate' and 'consistent with [their] evolving capacities' in accordance with Article 5 of the UNCRC, Article 18 seems to establish an overall obligation that states shall 'use their best efforts' to ensure that, in doing that, 'the best interests of the child will be [the parents'] basic concern'. This obligation is inevitably somewhat imprecise. Tobin and Seow (2019) suggest it should be considered 'equivalent to the obligation to take all appropriate measures', and that 'the most that can be reasonably expected of states is that they undertake their best efforts.' This can perhaps be reasonably understood in the sense of "do their best to".

Within this framework, the question explored here is, outside cases of abuse and neglect, what would "doing their best" look like in circumstances where parents are separating? On one view the problem is resolved by not involving the courts, or perhaps even the law, at all, and leaving the problem to the parents to work out between themselves. Courts are usually obliged to apply the "best interests" principle, and of course this is mandated by Article 3 of the UNCRC.[1] But, ironically, that could be the problem. Famously, Robert Mnookin (1975: 260) commented:

> Deciding what is best for a child poses a question no less ultimate than the purposes and values of life itself. Should the judge be primarily concerned with the child's happiness? Or with the child's spiritual and religious training? Should the judge be concerned with the economic 'productivity' of the child when he grows up?

---

[1] For further discussion of the relevance of context in the application of this principle, see Eekelaar (2015); Eekelaar and Tobin (2019).

These questions challenge the position that courts are best placed to make these decisions, or even whether it is appropriate at all that they do so. So Mnookin (1975: 266) concluded that, outside cases of abuse and neglect:

> ... there are affirmative justifications for making the family the presumptive locus of decision-making authority, particularly if there is no social consensus about what is best for children. Within the family, the child is more likely to have a voice in the decision, even if his wishes may not be determinative. Family members are more likely to have direct knowledge about a particular child. Affection for the child and mutual self-interest of family members are more likely to inform decisions.

However, somewhat reluctantly, Mnookin does not abandon the law (since, as he saw it, cases will continue to be decided by judges) but suggests three 'intermediate' rules through which the best interests test could be mediated:

> First, custody should never be awarded to a claimant whose limitations or conduct would endanger the health of the child under the minimum standards for child protection described above ... Second, the court should prefer a psychological parent (i.e., an adult who has a psychological relationship with the child from the child's perspective) over any claimant (including a natural parent) who, from the child's perspective, is not a psychological parent ...Third, subject to the two rules noted above, natural parents should be preferred over others (*ibid.*: 282–3).

Many years later, Mnookin (2014) advocated a presumption that the child's time with each parent after separation should approximate the times spent with each parent when they were together.

Mnookin's suggestion that, given the nature of the judgments that must be made, the matter should (at least presumptively) be left to the parents, was enthusiastically taken up by Kimberly and Robert Emery (2014), eminent advocates of mediation in the United States. In an article entitled, "Who knows what is best for children? Honoring agreements and contracts between parents who live apart", they attribute the reluctance of the law to become involved in ongoing marital relationships to an assumption 'that the interests of married parents and children are aligned, except in cases of abuse or neglect' (*ibid.*: 166) and argue that separated families are just another form of family, so the same assumption should apply to them. The "best interests" standard would remain, but courts would be explicitly required to accept what the parents agreed as satisfying that standard (except in cases of abuse and neglect) for, as they conclude in their article: 'Who knows what's best for children? In theory and in practice, the answer is their parents, whether married or living apart' (*ibid.*: 176).

If that is so, what is there left for the state to do apart from trying to bring about agreement between the parents in ensuring that parents treat their children's interests as their basic concern?

2   Privatisation and Liberalisation

This perspective has been given added impetus by a general movement towards privatisation of the resolution of (private) family disputes. This is a rather different process from the one usually described as "liberalisation" (see Antokolskaia, 2016). Liberalisation involved bringing the written law into line with what was often collusion on a grand scale, where couples manipulated fault-based grounds in order to achieve consensual divorce, as was the case in France and Germany before reforms in 2005 and 1976 respectively, and in England and Wales before the reform of 1971, although in the case of England and Wales (and to a lesser extent, Germany), such manipulation continued after the reforms. In English law this was because divorce could be obtained relatively quickly under the reformed law provided one party did not oppose an allegation of adultery or of 'unreasonable behaviour', which did not *necessarily* imply fault (though it usually did) but did assume a judgment about whether that party's behaviour was such that it would be unreasonable to expect the other to live with him or her: what could be characterised as "judgemental divorce".[2]

Liberalisation resulted in making divorce available more easily, either by agreement subject to some waiting period, of varying lengths,[3] or even without any waiting period, as in Sweden from 1973 if there were no minor children, or on the unilateral demand of one spouse after a short period of reflection, as also introduced by that Swedish law. This, of course, has strong elements of privatisation, but is not identical to it because some element of public involvement remained in the form of an order of a court or some administrative body, no matter how much this was a formality, and could also be present with respect to the arrangements regarding children, finances and property.

The movement towards privatisation in family law has been largely driven by concerns over its costs to the court system and legal aid budgets. (For examples of the extensive literature on this, see Eekelaar, 2011; Maclean *et al.* (eds.), 2015; Maclean and Eekelaar, 2019; Maclean and Dijksterhuis (eds.), 2019).

---

2   See, e.g., *Owens v. Owens* [2018] UKSC 41.
3   As in many US states.

This provided a powerful additional motivation for moving the resolution of family issues from the court system to the private arena. One of the most striking examples is the new divorce procedure introduced in France from 1 January 2017[4] which allows parties (who must both be French nationals) to agree the divorce and its financial and other consequences (Ferrand, 2018; Bastard, 2019). This requires that in such cases, to become effective, the agreement must be filed with a notary public, who simply carries out a document check. It must have been signed by each party, assisted by a lawyer, after a short (two-week) period of reflection. It is provided that the agreement must cover certain specified matters, which include whether compensatory payment should be made, and any division of property. Although not specifically mentioned, the agreement could cover matters concerning "parental responsibilities" (what would be called "child arrangements" in England and Wales). Any children must be informed, and given the opportunity to ask for the matter to go to a judge. If they do not, and these conditions are satisfied, the divorce becomes effective without its submission to a court, and the agreement could be enforced according to the principles of contract law.

The nature and extent to which a process can be said to be "privatised" can take a number of forms. At one extreme, suppose that no recourse is provided for public resolution of these matters even where the parties disagree. This might be the case where, for example, a marriage or a parental relationship is not recognised, or access to adjudication or resolution mechanisms is denied to one party on the grounds of gender, or of religion, or is effectively impossible because of absence of financial or other support. In such cases the parties are abandoned to their own arrangements, if any. They may agree or they may not, but in either case, without any prospect of recourse to some form of adjudication, the result to be expected is that the more powerful prevails. It is probable that in about half of cases where married or long-term unmarried relationships break down in England, the parties wish to settle matters 'without outside help' (Barlow *et al.*, 2017: 85–6).

But privatisation need not take such an extreme form. It may be mitigated, if, for example, the parties wish to take advantage of mechanisms provided by the state whereby agreements, if reached, can become enforceable in some way, thus promoting certainty over time. But this is still a strong form of privatisation, since the state gives its support to "private" arrangements, though the degree of its strength depends on the extent (if any) to which the state subjects such agreements to some form of scrutiny (the issue to be explored below). It

---

4 Law No. 2016–1547, 18 November 2016, Article 50, supplementing Code Civil, Article 229.

is also affected by the nature of any assistance provided towards reaching agreement.

3   Privatisation and De-legalisation

There is a further complication. A distinction should be drawn between privatisation and de-legalisation. For example, in the new "privatised" French divorce process, described above, the law is nevertheless very much present. Indeed, lawyers welcomed the measure as each party must appoint a lawyer to take care of their interests; the agreement must contain a list of items specified by law as to be agreed on and the agreement must be checked by and filed with a notary public. Furthermore, each spouse may apply for free legal advice, and it has even been doubted whether the result will reduce costs to the parties or the state compared to judicial divorce (Ferrand (2018: 200)). In contrast, Jana Singer (2014) has argued, with respect to parenting disputes, that the shift away from adjudication to alternative dispute resolution (ADR) had undermined not only the place of lawyers but also of legal norms in the process. 'No longer', says Singer, 'is the question, "Which, among a predetermined set of custody outcomes, would be right or best for this family according to some external set of criteria"? Rather the expectation is that the process itself will generate the options and the disputants will evaluate those options according to their own interests and values' (Singer, 2014: 187; see also Murphy and Singer, 2015).

4   Analysis

4.1   *Viability of the "Best Interests" Standard*
All this raises a number of points that require unpacking. It will be noted that Mnookin's concerns over the forward-looking and speculative nature of the best interests standard did not lead him to reject legal norms entirely. Indeed, he suggested, albeit reluctantly, that some types of legal presumption might be necessary simply in order to make decisions practicable. Singer, on the other hand, as noted above, argued that the very impracticality of that standard for traditional adjudication had led to greater use of ADR, which, in turn, weakened the relevance of legal norms.

It is possible that Mnookin's concerns about the best interests standard were exaggerated, or even misplaced. It is, of course, usually true that the longer-term outcomes of such decisions are impossible to know. That is also true for most decisions people make in their lives, whether for themselves (such as who to date, or to marry, what to study, what job to take, and so on) and, if they are parents, those touching their children (where to live, what interests to encourage, what books to read, what religion (if any) to follow). But that does not mean that rational decisions cannot be made regarding what is the best thing to do in such situations. They will, of course, reflect broad social values, which may be contested, but decisions can be made, based on the evidence available. There may be more than one option, between which reasonable choices may be made. In the case of children, this requires a conscious effort to focus on the child concerned, hearing the child's views and, while allowing for competence factors and not neglecting other interests completely, to seek an outcome most likely to enable the child to achieve what is of value to the child from the perspective of the child as a potential independent adult (Eekelaar (2017: 55–56, 59, 131–132)).

If we can accept that the best interests standard can be used in this way in deciding matters concerning children, the question remains as to where this decision is best made. Given the features of such decisions identified by Mnookin, it is hardly possible to compare empirically the long-term outcomes for children of decisions taken by their parents and those taken by others, including courts. In considering this matter, therefore, it is necessary to take into account the likely presence of factors that could undermine the quality of the decision from the child's perspective. In this respect, we need to compare the situations where parents, living together with the children, are not contemplating separation, and where they have separated, or are in the process of doing so.

The two situations share one important feature: the parents' power to affect the children's lives. That should put us on notice that there is an inherent risk of various forms of misuse of such power. However, there is a significant difference between the state imposing norms between people in ongoing intimate relationships, and regulating matters between them if they separate. In the former case, couples are engaged in a significant joint life project, involving the nature of intimacy, and the development of love and support in facing the joys, sorrows and difficulties of life. On a broader, social, perspective they are also involved in the inter-generational transmission of cultural or social values. In liberal societies, this ongoing joint project can best be achieved if the state respects the couple's own way of confronting the personal issues that might arise between them in providing the guidance required of them by Article 5, while providing them with advice and support at the same time. Who can say whether, in some objective sense, this is best for children? What *could* be said, however, is that, subject to the very important red lines which allow the welfare authorities to assume parental powers with respect to the child who has suffered, or is at risk of, significant harm, or where a court is required to resolve disputes over important matters, such as between the child's parents and medical personnel over the provision of treatment for the child,[5] when the court will act on its own judgment concerning the child's best interests, or over educational issues, where the state's interests in the values of society as a whole are implicated, in liberal societies, it is 'best that' children are brought up in this way. By allowing this the state is 'doing its best' in accordance with Article 18.

The situation is very different if the parents separate. The joint project has failed between them, and made considerably more difficult with regard to the children. Parents in an ongoing relationship, living with their children, may have their differences over some matters of upbringing, but they seldom go to the very nature of the relationship between the child and one or both of the parents as is potentially the case when parents separate. Importantly, the parents' own interests are likely to diverge more sharply after separation which could either divert attention from the children's interests, or colour the assessment of those interests by the strongly competing interests of the parents. And there is another difference which is present in many (though by no means all) cases where parents separate: that is, that the family re-organisation and legal procedures that sometimes accompany it provide a point of entry whereby external agencies acquire the opportunity to obtain information about, and influence, the position of the children.

4.2 Is Agreement Enough?

But, it may be said, it is still best, despite those tensions between separating parents, to seek a solution by way of agreement between them. The evidence is clear that conflict between the parents in itself damages the well-being of the children involved (Lamb, 2007: 19; Shaffer, 2007; Fehlberg *et al.*, 2015: 189), even if the arrangement has other benefits for the child, for example, by maintaining relationships with both parents (Nielsen, 2018), which indicates that the fact that the parents agree on post-separation arrangements regarding the children is in itself beneficial for the children. It might be concluded that the objective of resolution processes should therefore be to achieve such agreement, rather than to focus on the actual outcome for the child.

This is an important point. However, the fact that parties may have agreed does not necessarily mean there is no conflict, either because the agreement was reached reluctantly, or contains elements likely to induce conflicts later.

---

5 See *Yates and another v. Great Ormond Street Hospital* [2017] EWCA Civ. 410; *King's College Hospital NHS Foundation Trust v. Takesha Thomas, Laure Haastrup and Isaiah Haastrup* [2018] EWHC 127.

But even if there are no conflicts, what about the substance? An agreed solution may usually be better than disagreement, but that does not mean that the factors mentioned above that may be present between separating couples may not have made it less beneficial, or even less safe, for the child than a different solution could have achieved. Evidence from observations of mediation suggests that even though mediators may refer to the desirability of putting the children's interests first, the degree to which they balance that objective with achieving an outcome on which the parents agree seems to vary (Barlow et al., 2017: 201–202; Harada, 2019; Maclean and Eekelaar, 2016: 87–91; 122–129; Ryrstedt, 2012).

In 1958, advantage was taken in England and Wales, and Scotland, of the fact that divorce could provide a "point of entry" for examination of the position of the children. It was laid down that, before a divorce could be granted, any arrangements for children had to be submitted to the court for certification that they were 'satisfactory or the best that could be devised in the circumstances'.[6] This was confirmed in section 41 of the Matrimonial Causes Act 1973. It was applied by means of a private meeting between the judge and the parties (a 'children's appointment'), and this took place even after undefended cases involving children became subject in 1977 to the 'Special Procedure', which from 1973 had allowed divorce to be granted on the basis of submitted papers alone in undefended cases where no children were involved. But, somewhat oddly, the judge at the children's appointment was not supposed to consider any agreements over finances or property: that was a matter for the registrar when deciding whether to incorporate them into a Consent Order, where the welfare of the child was not given such prominence (Eekelaar, 1985).

The Matrimonial Causes Procedure Committee (Booth Committee) of 1985 (which anticipated recent moves towards allowing joint applications for divorce) sought to take this further, in an echo of much earlier debates over the role of the courts in private family disputes that include the (unsuccessful) attempts in the 1930s of the magistrate, Claud Mullins, and immediately post-war schemes, to enhance the welfare functions of the family courts. (See detailed discussions by Cretney (1998: chs. 5 and 6) and Murch (2018)). However, those earlier initiatives were primarily aimed at saving marriages. In contrast, the Booth Committee sought to enhance agreement, that is, conciliation rather than reconciliation, a shift also evident in the practice of the court welfare service (Dingwall and Eekelaar (eds.), 1988: ch. 1 and ch. 4 (by Adrian James)). The Committee distinguished between divorce cases involving children and those that did not and proposed that in all cases involving children, defended

---

6 Matrimonial Proceedings (Children) Act 1958.

or otherwise, there should be an initial, informal, hearing before a registrar with the objective of promoting and giving effect to agreements. Where agreement had been reached, the function would primarily be supervisory, combining the 'children's appointment' with giving first consideration to the welfare of any children in any financial and property orders agreed.[7] If so satisfied, the Consent Order could be made solely on the basis of the written documents.[8] At the same time it seemed that the role of the court as scrutineer of arrangements on behalf of the child might be enhanced. Section 3 of the Matrimonial and Family Proceedings Act 1984 required courts in England and Wales, when considering the matters it was to take into account when making financial and property orders, to give 'first consideration' to the 'welfare while a minor of any child of the family who has not attained the age of eighteen'.

However, the future went in the opposite direction. Already in 1977, research in England and Wales and in Scotland had demonstrated that almost nothing was achieved by the section 41 children's appointments, which consisted in a brief interview of the parents by the judge. Even where the process led to an investigation, it resulted in change in only 0.6 per cent of cases in England and Wales and only one in the sample of 203 cases in Scotland (where the process also applied) (Eekelaar and Clive, 1977). A devastating study carried out between May 1979 and June 1980 of these appointments in five courts in England revealed not only the stress they caused parents, but their overall failure to achieve any benefit (Davis, MacLeod and Murch (1983)). It seemed that even if the investigation brought to light a less than satisfactory situation, there was little or nothing which the court could do about it. In general, the parties made their own arrangements and the court accepted them. So, far from taking up the Booth Committee's suggestion about informal meetings, Guidance accompanying the Bill that was to become the Children Act 1989 observed that, 'children are generally best looked after within their families', which Lady Hale (2000: 463) defended on the ground that 'any civilised society has to start from the proposition that children are best brought up in their own families: it is the bedrock of society that children belong in families and not to the state.' In 1989

---

7 With respect to financial and property orders, Sir Roualeyn Cumming-Bruce remarked: ' ... if it had been intended to be paramount, overriding all other considerations pointing to a just result, Parliament would have said so. It has not. So I construe the section in requiring the court to consider all the circumstances, including those set out in subsection 2, always bearing in mind the important consideration of the welfare of the children, and then try to attain a financial result which is just as between husband and wife: *Suter v. Suter & Jones* [1987] Fam 111, 123.

8 Matrimonial and Financial Proceedings Act 1984, s. 7, inserting section 33A into the Matrimonial Causes Act 1973. See Eekelaar (1986).

the children's appointment system was abolished and the need for the court to certify, prior to granting divorce, that the child arrangements were 'satisfactory or the best that could be devised in the circumstances' was reduced to a duty to consider only whether the proposed arrangements for children called for a court order.[9] After further research showed how little time judges took doing this (about five minutes) and lack of clarity about how to apply it (Douglas, Murch, Scanlan and Perry (2000)), in 2014 this too was removed.[10]

So as a result it is now only if parties, having reached agreement, are *seeking a Consent Order implementing that agreement* that the position of the children will be monitored. This is because section 1 of the Children Act 1989 requires a court, when determining any question with respect to the upbringing of a child (essentially, 'child arrangements') to make the child's welfare its 'paramount consideration'. Making a Consent Order containing child arrangements would seem to be a 'determination' under section 1. There is no requirement that parties do seek such an order, but they may wish to do so because this makes anything they have agreed (if appropriate) enforceable as an order of court. Similarly, if financial or property matters are included in the order sought, the court must give 'first consideration' to the welfare of children as required by section 25 of the Matrimonial Causes Act.

How is this done? As regards financial and property orders, a perusal of information given on websites regarding preparing Consent Orders on these matters shows they often pay little or no attention to the effect on children. For example:

> Couples often assume that just because they have agreed a financial settlement that the Judge will grant them their order. However, this is a dangerous attitude to have as the Judge will only grant the order if he or she feels that the order is fair to both parties No, you do not need to physically attend a court to file a consent order; it is all done by post (Divorce Online).[11]

> The Court does not have to agree to the Consent Order, regardless of the fact that it has already been agreed by the couple. The Court will use their discretion to determine whether the agreement between the couple is

---

[9] Children Act 1989, Sch. 12, para. 31.
[10] Children and Families Act 2014, s. 17.
[11] https://www.divorce-online.co.uk/help-and-advice/consent-order-information/.

fair and whether each person can actually afford to fulfil their side of the agreement (Co-op Legal Services).[12]

The government site, "Get a Divorce: Step By Step", makes no mention of children when addressing money and property issues.[13] But AdviceNow (2019: 11), the website hosted by the charity, Law for Life, paints a very different picture, setting out the principles in this way:

> We explain these basic principles here: *The welfare of any child of the family under 18 years old. This* is a very important factor and will be the first thing a court considers. In many cases, it can mean that most, maybe all, of your joint resources should go towards providing a home for your children. Typically the children will live with the person mostly responsible for their day to day care. This is why it is common to come across situations where the person mainly looking after the children stays with them in the family home. Before you discuss it, think about what you want to agree. What is best for any children you may have?

In 2014, the Law Commission commented that:

> If there are children who must be cared for and limited resources available, the parent who primarily cares for those children should be securely housed in priority to the other parent. Preferably she or he and the children should remain in the family home after divorce if they wish and if that will not prevent the other parent from being able to be housed. If such an outcome would be unfair in terms of the capital split then the other parent could retain an interest in that property, under a trust or charge, that can be realised at a later date, usually on the youngest child leaving secondary or tertiary education. Alternatively, it may be that both parents can reasonably afford to retain or buy a property, perhaps by downsizing (Law Commission, 2014: [3.97]).

As regards child arrangements, the situation has been significantly affected by the introduction of the Children and Family Courts Advice and Support Service (Cafcass) in 2001. This is an independent body charged with the duty, 'in respect of family proceedings in which the welfare of children ... is or may be

---

12   https://www.co-oplegalservices.co.uk/media-centre/articles-sep-dec-2017/what-is-a-consent-order-in-a-divorce/.
13   https://www.gov.uk/money-property-when-relationship-ends/mediation.

in question' to (a) safeguard and promote the welfare of the children, (b) give advice to any court about any application made to it in such proceedings, (c) make provision for the children to be represented in such proceedings, and (d) provide information, advice and other support for the children and their families.[14] It was designed to integrate into one body similar services that were previously dispersed across the probation service, independent and local authority social workers acting as guardians ad litem and reporting officers and the Official Solicitor. The principal role of the Cafcass's Children and Family Reporter in private law proceedings has been described as being:

> ... to investigate and report on issues concerning the welfare of children involved in disputes about residence and contact, at the request of the court. The role has traditionally been described as "acting as the eyes and ears of the Court." The Children and Family Reporter may also assist parents to resolve any outstanding areas of disagreement, if this is possible during the course of their enquiries (House of Commons Select Committee on the Lord Chancellor's Department, 2003: ch. 2, [9]).

In the divorce context, the establishment of Cafcass seemed to provide an opportunity for intervention and support to occur at an early stage, with a strong focus on the children's welfare, making it more likely that agreements reached would reflect the children's interests. However, this was impeded by initial problems over management and personnel, followed by government austerity policies. Reviewing the situation in 2015, a Report from Relate (Marjoribanks, 2015) referred to the Cafcass website which 'provides information for children whose parents are involved in court proceedings', its piloting of 'SPIP Plus'[15] in some areas, which adds an additional hour where both parents attend together with a mediator, and its call centre including a free helpline in which 'callers speak to an experienced professional who talks through the difficulties with them, identifies needs and assess what support may be helpful, and offers impartial information and guidance on the most appropriate dispute resolution pathways'. Unsurprisingly, Murch (2018: 217) has described the opportunity as being 'largely undeveloped'.

With respect to the assistance that Cafcass gives to the court in cases where agreement has been reached, section 9, paragraph 41 of the Family Court Bench Book, published by the Judicial College in 2018, summarises the position thus:

---

14   Criminal Justice and Court Services Act 2000, s. 12.
15   Separated Parents Information Programme (see further below).

In all cases, it is for the court to decide if an order accords with the welfare of the child. Any proposed order, whether to be made by agreement or not, must be scrutinised by the court. The court must not make a consent order, or give permission for an application to be withdrawn, unless the parties are present in court, all initial safeguarding checks have been obtained by the court and an officer of Cafcass/CAFCASS Cymru has spoken to the parties separately, except where it is satisfied that there is no risk of harm to the child and/or the other parent in doing so. The court has to consider all the evidence and information available to help it decide if there is any risk of harm to the child.

However, despite the reference to the need for the parties to be present in court, the government digital "tool" advising people seeking a Consent Order regarding child arrangements[16] states that the parents must send in the appropriate documents, including a draft Consent Order, and adds:

> There's usually no court hearing. A judge will approve your Consent Order to make it legally binding if they think you've made decisions in your children's interest. If the judge does not think your consent order is in your children's interest they can: change your consent order or make a different court order to decide what's best for your children.

It is also interesting that the limited bases upon which Consent Orders can be set aside seem to be focused on matters, such as non-disclosure, that affect the fairness of holding one of the parties to the agreement,[17] and not the welfare of the children.

5   The Limits of Law

But the parents may not have brought the child arrangements, or even the financial or property issues, before the court at all: they may have just settled them between themselves, with or without professional (or other) help. There could be a case for restoring the requirement that divorcing parties set out their arrangements for the children as a condition for obtaining a decree, whether or not they desire a Consent Order. Something like this is required in a number of jurisdictions (Scherpe and Trinder, 2019: 15). It could concentrate

---

16   https://www.gov.uk/looking-after-children-divorce/if-you-agree.
17   *Livesey v. Jenkins* [1985] FLR 813; *Sharland v. Sharland* [2015] UKSC 60.

the parents' minds on the issue, and widen the possible points of entry if they reveal something truly unusual. The downside is that it could create an opportunity for a party to obstruct the divorce process itself, and in its recent review of divorce law, the government has not proposed it, commenting that in any case such an agreement presents only a 'snapshot in time and not reflecting the changing needs of children over time' (Ministry of Justice, 2019: 34). But Australian courts have said this is an important feature of their divorce process (Fehlberg et al., 2015: 111–2), and in some jurisdictions officials (sometimes) play an important role. Antokolskaia (2016: 76–7) gives examples of Portugal and Iceland.

What then should be the role of the courts in this matter? The possibilities will strongly reflect the legal and administrative "culture' of respective jurisdictions. For England and Wales, Douglas et al. (2000) have argued that courts should play a 'supportive' role, channelling people to agencies that could provide appropriate guidance, and in its recent review of the divorce law, the UK government stated that it would 'explore options for information sharing and signposting to encourage divorcing parents to make informal child-centred arrangements during the legal process of divorce, where making such arrangements is safe and appropriate' (Ministry of Justice, 2019: 34). At present courts may recommend, or indeed order, parents to attend special classes to guide them how best to cater for their children's interests after separation. The success of these is hard to evaluate. A 2011 study of the Parenting Information Programme (PIP) in England and Wales (Trinder et al., 2011) concluded that attending the programme (a group session) had no effect on parental relationships, though it did result in a higher rate of contact between the child and the non-resident parent, though there was no evidence that this was seen as being in the best interests of the child. A later study by the same researchers of an enhanced programme (now involving an additional joint session by the couple with an adviser) showed no change in effect on parental relationships, but a modest improvement in agreements reached, though again, whether these enhanced the interests of children was not known (Trinder et al., 2014). But such opportunities usually occur only if a dispute has come to court, and the conflict may have deepened.

The key seems to be the provision of good advice at an early stage. After all, independent legal advice is required by many jurisdictions for the enforceability of pre-marital agreements (Scherpe (ed.), 2012: 491–495). If legal oversight is deemed necessary to safeguard vulnerable adults in regard to their property interests, why should not something similar be required in the case of arrangements for children? The new French consensual divorce process mentioned earlier rests heavily on the requirement that each party must be advised by a lawyer, and the law mandates various matters to be covered in the agreement (Ferrand, 2018); Bastard, 2019). The lawyers should be well acquainted with the relevant norms, and English courts have tended to place great reliance on the presence of legal advice as an important means of safeguarding the interests of parties entering such agreements. But each party will be the client of each lawyer, and it may be hard for the lawyers not to put the satisfaction of their clients first, even if this may not be best for the children.

It might be easier for a lawyer to act more objectively with regard to the children's interests if the same lawyer was advising the clients jointly. There is resistance to this among solicitors, who are required not to act, 'if there is a client conflict, or a significant risk of a client conflict'. But there is an exception if the clients have a substantially common interest in relation to a matter or a particular aspect of it', the clients have given informed consent to it, and if the solicitor thinks this is in their best interests and the benefits outweigh the risks. The substantial common interest could be the duty to make their children's interests their 'basic concern'. Such a process, which Mavis Maclean and I have proposed should be allowed to be undertaken by lawyers with mediation training in what we called 'legally-assisted family mediation' (Maclean and Eekelaar, 2016: 129–137), places the lawyer-mediator in an advisory role that not only facilitates agreement, but one performed by someone with knowledge of the relevant legal norms, with their focus on the child's interests, and also the best legal means of achieving this (Maclean and Eekelaar, 2019: 17–18).

But it is arguable that the advice need not be from a lawyer: indeed, expertise other than legal may be equally, if not more, important. Already, agreed child arrangements are referred to Cafcass for a safeguarding check. Might it be possible to involve Cafcass at an even earlier stage, perhaps by requiring parties to have submitted their agreed proposals to a Cafcass officer before applying to the court, and even giving Cafcass officers power to refer parties to counselling or other services, as proposed by Murch (2018: 332)? In 2019 a Working Group of professionals reporting to the President of the Family Division on the way the Child Arrangements Programme (CAP)[18] was operating, expressed its belief that such issues are best dealt with outside the court, and that 'a national non-court dispute resolution ("Family Solutions") service should be actively considered' (Private Law Working Group, 2019: [9]). However, it thought that, 'radical reform of the way society deals with children disputes following family breakdown away from the court would only be likely to be effective if supported

---

18　The CAP sets out practices to be followed when a dispute arises between separated parents and/or families about arrangements concerning children: Family Proceedings Rules 2010, Practice Direction 12B.

by a public education campaign; cultural change would be necessary in order to deliver it'. In Denmark in 2019 a new administrative authority, the Agency for Family Law (Familieretshuset), was established which parents must initially approach before accessing the court. The Agency will perform a triage function and can provide measures such as counselling and other assistance, with the primary goal of protecting the children's interests. The Agency can also make final decisions in some matters, which are appealable to the court. Might the role of Cafcass be developed along these lines (Singer, 2020)?

But, as in the case of ongoing families, there are limits to the degree of proactive intrusion liberal societies can exercise with regard to family life. This has been called the "liberal compromise", a feature of which is the so-called "rule of optimism" that parents generally treat their children as well as they can. This does not imply an assumption that professionals coming into contact with families, whether ongoing or separating, will be disposed always to believe that is happening in each case. Far less is it an application of the view of Kimberly and Robert Emery that as a matter of fact, parents always know what is best for their children. Rather, as Robert Dingwall has put it in the context of child protection services, the rule 'is a dimension of the organizational culture of (those services) which is founded on the deep ambivalence that we feel in a liberal society about state intervention in families' (Dingwall et al., 1995: 247). We therefore should perhaps recognise that the claim that "parents know best" is not so much a statement that this is always, or even mainly, the case, but that in 'doing their best' under Article 18 to ensure that parents do treat their children's best interests as their basic concern when fulfilling their Article 5 duties, the best interests principle must be tempered by the need for constraints on institutional intrusion into the arrangements parents make for their children.

References

AdviceNow, *A survival guide to: Sorting out your finances when you get divorced*, 2019.

Antokolskaia, M., "Divorce law in a European perspective" in J. M. Scherpe (ed.), *European Family Law, Vol. III, Family Law in a European Perspective* (Cheltenham: Edward Elgar, 2016).

Barlow, A., Hunter, R., Smithson, J. and Ewing, J., *Mapping Paths to Family Justice: Resolving Family Disputes in Neoliberal Times* (London: Palgrave Socio-Legal Studies, 2017).

Bastard, B., "Family Justice in France: Two Dimensions of 'Digitisation'", in M. Maclean and B. Dijksterhuis (eds.), *Digital Family Justice: from Alternative Dispute Resolution to Online Dispute Resolution?* (Oxford: Hart Publishing, 2019).

Cretney, S. M., *Law, Law Reform and the Family* (Oxford: Oxford University Press, 1998).
Davis, G., MacLeod, A. and Murch, M., "Undefended Divorces: Should Section 41 of the Matrimonial Causes Act 1973 be repealed?", *Modern Law Review*, 1983 (46), 121–46.
Dingwall, R. and Eekelaar, J., *Divorce, Mediation and the Legal Process* (Oxford: Clarendon Press, 1988).
Dingwall, R., Eekelaar, J. and Murray, T., *The Protection of Children* (2nd edn., Aldershot: Avebury, 1995).
Douglas, G., Murch, M., Scanlan, L. and Perry, A., "Safeguarding Children's Welfare in Non-Contentious Divorce: Towards a New Conception of the Legal Process?", *The Modern Law Review* 2000 (63), 177–96.
Eekelaar, J., "Consent Orders – in Whose Interests?", *Law Quarterly Review* 1985 (101), 318–22.
Eekelaar, J., "Divorce English Style – A New Way Forward?", *Journal of Social Welfare Law* 1986, 226–36.
Eekelaar, J., "'Not of the First Importance': Family Justice under Threat", *Journal of Social Welfare and Family Law* 2011 (33), 311–317.
Eekelaar, J., *Family Law and Personal Life* (2nd edn., Oxford: Oxford University Press, 2017).
Eekelaar, J., "The role of the best interests principle in decisions affecting children and decisions about children", *International Journal of Children's Rights* 2015 (23), 3–26.
Eekelaar, J. and Tobin, J., "Article 3: The Best Interests of the Child" in J. Tobin (ed.), *The UN Convention on the Rights of the Child: A Commentary* (Oxford: Oxford University Press, 2019).
Eekelaar, J. and Clive, E., *Custody after Divorce* (Oxford: SSRC Centre for Socio-Legal Studies, 1977).
Emery, K. C. and Emery, R. E., "Who knows what is best for children? Honoring agreements and contracts between parents who live apart", *Law and Contemporary Problems* 2014 (77), 151–176.
Fehlberg, B., Kaspiew, R., Millbank, J., Kelly, F. and Behrens, J., *Australian Family Law: The Contemporary Context* (2nd edn.), Melbourne: Oxford University Press, 2015).
Ferrand, F., "Non-Judicial Divorce in France: Progress or a Mess?", in G. Douglas, M. Murch and V. Stephens (eds.), *International and National Perspectives on Child and Family Law: Essays in Honour of Nigel Lowe* (Cambridge: Intersentia, 2018).
Hale, B., "In Defence of the Children Act", *Archives of Disease in Childhood* 2000 (83) 463–6.
Harada, E., "Family Reorganization in the Japanese Family Conciliation System: Resolving Divorce Disputes involving Minor Children", *International Journal of Law, Policy and the Family* 2019 (33(1)), 75–103.
House of Commons Select Committee on the Lord Chancellor's Department, Third Report (Session 2002–3).

Judicial College, *Family Court Bench Book*, 2019.

Lamb, M. E., "Parent–child contact in Separating Families" in M. Maclean (ed.), *Parenting after Partnering: Containing Conflict after Separation* (Oxford: Hart Publishing, 2007).

Law Commission, *Matrimonial Property: Needs and Agreements* (Law Com. No. 343, 2014).

Maclean, M., Eekelaar, J. and Bastard, B. (eds.), *Delivering Family Justice in the Century 21st*(Oxford: Hart Publishing, 2015).

Maclean, M. and Eekelaar, J., *Lawyers and Mediators: The Brave New World of Services for Separating Families* (Oxford: Hart Publishing, 2016).

Maclean, M. and Eekelaar, J., *After the Act: Access to Family Justice after LASPO* (Oxford: Hart Publishing, 2019).

Maclean, M. and Dijksterhuis, B. (eds.), *Digital Family Justice: from Alternative Dispute Resolution to Online Dispute Resolution?* (Oxford: Hart Publishing, 2019).

Marjoribanks, D., *Breaking up is hard to do: Assisting families to navigate family relationship support before, during and after separation* (Relate, 2015).

Ministry of Justice, *Reducing family conflict: Government response to the consultation on reform of the legal requirements for divorce* (Ministry of Justice, CP 59, 2019).

Mnookin, R. H., "Child Custody Adjudication: Judicial Functions in the Face of Indeterminacy", *Law and Contemporary Problems* 1975 (39), 226–293.

Mnookin, R. H., "Child Custody Revisited", *Law and Contemporary Problems* 2014 (77), 249–270.

Murch, M., *Supporting Children when Parents Separate: embedding a crisis intervention approach within family justice, education and mental health policy* (Bristol: Policy Press, 2018).

Murphy, J. C. and Singer, J. B., *Divorced from Reality: Rethinking Family Dispute Resolution* (New York: New York University Press, 2015).

Nielsen, L., "Joint Versus Sole Physical Custody: Children's Outcomes Independent of Parent–Child Relationships, Income, and Conflict in 60 Studies", *Journal of Divorce & Remarriage*, 2018 DOI: 10.1080/10502556.2018.1454204.

Private Law Working Group, *A review of the child arrangements programme (CAP) [PD12B FPR 2010]: Report to the President of the Family Division*, 2019.

Ryrstedt, E., "Mediation regarding children – is the Result always in the Best Interests of the Child? A View from Sweden", *International Journal of Law, Policy and the Family* 2012 (26), 220–241.

Scherpe, J. and Trinder, L., *Reforming the Ground for Divorce: Experiences from other Jurisdictions* (London: Nuffield Foundation, 2019).

Scherpe, J. M. (ed.), *Marital Agreements and Private Autonomy* (Oxford: Hart Publishing, 2012).

Shaffer, M., "Joint Custody, Parental Conflict and Children's Adjustment to Divorce: What the Social Science Literature does and does not tell us", *Canadian Family Law Quarterly* 2007 (26), 286.

Singer, A., "Parenting issues after separation: a Scandinavian perspective" in J. Eekelaar and R. George (eds.), *Routledge Handbook of Family Law and Policy* (2nd edn. Abingdon: Routledge, 2020).

Singer, J. B., "Bargaining in the Shadow of the Best-Interests Standard: the Close Connection between Substance and Process in resolving Divorce-related Parenting Disputes", *Law and Contemporary Problems* 2014 (77), 177–194.

Tobin, J. and Seow, F., 'Article 18: Parental responsibilities and State Assistance' in Tobin J. (ed.), *The UN Convention on the Rights of the Child: A Commentary* (Oxford: Oxford University Press, 2019).

Trinder, L., Bryson, C., Coleman, L., Houlston, C., Purdon, S., Reibstein, J., Smith L. and Stoilova, M., *Building Bridges? An Evaluation of the Costs an Effectiveness of the Parenting Information Programme (PIP)* (London: Department for Education, DFE RR140, 2011).

Trinder, L., Bryson, C., Coleman, L., Houlston, C., Purdon, S., Reibstein, J., Smith, L. and Stoilova, M., *Evaluation of the SPIP Plus: (SPIP Plus) Project* (London: Department for Education, 2014).

CHAPTER 7

From Reasonable to Unreasonable

Corporal Punishment in the Home

Trynie Boezaart

1   Introduction

In 2020 the Global Initiative to End All Corporal Punishment of Children reported that children are protected by law from corporal punishment in all settings, that is, in the criminal justice system, in schools, other institutions and in the home in 60 states all over the world (http://www.endcorporalpunishment.org). This is 40 years since Sweden took the lead in eradicating this way of punishing children. South Africa seems to be in a peculiar position and this chapter aims at providing some understanding of the status quo, evaluate the international benchmarks and critically analyse the progress towards achieving protection for children from corporal punishment in the home. In South Africa, the Constitutional Court has been on the forefront guiding the boundaries of children's constitutional rights in general and more specifically their rights involved in the corporal punishment debate. It pronounced in *S v Williams* (1995 (3) SA 632 (CC)) that the whipping of child offenders in the criminal justice system is unconstitutional. Chief Justice Langa (in a unanimous judgment) explicitly made the point that by abolishing corporal punishment, the state was breaking away from the past and the authoritarian approach to disciplining children (para. 50). In South Africa, this authoritarian approach has unsurprisingly also been linked to the system of Apartheid (Dawes, *et al.*, 2005). The court found that maintaining authority through violence was inconsistent with the South African Constitution (paras. 38, 52). As *S v Williams* was decided on the interim Constitution, (Constitution of the Republic of South Africa Act 200 of 1993, ss. 10 (human dignity) and 11(2) (freedom and security of the person)) the corresponding sections, namely sections 10 and 12(1)(*e*) of the Constitution of the Republic of South Africa, 1996 will be dealt with in paragraph 4.2 below. It should be noted that the right 'to be free from all forms of violence from either public or private sources' that is part and parcel of the 1996 Constitution (s. 12(1)(*c*)), was not available in the interim Constitution.

Just four years later, in *Christian Education South Africa v Minister of Education* (2000 (4) SA 757 (CC)) the Constitutional Court gave the final judgment in a case where an organisation contested the constitutionality of the abolition of corporal punishment in schools, with reference to the parents' individual, parental and community rights to practice their religion. According to the applicants their privacy (s. 14), freedom of belief and religion (s. 15), the right to maintain independent schools (s. 29(3)), language and culture (s. 30) and cultural, religious and linguistic communities (s. 31) in the Constitution have been infringed. This gave the Constitutional Court the opportunity to contextualise the abolition of corporal punishment in schools in terms of the then new constitutional value system. The court considered sections 9 (equality), 10 (human dignity), 12 (security of the person) and 28 (children's rights) (para. 15). This court's engagement with these underlying values has made this case being preferred to similar cases in other jurisdictions (Eekelaar, 2003: 373, comparing it with *R (on the application of Williamson and others) v Secretary of State for Education and Employment* 2002 EWCA Civ. 1820, [2002] 1 All E. R. 385). Justice Sachs (in an unanimous judgment) emphasised that the right to be free from all forms of violence (s. 12(1)(*b*)) and the right not to be punished in a cruel, inhuman or degrading way (s. 12(1)(*e*)) constitute separate rights and that the one does not substitute the other (para. 47). He added that the state 'must respect, protect, promote and fulfil' these rights and that this provision obliges the state to act accordingly (s. 7(2)) over and above the constitutional injunction to develop the common law to give effect to fundamental rights in this regard (s. 8(3)(*a*)). Justice Sachs added this important sentence: 'It [the state] must accordingly take appropriate steps to reduce violence in public **and private life**' (own emphasis). These words encouraged the argument that the state's responsibility be applied beyond the public and into the private domain to challenge the common-law defence of reasonable chastisement (Skelton, 2015: 337). He also referred to the special duty owed by the state to children and mentioned that ratifying international documents also required appropriate measures (paras. 47, 40). Unfortunately, the facts of the *Christian Education* case did not ask of the court to decide on whether corporal punishment in the home would amount to a form of violence from a private source (para. 48). A few years later the same court did find (in *S v Baloyi (Minister of Justice and Another Intervening)* 2002 (2) SA 425 (CC) para. 11, in the context of the Domestic Violence Act 116 of 1998) that the state is obliged 'to protect the right of everyone to be free from private or domestic violence'.

Thus far, the legislator played its part. Section 10 of the South African Schools Act 84 of 1996 criminalises the administering of corporal punishment to a learner at both public and independent schools. The ban on corporal punishment is supported by the provision in the Act for a Code of Conduct to enhance discipline in a positive way while respecting the rights of learners at the same time (s. 8, read with s. 20(1)(*d*) of the Schools Act and paras. 1.4, 4.4.1 of the *Guidelines for the Consideration of Governing Bodies in Adopting a Code of Conduct for Learners* (1998) GG 18900). This laid the foundation for school-discipline to be part of an empowering learning experience (Joubert, 2017: 605–608, National Department of Education 2001). Regulations were also promulgated in terms of the now repealed Child Care Act 74 of 1983 to abolish corporal punishment in institutional settings taking care of children, such as children's homes and child care centres (regulations 30A, 31A *GG* 18770 of 31 March 1998).

2   Legislative Reform

The South African Law Reform Commission (SALRC) initially proposed abandoning the reasonable chastisement defence in a report in 2002 (120–1). Another attempt to abolish corporal punishment in the home was made during 2006 in the Children's Amendment Bill (Children's Bill [B19 of 2006]), clause 139. Unfortunately this section was not included in the Children's Act (Waterhouse, 2007: 3).

During 2018 we saw a renewed attempt in another Amendment Bill [B – 2018] to the Children's Act 38 of 2005. The Draft Bill inserted an entire new section 12A in which persons caring for a child, including persons with parental responsibilities and rights, are instructed not to punish a child in any cruel, inhuman or degrading way when disciplining the child (s. 12A(1)). It completely abolished the defence of reasonable chastisement (s. 12A(2)). Once a person has been reported subjecting a child to any inappropriate punishment, including corporal punishment, that person must be referred to a prevention and early intervention programme focusing on developing appropriate parenting skills including positive, non-violent forms of discipline (s. 12A(3), referring to s. 144 of the Children's Act on prevention and early intervention programmes). The Department of Social Development is obliged to take all reasonable steps to implement awareness-raising programmes concerning the ban on corporal punishment and the abolition of the common-law defence of reasonable chastisement and run programmes promoting positive discipline (s. 12A(4)). When prevention and early intervention services are inappropriate or have failed and the child's safety and well-being is at risk, a designated social worker must assess the child and if necessary, take measures to protect the child (s. 12A(5)).

Unfortunately this "new" section 12A disappeared from the Bill when these provisions were very unexpectedly recalled by the Department – and this, after being relied upon in the Constitutional Court (para. 8 below). This Amendment Bill [B18 – 2020] was heading for Parliament by the end of August 2020 and tabled during the first week of September without even mentioning the controversial issue of corporal punishment in the home. The question now remains, where in the world are we when the lawmaker refrains from making law?

3   Reasonable Chastisement as a Ground of Justification

If the answer to this question is to be found in common law, common law recognises that reasonable chastisement is a defence that parents may raise as a ground of justification in relation to their children's discipline in the home (*R v Janke and Janke* 1913 TPD 382; *R v Scheepers* 1915 AD 337). In the South African context, common law is non-enacted law, primarily Roman-Dutch in its origins but also influenced by English law and adapted by the courts (Du Bois, 2010: 64). The common law derives its authority from the Constitution (*Pharmaceutical Manufacturers Association of SA: In re Ex parte President of the Republic of South Africa* 2000 (2) SA 674 (CC) para. 49).

Viewed from this angle, the parent-child relationship and the responsibilities and rights it entail are considered special circumstances that justify the *prima facie* unreasonable or unlawful violation of interests and render it reasonable/lawful. Wrongful conduct is not only to be found in the definition of assault (i.e. the wrongful or unlawful and intentional application of force to the person of another or at least inspiring such a belief in the person) within the boundaries of criminal law but wrongful and culpable conduct is also addressed by private law and more particularly in the law of delict (or tort law).

The South African law of delict follows a generalised approach where the general principles or requirements, commonly referred to as the elements, regulate delictual liability (Neethling and Potgieter, 2015: 4). As a general rule, you will be liable in delict if your wrongful, culpable conduct is causally connected to the harm that another person suffers. Wrongfulness thus constitutes an essential element. It entails that the conduct should not only have caused a harmful result but a legal norm must be violated in doing so. The *boni mores* (or, the legal convictions of the community), which is based on reasonableness (*Lee v Minister for Correctional Services* 2013 2 SA 144 (CC) 167), plays an important role in this enquiry (*NM v Smith (Freedom of Expression Institute as amicus)* 2007 5 SA 250 (CC) 274).

The bottom line is therefore that, whether parents are criminally charged or held to account in delict (*Hiltonian Society v Crofton* 1952 (3) SA 130 (A)), South African law recognised that parents may use moderate force to discipline their children (Schäfer, 2011: 133). It is noteworthy that this defence was not only available to the parents, but to persons *in loco parentis* as well (*Du Preez v Conradie* 1990 (4) SA 46 (B) 54). The authority of persons *in loco parentis* to discipline children was original, and therefore a parent was not able to unilaterally restrict or suspend a step-parent's power to mete out corporal punishment. This is why educators and even prefects were in a position to use this type of punishment (*Hiltonian Society v Crofton* 1952 (3) SA 130 (A) 134–5). Boberg so eloquently stated, '[t]hus a scoutmaster, friend, relative or babysitter may have a limited right of punishment, proportionate to the degree and duration of his [or her] responsibility' (1984: 845). However, this defence was not at the disposal of foster parents (General Regulations Regarding Children GN R261 in *GG* 33076 2010 reg. 65(1)(*h*)) and also not in Child and Youth Care Centres (reg. 76(2)(*d*)).

The person on whom the law conferred the power to discipline had a discretion regarding the form of punishment to be meted out including whether or not to use corporal punishment. A certain level of arbitrariness was thus implicit. The court interfered only if the discretion was exercised in an unreasonable manner. The test for reasonableness is objective and the following factors were considered (*R v Janke and Janke* 1913 TPD 382 at 385–6): The nature and seriousness of the transgression; the degree of punishment or force inflicted; the physical and psychological condition of the child; the nature of the instrument used; and the purpose and motive of the parent inflicting the punishment.

The purpose of the punishment must be correction. Malice and improper motive are indicative of unreasonable/wrongful punishment. However, there was a presumption that chastisement meted out for the purpose of correction was exercised reasonably and without malice (*R v Janke and Janke* 1913 TPD 382 at 385; Boberg, 1984: 843–4). A person/party who asserts the contrary will have to prove it (*Hiltonian Society v Crofton* 1952 (3) SA 130 (A)). In the criminal law context the state had to prove that the parent exceeded the boundaries of the defence (Van Heerden *et al.*, 1999: 671).

4   The Unreasonableness of Corporal Punishment

Nearly a century ago the court remarked that the old saying 'spare the rod and spoil the child' has long ago been abolished (*Rex v Theron* 1936 OPD 166 at 172). Reading through the literature on this point it is apparent that this defence is out-dated (Neethling & Potgieter, 2015: 121). It is impossible to explain the concept thereof without referring to either parental (and quasi-parental) authority, that is the parent's right to demand that their children pay due reverence and obey their orders; or parents' power to chastise and control their children to correct deviant behaviour (*Germani v Herf and*

Another 1975 (4) SA 887 (A) 902B; Van Heerden *et al.* 1999, 668–669). And the state has always been reluctant to interfere with the exercise of the rights and duties of parents in rearing their children (Burchell and Hunt, 2008: 117). While parents' rights took centre stage in common law a few decades ago, the scene has completely changed in the past twenty years. There has been a paradigm shift from parents' rights to children's rights (*S v M (Centre for Child Law as Amicus Curiae)* 2008 (3) SA 232 (CC) paras. 18–19). Revolutionary changes were brought about by the Constitution, supported, and in some instances initiated by international law (notably art. 5 of the CRC; GC No. 8 paras. 22–5; Tobin and Varadan 2019: 174), and in the legislative reform that followed it through.

The Constitution spells out specific rights that every child has and pertinent to the corporal punishment issue is the child's right 'to be protected from maltreatment, neglect, abuse or degradation' (s. 28(1)(*d*)). Furthermore, in South Africa the best interests-standard has been adopted in the Constitution and elevated to the paramount consideration (s. 28(2)). The paramountcy of the best interests of the child in every matter concerning him or her is a separate right (*Minister of Welfare and Population Development v Fitzpatrick* 2000 (3) 422 (CC) para. 18) and it is echoed in the Children's Act 38 of 2005 (s. 9, and the factors that have to be considered whenever the child's best interests are at stake is in s. 7 of the Children's Act and note s. 7(1)(*h*) regarding the child's physical and emotional well-being).

The Children's Act is the primary legislation that establishes a detailed framework for the protection of children. Its objectives are to *inter alia* 'give effect to the constitutional rights of children, including the right to be protected from maltreatment, neglect, abuse or degradation' and 'give effect to South Africa's obligations concerning the well-being of children in terms of international instruments binding on it' (s. 2(*b*)-(*c*)). Both the child's right to be protected from maltreatment and the paramountcy of the child's bests interests are echoed in the Children's Act. The child's right to be protected from maltreatment, degradation, neglect, abuse (definition of "abuse" in s. 1(1), read with s. 305(3)(*a*) which criminalises abuse and deliberate neglect) finds its correlative in the duty of parents to protect them from exactly these things and any physical, emotional or moral harm (s. 1(*c*) under the definition of "care" and a regime to deal with abuse involving social workers, police investigations, the Children's Court etc., e.g. ss. 46, 104, 110, 150, 155). More broadly stated, parents have a duty to protect, respect, promote and secure the fulfilment of, and guard against any infringement of the child's Bill of Rights-rights. However, to date there is no prohibition of corporal punishment to be found in the Children's Act.

5 International Benchmarks

5.1 Role of International Law in South Africa

South Africa follows a dualist approach to international law which means that international law must be domesticated to have the force of law. The Constitution and the legislation dealing with children's rights have to a large extent done exactly that. Furthermore, the importance of international law has been constitutionalised in section 39(1) on the interpretation of the Bill of Rights. In terms of this provision a court, tribunal or other forum must consider international law when interpreting the Bill of Rights (s. 39(1)(c)). Moreover, the Constitution also provides that when interpreting any legislation the court has to prefer any reasonable interpretation that is consistent with international law (s. 233). Very important in this debate revolving around human rights is also that customary international law is the law in South Africa unless it is inconsistent with the Constitution or an Act of Parliament (s. 232).

5.2 Convention on the Rights of the Child

In *S v M (Centre for Child Law as Amicus Curiae)* (2008 (3) SA 232 (CC) para. 16) the Constitutional Court noted the significance of the Convention on the Rights of the Child (CRC, that South Africa ratified on 16 June 1995) in that it had 'become the international standard against which to measure legislation and policies, and has established a new structure, modelled on children's rights', and that this involved 'a change in mindset, one that takes appropriately equivalent account of the new constitutional vision'. These remarks were made in the context of the criminal justice system and are important principles of general application (approved and applied by Keightley J in *YG v S* 2018 (1) SACR 64 (GJ) para. 45 discussed in para. 6 below).

Article 5 of the CRC provides a crucial international benchmark regarding the way parents and others that are legally responsible for children should exercise their responsibilities and rights and the state's overseeing thereof ('States Parties shall respect the responsibilities, rights and duties of parents or, where applicable, the members of the extended family or community as provided for by local custom, legal guardians or other persons legally responsible for the child, to provide, in a manner consistent with the evolving capacities of the child, appropriate direction and guidance in the exercise by the child of the rights recognized in the present Convention'). It provides the normative standard for the triangular relationship between the state, the parents and their children (Tobin and Varadan 2019: 161).

The state must respect the responsibilities and rights of the parents (and others) and in doing so the state acknowledge that the parents bear the primary responsibility for the upbringing of their children. But the state's obligations in terms of this article extends beyond providing a safety net if the primary caregivers cannot fulfil their responsibilities. The state also have a duty to clearly articulate the legally accepted norms (e.g. in legislation), take appropriate measures to educate parents regarding the type of parenting that article 5 requires (Tobin and Varadan 2019: 163) and encourage compliance even on a broader scale (e.g. educate state and non-state actors and run awareness raising programmes for parents and the public at large).

In the second part of this unique article the Convention spells out how the parents have to exercise these responsibilities and rights. They have to provide appropriate direction and guidance to the child taking due regard of the evolving capacities of the child. Article 5 thus lays down the basic "rules" for this state-parent-child relationship and it does so in a very radical way. The pertinent question now becomes whether it is possible for parents to meet out corporal punishment to their children without transgressing the "article 5-rules" and to answer the question, the exact wording of the article becomes very important.

Parents have a responsibility in terms of article 5 to appropriately direct and guide their children in the exercise of their, the children's, rights. The CRC Committee calls this direction and guidance "child-centered" and proposes that example and dialogue would enhance children's capacities to exercise their rights (GC No. 7 (2005) para. 17). The word "appropriate" is very powerful in this context and the CRC Committee has been vocal in explaining that corporal punishment is incompatible with several provisions of the CRC (GC No. 8 para. 28, Tobin and Varadan 2019: 172). '[I]n a manner consistent with the evolving capacities of the child' means that the parents will have to continually adjust their guidance to further their children's development through an enabling process into independent adulthood (GC No. 7 para. 17).This process of continually adjusting the guidance will inevitably mean that the parents will have to acknowledge and have respect for the evolving capacities of the child (GC No. 14 (2013) para. 44; GC No. 20 (2016) para. 18). This respect will certainly include recognising *inter alia* the child's autonomy (Tobin and Varadan 2019: 161, 173). The evolving capacities of the child in article 5 becomes an overarching enabling principle of the CRC (Tobin and Varadan 2019: 178).

The relationship between parents and children that article 5 deals with (Varadan, 2019: 316) is a respectful parent-child relationship and overrules all the out-dated and authoritarian conceptions regarding this relationship (Tobin and Varadan 2019: 161). In the parent-child relationship that the CRC creates the bottom-line is that '[t]he best interests of the child will be their basic concern' (art. 18(1) and similar is UN Declaration on the Rights of the

Child (1959) prin. 7)). The Convention then builds on this foundation in many other articles such as articles 12 (on the child's opinion and participation) and 14 (on freedom of thought, conscience and religion) in the development of the child's capacities towards adulthood. What stands out is that article 5 is about respect for the child's rights. The Convention also takes the respect that a child has to have further (in art. 29).

The Children's Act is to some extent aligned with international law on this point (Freeman, 2010: 216; Schäfer, 2011: 137). Included in the definition of the concept "care" is a duty on parents to guide the behaviour of the child in 'a humane manner' while 'guiding, directing and securing the child's education and upbringing, including religious and cultural education and upbringing, in a manner appropriate to the child's age, maturity and stage of development' (subs. 1(*g*), 1(*e*)). The challenge in the corporal punishment debate is to internalise that corporal punishment is not humane. Fortunately, one of the underlying objectives of the Children's Act is to promote positive parenting (subs. 1(*d*), 46(*g*), 46(*h*)).

The CRC also strives to protect children from all forms of physical (and mental) violence while 'in the care parent(s), legal guardian(s) or any other person who has the care of the child' by instructing states to take legislative, administrative, social and educational measures to that effect (art. 19(1)). These protective measures are taken further in the same article when stipulating that it should *inter alia* include effective procedures regarding social programmes, prevention, identification and reporting (art. 19(2); CRC Committee GC No. 8 paras. 48–9).

These provisions run deep in the Children's Act. Protection from maltreatment, neglect, abuse or degradation (s. 2(*b*)) and providing for structures, services and means in achieving the physical and mental well-being of children (s. 2(*d*)) are important objectives of the Act. Subjecting a child to violence goes against the best interests of the child which is paramount (subss. 7(*l*)-(*m*) read with s. 9). There are ample provisioning on prevention and early intervention programmes including programmes to develop appropriate parenting skills to promote 'positive non-violent forms of discipline' (ss. 143–149), identification (ss. 45(*f*), 150 and a National Child Protection Register to record and monitor abuse: s. 113), reporting (s. 110,) and the criminalisation of abuse of a child by a parent or other persons with parental responsibilities and rights (s. 305(3)).

Article 37(*a*) puts the final responsibility to ensure that '[n]o child shall (note the imperative) be subjected to torture or other cruel, inhumane or degrading treatment or punishment' squarely on the state parties. Like the UN Declaration on the Rights of the Child (prin. 2) the CRC evokes the child's dignity in the administration of discipline (Freeman, 2010: 215). This principle is also repeated in the context of school discipline (art. 28(2)). The CRC Committee has made it clear that with "discipline" is meant the 'necessary guidance and direction' (GC No. 8 para. 13).

Referring to the remainder of the CRC the requirement (or general principle) that 'the best interests of the child shall be a primary consideration' (art. 3(1)) is very important (although the wording is not as strong as 'the paramount consideration' of the UN Declaration on the Rights of the Child prin. 2). Many books have been written on the pros and the cons of the best interests standard but I endorse Freeman's viewpoint (2010: 216) that no matter how indeterminate, subjective or value-laden the child's best interests might be, violence against a child is not in a child's best interests (GC No. 8 paras. 26 and 28). I find the argument regarding the best interests of the present that have to be sacrificed in favour of the best interests being savoured later, unconvincing. When this viewpoint is being held in the corporal punishment debate, it narrows the investigation to exclude the consideration of all other forms of discipline (Mnookin, 1975: 260; Thèry, 1989: 82 *et seq.*). Children thus have a right to be protected from violence and all forms of abuse and neglect have to be eliminated to realise the best interests of the child as a primary consideration (Freeman, 2007: 52).

In actual fact, all the general principles come to play in the corporal punishment debate. Over and above the best interests of the child (art. 3) and child participation (art. 12) in parental guidance and support, the child's right to life, survival and development is the overarching concern (art. 6). Less obvious could be the fact that the principle of non-discrimination also addresses punishment and in this case punishment of the child based on the parent's/parents' opinions or beliefs (art. 2(2); Besson and Kleber, 2019: 61). It will be evident in the case law that these are all too often the reason behind corporal punishment (e.g. the *YG* case in para. 6 below).

The CRC Committee addressed the child's right to be protected from corporal punishment very specifically in 2007 (GC No. 8) following on general discussions and international studies on violence against children (paras. 1, 4). The Committee provided a very broad and inclusive definition of corporal punishment which encompasses 'any punishment in which physical force is used and intended to cause some degree of pain or discomfort'. This definition goes beyond hitting and includes, for example kicking, shaking, and pulling hair, biting and any punishment which belittles, humiliates or threatens the child. It thus also includes non-physical punishment (para. 11). The Committee explicitly stated that corporal punishment is invariably degrading and all children have the right to be free from all forms of cruel and degrading treatment (paras. 7, 12, 18).

In the same General Comment the Committee responded to the corporal punishment and religious teaching debate and highlighted the fact that religion must be consistent with respect for human dignity and does not enjoy unlimited protection (para. 29). The Committee supports a positive concept of discipline if the necessary guidance is provided in line with the child's evolving capacities (GC No. 8 para. 13) and very pertinently referred to the common-law defence of reasonable chastisement. It held the opinion that state parties should in view of the 'traditional acceptance of corporal punishment' adopt legislative measures clearly prohibiting and criminalising its use in the relevant settings (GC No. 8 paras. 28, 31, 33–35).

In another General Comment (No. 13) on the right of the child to freedom from all forms of violence, the Committee elaborated on the dignity of the child in a child-rights approach to the surge of violence towards children, the majority of which takes place in the family context (paras. 3, 14). It comes very close to addressing the defence of reasonable chastisement, albeit not using exactly this terminology, when it notes that national laws should 'in no way erode the child's right to human dignity and physical and psychological integrity by describing some forms of violence as legally … acceptable' (para. 17).

The CRC Committee has also been vocal on the corporal punishment debate in its reviews on South Africa's country reports. Already in 2000 it expressed concern that corporal punishment is 'still permissible within families' and recommended that measures should be taken 'to prohibit [it] by law' (Concluding Observations para. 28). The same happened in 2016 (Concluding Observations para. 34).

5.3 *African Charter on the Rights and Welfare of the Child*

Unfortunately physical punishment of children is prevalent in Africa (Morrell, 2001: 297. Hesselink & Dastile, 2016: 14–5 depicts it as a world-wide phenomenon but more severe in impoverished and rural households). At regional level the African Charter on the Rights and Welfare of the Child (ACRWC) (1990) (that South Africa ratified in 2000) does not contain any provision that resembles article 5 of the CRC, underscoring the uniqueness of the latter. The ACRWC contains an article (art. 16(1): 'States Parties to the Present Charter shall take specific legislative, administrative, social and educational measures to protect the child from all forms of torture, inhuman or degrading treatment and especially physical or mental injury or abuse, neglect or maltreatment including sexual abuse, while in the care of the child') that is very closely aligned to the more general measures on the protection of children against all forms of violence in the CRC (19(1)). The ACRWC uses stronger language when the best interests of the child are at stake requiring that the best interests of the child 'shall be the primary consideration' in all actions concerning a child 'undertaken by any person or authority' (art. 4(1)).

Unfortunately the ACRWC also contains sections that could be interpreted either for or against corporal punishment. A few examples will suffice. Article 11(5) provides that state parties shall take all appropriate measures to ensure that a child who is subjected to discipline, either at school or in the home, shall be treated with humanity while respecting the child's inherent dignity. On the one hand it seems to set the boundaries when corporal punishment is administered and on the other hand it seems not possible to administer this type of punishment without overstepping these limits (Mezmur, 2006: 9). Likewise article 20(1)(c) provides that parents have the duty 'to ensure that domestic discipline is administered with humanity and in a manner consistent with the inherent dignity of the child'. Mezmur puts forward a very powerful argument that if corporal punishment is part and parcel of African culture and tradition, all appropriate measures must be taken to eliminate it in terms of article 21(1) which obliges state parties 'to eliminate harmful social and cultural practices'. It is noteworthy that several African countries have abolished corporal punishment in full in spite of its cultural and/or traditional links (Mezmur, 2006: 10).

The African Committee of Experts on the Rights and Welfare of the Child addresses the dichotomy in South African law in its Concluding Recommendations on the country's initial report in 2014 urging South Africa to ban corporal punishment in the home, harmonise its own laws on the chastisement of children and promote and provide information and training on positive disciplining (para. 35).

5.4 Concluding Remarks Regarding International and Regional Documents and Bodies

Many other international and regional documents could be referred to in which violence and or corporal punishment is condemned and just a few examples will suffice. At international level the Universal Declaration of Human Rights (UDHR, 1984) (ss. 1, 3, 5, 7, 18, 27) and the International Covenant on Civil and Political Rights (ICCPR, which South Africa ratified in 1998, ss. 3, 4, 7, 10, 24, 26) stand out and at regional level the same applies to the European Convention on Human Rights of 1950 (art. 3) and the African Charter on Human and People's Rights of 1982 (arts. 2, 3, 5, 8, 19, 25). (For a very comprehensive discussion on the European Convention on Human Rights and the European bodies concerned with the matter, see Freeman, 2010: 232 *et seq.* and 238 *et seq.* respectively, and regarding other regions, e.g. the American States (248–9) and Asia (249–50).) It is relevant in the discussion that follows to note that the European Committee of Social Rights (ECSR) which monitors compliance with the

European Social Charter and the Revised Social Charter observed that article 17 of the Social Charter which aims at protecting children against *inter alia* violence requires a legislative prohibition against any form of violence in all settings (Council of Europe, 2008: 5).

An obvious conclusion to draw from the above, is that South Africa has ratified international documents that requires corporal punishment in the home to be outlawed in legislation. Various international bodies have responded hereto. The Human Rights Council has on three occasions (in the Universal Review Process in 2008, 2012 and 2017) recommended to the Government of South Africa to prohibit corporal punishment in all settings, including in the home (Mezmur, 2018: 81). The Human Rights Committee, the body that monitors the implementation of the ICCPR, made similar recommendations (2016: para. 25).

6   Transformative Constitutionalism

The role of the Constitution should never be underestimated. South African law is slowly but surely transforming to align itself with the values and prescripts of the Constitution (s. 8(1), read with ss. 8(3), 39(2)). Although inroads have been made (e.g. *H v Fetal Assessment Centre* 2015 (2) SA 139 (CC) for a case in the law of delict), much more will have to be done to transform all the common-law principles involved to reflect constitutional values such as human dignity and equality (Skelton, 2015: 347–8). This transformative process is in the hands of the legislature or, if it has to be done on a case by case basis, the courts.

Regarding the defence of reasonable chastisement, it seems that the legislature have been extremely reluctant to respond to both international law and the Constitution. The courts have thus taken the lead and the first bold step in this transformative process has been made in the case of *YG v S* (2018 (1) SACR 64 (GJ)) that reached the High Court in 2017. In that instance a father appealed a magistrate court's judgment convicting him of common assault of his 13-year-old boy. The facts relating to this conviction indicate that the father accused his son of viewing pornographic material on an iPad which the boy denied repeatedly. (He was also found guilty of assaulting his wife on the very same day alleging that she is involved in an extra-marital affair.) The appellant's case was that he chastised his child by meting out reasonable corporal punishment because pornography is strictly forbidden by their religion. The court therefore had to decide whether the common-law defence was compatible with the Constitution (para. 10). The court requested counsel on both sides and the

Ministers of Justice and Correctional Services and Social Development to make submissions and issued directions inviting interested parties to join as *amici*. Written submissions were received from the Minister of Social Development and four *amici* were admitted (paras. 11, 12), but the position of the Department of Social Development in this matter is not clear. In the written submissions that the Department made to the court it quoted a Draft Policy in which the premise is apparently that the defence of reasonable chastisement is not part of South African law anymore. However, when *YG v S* was passed, it was the law (para. 58). The Centre for Child Law at the University of Pretoria represented the first three *amici* (The Children's Institute at the University of Cape Town, the Quaker Peace Centre and Sonke Gender Justice). The fourth *amicus* was Freedom of Religion South Africa (FORSA, a non-profit company that aims at advancing freedom of religion and claim to represent 6 million people in South Africa spanning various denominations and faith groups).

Interestingly the constitutional issue was first raised by the court of appeal, but Keightley J pointed out that the Constitutional Court held that a High Court may raise constitutional issues of its own accord when it is necessary for purposes of disposing of the case before it or when there are compelling reasons to adjudicate on the matter in the interest of justice (para. 20, in line with *Director of Public Prosecutions, Transvaal v Minister of Justice* 2009 (2) SA 222 (CC)). The court found that the present case requires consideration of the constitutionality of the common-law defence of reasonable chastisement in the interest of justice because it is necessary for parents to know whether the defence is available or not (para. 25). Keightley also considered the constitutional obligation that courts has to develop the common law to be in line with the values that underlie our Constitution (para. 27, referring to s. 39(2) of the Constitution). The court also acknowledged the role of international law on the issue of corporal punishment, referring to the CRC, the recommendations South Africa received from the Committee on the Rights of the Child as well as their General Comments 8 and 13 and the African Committee of Experts on the Rights and Welfare of the Child (paras. 54, 55).

Keightley J penned a ground-breaking judgment based on the fact that the Constitutional Court recognises that children are constitutional rights holders 'in their own respect, not through their parents' (para. 61, referring to *S v M* 2008 (3) SA 232 (CC) paras. 18–19). In her judgment she expanded on the development of the reasonable chastisement defence and indicated that this parent-centered defence is at odds with the child-focused Constitution (paras. 62–64). The judgment gave a very concise account of the constitutional protection afforded to children in the Bill of Rights finding that physical chastisement breaches a child's right to –

- dignity (paras. 71–72, referring to s. 10 of the Constitution that grants everyone inherent dignity and the right to have their dignity respected and protected);
- equal protection under the law (paras. 73–74, referring to s. 9(1) of the Constitution). Children therefore have no less dignity or physical integrity than adults/parents. This links with section 9(3) that children may not be discriminated against because of their age (paras. 75–76);
- be free from **all** forms of violence from either public or **private** sources (para. 69, referring to s. 12(1)(c));
- not be treated or punished in a cruel, inhuman or degrading way (referring to s. 12(1)(e) of the Constitution, which is a non-derogable right in terms of s. 37(5)(c));
- bodily and psychological integrity (para. 69, referring to s. 12(2));
- be protected from maltreatment, abuse or degradation (s. 28(1)(d), which is one of the child-specific right); and
- have his or her best interests being considered of paramount importance in every matter concerning the child (para. 76, referring to s. 28(2)).

She also found that the limitations imposed by the reasonable chastisement defence are not constitutionally justifiable under the limitation clause (s. 36), and that children deserve special protection (paras. 77–85). It is stated very clearly in her order that the development of the common law (and thus the order declaring the defence unconstitutional) is prospective and not retrospective (para. 107). This is very significant because the appellant can then only appeal the judgment on the narrow point that affects him, that is, did he exceed the boundaries of the defence. This court found that there is no merit in his appeal (para. 95) and one would think that the matter was disposed of in this way.

However, FORSA, one of the *amici*, lodged an application to the Constitutional Court, first for standing and, secondly, for leave to appeal (*Freedom of Religion South Africa v Minister of Justice and Constitutional Development and others* 2020 (1) SA 1 (CC)). Interestingly, there is a precedent (*The Campus Law Clinic (University of Kwazulu-Natal Durban) v Standard Bank of South Africa Ltd and Minister for Justice and Constitutional Development* 2006 (6) SA 103 (CC)), where an application for leave to appeal was lodged in the Constitutional Court by an applicant that was, like FORSA, not a party to the case. In that case the Constitutional Court found that the *Campus Law Clinic* had standing to bring an application for leave to appeal in terms of section 38 of the Constitution (para. 22). This section provides that if rights in the Bill of Rights are infringed, or threatened to be infringed, a list of people has the right to approach an appropriate court (s. 38(d) and (e)). This list *inter alia* includes anyone acting in the public interest and an association acting in the interest of its members, and has introduced a radical departure from the common law in relation to standing. Potentially it includes associations like FORSA.

Another important fact to note regarding the High Court judgment in the Gauteng Local Division is that it has the force of law only in one of the nine provinces, namely Gauteng. It may have persuasive force in the remainder of the country, but the Gauteng Local Division has jurisdiction in that province only. There was thus a need for uniformity and finality on this issue.

It is striking that in the same year (2017), in the High Court in neighbouring Zimbabwe, that share a Roman-Dutch based English law influenced common law system with South Africa, Linah Pfungwa and the Justice for Children Trust applied for a constitutional declaratory order that corporal punishment in schools and in the home violates children's rights as set out in sections 51 (the right to human dignity), 53 (freedom from torture or cruel, inhuman or degrading treatment or punishment) and 81 (child-specific rights) of the Constitution of Zimbabwe Amendment (No. 20) Act, 2013 (*Pfungwa and Justice for Children v Headmistress Belvedere Junior Primary School, Minister of Education, Sport and Culture, Minister of Justice, Legal and Parliamentary Affairs* [2017] ZWHHC 148). In this case a teacher severely assaulted a 7-year-old girl with a rubber pipe because her mother failed to sign a book to confirm that the child did her homework. The mother took to social media and shared photos of the deep bruises on a WhatsApp group to discover that other children had also been assaulted. The applicants filed their application in terms of section 85(1)(*d*) of the Zimbabwean Constitution that is remarkably similar to section 38 of the South African Constitution and proved, in what eventually turned out to be an unopposed application, that the new Constitution is indeed a transformative document.

However, Sloth-Nielsen (2018: 263) indicates that other neighbouring countries with similar common law roots (i.e. Botswana and Namibia), have less impressive track records. What we seem to have in common, are progressive courts and resistance by parliamentarians.

7 Religious and Cultural Perceptions

In the *YG* case FORSA contended that it acts for millions of religious believers who believe that their scriptures and other holy writings permit (if not command) reasonable and moderate correction of their children. The father in the *YG* case was a devout Muslim and he averred that he chastised his son as per his religious beliefs. FORSA argued in the High Court that several constitutional rights of parents are implicated, such as the right to freedom of religion, belief and opinion (s. 15 of the Constitution), the right to human dignity (s. 10) and the rights of cultural and religious communities (s. 31 of the Constitution) and that it would be 'unconscionable and unconstitutional to undermine these rights by doing away with the defence' (para. 82).

Although the right to freedom of religion and belief is recognised in many international and regional human rights instruments (e.g. arts. 18 of the UDHR and 18(1) of the ICCPR), this argument is in direct conflict with international law, various constitutional rights and the constitutional imperative regarding the child's best interests. In establishing the parameters of the parents' right to religious beliefs and cultural practices Keightley J found that the child's right to dignity, physical integrity and the importance of the principle of the best interests of the child justify the limitation of the parents' rights (para. 84). The boundaries of the parents' rights are also affected by the arbitrariness regarding what actually constitutes "reasonable" chastisement. Furthermore, the vulnerability of children and the fact that children enjoy less protection than adults are clearly displayed in the *YG* case (Mezmur, 2018: 90). The same man was found guilty of abusing both his wife and his son on the very same day but the reasonable chastisement defence only applied to the incident involving the child (paras. 75–76, in conflict with the Constitution, s. 9(1)). It is also important in the discussion that follows to note that the Department of Social Development was on board in the *YG* case referring to a Draft Policy that depicts corporal punishment as inappropriate and supports positive discipline with prevention and early intervention services (para. 81).

8   Constitutional Court's Contribution

In *Freedom of Religion South Africa v Minister of Justice and Constitutional Development* (2020 (1) SA 1 (CC)) Mogoeng CJ. paid some homage to religion by referring to a verse from the Bible (Proverbs 13: 24) in the first paragraph of his judgment and assuming the challenge to add 'Solomonic wisdom' 'on a sensitive, complex and controversial matter of national importance – child discipline'. The Constitutional Court granted FORSA direct access (in terms of s. 167(6)(*b*) of the Constitution) and leave to intervene in the following words (para. 20):

> Legal principles exist to facilitate rather than to frustrate the attainment of a just, equitable and definitive outcome. The issue of discipline, its positive and negative aspects, and the need for certainty on the disciplinary

options available to parents cry out for the attention of this court. A pronouncement by the apex court on whether the common law defence of reasonable and moderate chastisement is constitutionally invalid would clearly serve the interests of the public.

In delivering judgment for an unanimous court the Chief Justice indicated that what is in the best interests of children lies at the heart of this application (para. 24), but he chose to resolve the constitutionality of reasonable chastisement primarily on the right of everyone (thus not a specific children's right) 'to be free from all forms of violence from either public or private sources' (s. 12(1)(c)) and the right to 'inherent human dignity' (s. 10). Unfortunately it seems that the judgment on the constitutionality of the defence of reasonable chastisement is restricted to the criminal law setting (para. 37) instead of acknowledging the applicability thereof in the law of delict as well. The judgment very clearly finds that a contextual and purposive interpretation of the word "violence" in section 12(1)(c) converges on the definition given to assault (see para. 3 above): 'Violence is not so much about the manner and extent of the application of the force as it is about the mere exertion of some force or the threat thereof' (para. 38). Reasonable chastisement thus falls within the category of violence envisaged in section 12(1)(c) because of the force or threat of force with which it is applied (para. 40). Reasonable chastisement also limits everyone's right to dignity, including children (para. 45).

The court then had to consider whether the limitation of these rights was reasonable and justifiable (para. 50). The court very carefully considered the difference between chastisement administered by a parent, and by an institution (para. 51); that invalidating the defence might remove a culturally or religiously directed form of child discipline (para. 52); the vulnerability of children (para. 55), the constitutional obligation to protect children's rights (para. 56) and the paramountcy thereof (paras. 57–60). The court found in this regard that the paramountcy of children's rights (s. 28(2) of the Constitution) 'is crafted in terms so broad as to leave no doubt about the choice it makes between the best interests of the child and the parent's perceived entitlement to resort to unreasonable and immoderate chastisement meant to procure a child's obedience to a parent's legitimate directive and orders' (para. 61).

The Constitutional Court found that neither the parents' right to freedom of religion or culture nor their 'right to parenting' provide for parental entitlement to administer chastisement to the child (para. 63). Furthermore, the right to religion is a right of the parent **and** the child (*Kotze v Kotze* 2003 (3) SA 628 (T)) and has a voluntary nature (MEC *for Education, KwaZulu-Natal v Pillay* (2008 (1) SA 474 (CC) paras. 60–67). The Constitutional Court acknowledged that positive parenting reduces the need to enforce discipline by resorting to violence (para. 64) and that there are less restrictive means to instil discipline (para. 68).

In the concluding remarks the Constitutional Court enjoins Parliament to consult widely before providing an 'appropriate regulatory framework' (para. 74) which apparently assumes legislation on the matter. It also advises law enforcement agencies to deal with reported cases of child abuse flowing from this declaration of unconstitutionality on a case-by-case basis (para. 75) once more assuming some legislative guidance. The Constitutional Court declared the common law defence of reasonable chastisement inconsistent with sections 10 and 12(1)(c) of the Constitution and dismissed the application for leave to appeal.

9 Concluding Remarks

The unreasonableness of corporal punishment in the home is evident. It is not right for children if parents assault them when they are supposed to sensitively direct and guide them (CRC, art. 5). It is not right for children if their parents undermine, instead of respect their inherent dignity (Freeman and Saunders 2014: 701). It is not right for children to be subjected to corporal punishment in the home when they/everybody should be free from all forms of violence (CRC, art. 19).

Research has indicated that corporal punishment is ineffective, in both the short-term and long-term (Gershoff 2013: 133–7). Furthermore, the negative effects of corporal punishment on children have been spelt out in various studies, both locally (e.g. by Burton, et al. 2015: 17–20; Breen, et al. 2015: 131–139) and internationally (e.g. GC No. 8 paras. 37, 48; Gershoff 2013: 133–137). These negative effects include behavioural problems, especially with aggression, emotional and mental health problems, like depression and the impact thereof may extend into adult life (Gershoff 2013: 133–137; Freeman and Saunders 2014: 688). Studies also abound highlighting the vulnerability of especially young children due to their age, size and developmental status to corporal punishment (Richter, et al. 2018: 181–186; Bower and Dawes 2014: 58). The younger the children are the more vulnerable they become to the long-term negative consequences, which could include lasting neurological and psychological damage (Bower and Dawes 2014: 58, 60, 62.). Child deaths have also been associated with corporal punishment in the home (Mathews, et al. 2016: 851–852).

In the YG case, Keightley J. pointed out that '[i]t is time for our country to march in step with its international obligations under the CRC…' (para. 85). Eliminating violent and humiliating punishment of children through law reform is an immediate and unqualified obligation on state parties (CRC art. 5, GC No. 8 para. 22; GC No. 20 para. 49) and South Africa is yet to comply with this obligation.

There seems to be two routes to take to what is right for children. The one-stop legislative route underpinned by awareness raising and community education. Sadly, South Africa has missed this opportunity when article 12A disappeared from the 2018 Amendment Bill (para. 2 above). The other route is judicial decision-making backed by subsequent law reform (like Israel, where the Supreme Court of Appeal banned the common law defence in 2000 and followed through with subsequent law reform in the same year: Mezmur 2018: 82–85; Morag 2018: 225). The latter should include providing parenting programmes, for instance on 'positive disciplining', to high risk families in communities for instance where crime, violence and alcohol abuse are common (Bower and Dawes 2014: 59, 61). Parental training and community awareness programmes are of the utmost importance and have to be prioritised in this scenario. Compared to the pointed provisions that were in the 2018 Amendment Bill, it is doubtful whether the early intervention provisions in the Children's Act (paras. 4 and 5.2 above) are sufficiently tailor-made to address this need.

Legislation should have ensured that the direction and guidance provided by the parents are in conformity with all the provisions of the Convention on the Rights of the Child (CRC, art. 5, GC No. 8 paras. 5, 18). A clear legislative regime should have criminalised corporal punishment in the home (GC No. 8 para. 39 while retaining the *de minimis non curat lex* principle, para. 40) and provided for appropriate education and training for all the parties (para. 5.1 above). If the law can change attitudes and behaviour (Freeman and Saunders 2014: 701; Dodd 2018: 122), why is the legislative process in South Africa so slow (*YG* case para. 85) and now completely non-existent? A unanimous decision of the Constitutional Court should inform and be able to move an apparently reluctant parliament to give life to the 'appropriate regulatory framework' that the Chief Justice envisioned (*Freedom of Religion South Africa* para. 74).

Acknowledgements

This material is based upon work that was supported financially by the National Research Foundation (NRF). Any opinions, findings, conclusions or recommendations expressed in this material are those of the author and therefore the NRF does not accept any liability with regards thereto.

References

African Committee of Experts on the Rights and Welfare of the Child, Concluding Recommendations by the African Committee of Experts on the Rights and Welfare of the Child on the Republic of South Africa Initial Report on the Status of Implementation of the African Charter on the Rights and Welfare of the Child, (2014).

Besson, S. and Kleber, E., "Article 2. The right to non-discrimination", in J. Tobin (ed.), *The UN Convention on the Rights of the Child: A Commentary* (Oxford: Oxford University Press, 2019).

Boberg, P. Q. R., *The Law of Delict* (Cape Town: Juta, 1984).

Bower, C. and Dawes, A., "Young children: Preventing physical abuse and corporal punishment" in *South African Child Gauge* 2014, 58–64.

Breen, A., Daniels, K. and Tomlinson, M., "Children's Experiences of corporal punishment: A qualitative study in an urban township of South Africa", *Child Abuse and Neglect* 2015 (48), 131–139. DOI: 10.1016/j.chiabu.2015.04.022 2015.

Burchell, E. M. and Hunt, P. M. A., (3rd. ed. by J. M. Burchell), *South African Criminal Law and Procedure* (Cape Town: Juta, 2008).

Burton, P., Ward, C. L., Artz, L. and Leoschut, L., *The Optimus Study on Child abuse, Violence and Neglect in South Africa* (Cape Town: Centre for Justice and Crime Prevention, 2015).

Council of Europe, Commissioner for Human Rights, Children and Corporal Punishment: "The Rights not to be Hit, Also a Children's Right" (2006) CommDH/IssuePaper(2006)1, (Updated version, 2008).

Council of Europe, European Social Charter (Revised), 3 May 1996, ETS 163.

Council of Europe, European Social Charter, 18 October 1961, ETS 35.

Dawes, A., De Sas Kropiwnicki, Z., Kafaar, Z. and Richter, L. "Corporal punishment of children: A South African National Survey", Paper prepared for distribution at regional consultation of the UN study on violence against children (July 2005) available at www.hsrc.ac.za.

Dodd, C. "Towards Universal Prohibition of Corporal Punishment of Children – Religious Progress, Challenges and Opportunities", in B. J. Saunders, P. Leviner and B. Naylor, *Corporal Punishment of Children Comparative Legal and Social Developments towards Prohibition and Beyond* (Leiden: Brill Nijhoff, 2018).

Du Bois, F., "Sources of law: Common law and precedent" in F. du Bois (ed.), *Wille's Principles of South African Law* (Claremont: Juta, 2010).

Eekelaar, J., "Corporal punishment, parents' religion and children's rights", *Law Quarterly Review* 2003 (119), 370–375.

Freeman, M. D. A., "Upholding the dignity and best interests of children: International law and the corporal punishment of children", *Law and Contemporary Problems* 2010 (73), 211–251.

Freeman, M. D. F. and Saunders, B. J., "Can we conquer child abuse if we don't outlaw physical chastisement of children?", *International Journal of Children's Rights* 2014 (22), 681–709. DOI: 10.1163/15718182-02204002.

Freeman, M., "Article 3: The best interests of the child" in A. Alen, J. Vande Lanotte, E. Verhellen, F. Ang, E. Berghmans and M. Verheyde (eds.), *A Commentary on the United Nations Convention on the Rights of the Child* (Leiden: Martinus Nijhoff, 2007).

Gershoff, E. T., "Spanking and Child Development: We know enough now to stop hitting our children", *Child Development Perspectives* 2013 (7(3)), 133–137. DOI: 10.1111/cdep.12038.

Hesselink, A. E. and Dastile, N. P., "Vulnerable children in the South African context" in R. Songca, *et al.*, *Vulnerable Children in South Africa* (Claremont: Juta, 2016).

Human Rights Committee, Concluding Observations, South Africa Initial Report, April 2016, CCPR/C/ZAF/CO/1.

Joubert, R., "School discipline" in T. Boezaart (ed.), *Child Law in South Africa* (Claremont: Juta, 2017).

Mathews, S., Martin, L. J., Coetzee, D., Scott, C., and Brijmohun, Y., "Child deaths in South Africa: Lessons from the child death review pilot", *South African Medical Journal* 2016 (106 (9)), 851–852. DOI:10.7196/SAMJ.2016.v106i9.11382.

Mezmur, B. D., "'Don't try this at home?': Reasonable or Moderate Chastisement, and the Rights of the Child in South Africa with *YG v S* in Perspective", *Speculum Juris* 2018 (32 (2)), 75–92.

Mezmur, B. M., "The African Charter on the Rights and Welfare of the Child and corporal punishment: Spare the rod, spare the child", *Article 19* 2006, 8–10.

Mnookin, R. H., "Child-Custody Adjudication: Judicial Functions in the Face of Indeterminacy", *Law and Contemporary Problems* 1975 (39), 226–293.

Morag, T. "The Ban on Parental Corporal Punishment in Israel – What Facilitated the Change", in B. J. Saunders, P. Leviner and B. Naylor, *Corporal Punishment of Children Comparative Legal and Social Developments towards Prohibition and Beyond* (Leiden: Brill Nijhoff, 2018).

Morrell, R., "Corporal punishment in South African schools: a neglected explanation for its persistence", *South African Journal of Education* 2001 (21(4)), 292–299.

National Department of Education, Guidelines for the Consideration of Governing Bodies in Adopting a Code of Conduct for Learners, 1998, Government Gazette 18900.

National Department of Education, The Alternatives to Corporal Punishment: The Learning Experience, 2001.

Neethling, J. and Potgieter, J. M., *Neethling-Potgieter-Visser Law of Delict* (Durban: LexisNexis, 2015).

OAU African Charter on the Rights and Welfare of the Child, (1990) CAB/LEG/24.9/49.

Richter, L. M., Mathews, S., Kagura J. and Nonterah, E., "A longitudinal perspective on violence in the lives of South African children from the Birth to Twenty Plus cohort study in Johannesburg-Soweto", 2018 (108(3)), 181–186. DOI: 10.7196/SAMJ.2018. v108i3.12661.

Schäfer, L., *Child Law in South Africa: Domestic and International Perspectives* (Durban: LexisNexis, 2011).

Skelton, A., "*S v Williams*: A springboard for further debate about corporal punishment", *Acta Juridica* 2015, 336–359.

Sloth-Nielsen, J., "Southern African Perspectives on Banning Corporal Punishment – a Comparison of Namibia, Botswana, South Africa and Zimbabwe" in B. J. Saunders, P. Leviner and B. Naylor, *Corporal Punishment of Children Comparative Legal and Social developments towards prohibition and Beyond* (Leiden: Brill Nijhoff, 2018).

South African Law Reform Commission, Report on the Review of the Child Care Act Project 110, 2002.

Thèry, I. "'The interest of the child' and the regulation of the post-divorce family" in C. Smart, and S. Sevenhuijsen, (eds.), *Child Custody and the Politics of Gender* in (Routledge, 1989).

Tobin, J. and Varadan, S. "Article 5 The Right to Parental Direction and Guidance Consistent with a Child's Evolving Capacities" in J. Tobin (ed.), *The UN Convention on the Rights of the Child: A Commentary* (Oxford: Oxford University Press, 2019).

UN Committee on the Rights of the Child, Concluding Observations, South Africa Initial Report, February 2000, CRC/C/15/Add.122.

UN Committee on the Rights of the Child, Concluding Observations, South Africa Second Periodic Report, September 2016, CRC/C/ZAF/CO/2.

UN Committee on the Rights of the Child, General Comment No. 13 (2011), The right of the child to freedom from all forms of violence, 18 April 2011, CRC/C/GC/13.

UN Committee on the Rights of the Child, General Comment No. 14 (2013), on the right of the child to have his or her best interests taken as a primary consideration (art. 3 para. 1), 29 May 2013, CRC/C/GC/14.

UN Committee on the Rights of the Child, General Comment No. 20 (2016), Implementation of the rights of the child during adolescence, 6 December 2016, CRC/C/GC/20.

UN Committee on the Rights of the Child, General Comment No. 7 (2005), Implementing child rights in early childhood, 20 September 2006, CRC/C/GC/Rev.1.

UN Committee on the Rights of the Child, General Comment No. 8 (2006), The right of the child to protection from corporal punishment and other cruel or degrading forms of punishment (arts. 19; 28 para. 2 and; 37 inter alia), 2 March 2007, CRC/C/GC/8.

UN General Assembly, Convention on the Rights of the Child, 20 November 1989, 1577 UNTS 3 UN.

UN General Assembly, Declaration on the Rights of the Child, 20 November 1959, GA Res. 1386 A/4354.

UN General Assembly, International Covenant on Civil and Political Rights, 16 December 1966, Res. 2200A (XXI).

UN General Assembly, Report of the independent expert for the United Nations study on violence against children, August 2006, A/61/299.

UN General Assembly, Universal Declaration of Human Rights, 10 December 1948, Res. 217 A.

Unicef, Global Initiative to End All Corporal Punishment of Children, available at www.endcorporalpunishment.org accessed on 9 January 2020.

Van Heerden, B., Cockrell, A. and Keightley, R., (eds.), *Boberg's Law of Persons and the Family* (Kenwyn: Juta, 1999).

Varadan, S., "The Principle of Evolving capacities under the UN Convention on the Rights of the Child", *International Journal of Children's Rights* 2019 (27), 306–338. DOI:10.1163/15718182-02702006.

Waterhouse, S., "Status of corporal punishment in the South African Children's Amendment Bill Law Reform Process", *Article 19* 2007 (3(3)), 1–3.

CHAPTER 8

Parental Responsibilities and Rights during the "Gender Reassignment" Decision-Making Process of Intersex Infants

Guidance in Terms of Article 5 of the Convention on the Rights of the Child

Lize Mills and Sabrina Thompson

1   Introduction

A parent, in terms of a dictionary definition, is 'a person who is a father or mother: a person who has a child; ... one that begets or brings forth offspring; ... a person who brings up and cares for another' (*Miriam Webster Online Dictionary*, 2018). In most instances, the news that offspring and impending parenthood are on its way, is met with excitement and delight. Expecting parents will often prepare their home and family in anticipation of the new arrival, and one of the first and most frequently asked questions is whether they are expecting a boy or a girl. This determination has an effect on many of the preparations: it may determine the colour of the baby room and the clothes and toys to be bought, while a current trend is to host "gender reveal" parties, during which the sex of the awaited baby will be revealed to friends and family (DeLoach, 2018). As a result, the birth of a child with ambiguous sexual characteristics may present practical, medical, legal and ethical issues (Ahmed, Morrison and Hughes, 2004).

Every year, approximately two million infants displaying intersex[1] characteristics, are born (Horowicz, 2017). It is estimated that approximately 1.7 per cent of live births, 'do not conform to a Platonic ideal of absolute sex chromosome, gonadal, genital, and hormonal dimorphism' (Blackless *et al.*, 2000: 161).[2] Children born with intersex characteristics are likely to be subjected to medi-

---

1   "Intersex" is a broad term that encompasses various physiognomies with which an individual is 'born with a sexual or reproductive autonomy' that does not correspond with the accepted physical binary definitions of male and female. See also further explanation below.
2   This means that generally there are the same amount of intersex people in the world as the amount of people that have red hair (The United Nations Free and Equal Campaign, 2019).

cal intervention during the early years of infancy (Haas, 2004).[3] The rationale for medical intervention is often socially driven as it is considered "necessary" to allocate a conclusive sex to an intersex child (Kennedy, 2016). Surgical intervention is considered to be the answer to ambiguous genitalia (White, 2014) although it is broadly observed that there are only three instances where "gender re-assignment surgery" for intersex infants is medically necessary (Human Rights Watch and Interact, 2017).[4] In the majority of instances, such surgeries are cosmetic[5] and unnecessary but are performed with the stated aim of making it easier for intersex children to grow up "normal" (Human Rights Watch and Interact, 2017).

Since infants are unable to make this decision for themselves, parents of intersex children are faced with the agonising choice as to whether or not to consent to their intersex baby undergoing sex alteration surgery. They will rely predominantly on the information provided to them by medical experts, who may often presuppose that parents will not be able to accept their intersex child unless the sex alteration surgery is performed. Parents are often misinformed about the nature of their child's "condition", as well as the potential risks (both physical and psychological) that can occur throughout childhood, and evidently further into adulthood, if the surgery is performed at such a young age (Tamar-Mattis, 2006). A potential consequence of surgery being performed while a child is still in infancy, is the likelihood that the child will not identify with the sex that is assigned to her, causing many physiological challenges later in life (White, 2014) and there is a risk of sterility and other complications regarding sexual function (Bird, 2005; Minto *et al.*, 2003). Making this decision as to whether or not surgical intervention will be used at this very

---

3 In certain jurisdictions the general position in regards to surgery on intersex infants, is that surgery on the external genitalia will be performed within the first week of infancy, in order to allow parents to raise their child in a clearly defined and gendered role. In Denmark and Germany it is estimated that infants born with atypical characteristics will face up to five surgeries before they reach the age of one (Barry, 2018).

4 First, in the case where the internal organs are externally situated on the body; secondly, to ensure that there is a place provided for urine to be expelled; and thirdly if there is a risk of gonadal cancer.

5 The Cambridge Dictionary defines "cosmetic surgery" as: 'any medical operation that is intended to improve a person's appearance rather than their health' (Cambridge Academic Content Dictionary, n.d.) (O'Connor, 2012: 172) remarks that cosmetic surgery actually impedes the authenticity of medical ethics, as by performing the surgery, one actually enhances the social perceptions of what constitutes "normality". Therefore, we are of the view that performing cosmetic surgery on children tells them that there is something wrong with their bodies, when actually there is something wrong with society and those that bully them.

early stage of their child's life, is a parental responsibility that will affect the child's identity, physical and psychological integrity and well-being for the rest of her life.

This chapter seeks to evaluate some aspects of the legal position in these circumstances. It will not focus on the rights of the child that may be affected by this decision but rather on the role and duty of parents during the decision-making process, as explained by Article 5 of the 1989 UN Convention of the Rights of the Child ("CRC"). It will evaluate the effect of Article 5, which provides that, 'States Parties shall respect the responsibilities, rights and duties of parents ... to provide, in a manner consistent with the evolving capacities of the child, appropriate direction and guidance in the exercise by the child of the rights recognized' in the CRC. We will argue that this means that States must respect that parents of intersex children have the right to make these life-altering decisions, especially when the child is at an age where she does not yet have the capacity to do so. However, the CRC also provides that parents have to perform their responsibilities, rights and duties in such a manner that their children's best interests always remain their basic concern (see, in particular, Articles 3, 5 and 18). In this respect, States must 'render appropriate assistance to parents and legal guardians in the performance of their child-rearing responsibilities' (Article 18(2)). Although the drafters of the CRC may have had no intention to regulate private family decisions (Alston, 1994), it has been established that the general duty of promoting the best interests of the child, imposed by, *inter alia*, the CRC,[6] may be firmly laid at the door of parents, caregivers and other adults responsible for the child.[7] Therefore, parents of intersex babies have the responsibility to take the decision as to sex alteration surgery with their child's best interests as their basic concern, but they must receive appropriate direction and guidance when making this decision.

---

6 See, for example, also Art. 4 of the African Charter on the Rights and Welfare of the Child, 1990; a number of national constitutions, including that of Ethiopia, Columbia, Paraguay, and Sri Lanka and South Africa; and legislation of juridictions such as Indonesia, the Philippines, Tunisia, Egypt, Colombia, Romania, South Africa, Sweden, Italy, Quebec and the UK (The UNICEF Innocenti Research Centre, 2007).

7 This interpretation is in line with the approach which has been adopted by the South African Legislature when it enacted the Children's Act. In s. 1 of the Act, one of the responsibilities of a parent, namely that of "care", is defined as, *inter alia*, 'ensuring that the best interests of the child is the paramount concern in all matters affecting the child.'

2 Born Intersex[8]

The term "intersex" is an intricate concept with many variations (Sloth-Nielsen, 2018). This term has replaced the term "hermaphrodite" that was previously used to describe persons who were born with both female and male reproductive organs (White, 2014). Intersex persons are normally described as persons 'born with sex characteristics[9] (including genitals, gonads and chromosome patterns) that do not fit typical binary notions of male or female bodies' (United Nations Office of the High Commissioner for Human Rights, 2018: 1). Therefore, it can be said that "intersex" is a heterogeneous term that is used to explain a variety of bodily differences. In some instances, these intersex variations are immediately apparent upon birth, while some only become apparent upon puberty, and in certain instances, specific chromosomal intersex traits are not physically visible at all (*ibid.*).[10] Generally, a medical diagnosis of intersex infants are determined by the visible ambiguous genitalia and concentrates on the 'size, shape and the cosmetic appearance of the organ' (Ford, 2001: 470) that develops into either a penis or a clitoris. It should be noted that by the introduction of advanced scientific knowledge, it is increasingly evident that biological sex does not conform to a binary model. Intersex variations are no longer being considered phenomena but rather a difference of human physiology (Human Science Research Council & The Other Foundation, 2016).

Furthermore, it must be noted that the terminology used for the surgery that intersex infants undergo, is incorrect in its current format. "Gender" is a fluid concept concerning an individual's 'culture and psychology' (Barnes, 2007: 165), whereas "sex" refers to an individual's biological features. "Gender reassignment" or "gender normalisation" surgery, per definition, refers to the alteration of an individual's personal psychology and individual identity, not necessarily their anatomical features. In actual fact, the surgery involves the physical alteration of the external genitalia and potentially the removal of

---

[8] Some of the ideas expressed here are also contained in S. Thompson, "Parental responsibilities and rights during the 'gender re-assignment' decision making process of intersex infants in South Africa", unpublished LLB paper at Stellenbosch University (2018).

[9] Newcombe explains that there are a variety of factors that need to be considered when attempting to determine one's sex (Newcombe, 2017: 227). Kusum lists the factors, which include chromosomal presentation, gonadal presentation, the presentation of genital organs and the secondary sex characteristics displayed by the individual (Kusum, 1983: 74).

[10] Ben Asher describes intersex individuals as those 'who are not considered by medical experts as "normal" males or females. The intersex category today covers: (1) chromosomal variations, (2) gonadal variations (atypical ovaries or testes), (3) hormonal variations, and (4) external morphologic variations (genitalia that is neither clearly male of female)' (Ben-Asher, 2006: 51, fn 2).

the internal sex reproductive system. "Normalisation", in turn, denotes a relatively derogatory connotation of "abnormality" and "malformation", thereby othering the intersex person to be "less human". We are of the view that the incorrect use of terminology has contributed to the social stigma that is attached to this set of circumstances. Therefore, it is our submission that "sex alteration" surgery is a more inclusive term to use in the circumstances.

An ambiguous body has always tended to generate uncertainty and social anxiety, even if Hippocrates proposed to include "intersex" as a third sex (Rosin, 2005). During the Middle Ages, "hermaphrodites" were even considered monstrosities and were ostracised from the society in which they lived (Kennedy, 2016). In the 16th century, English society would not allow an intersex child to be baptised until they were categorised according to a heteronormative sex (Horowicz, 2017). In the 17th century, practitioners were consumed with the idea of protecting sexual "purity" and preventing against sexual deviance and dishonesty, which was associated with intersexed bodies (Carpenter, 2018). Hermaphroditism coincided with the concerns surrounding homosexuality and the rise of "deviant" sexual conduct (Kennedy, 2016).[11] Towards the end of the 19th century and at the start of the 20th century, as scientific knowledge about endocrinology and genetics expanded and the complexity of sex development *in utero* became apparent, intersex was determined on a case-by-case approach (Kennedy, 2016). In terms of this approach, doctors made an approximation of the sex of the intersex infant and advised parents to wait and determine if contradictions occurred during puberty (Redick, 2005).

However, in the latter half of the 20th century, sexologist Dr. John W Money, proposed an alternative approach (Kennedy, 2016). Sex alteration surgery became common practice under the guidance of Dr. Money. Money hypothesised that children are not born with a gender identity, but rather that gender is learned behaviour (Haas, 2004). The "John/Joan" study is famous as it postulated Money's theory of gender identity: he theorised that genital alteration, if never revealed to the intersex child, would allow the child to develop a gender identity corresponding with their assigned sex (White, 2014; Redick, 2005). It was Money's belief that as long as children were raised in a gender role that corresponded with their genitalia, their gender identity would develop according to their "assigned" sex (Kennedy, 2016). The 'traditional paternalistic

---

11   Kennedy further explains that, '[i]f a person was truly female but they had ambiguous genitals, such as an enlarged clitoris that looked like a penis, then there was a real possibility that they might engage in homosexual activity if their status was not discovered and disclosed' (Kennedy, 2016).

treatment model' inspired by Money's theory was the predominant approach used in cases concerning intersexed children (Lareau, 2003). Money's model determined that sexual ambiguity in an infant could be classified as a 'psychological emergency' (Lareau, 2003: 131). It was the general opinion that parents would not be comfortable with their child's sexual ambiguity and subsequently, immediate rectification was required in order to mitigate against the potential stigma that was associated with intersexuality (Lareau, 2003; Newcombe, 2017).

At the outset, Money's theory seemed to be a success and in intersex children's best interests. His rationale was based on his belief that if genital alteration is never revealed to the intersex child, the child would develop a gender identity that matches the sex chosen by the medical practitioner (White, 2014). One example from Money's "John/Joan" study did not involve an intersex child but rather that of a boy, David Reimer, who was born biologically male and was subject to sex alteration surgery after a failed circumcision. Money persuaded the parents of David (who was originally named Bruce), to raise him as a female and was given permission to construct "normal" female genitalia for David. Subsequently, David was raised as female and was renamed Brenda by his parents. Despite Money's claims to the contrary, the case did not have a successful outcome. David always identified as male and later underwent sex alteration surgery to construct male sex organs (White, 2014). The physiological trauma that resulted from the procedure in his childhood contributed to a life-long battle with depression (Haas, 2004).[12] Despite David's ultimate transition to male, the damage had been done, and in 2004, at the age of 38, he committed suicide (White, 2014).

Today medical experts continue first to suggest sex alteration surgery and frequently place pressure on parents to make a decision about assigning their child a gender and binary sex. Parents are often not informed about the potential psychological risks involved, nor are they offered any form of counselling as to how to approach this very challenging situation (Haas, 2004). The example of David is one of many that demonstrates the lived reality of intersex persons who had undergone sex alteration surgery as infants and developed gender dysphoria at a later stage in life. A 2012 study determined that approximately 47 per cent of intersex persons who have undergone sex alteration surgery at an early age, were dissatisfied (White, 2014).[13] Many reported consequences

---

12   David attempted suicide on several occasions as a result of the trauma after discovering the truth at age 14.
13   The study by Köhler *et al* also found that, '[e]arly sex assignment surgery for intersex individuals ... has been shown to create adult risks of sexual anxiety, impotence, minimal clitoral arousal, and overall dissatisfaction with one's sex life.' White further explains that a

such as sexual and psychological complications, resulting from such surgeries, which continue from childhood into adulthood (*ibid.*).

3 Applying Article 5 of the CRC

3.1 *"States parties shall respect the responsibilities, rights and duties of parents"*

3.1.1 Parental Responsibilities and Rights: A 21st Century Perspective[14]

Despite the fact that the emphasis has moved away from the power and authority of parents over their children, the relationship between parents and children is still often formulated in terms of the rights that parents have over their children. The notion of parental authority, which has been described as the sum of all of the rights and responsibilities a parent has over a child (Spiro, 1985; Human, 2000; Skelton, 2009), is one that will not easily disappear. Ownership is embedded in the concept of parental authority, accompanied by a sense of entitlement that a parent has over a child. In terms of this model, parents primarily have fundamental rights merely because of their status as parents and their responsibilities play a secondary role (Human, 2000). Since parents "own" their children, and parents are expected to develop their children into particular types of persons, parents have the right to take decisions for and on behalf of their children. Peleg describes this type of approach as the 'human becomings conception of childhood' (Peleg, 2014: 388), in terms of which the child's right to development can only be interpreted as 'a right of the child to become an adult' (*ibid.*: 389).

This type of reasoning was especially evident in the arguments raised by the applicant mother in (*Gillick v. West Norfolk and Wisbech Area Health Authority* [1986] 1 AC (HL) 112) ("*Gillick*"). However, the now well-known statement of Lord Scarman, writing for the majority, declared that 'parental rights are derived from parental duty and exist only so long as they are needed for the

---

'2004 Meyer-Bahlburg study, though, stated that only thirty-two percent of intersex adults are actually dissatisfied with their gender after having undergone genital-normalizing procedures as a child' (White, 2014: 790). According to White, the conclusions of the 2004 Meyer-Bahlburg study, however, were refuted by Morgan Holmes in her book, *Intersex: A Perilous Difference*. Holmes questioned the validity of the 2004 Meyer-Bahlburg study due to its inherent bias with weighting of questions, limited survey population and insufficient data to create a diversified analysis of the survey population (White, 2014).

14 Some of the thoughts and ideas expressed here were originally formulated in L. Mills, "Considering the Best Interests of the Child when Marketing Food to Children: An Analysis of the South African Regulatory Framework", unpublished LLD thesis, Stellenbosch University (2016), available at: https://scholar.sun.ac.za/handle/10019.1/100245 (accessed on 4 May 2019).

protection of the person and property of the child' (*ibid.*: 184B). Lord Fraser agreed with him in explaining the more contemporary approach to parenthood in the following terms:

> [P]arental rights to control a child do not exist for the benefit of the parent. They exist for the benefit of the child and they are justified only in so far as they enable the parent to perform his duties towards the child, and towards other children in the family (*ibid.*: 170D).[15]

In terms of this approach, parents have responsibilities and rights over their children so as to fulfil their duties towards children. Parents are to take decisions for their children insofar as their children cannot do so themselves (Human, 2000) but have to do so for the benefit of their children. Bainham has explained this ideology as one in terms of which parental powers only survive unless the best interests of the child 'demand that they are overridden' (Bainham, 1986: 51). In line with the notion that to act in the best interests of children is to have a concern for their welfare, Bainham explains as follows:

> This could be interpreted as a reiteration of the familiar welfare principle but with the significant modification that the assessment of the child's best interests (upon which depends the lawfulness of the parents' proposals) would be made by third parties dealing with the child and/or the parents and not by the courts (*ibid.*: 52).

Therefore, it can be said that parents, as the primary care-givers, are predominantly responsible for the welfare of and meeting the basic needs of their children. While acknowledging the parental right to freedom of choice in making the decisions as to the daily methods of care of their children, the most important and general of the duties of parents and other care-givers of children is that of promoting the best interests of the child. In fact, a Committee of Ministers of the European Union described parental responsibilities in an Explanatory Memorandum, in the following terms:

> [a] modern concept according to which parents are, on a ... basis of equality ... and in consultation with their children, given the task to educate, legally represent, maintain, etc their children. In order to do so they

---

15 Woolf J. from the Queen's Bench Division of the High Court even questioned the existence of parental rights, asking whether it was accurate to state that parents have rights at all, and thought it more appropriate to only refer to parental responsibilities and duties (see also Bainham, 1986).

exercise powers to carry out duties in the interests of the child and not because of an authority which is conferred on them in their own interests (Council of Europe, Committee of Ministers, 1984).

In line with this approach to parenthood, it would appear that the legislative trend is to define activities of parental care in terms of responsibilities, connoting a sense of duty rather than that of rights. The 2005 South African Children's Act ("Children's Act") explains that the parental responsibilities and rights that a person may have in relation to a child, include the responsibilities and rights of caring for a child; maintaining contact with a child; to act as a guardian; and to contribute to the maintenance of a child. "Care" is defined, *inter alia*, as:

> (b) safeguarding and promoting the well-being of the child;
> (c) protecting the child from maltreatment, abuse, neglect, degradation, discrimination, exploitation and any other physical, emotional or moral harm or hazards;
> (d) respecting, protecting, promoting and securing the fulfilment of, and guarding against any infringement of, the child's rights set out in the Bill of Rights and the principles set out in Chapter 2 of this Act;
> ...
>
> (f) guiding, advising and assisting the child in decisions to be taken by the child in a manner appropriate to the child's age, maturity and stage of development;
> ...; and
> (j) generally, ensuring that the best interests of the child is the paramount concern in all matters affecting the child.[16]

Section 1(1)(h) further explains that care also requires 'accommodating any special needs that the child may have'. Therefore it may be said that it is a parent's role to encourage a child's development, to protect the child and her rights and best interests whilst accepting any unique characteristics that the child may have.

---

16   Section 1 of the Children's Act. A "care-giver" is defined as being 'any person other than a parent or guardian, who factually cares for a child and includes- (a) a foster parent; (b) a person who cares for a child with the implied or express consent of a parent or guardian of the child; (c) a person who cares for a child whilst the child is in temporary safe care; (d) the person at the head of a child and youth care centre where a child has been placed; (e) the person at the head of a shelter; (f) a child and youth care worker who cares for a child who is without appropriate family care in the community; and (g) the child at the head of a child-headed household'.

The definition of "parental responsibilities" found in section 41 of the Family Law Act of British Columbia in Canada is similar to the definition of "care" found in the South African Children's Act. However, this provision explicitly explains that parental responsibilities also include 'giving, refusing or withdrawing consent to medical, dental and other health-related treatments for the child ...; giving, refusing or withdrawing consent for the child, if consent is required; ... requesting and receiving from third parties health, education or other information respecting the child;' and 'exercising any other responsibilities reasonably necessary to nurture the child's development.' Also in Australia, section 19 of the Children and Young People Act 2008 of the Australian Capital Territory, describes "daily care responsibility" as including making decisions about a child or young person's daily activities and care.

The South African Children's Act further stipulates that '[i]n all matters concerning the care, protection and well-being of a child the standard that the child's best interest is of paramount importance, must be applied' (s 9). This piece of legislation therefore confirms that the duty upon parents and care-givers is to safeguard the best interests of their children. They must ensure that none of the rights which their children have, are violated; that, as far as is within their control, their children remain both physical and mentally healthy; and that they guide their children in making responsible decisions when they reach a level of maturity and understanding to do so. It is the obligation of parents to look out for their children's welfare and to protect them from harm.

3.1.2 The Parental Responsibility of Taking Medical Decisions on Behalf of a Child

As has been explained above, parents also have the responsibility to make decisions on behalf of their children relating to their children's healthcare. Since informed consent is pivotal to all medical procedures and since some children are unable to provide such consent, parents have to consent to medical intervention that are to be effected upon their young children. A child can consent to medical treatment if such a child has adequate understanding and intelligence at common law, in spite of an absence of parental consent or any other prohibition made by them (Harper, 1999). This is known as the *Gillick*-competency test, in terms of which a child is capable of consenting to medical treatment when the child has the necessary intelligence and maturity to fully understand what is being proposed (Weston-Scheuber & Parlett, 2004). An important component to determine whether a child is *Gillick* competent, is whether a child can fully comprehend the consequences of the medical procedure, not only the procedure itself (Herring, 2004). The *Gillick* competency test therefore arguably allows parents of intersex babies to make the decision as to whether their child will be receiving treatment and surgery to alter the child's sexual characteristics to such an extent that it conforms to being either male or female. However, as is the case with all parental responsibilities, this decision must be made with the best interests of the child as the basic concern.

3.2 "To provide, in a manner consistent with the evolving capacities of the child"

Although at first glance, it would appear that the evolving capacities of infants are irrelevant, since the law does not recognise babies and toddlers to have too many capacities (Skelton and Kruger, 2010), this particular phrase of the provision of the CRC is also important in the context of the sex alteration decision-making process of intersex infants. The exercise of any parental responsibilities must be performed in such a way that the child will be able to evolve into making their own decisions, while also taking into account that different levels of development require different levels of guidance. In the words of the former Chair of the Committee on the Rights of the Child, Article 5 of the CRC "recognises the role of the parents, but also expresses that the role changes over time, with the evolving capacities of the child' (Sandberg, 2015: 346).

Lord Denning powerfully explained that the scope of parental authority 'starts with a right to control and ends with little more than advice' (Hewer v Bryant (1970) 1 QB 357: 369). This approach appealed to both Lord Fraser and Lord Scarman in the *Gillick* decision, quoting Lord Denning with approval and finding that parental rights will yield to the child's right to make her own decisions when she 'reaches a sufficient understanding and intelligence to be capable of making up his own mind on the matter requiring decision' (Gillick: 186D). This is also the view of the Committee on the Rights of the Child, who has commented as follows:

> These adjustments [to the levels of support and guidance parents offer their child] take account of a child's interests and wishes as well as the child's capacities for autonomous decision-making and comprehension of his or her best interests. While a young child generally requires more guidance than an older child, it is important to take account of individual variations in the capacities of children of the same age and of their ways of reacting to situations. Evolving capacities should be seen as a positive and enabling process, not an excuse for authoritarian practices that restrict children's autonomy and self-expression and which have traditionally been justified by pointing to children's relative immaturity and their need for socialization. Parents (and others) should be encouraged to offer "direction and guidance" in a child-centred way, through dialogue and

example, in ways that enhance young children's capacities to exercise their rights, including their right to participation (art 12) and their right to freedom of thought, conscience and religion (art 14). (Committee on the Rights of the Child, 2005: 8).

We are of the view that the Committee here emphasised an important aspect of the recognition of the rights intersex infants: their evolving capacities should be seen as a positive and enabling process, one that will allow them to eventually also make their own decisions. Even more important though, is that the Committee also urges an appreciation of the possibilities that lie within babies and that parents are the ones to nurture and unlock this potential by teaching the child to think and act for itself:

> Babies and infants are entirely dependent on others, but they are not passive recipients of care, direction and guidance. They are active social agents, who seek protection, nurturance and understanding from parents or other caregivers, which they require for their survival, growth and well-being. Newborn babies are able to recognize their parents (or other caregivers) very soon after birth, and they engage actively in non-verbal communication. Under normal circumstances, young children form strong mutual attachments with their parents or primary caregivers. These relationships offer children physical and emotional security, as well as consistent care and attention. Through these relationships children construct a personal identity and acquire culturally valued skills, knowledge and behaviours. In these ways, parents (and other caregivers) are normally the major conduit through which young children are able to realize their rights (*ibid.*).

Furthermore, in terms of this approach, it becomes clear how important it is that parents themselves must be appropriately guided and equipped, in order to enable their children to make decisions that are in their own best interests.

3.3 *"Appropriate direction and guidance"*
The responsibility of parents to direct and guide their children must be respected. The State, even in its capacity as *parens patriae*, cannot dictate to parents how to raise their children (Bridgeman, 2007). In fact, Lord Templeman explained that "[t]he best person to bring up a child is the natural parent. It matters not whether the parent is wise or foolish, rich or poor, educated or illiterate, provided the child's moral and physical health are not in danger.

Public authorities cannot improve on nature" (Re KD (A Minor: Ward: Termination of Access [1988] 1 AC 806: 812). Nonetheless, the drafters of the CRC thought it necessary to qualify this type of guidance and direction described in Article 5, with the word "appropriate". Unfortunately, the word "appropriate" was not given content, nor can it ever be sufficiently explained without a relevant context. Once again, we submit that the standard of the best interests of the child must be the guiding principle. To this end, Article 18(1) and (2) of the CRC provide further instruction: the State has the obligation to provide parents with the guidance and assistance to be able to know what their parental responsibilities are and how to perform them to the best of their abilities and in their children's best interests. Although some parents may be "wise" and "educated", and able to make many decisions on behalf of their child, there are also numerous instances in which parents will not necessarily be best equipped to make decisions about their children's interests. One such instance may exist in circumstances where medical professionals need to advise as to the best option in respect of the medical treatment of a child. The challenge for the State, and indeed for the law, is to encourage parents to make all of their decisions in the interests of their children, rather than in the interests of themselves (Scott, 2003).

It is submitted that, in the context of children who are born intersex, this is a particularly complex challenge and one that cannot be dismissed as an easy choice. Parents may consider it to be in their child's best interests to be subjected to sex alteration surgery. They may regard it as crucial in order to prevent their child from being ridiculed, bullied and ostracised. Parents may feel that it is their duty to protect their child and that they should try to make life as easy and uncomplicated for their child. In a world where a binary concept of sex is the norm and where the registration of a birth, which is a prerequisite to unlock a number of other services such as health care and education, requires the ticking of either the 'male' or 'female' box, it is understandable that parents would accept sex alteration surgery as the solution. In addition, one can hardly blame parents for taking this decision when a medical practitioner, being the relevant expert in these circumstances, directly or indirectly pressures or forces parents to make the decision to have the surgery performed.

As a result, it must be stressed that parents cannot be judged or condemned for making a decision that they believe are in the best interests of their child. However, since the State has the obligation to provide parents with the necessary guidance and render appropriate assistance to them 'in the performance of their child-rearing responsibilities', (Art 18(2) CRC) it is our submission that the State must provide the parents of intersex infants with sufficient knowledge, support and an enabling environment that will allow them to leave the decision to be made by their child. In fact, the Yogyakarta Principles[17] provide further instruction in this respect by stipulating that States have the obligation to '[e]nsure that education methods, curricula and resources serve to enhance understanding of and respect for, *inter alia*, diverse sexual orientations and gender identities, including the particular needs of students, their parents and family members related to these grounds' (Principle 16). To ensure that the stigma associated with being born intersex is diminished, States must put measures in place that will dispel the myths and enable an appreciation of the truth. The Principles clearly call for raising awareness of the reality of transgender and intersex people by urging governments to '[d]evelop, implement and support education and public information programmes to promote human rights and to eliminate prejudices on grounds of sexual orientation, gender identity, gender expression and sex characteristics' (Principle 30). Furthermore, it stipulates that everyone has the right to identity documents and birth certificates, regardless of "sex characteristics" (Principle 31), meaning that States should not oblige a person to divulge details of her sex in order to receive such important and enabling documentation. It is submitted that such measures will provide a more conducive environment for parents to be able to make the decision that truly is in the best interests of their child.

It is our argument that States have to put in place policies and procedures that will ensure that medical experts advise parents of intersex infants truthfully and without placing undue pressure on them. Medical practitioners need to provide parents with the real facts as to when surgery will truly be a necessity, and not merely a method to try and make a child look "normal". Social and psychological concerns may not be used to justify irreversible medical surgery (Lareau, 2003). In terms of the informed consent doctrine, physicians must disclose all pertinent information and options, including the option of no intervention, and doctors must ensure that parents understand the full extent of their possible decision to have their child's genitals altered (Newcombe, 2017). As a result, medical experts also have the duty to provide appropriate direction

---

[17] 'Principles on the application of international human rights law in relation to sexual orientation and gender identity', agreed to in Indonesia in 2006. The Yogyakarta Principles address a broad range of international human rights standards and their application to Sexual Orientation/Gender Identity issues. On 10 November 2017 a panel of experts published additional principles expanding on the original document reflecting developments in international human rights law and practice since the 2006 Principles namely, The Yogyakarta Principles plus 10. The new document also contains 111 'additional state obligations', related to areas such as torture, asylum, privacy, health and the protection of human rights defenders. The full text of the Yogyakarta Principles and the Yogyakarta Principles plus 10 are available at: www.yogyakartaprinciples.org.

and guidance, without allowing their own prejudices to cloud their professional opinion.

3.4 *"In the exercise by the child of the rights recognized"*

This final part of Article 5 indicates that the child is not only a passive bearer of rights, but is the person who is entitled to use these rights in her own capacity. Furthermore, the CRC stipulates that children who have the capacity to form their own opinions, have the right to freely express themselves in all matters that concern them (Article 12 CRC; see also Kruger, 2018). This premise is also reflected in the ACRWC, emphasising that children must be allowed to openly express their views and have them considered (Article 7; Kruger, 2018). In South Africa, sections 10 and 31 of the Children's Act grant a child the right, depending on their 'age, maturity and stage of development', to participate in all matters that affect them, and their opinions must be given consideration when making such a decision.

When parents make the decision to have their baby's genitals altered, they are not only determining their child's sex but also the child's gender. The physiological ramifications may be severe in the event that parents did not elect the 'correct' sex for their child, and there is a probability that the child may, at a later stage in life, experience gender dysphoria.[18] As an adolescent, the child may also carry a fear of disappointing her parents for not being what her parents wanted her to be, and feelings of guilt, lack of identity and self-esteem may have dire, and even fatal, consequences.

These consequences may be prevented. As difficult as it may be, parents have to realise that this is a decision that their child has to make. This choice is one that affects a person's identity, dignity, privacy, mental and physical health and bodily and physiological integrity.[19] If surgical intervention is not medically necessary, there should not be a reason to take this choice from the person whose rights will be affected most.[20] The child's best interests – especially

---

18 The American Psychological Association describes *Gender Dysphoria* as a cognitive discontent experienced by an individual with their biological sex (American Psychiatric Association, 2013). See also the other possible consequences, as discussed above.

19 See, for example, Newcombe listing a number of international human rights organisations calling for the infringement of these rights of intersex infants to stop, often framing it as "genital mutilation" (Newcombe, 2017: 248–252).

20 See also principle 18 of the Yogyakarta Principles, which provides that 'no person may be forced to undergo any form of medical or psychological treatment, procedure, testing, or be confined to a medical facility, based on sexual orientation or gender identity. Notwithstanding any classifications to the contrary, a person's sexual orientation and gender identity are not, in and of themselves, medical conditions and are not to be treated, cured or suppressed.' To this end, the Principles further state that State Parties must take 'all

long-term interests – are to be considered as paramount and if the decision as to what sex the child identifies with can be made in a couple of years by that very person whose sex is in question, it should be that person who exercises that choice.

Once again it must be emphasised that it must be incredibly difficult for parents to not make this decision on their child's behalf. Parents will have to first accept the fact that their child is intersex before they can guide the child to accept herself. The South African Constitutional Court in *S v M (Centre for Child Law as Amicus Curiae)* recognised that a child is constitutionally envisaged as an individual with their own distinct personality and with "his or her own dignity", and cannot merely be considered to be an extension of his or her parents (2008 3 SA 232 CC: para. 18). Parents have to realise that their children are individuals with their own identity and autonomy (*ibid.*: para. 19), that they are not mere human 'becomings' but already human beings. Children, individually and collectively, have a right to get to know their own bodies, to learn how they should act and make decisions in order for them to become functioning members of the adult world (*ibid.*: para. 18).

4 A Comparative Perspective[21]

A number of jurisdictions have gradually begun to implement mechanisms to aid parents in making decisions that would be in their interest child's best interests. There is a growing trend of calls to States 'to repeal any law allowing intrusive and irreversible treatments, including forced genital-normalizing surgery, involuntary sterilization, unethical experimentation, medical display, "reparative therapies" or "conversion therapies", when enforced or administered without the free and informed consent of the person concerned' (UN Special Rapporteur, 2013: 23).[22] However, development in this regard continues to piecemeal and limited.

---

necessary legislative, administrative and other measures to ensure that no child's body is irreversibly altered by medical procedures in an attempt to impose a gender identity without the full, free and informed consent of the child in accordance with the age and maturity of the child and guided by the principle that in all actions concerning children, the best interests of the child shall be a primary consideration'.

21 Some of the ideas expressed here are also contained in S Thompson "Parental responsibilities and rights during the 'gender re-assignment' decision making process of intersex infants in South Africa", unpublished LLB paper at Stellenbosch University (2018).

22 See also Principle 18 of the Yogyakarta Principles, refered to above at footnote 20, and a resolution of the Parliamentary Assembly of the Council of Europe on Promoting the human rights of and eliminating discrimination against intersex people, calling on States to

4.1 *Colombia*

Colombia was one of the first countries to recognise the problem with subjecting minor intersex children to surgery for the permanent alteration of their genitalia (Hupf, 2015: 98). The country's attempt to regulate against non-consensual sex alteration surgery has been somewhat successful, especially at the outset. The courts have observed that sex alteration surgery is often motivated by parents' own person intolerance of sexual differences (Greenberg & Chase, 1999). Therefore, it can be argued that the attitude of parents plays an essential role in the making of this decision.

The Colombian courts have handed down diverging decisions, each resulting in implications for the intersex community. In the decision of *Sentencia No. T-477/95* ("*Gonzalez*") it was determined that doctors are legally prohibited from surgically altering the 'gender' of a patient, regardless of their age. A medical practitioner will need the patient's express consent in order to perform sex alteration surgery (Hupf, 2015). The role of parents of intersex children has also been redefined through the Colombian Courts. In the case of *Sentencia No. SU-337/99* ("*Ramos*") the court refused to accept the proxy consent of a parent on behalf of an intersex child. The court came to this conclusion on the basis that the decision should rest with the child and that is not a decision that could be taken by anyone else. This case illustrated a growing trend that parents should not be the ultimate decision makers, when their child's sex is under debate. However, in *Sentencia No. T-551/99* ("*Cruz*") the court qualified that parents should be able to consent to surgery if the intersex child is under the age of five because at that age children lack a gender identity. The qualification to the consent is that it must be "informed consent" (*ibid.*). "Informed consent" in accordance with the Colombian standard, requires doctors to ensure that parents are provided with all the information relating to the intersex condition over a long period of time. Doctors are also required to inform the parents about surgical and non-surgical options for their intersex child, as well as refer parents to organisations that provide support for intersex persons (*ibid.*). This aims to ensure that parents are not coerced into choosing gender re-assignment surgery and that there are other options available. However, although the Colombian court tried to institute a means of regulation, the reality is that intersex infants are still at the 'mercy' of their parents and regardless of these safety measures parents can make decisions that are clouded by their own personal beliefs, rather than what is in their child's best interests.

---

prohibit medically unnecessary sexnormalising surgery, sterilisation and other treatments practised on intersex children without their informed consent (Parliamentary Assembly Council of Europe, 2017).

4.2 Malta

Malta has one of the most inclusive laws protecting transsexual and intersex people in the world (Morgan, 2015). This inclusivity is a result of the Maltese Gender Identity, Gender Expression and Sex Characteristics Act 2015 ("GIGESC"). Malta has received much praise from the intersex community, as it was 'the first time in history a government anywhere has adopted laws to protect intersex people from the human rights abuses directed at them simply for their state of being' (Hupf, 2015: 103). The GIGESC prohibits cosmetic, non-consensual, sex assignment surgery of intersex persons (Hupf, 2015). Section 14 of GIGESC is arguably the most pioneering aspect of the Act (Mhuirthile, 2018). Performance of sex alteration surgery on minors is criminalised if the treatment or surgery is capable of being postponed until an individual is capable of giving informed consent (*ibid.*). By introducing this mechanism, the GICESC reiterates the significance of the right of bodily integrity and personal autonomy through its implementation (Hupf, 2015).

A new paradigm of legal innovation was introduced by the GIGESC in that it introduced a method to dispute gender "determined" at birth (Mhuirthile, 2018). Previously the position in Malta echoed that of the rest of the world: that gender is binary and one needs to be recorded as male or female in order to achieve legal recognition. Thus, by providing a delay for gender determination for minors, the Act enables children to make their own autonomous decisions (Mhuirthile, 2018). An important aspect that resulted from the introduction of this piece of legislation is that it decreases social pressures on parents to make decisions that are not medically necessary for their intersex children (*ibid.*). Section 7 of the GIGESC states that a person who exercises parental authority over a minor can apply to the court to change the recorded gender of the child as well as the child's name in order to reflect the child's true gender identity.

4.3 United States of America

The case of (*MC v Amrhein et al,* 2015)[23] provides a unique perspective on the question of consent during the decision-making process, since in this case, the parents of a child who was subjected to sex alteration surgery, realised that the decision was the child's to make. MC was born intersex with both male and female internal reproductive organs. MC was given up for adoption by his biological parent at birth and in state care at the time the sex alteration surgery was performed (White, 2014). The South Carolina Department of Social Services consented to the procedure on his behalf (Lane, 2018). MC's adoptive

---

23 The case is frequently also referred to as *MC v Aaronson,* 13-2183 originating case number 2:13-cb-01303-DCM.

parents raised him as the girl that the surgery changed him to, 'with full awareness of the psychological and social hardships MC may face while growing up' (Baumgartner, 2017: 45). At the age of eight, MC asked his parents when he would be growing a penis, since he identified as a male (*ibid.*: 46).

MC's parents filed a suit against the hospital and medical team that performed the surgery and the Department of Social Services (Lane, 2018: 5) and asserted that the defendants violated MC's constitutional rights, including his right to procreation (Baumgartner, 2017: 52). In 2015 the 4th US Circuit Court of Appeals found that, in 2006 when the surgery was performed, 'reasonable officials ... did not have fair warning that they were violating MC's clearly established rights by not seeking a hearing before performing, or consenting to, the sex alteration surgery' (*MC v Amrhein et al*, 2015: 15). The Court found it necessary to also explain that

> [i]n concluding that these officials did not have fair warning, we do not mean to diminish the severe harm that M. C. claims to have suffered. While M. C. may well have a remedy under state law, we hold that qualified immunity bars his federal constitutional claims because the defendants did not violate M. C.'s clearly established rights (*ibid.*: 16).

In 2017, the case was settled with a monetary settlement paid by the defendant to MC (Lane, 2018: 5).

5 Conclusion

It is a well-established principle of international and national law that the best interests of children are an important consideration in all matters that concern them. It is also the duty of parents to consider it, and in most instances, the presumption is that parents want to act in their children's best interests. The majority of parents do not want their child to experience hardship, ridicule or feelings of not belonging or being abnormal. Therefore, it is understandable that parents would want to make use of all options to prevent their children from suffering.

Article 5 of the CRC, however, also obliges Member States to provide appropriate direction and guidance that will enable parents to make the best possible decisions on behalf of their children. In the case of children born intersexed, parents need to be given the best possible advice as to the probable impact of a decision to change their child's sex by altering their child's genitals. Parents first have to accept their child and her true identity, whilst providing that child with the tools to grow up and develop to become the best versions of herself. Unfortunately the current reality is that an intersex child will face many hardships growing up in a binary world, as many social conventions dictate that only "male" and "female" sex is accepted. Therefore, our submission is that in terms of the CRC, and in particular, Article 5, States have the duty to provide the parents of intersex infants with sufficient knowledge and support, and to create a society that appreciates the complexities of being born intersexed. In this respect, States must regulate the medical advice that parents receive and abolish bureaucratic systems that compel or unduly induce parents to make a decision that will not be in their child's best interests. Although not fully explored in this chapter,[24] that decision ultimately is one that has to be exercised by children themselves when their capacities have evolved and developed to such an extent that they can make an informed and dignified choice.

Acknowledgement

Some of the ideas expressed in this chapter are also contained in an unpublished LLB research paper, entitled "Parental responsibilities and rights during the 'gender re-assignment' decision making process of intersex infants in South Africa", written by Sabrina Thompson in 2018, and in an unpublished LLD thesis, entitled "Considering the Best Interests of the Child when Marketing Food to Children: An Analysis of the South African Regulatory Framework", written by Lize Mills in 2016.

Bibliography

Ahmed, S. F., Morrison, S., & Hughes, I. A. (2004). Intersex and gender assignment; the third way? *Archives of Disease in Childhood*, 847–850.

Alston, A. (1994). The best interests principle: towards a reconciliation of culture and human rights. *International Journal of Law, Policy and the Family*, 1–25.

American Psychiatric Association. (2013). *American Psychiatric Association Diagnostic and Statistical Manual of Mental Disorders (DSM-5)*.

---

24 This chapter sought to analyse the matter from the limited perspective of Art 5 of the CRC. In order to fully appreciate the complexity of this situation, a much more indepth examination of the applicable children's rights is also required.

Bainham, A. (1986). The balance of power in family decisions. *Cambridge Law Journal*, 262–284.

Barnes, L. (2007). Gender Identity and Scottish Law the Legal Response to Transsexuality. *Edinburgh Law Review*, 11, 162–186.

Barry, S. (2018, August 29). *gcn*. Retrieved October 18, 2018, from ntersex Rights Legally Recognised for the First Time in California: https://gcn.ie/intersex-rights-legally-recognised-first-time-california.

Baumgartner, N. (2017). Intersex Parenting: Ethical and Legal Implications of the Treatment of Intersex Infants and the Ramifications for Their Families. *Women Leading Change: Case Studies on Women, Gender, and Feminism*, 3(1), 45–55. Retrieved May 24, 2019, from https://journals.tulane.edu/index.php/ncs/article/view/1121/1015.

Ben-Asher, N. (2006). The Necessity of Sex Change: A Struggle for Intersex and Transsex Liberties. *Harv J L & Gender*, 51–98.

Bird, J. (2005). Outside the Law: Intersex, Medicine and the Discourse Rights. *Cardozo Journal of Law & Gender*, 12, 65–80.

Blackless, M., Charuvastra, A., Derryck, A., Fausto-Sterling, A., Lauzanne, K., & Lee, E. (2000). How sexually dimorphic are we? Review and synthesis. *American Journal of Human Biology*, 12(2), 151–166. doi:10.1002/(SICI)1520-6300(200003/04)12:2<151::AID-AJHB1>3.0.CO;2-F.

Bridgeman, J. (2007). Accountability, support or relationship? Conceptions of parental responsibility. *Northern Ireland Legal Quarterly*, 307–324.

Cambridge Academic Content Dictionary. (n.d.). Retrieved August 22, 2019, from https://dictionary.cambridge.org/dictionary/english/cosmetic-surgery.

Carpenter, M. (2018). The "Normalization" of Intersex Bodies and "Othering" of Intersex Identities in Australia (2018) 15 487 488. *Bioethical Inquiry*, 487 – .

Children and Young People Act of the Australian Capital Territory, 2008.

Committee on the Rights of the Child. (2005). *Implementing child rights in early childhood*.

Committee on the Rights of the Child. (2013). *General Comment No 15 on the right of the child to the enjoyment of the highest attainable standard of health (art 24)*.

Council of Europe, Committee of Ministers. (1984). *Recommendation No R (84) 4 (adopted by the Committee of Ministers on 28 February 1984 at the 367th meeting of the Ministers' Deputies)*.

Family Law Act of British Colombia.

DeLoach, C. (2018). *How to Host a Gender Reveal Party*. Retrieved March 19, 2019, from Parents: https://www.parents.com/pregnancy/my-baby/gender-prediction/how-to-host-a-gender-reveal-party.

Ford, K. (2001). First, Do No Harm – The Fiction of Legal Parental Consent to Genital-Normalizing Surgery of Intersex Infants (2001) 19 Y 469. *Yale L & Pol'y Rev*, 19, 469–488.

Gillick v West Norfolk and Wisbech Area Health Authority (1986 1 AC (HL) 112).

Greenberg, J. A., & Chase, C. (1999). *Background of Colombia Decisions*. Retrieved October 10, 2018, from Intersex Society of North America: http://www.isna.org/node/21.

Haas, K. (2004). Who will make room for the intersexed? (2004) 30 41 51 (fn 117):. *American Journal of Law and Medicine, 30,* 41–68.

Harper, S. (1999). Medical Treatment and the Law: The Protection of Adults and Minors in the Family Division. In H. S, *Family Law* (p. 85). Bristol.

Herring, J. (2004). *Family Law* (2nd ed.). Longman.

Hewer v Bryant 1970 1 QB 357 369.

Horowicz, E. M. (2017). Intersex children: Who are we really treating? *Medical Law International, 17,* 183.

Human Rights Watch and Interact. (2017, July 23). *Human Rights Watch*. Retrieved from 'I want to Be Like Nature Made Me' Medically Unnecessary Surgeries on Intersex Children in the US: https://www.hrw.org/sites/default/files/report_pdf/lgbtintersex0717_web_0.pdf.

Human Science Research Council & The Other Foundation. (2016). *Progressive Prudes: A survey of attitudes towards homosexuality & gender non-conformity in South Africa.* Retrieved from HSRC: https://theotherfoundation.org/wp-content/uploads/2016/09/ProgPrudes_Report_d5.pdf.

Human, C. (2000). Kinderregte en ouerlike gesag: 'n Teoretiese perspektief. *Stellenbosch Law Review,* 71–.

Hupf, R. (2015). Allyship to the Intersex Community on Cosmetic, Non-Consensual Genital "Normalizing" Surgery. *William & Mary Journal of Race, Gender, and Social Justice,* 73–104.

Kennedy, A. (2016). Fixed at Birth: Medical and Legal Erasures of Intersex Variations. *University of New South Wales Law Journal, 39,* 813–842.

Kruger, H. (2018). The realization of children's rights to participate in selected medical decisions in South Africa. *South African Law Journal, 135,* 73–100.

Kusum. (1983). Legal Implications of Sex Change Surgery. *Journal of the Indian Law Institute, 25,* 73–89.

Lane, J. M. (2018, March). Reproducing Intersex Trouble: An Analysis of the MC Case in the Media. South Florida: Scholar Commons University of South Florida Graduate Theses and Dissertations. Retrieved May 24, 2019, from https://scholarcommons.usf.edu/etd/7187/.

Lareau, A. C. (2003). Who Decides- Genital-Normalizing Surgery on Intersexed Infants. *Georgetown Law Journal,* 129–151.

MC v Amrhein et al, No. 13-2178 (US Court of Appeals for the Fourth Circuit January 26, 2015). Retrieved from https://cases.justia.com/federal/appellate-courts/ca4/13-2178/13-2178-2015-01-26.pdf?ts=1422302488.

Mhuirthile, T. N. (2018). Malta. In J. D. Scherpe, *The legal status of intersex persons* (pp. 357–367). Intersentia.

Mills, L. "Considering the Best Interests of the Child when Marketing Food to Children: An Analysis of the South African Regulatory Framework" Unpublished LLD thesis, Stellenbosch University (2016), available at https://scholar.sun.ac.za/handle/10019.1/100245 (accessed on 4 May 2019).

Minto, C. L., Liao, L.-M., Woodhouse, C. R., Ransley, P. G., & Creighton, S. M. (2003). The effect of clitoral surgery on sexual outcome in individuals who have intersex conditions with ambiguous genitalia: a cross-sectional study. *The Lancet, 361*(9365), 1252–1257. doi:https://doi.org/10.1016/S0140-6736(03)12980-7.

Miriam Webster Online Dictionary. (2018). *"Parent", noun*. Retrieved February 13, 2019, from http://www.merriam-webster.com/dictionary/parent.

Morgan, J. (2015). *Attorneys for the Rights of the Child Newsletter Academic OneFile*. Retrieved October 10, 2018, from Malta now has one of the best trans and intersex laws in the world: http://link.galegroup.com/apps/doc/A466617464/AONE?u=27uos&sid=AONE&xid=a823ce1f.

Newcombe, P. (2017). Blurred Lines – Intersexuality and the Law: An Annotated Bibliography. *Law Library Journal*, 221–267.

O'Connor, D. (2012). A Choice to Which Adolescents should Not Be Exposed: Cosmetic Surgery as Satire. *J Health Care L & Pol'y, 15*, 157–172.

Parliamentary Assembly Council of Europe. (2017). *Promoting the human rights of and eliminating discrimination against intersex people – Resolution 2191*. Retrieved from Parliamentary Assembly: https://assembly.coe.int/nw/xml/XRef/Xref-XML2HTML-EN.asp?fileid=24232&lang=en.

Peleg, N. (2014). Reconceptualising the Child's Right to Development: Children and the Capability Approach. In F. M, *The Future of Children's Rights* (pp. 386–404). Leiden: Koninklijke Brill NV.

"Principles on the application of international human rights law in relation to sexual orientation and gender identity", agreed to in Indonesia in 2006 (The Yogyakarta Principles).

Re KD (A Minor: Ward: Termination of Access) [1988] 1 AC 806 812.

Redick, A. (2005). What Happened at Hopkins: The Creation of the Intersex Management Protocols. *Cardozo Journal of Law & Gender*, 289–296.

Rosin, M. (2005). Intersexuality and Universal Marriage. *Law & Sexuality: Rev. Lesbian, Gay, Bisexual & Transgender Legal Issues*, 51–133.

S v M (Centre for Child Law as Amicus Curiae) 2008 3 SA 232 CC para 18.

Sandberg, K. (2015). The Rights of LGBTI Children under the Convention on the Rights of the Child. *Nordic Journal of Human Rights, 33:4*, 337–352.

Scott, E. (2003). Parental Autonomy and Children's Welfare. *William and Mary Bill of Rights Journal*, 1071–1100.

Skelton, A. (2009). Parental Responsibilities and Rights. In B. (ed), *Child Law in South Africa* (pp. 63–).

Skelton, A., & Kruger, H. (2010). *The Law of Persons in South Africa*. Cape Town: Oxford University Press.

Sloth-Nielsen, R. (2018). Gender Normalisation and he Best Interest of the Child. *Stellenbosch Law Review*, 48–72.

Spiro, E. (1985). *The Law of Parent and Child*. Cape Town: Juta.

South African Children's Act 38 of 2005.

Tamar-Mattis, A. (2006). Exceptions to the Rule: Curing the Law's Failure to Protect Intersex Infants. *Berkeley Journal of Gender, Law & Justice, 21*, 59–110.

The UNICEF Innocenti Research Centre. (2007, December). *Law Reform and Implementation of the Convention on the Rights of the Child*. Retrieved from UNICEF Office of Research-Innocenti: http://www.unicef-irc.org/publications/pdf/law_reform_crc_imp.pdf.

The United Nations Free and Equal Campaign. (2019). *What does Intersex mean?* Retrieved March 19, 2019, from https://www.unfe.org/wp-content/uploads/2018/10/Intersex-English.pdf.

Thompson, S. "Parental responsibilities and rights during the 'gender re-assignment' decision making process of intersex infants in South Africa", unpublished LLB paper at Stellenbosch University (2018).

UN Special Rapporteur on torture and other cruel, inhuman or degrading treatment or punishment. (2013). *A/HRC/22/53*. Geneva: Human Rights Council.

United Nations Human Rights Office of the Human Rights Commissioner. (2018, October 28). *Intersex Fact Sheet*. Retrieved November 8, 2018, from UNHRC Free and Equal: https://unfe.org/system/unfe-65-Intersex_Factsheet_ENGLISH.pdf.

Weston-Scheuber, K., & Parlett, K. M. (2004). Consent to treatment for transgender and intersex children. *Deakin Law Review*, 375–397.

White, R. L. (2014). Preferred Private Parts: Importing Intersex Autonomy for MC v Aaronson. *Fordham Int'l LJ, 37*, 777–821.

PART 4

The Impact of Article 5 in Adoption Proceedings

CHAPTER 9

Children's Capacities and Role in Matters of Great Significance for Them

An Analysis of the Norwegian County Boards' Decision-Making in Cases about Adoption from Care

Amy McEwan-Strand and Marit Skivenes

1   Introduction

> Boy (12) has expressed his views in the case, ... He wants to be adopted, and his wish will be assigned considerable weight, ... He has been preoccupied with his belonging to the foster home since he was 4–5 years old. There is no information about the boy's functioning or maturity, nor in the case otherwise, that would indicate that he doesn't understand what an adoption entails (NA44).

This excerpt illustrates a decision-maker's consideration of a boy's capacities and his opinion about being adopted from care. The cognitive functioning of the boy is emphasised, combined with his long-standing concern about belonging in the family. These factors, as well as others, are not uncommon for decision-makers to assess when considering if an opinion is rational and should be given weight (Archard and Skivenes, 2009, 2009a; Le Grand and New, 2015). However, as much research has revealed, it is difficult for decision-makers to assess when and how a child should participate in his or her own case, (see for example Gal and Duramy, 2015; Magnussen and Skivenes, 2015; Porter, 2019).

The United Nations Convention on the Rights of the Child of 1989 (CRC) clarifies in Article 5 that states should ensure and protect children's right to be involved in decisions that concern them – from the earliest possible age, in recognising parents' and others' rights and responsibilities to give: '... in a manner consistent with the evolving capacities of the child, appropriate direction and guidance in the exercise by the child of the rights recognized in the present Convention.' The presumption in the CRC is that children are capable of being involved in matters of importance to them (GC 12, para. 20; Varadan, 2019). The right to express their views is accorded to all children 'capable of forming his or her own views' (CRC, Article 12). Thus, children shall have a form of agency in matters concerning them, which starts with the presumption that they have the capacity to participate and to make and to express their views and that exceptions must be justified. It follows from the rights perspective that the child's capacities should set the threshold for the child's ability to form an opinion. Furthermore, it is an obligation to enable children to participate and be involved in matters concerning them, and in terms of giving due weight to a child's view or opinion, it is an obligation to assign increasing weight in accordance with the child's capacities and maturity.

For decision-makers in courts or public administration, the CRC provides clear directions on how to proceed. The crux is to interpret what is meant by capacities and to identify the capacity of a specific child. Developmental psychology provides us with general insight into children's abilities, although there are different schools of thought (Smith *et al.*, 2015; Miller, 2016). The typical proxy for children's competency and abilities is age. At age 18 years, an individual is by definition an adult, and by age 15 and 12 years, children in many states are defined as being capable of making certain decisions, or their views should be given great weight. Although using age as a marker for competency in some areas makes sense, it is not recommended by the CRC committee (GC 12, para. 21) because it becomes a crutch, and decision-makers fail to fulfil their obligation to assess each individual child's capabilities (see Magnussen and Skivenes, 2015; Hultman *et al.*, 2019).[1] In decisions and matters of direct concern for a child, it is clear that the *ability to form an opinion* is the criterion and the threshold that shall be met as to whether to involve a child.

In this chapter, we examine decisions of direct concern and importance for children, namely decisions in which the judiciary must decide if a child should be adopted from care or continue their stay in public care. These decisions are made after a two- to three-day hearing involving all legal parties concerned by the decision. Typically, only children above 15 years old are present in the hearing, and younger children may have a spokesperson and/or speak with a psychologist or social worker. It is the County Board's responsibility to ensure that all relevant information is included in the case (Section 19-6 of The Dispute Act 2005). We are curious to find out how the Norwegian system involves and includes the child when making these decisions. We have examined all judgments made by the County Social and Child Welfare Boards

---

[1] This does not mean that age should never be used as a proxy for competency, as discussed by, for example, Archard (2015). Setting an age limit for when a person can apply for a driver's licence is efficient and cost effective.

(County Board)[2] in the period 2011–2016 in Norway in which the child is four years or older (n=179 children, n=169 cases). We first identified if the County Boards considered the child's competency by assessing his or her ability to form an opinion or view about the matter at stake. If yes, what factors do the County Boards rely on? Second, we identify if the County Boards have presented the child's view and, if yes, what this view is and how it is interpreted. Third, we analyse if and how the County Boards assign weight to the child's opinion.

The structure of the paper is as follows: in the next section, CRC, Articles 5 and 12 are outlined. Thereafter, the theme of adoption from care and the Norwegian decision-making system are presented. Following that, the legal platform and theories of what promotes and hinders children's involvement are presented, including an overview of research on children's involvement in adoption proceedings. A section on the methodological approach, data material and ethical approvals follows. We then present findings, followed by a discussion section and concluding remarks.

2 Evolving Capacities – Rights and Theory

2.1 *Evolving Capacities*

Article 5 of the Convention on the Rights of the Child is titled "Parental guidance and the child's evolving capacities" and reads as follows:

> States Parties shall respect the responsibilities, rights and duties of parents or, where applicable, the members of the extended family or community as provided for by local custom, legal guardians or other persons legally responsible for the child, to provide, in a manner consistent with the evolving capacities of the child, appropriate direction and guidance in the exercise by the child of the rights recognised in the present Convention.

For our purposes, we are concerned with the concept of children's *evolving capacities*, and in one of the few discussions of the concept, UNICEF 2005, three interlinked strands are identified: (1) the developmental dimension of the convention, (2) the participatory/emancipatory dimension, (3) the protective concept of evolving capacities. These are presented as conceptual frameworks through which the concept should be understood and examined.

---

[2] Norway has a unitary court system, and establishment of the Social County Board in 1994 constituted an anomaly because the County Board is a "court-like" decision-making body. However, the County Boards are considered a "court" according to ECHR, Art. 6 due to its independent position and procedural guarantees. See Skivenes and Søvig (2017) and Skivenes and Tonheim (2016) for details of the County Board's working methods.

The participatory/emancipatory dimension is especially interesting for our purposes because it imposes on states a duty to respect the rights of children to have their capacities recognised in accordance with their level of competence and to shift the level of responsibility for the exercise of rights from parents to children accordingly (Landsdown, 2005: 15). In this respect, we cannot mention Article 5 without Article 12 of the CRC, on the child's right to be heard, which likewise establishes children as agents with autonomy, with the right to participate in matters affecting them (see also Archard and Skivenes, 2009). Varadan (2019) suggests that the concept of evolving capacities has been treated as (1) an enabling principle, (2) an interpretive principle, and (3) a policy principle (Varadan, 2019: 11). In terms of being an enabling principle, the concept of evolving capacities serves four functions: (1) affirming children as rights holders and recognising their increased capacity and agency as they grow, (2) supporting children's agency in decision-making, (3) recognising that all – even very young – children should be engaged in the exercise and promotion of their own rights, (4) clarifying the duties of parents and legal guardians in supporting and guiding their children's enjoyment of their own rights under the CRC (Varadan, 2019: 317).

We find two main messages from the literature on Article 5 of the CRC to be of particular importance: first, the imperative to move away from age as determinant but rather focusing on capacity (Landsdown, 2005). As discussed elsewhere (for example, Archard, 2005; Archard and Skivenes, 2009; Daly, 2018), age as a proxy for a linear progressive development in terms of maturity and competency to apply equally to all children is highly problematic. Following the CRC, decision-makers in adoption proceedings have an obligation to assess each child's ability to form an opinion and make sure the child is involved accordingly in the proceedings.

Second, the *rights* of children are the same, but their needs and capacities vary (Landsdown, 2005). The balance to be struck is recognising children as autonomous rights holders with respect to their relative capacity, without exposing them to responsibilities prematurely. It also needs to be said that evolving capacities is not about rights as such, rather, it concerns the *exercise* of rights and where the responsibility to do so lies (Landsdown, 2005). While the concept recognises children as active agents with autonomy, it also recognises their need for protection and how competency and the need for protection will vary between children and situations, and evolve as children grow both with age and life experience. A summary of how to think about children's involvement, which we concur with, is laid out in a piece by Archard and Skivenes:

> ... we do not seek the views of the child simply in order to demonstrate the child's possible competence to decide for himself or herself; nor

only so that they might play a consultative role in helping adult decision-makers judge what is in the overall best interests of the child. We think that the expression by a child able to do so of his or her views has independent value as an essential element in the decision-making process. The value derives from the fundamental respect a child is owed as a distinct individual in that process (Archard and Skivenes, 2009: 392).

Moving forward from this platform, the question is how children may be barred from involvement and how they can be involved in decision-making.

2.1.1 Barriers for Involving Children

There are several reasons why decision-makers in the child welfare service and in courts do not involve children adequately. We do not have systematic research knowledge about this, but some explanations do emerge. In Skivenes (2018), five barriers for decision-makers that hinder the involvement of children are presented. The first one is about decision-makers' (and adults') desire to protect children from potential re-traumatisation and from reliving pain they have experienced. Furthermore, decision-makers do not want to place the child in a difficult conflict of loyalty or further burden the child. They have thoughts of the child as vulnerable and that they should not give the child additional experiences they cannot handle. Second, many decision-makers believe that children do not have sufficient ability and maturity to get involved or to have reasonable perceptions about a case or the matters at stake. Third, there may be a perception among decision-makers that it does not matter to the decision whether the child participates. If the risk to the child is considered high, the decision-makers may think that one must do what is necessary – regardless of what the child thinks. Fourth, decision-makers lack the competence and training in talking about difficult and sensitive issues with children. Finally, there are not sufficient organisational structures or bureaucratic case management rules for involving children, and the decision-makers may have high time pressure and physical surroundings designed for interacting with adults (see Skivenes, 2018 for details; cf. also Hultman *et al.*, 2019). The first three barriers are about individual features and attitudes, whereas the final two barriers are about structures for building competence through education and training, as well as in organisations.

2.1.2 Involving Children in Decision-making

A child can be involved in various ways: directly if the child provides oral testimony or submits a written statement, or indirectly through the intermediary of an adult such as a specially trained legal advocate or a relevant professional.

Clearly, in any interaction with children, one seeks the child's authentic voice, and the decision-making must be a deliberative process, in the sense that arguments and new information will influence decision-makers' opinions and considerations (Archard and Skivenes, 2009, 2009a). As much scholarship has demonstrated, children are involved in many ways; some experience real involvement, while some are on the opposite end, experiencing tokenism or simply exclusion (Hart, 1992; Shier, 2001).

Involvement of children (and any person for that matter) in decision-making aiming to withstand rational critique (see Habermas, 1981; Eriksen and Weigård, 2004; Archard and Skivenes, 2009; Magnussen and Skivenes, 2015) must ensure that all participants involved in the case must be given the opportunity to participate. There must be an appropriate location for the presentation of opinions and arguments, and important differences between the participants in their ability to articulate a point of view, advance a claim or understand the terms of the case should be compensated. The decision-making process should be transparent so that everyone participating hears everything that everyone else has to say, and the process must be accountable to avoid peculiar customs and illegitimate arguments. In the methods section, we operationalise how to identify children's involvement in a written judgment, but first, we will address the scholarship on adoptions from care and children's involvement, followed by an outline of the Norwegian system on adoptions from care and the research available on this theme.

2.2 *Children's Involvement in Adoption Proceedings*

There is vast variation across European countries in their legal regulation of children's involvement in adoption proceedings, and the revised European Convention on the Adoption of Children (2008)[3] states that *if* the child's consent is required, the age should not be set higher than 14 years (Article 5(1)b). Some countries in Europe, for example Switzerland and Ukraine, do not operate with an age limit but solely require an assessment of the child's capacities to consent or not. In some countries, for example England, Ireland and Austria, the child's consent or lack thereof is at no point legally determinative (Fenton-Glynn, 2013).

Although the CRC does not set as an *obligation* that the child should determine to be adopted or not (Fenton-Glynn, 2013: 593), it is clear that it is an obligation that states hear the child's opinion and give it due weight according to age and competency. While states vary signifcantly in how they regulate this,

---

3   Ratified by 11 countries (in 2019): Belgium, Czech Republic, Denmark, Finland, Germany, Malta, Netherlands, Norway, Romania, Spain, Ukraine.

age as a proxy for competency is widespread throughout Europe. Thirty European countries use only age to determine if consent to an adoption is necessary: age 10 years in, for example, Estonia, Lithuania, and Russia; age 11 years in Malta; age 12 years in, for example, Belgium, Portugal, and Spain; age 13 years in Poland and France; age 14 years in, for example, Germany and Italy; and age 15 years in, for example, Monaco (see Fenton-Glynn, 2013: 594-5 for a full overview). Some countries – Finland, Hungary and the Netherlands – have chosen a combination of an age limit that can be deviated from if a younger child is found mature and competent. Other countries, Denmark, Sweden, Iceland and the Czech Republic, allow for dispensing of the requirement of consent from the child at a set age, based on a best interests' consideration (Fenton-Glynn, 2013). In Norway, the country from which we have empirical material, a child must consent to adoption if 12 years or older.

To our knowledge, there is little research on children's position and views in cases about child protection adoptions or other types of adoptions (see Helland and Skivenes, 2019). Tregeagle *et al.* (2019) recently published a study on the adverse childhood experiences of vulnerable children adopted from care in Australia. Palacios and a wide interdisciplinary group of researchers (2019) argue that adoption is an important and legitimate model for the care of children when made within a rights-and-ethics framework that emphasises children's best interests. Two studies directly address children adopted from care, Berg (2010) interviewed 12 children adopted from care in Norway about their experiences, but this did not relate to court proceedings. Thomas *et al.* (1999) interviewed 41 children adopted from care in England, and they were also asked about the court proceedings. This study shows that half of the children were concerned about the court proceedings, both in terms of the actual court hearing, meeting a judge and being in the court-room, but also worried about the outcome of the proceeding and if the judge would, for example, say no to an adoption and what would happen then (69). The long waiting period before the court hearing was also mentioned as difficult for about half of the children (70 ff). In conclusion, questions about if and how children are involved, whether children provide their consent, whether children have views on foster home versus adoption as a placement alternative, and if children have a view on their contact with the birth family, are to a large degree left unanswered (Helland and Skivenes, 2019). There is research on children's involvement in child protection cases in general and also on legal proceedings, such as the Norwegian Expert by Experience group, the Change Factory, which has collected information from 130 children (Expert by Experience Report, 2019). We return to these findings in the discussion section.

3 Background – Adoption from Care in the Norwegian Child Protection System

Research on Norwegian adoption cases is scarce. In Norway, around 50 children are adopted from care each year and about 8,000 children are at any given day placed out of home due to a care order. A general outline of adoption from care in Norway is presented in Skivenes and Thoburn (2016) and in Helland and Skivenes (2019; in press).[4] Adoption from care is regulated by the Norwegian Child Welfare Act 1992 (section 4-20) as well as the Adoption Act 2017 (section 12, second sentence). The Child Welfare Act states in Section 4-20, Deprival of parental responsibility. Adoption, that:

> If the county social welfare board has made a care order for a child, the county social welfare board may also decide that the parents shall be deprived of all parental responsibility. If, as a result of the parents being deprived of parental responsibility, the child is left without a guardian, the county social welfare board shall as soon as possible take steps to have a new guardian appointed for the child.

When an order has been made, depriving the parents of parental responsibility, the county social welfare board may give its consent for a child to be adopted by persons other than the parents.

Consent may be given if:
a) it must be regarded as probable that the parents will be permanently unable to provide the child with proper care or the child has become so attached to persons and the environment where he or she is living that, on the basis of an overall assessment, removing the child may lead to serious problems for him or her; and
b) adoption would be in the child's best interests and
c) the adoption applicants have been the child's foster parents and have shown themselves fit to bring up the child as their own and
d) the conditions for granting an adoption pursuant to the Adoption Act are fulfilled.

When the county social welfare board consents to adoption, the Ministry shall issue the adoption order (Section 4-20, Norwegian Child Welfare Act 1992).

---

4 An outline of the Norwegian child protection system can be found in Skivenes (2011) and Falch-Eriksen and Skivenes (2019), and details on various processes of child protection removals are specified in Skivenes and Søvig (2017).

Thus, the legislation provides for adoption of children placed in long-term public care, provided it is in the child's best interests. Post-adoption contact with birth parents may be a formalised arrangement decided by the County Board (see Section 4-20 a). The legislator has assumed this contact to be limited, stipulated in extent by the decision-maker, and can only be granted if the adoptive applicants agree and it is considered in the child's best interests.

3.1   County Board Proceedings

The child protection service prepares an application for an adoption from care, and the County Boards make the decision. The County Board typically consists of three decision-makers: a lawyer (the Board's chair), an expert member and a lay member. The main principles for the proceedings and strict due process requirements are outlined in the Child Welfare Act of 1992, Section 7-3. Typically, decision-makers in adoption proceedings will have been provided with extensive written material by the public and private parties in the case. However, children are parties to the case only when they are 15 years or older (or younger if the case is due to the child's own behaviour). There will be an *in-camera* hearing of two to three days, ensuring that all arguments are heard and addressed. The County Board has an obligation to ensure that 'an independent and genuine assessment of the basis for decision-making' (Child Welfare Act of 1992, Section 7-3 e) is undertaken. The chair and the co-decision-makers meet after the last day of hearings, discuss the case, and make a decision. Typically, in adoption cases, these decisions are unanimous (Helland and Skivenes, 2019). The written judgment should be ready no later than two weeks after the hearing and must include all relevant reasons and arguments on which the County Board has based its decision. The written judgment will be around 10–15 pages long.

3.2   On Child Participation in Adoption Proceedings

In adoptions from care, the Norwegian Child Welfare Act 1992 sets out the general rules of procedure. In accordance with Section 6-3 of the Act,

> A child who has reached the age of 7, and younger children who are capable of forming their own opinions, shall receive information and be given an opportunity to state his or her opinion before a decision is made in a case affecting him or her (Section 6-3 first sentence, Norwegian Child Welfare Act 1992).

The law further specifies that 'Importance shall be attached to the opinion of the child in accordance with his or her age and maturity' (section 6-3 second sentence). The Adoption Act (section 9, second paragraph) also sets out requirements on children's participation in adoption proceedings, largely echoing that of the Child Welfare Act Section 6-3. However, the Adoption Act (*ibid.*) further specifies that children aged 12 years or older can only be adopted with their consent. This does not apply, however, if the child, due to mental disability or physical or mental illness, is clearly not able to understand what consent entails. The requirement of consent from children aged 12 years or older was also stated in the previous adoption law of 1986 (Norwegian Adoption Act 1986, section 6-2), which was repealed by the 2017 legislation.

The requirements for children's involvement are further anchored in the Norwegian Constitution §104, which states that children – regardless of age – have the right to be heard in questions relating to them and, in so doing, consideration should be had to their age and development. Moreover, the Norwegian Children Act 1981 (section 31) sets out children's right of co-determination, providing that children who are able to form their own point of view in matters that concern them shall have their opinion considered before someone makes a decision on their personal situation. This Act echoes the guiding age of seven years, stating (*ibid.*) that, 'A child who has reached the age of seven and younger children who are able to form their own points of view must be provided with information and opportunities to express their opinions', and 'When the child has reached the age of 12, the child's opinion shall carry significant weight.'

Thus, it is clear that children's involvement is extensively and cohesively provided for in Norwegian legislation concerning adoption from care. The Norwegian legislation does not set out a strict age limit as such; rather, a combination of age, capacity and maturity is to be considered when assessing whether the child should be involved, i.e. receive information and state their opinion. However, age is important because the ages 7 and 12 years are key in assessing the maturity of the child. While age 12 years is an absolute age limit for consent, with only limited exceptions, age 7 years is worded as a guiding age; children above this age *should* be heard, while children below this age *may* be heard, all the while assessing their capabilities. The law does not specify the issue of consent for children below the age of 12 years; rather, the law provides an obligation to involve the child, not a duty placed on the child that she or he should have to decide on the outcome.

In County Board proceedings, children will not be directly involved in the proceedings unless they are a party to the case at age 15 years and older. This means the decision-makers in the County Board do not meet the children, and they are dependent on the information provided by the parties in the case. A spokesperson may also speak with the child to identify the child's view on the situation and give testimony before the County Board (in person or by video conference). A spokesperson will typically meet with the child a couple of times for a few hours. In Enroos *et al.* (2017), details on the spokesperson system are outlined, and one of the findings is that the spokesperson arrangement is not sufficiently resourced to provide for children's involvement on their own standing (*ibid.*). The arrangement with a spokesperson is much used for children aged seven years and older, but rarely for children under seven years (Magnussen and Skivenes, 2015).

4 Methodological Approach

The study reported here is part of a larger project relating to decision-making in child protection, funded by Bufdir (The Norwegian Directorate for Children, Youth and Family Affairs) and the European Research Council. Detailed information about ethical approvals and data collection procedures is available in Helland and Skivenes (2019). Permission to access the cases was given by The Norwegian Data Protection Authority and the Council for confidentiality and research, and the project is reported to Data Protection Services and the University of Bergen's Ombudsman for Personal Data and Privacy. Only select named researchers could access the cases. Our data material consists of written judgments. We have examined all judgments on adoption from care decided by the County Boards over a six-year period (2011-2016). The written decisions are statements that consist of four parts: 1) an objective (non-contested) summary of the case, then 2) and 3) the two (usually) contested parts, each with a presentation of the viewpoints and the arguments of the parties (public and private), and 4) finally the County Board's considerations and conclusion(s). The judgments are required to include all information and arguments relevant to the decision-maker's decision (see Section 19-6 of the Dispute Act 2005; cf. Skivenes & Tonheim, 2017). Thus, if children have been assessed or their views have been considered, this should be evidenced in the County Board's written justification of its decision (read more here: https://www.discretion.uib.no/wp-content/uploads/2019/10/FORMAL-LEGAL-REQUIREMENTS-FOR-JUDGMENTS-IN-CARE-ORDER-DECISIONS-IN-8-COUNTRIES.pdf). In the analysis of the data material we have only used the County Board's considerations and conclusion(s), each typically three to five pages, to examine if and how the child's capacities and views have been considered by the decision-makers.

In the six-year period covered, a total of 283 cases have been decided on adoption from care, involving 302 children. For our study, we have included all cases with children between 4 and 17 years (n=169 cases and n=179 children), and excluded children who have not yet turned 4 years (n=122 children; n=120 cases). We collected all the information about the children in these cases. Our research approval[5] only allows us to keep a limited sample of cases for a longer period, and thus we deleted all cases for the years 2012-2015 after extracting the information about children in each case. Thus, we cannot review these cases again, for example, if we wish to extract new information. The reason we excluded cases with children younger than four years is that we believed it likely that they would not be involved. To check if this assumption is accurate, we conducted a systematic check of all the cases with children below four years of age from the years 2011 and 2016 (the years we have complete case material of all age levels). A total of 34 children were below the age of four years old, and in none of these cases was the child's opinion mentioned, nor had the child been appointed a spokesperson. In two cases (both from 2016), there had been an assessment of the child's ability in the sense that it was stated that due to the children's young age, their opinion would not be heard.

We used an analytical and conceptual strategy (Coffey and Atkinson, 1996: 26) by gaining an overall impression of the County Board's reasoning, and thereafter specifically identifying a) whether the child's views and opinions are mentioned by the Board in its assessment; b) how much weight the Board will give the child's views and opinions in its assessment (no weight, weight not mentioned, weight mentioned but unspecified how much, some, a lot); c) what the child's opinion and view towards adoption is (positive, negative, neutral). In Table 1 below, the codes and code descriptions are set out. To ensure the validity of the interpretations and categorisations, both researchers were involved in discussing and determining the codes, and one researcher was responsible for the coding. The text analysis program Nvivo 12 Pro was used for the coding process. The reliability of the coding was secured by a third person independently checking the coding. Only a few differences were detected, and these were discussed and then given a final code.

We use quotes to illustrate typical statements and findings from the material. The quotes are de-identified, and we sometimes also alter gender to ensure anonymity. Cases are referred to by numbers, and we have ordered the cases in alphabetical and chronological order, starting at number 1 for the first case in 2011 (by alphabetical order) and number 169 for the last case in 2016. All translations from Norwegian to English were done by the authors and have been independently checked by a third person. In an online appendix, we have included additional findings for readers who have an interest in the

---

5   Please read here about storage of sensitive data material: https://www.discretion.uib.no/wp-content/uploads/2019/11/SAFE-STORAGE-OF-CHILD-PROTECTION-JUDGMENTS-.pdf.

TABLE 1   Code descriptions

Whether the board assesses the child's capabilities: Statements in which the County Board has assessed the child's ability to form an opinion or the child's ability to be involved in the process. We also include here the indirect assessment of abilities, when an opinion is in fact included. We code "yes" if the child's abilities are assessed by the board, "no" if not.

Whether the board mentions and presents the child's views and opinions in the case: References to direct statements from the child to their spokesperson, or indirect statements where the child has expressed their opinions to other persons (parents, foster parents, child welfare services etc.). We code "yes" if the child's opinion is mentioned by the board, "no" if not.

Whether the board considers and relies on the child's opinion in their decision: Includes statements from the County Board on whether they will assign weight to the child's opinion in their decision. This can be direct statements from the board that they will or will not rely on the child's opinion, e.g. 'the perhaps most important argument for adoption, in this case, is still the child's clear and well-reflected wish to be adopted'. Indirect statements may express an evaluation on the board's part of the child's opinion, such as, 'the board considers that child X has not understood what adoption implies'. We interpret this as the perception that the view is rightly held, implying it will not be relied upon by the board. We register results in the following six categories:

- Yes: the board indicates that the opinion is relied upon, but there is no mention of the degree
- Yes – a lot: the board indicates that the opinion is relied upon and weighed heavily
- Yes – some: the board indicates that the opinion is relied upon to some extent
- Not mentioned: the opinion is merely mentioned by the board with no indication of whether it is relied upon[a]
- No: the opinion is not relied upon, either by express statement or because the opinion is devalued by the board
- Not relevant: the opinion is not mentioned by the board

The child's opinion towards adoption: Statements that describe what the child's opinion towards adoption is, categorised according to positive, neutral, and negative.

- Positive: the child is positive towards adoption. This can be assessed either from direct statements or indirect statements or actions.

TABLE 1   Code descriptions (*cont.*)

- Direct statement: 'the child has been heard in this case, as is stated above. He wants to be adopted, and his wish will be assigned considerable weight'.
- Indirect statement: 'the child has been preoccupied with not having the same last name as the foster parents, and she is very quick to point out specifically that she belongs to the foster family and is a part of the family'.
- Neutral: there is no indication of whether the child is positive or negative to adoption, or there is an indication that the child is unsure.
- E.g. 'the child did not have any opinions on what adoption entails, but did express that she belongs to the foster home and the network around them'.
- Negative: The child is negative or has doubts concerning adoption.
- E.g., 'in her latest conversation with the spokesperson, the child expressed she did not want to be adopted if this means less contact with her father'.

[a] There are nuances as, for example, reference to a repeated wish over the years could be interpreted as implicitly assigning weight. However, we do not stretch the interpretation on behalf of the County Board, and thus categorise this as not mentioned.

details of the material: https://www.discretion.uib.no/wp-content/uploads/2019/11/McEwan-Strand-Skivenes.-Childrens-Capacities.pdf.

There are limitations to our study. We do not learn if the children themselves feel they have been involved. Although our data material is comprehensive, we have only examined the written judgments and do not have access to the full case files submitted to the County Boards. We do not know if the County Boards have included children or met with the children without this being mentioned in the judgments. However, our enquiries about this to the County Boards indicate that this rarely happens. Our data collection procedure, extracting information for a specific part of the judgments, hinders us checking other parts of the judgment for 2012–2015. We experience this to be a limitation in regard to the consent issue of the findings because the County Board may have mentioned this in the facts section, although we do not have reason to believe this has happened on a general basis.

5   Findings

The 179 children in our sample were on average 7 years old at the time of the adoption and included 88 boys and 91 girls. A total of 171 (95 per cent) of the children were adopted. Most of the County Board decisions (163 out of 169) were unanimous. The questions we address in the findings section are threefold. First, we examine if the County Boards have considered the child's abilities to form an opinion or view about the matter at stake and, if so, what factors do the County Board rely on. Second, when the County Boards present the child's opinion, what is the content of the child's opinion, and how does the County Board interpret the opinion. Third, we examine if and how the County Board gives weight to the child's opinion.

5.1 *Ability to Form an Opinion?*

The County Board undertook some form of assessment for half of the children (n=90), leaving 89 children excluded (see Table 2). Most of these children had their opinion mentioned (n=73), and thus the County Board did not make an explicit assessment of their capacity to form an opinion. For only 17 children, the County Board undertook an assessment of the capacity of the children. Of these, none were deemed to have the ability to be involved or to have their opinion heard. Sixteen children were too young, according to the County Board, without any additional reason. These children were on average 4.3 years

TABLE 2   Children's ability assessed or view included. N=179 children.

Child's age	Number of children	Ability assessed or child's opinion included			
		Yes (N=)	Yes (%)	No (N=)	No (%)
All ages	179	90	50%	89	50%
4	50	13	26%	37	74%
5	33	9	27%	24	73%
6	29	7	24%	22	76%
7	7	6	86%	1	14%
8	15	15	100%	0	0%
9	12	10	83%	2	17%
10	7	7	100%	0	0%
11	3	2	67%	1	33%
12	8	7	88%	1	12%
13	4	4	100%	0	0%
14	2	2	100%	0	0%
15	6	5	83%	1	17%
16	1	1	100%	0	0%
17	2	2	100%	0	0%

old (median age 4 years). For one of these children, the Board expresses what seems to be a direct misrepresentation of the law: 'Child x is only four years old, meaning there is no requirement for her to be given the opportunity to provide her opinion in this case' (NA153). However, the law requires an assessment of a child's abilities to form an opinion, regardless of age, as we have set out above. For one child (out of the 17 children), the County Board provides a reason for its assessment of the child's capacity that is directly related to the specific child in the case: 'It has been shown that Child x at this time is not able independently to form an opinion on whether or not he wants his foster parents to adopt him' (NA81).

For those 89 children who were absent from the County Boards' considerations, without a justification for this exclusion, most of the children (n=83) were between four and six years old, indicating that the County Board does not consider it a legal obligation to assess the abilities or listen to children below the age of seven years. Six of the excluded children ranged in age from 7 to 15 years old. The 15-year-old did have legal representation in his/her case, but nevertheless his/her opinion was not mentioned by the County Board in its assessment. Furthermore, while children above the age of 12 years must consent to adoption, we see that for one of the 12-year-olds in this sample, the child's opinion, views or consent are absent from the County Board's reasoning. We return to the issue of consent below.

For seven children, the County Boards seem to consider the right to be involved as negative for the child, as illustrated in these two quotes, both concerning children aged four years old:

> The boy has been too young to be involved in the process so far. In not too long, the boy will reach the age where the law requires that he has the right to be heard in any future proceedings. In the County Board's opinion, this right on behalf of the boy seems more like a disadvantage, rather than a benefit (NA135).

> The mother has also stated that it might become natural with more contact in future if the child wants to. It might, therefore, be important to consent to adoption before the child is at an age where she will need to be involved in the proceedings before the County Boards or courts (NA119).

According to the County Board in these cases, reaching an adoption decision before the child is old enough to be heard is positive, because it would protect the child against the insecurity of having to be involved in future processes.

5.2 Opinion included in the Judgments?

Around 40 per cent (n=73) of the children in the adoption judgments were considered to have the ability to form an opinion, whereas, for 59 per cent (n=106) of the children, there is no mention of the child's view or opinion by the County Board. This is correlated with the age of the child because younger children's views are mentioned to a lesser degree, see Table 3.

As can be seen from the table, most children aged seven years and above did have their opinion mentioned by the Board, with the exception of six children. Of these, three judgments made no reference to the views or opinions of the child at all (children aged 9, 11, and 12 years), and it would be difficult to point to any reason as to why their opinion would not be mentioned. In the case concerning a child aged 15 years, the child did have legal representation, thus

TABLE 3   Overview of children's view reflected in judgment in adoption cases. N=179 children

Child's age	Number of children	The opinion is included. N/%		The opinion is excluded. N/%		View is mentioned and given weight N=number of children
All children	179	73	41%	106	59%	53
4	50	1	2%	49	98%	1
5	33	4	12%	29	88%	3
6	29	7	24%	22	76%	3
7	7	6	86%	1	14%	1
8	15	15	100%	0	0%	9
9	12	10	83%	2	17%	8
10	7	7	100%	0	0%	7
11	3	2	67%	1	33%	2
12	8	7	88%	1	13%	5
13	4	4	100%	0	0%	4
14	2	2	100%	0	0%	2
15	6	5	83%	1	17%	5
16	1	1	100%	0	0%	1
17	2	2	100%	0	0%	2

the view of the child was present in the judgment but was not part of the Board's assessment of the case. In the two remaining cases, there was mention of the child's spokesperson, but no mention of the child's opinion. In one case (child aged nine years), the child had been offered a spokesperson but refused. In the second case (child aged seven years), the child did have a spokesperson, and the Board concluded that nothing the child had told the spokesperson would indicate that adoption would not be in the child's best interest, without making any further mention of what the child's views might have been. Thus, it would seem that this particular Board holds the view that the spokesperson's task is to assess whether adoption would be in the child's best interest, and not necessarily to ascertain the child's views or opinions.

5.3   Consent to Adoption

Children must by law consent to adoption when 12 years and older,[6] and for the judgments in our sample, consent could have been provided by the child orally or in written form, and we expect it to be mentioned by the County Board in the judgment. A total of 23 children in our sample should give consent, but for only three children was this mentioned in the County Board's reasoning for its conclusion, and in one case it was mentioned in the facts section of the case. For 21 children, their views on adoption were presented (20 expressed a positive view on adoption), one had legal representation and one was absent from the County Board's reasoning.

5.4   The Views of the Children

Out of the 73 children who had their views represented in the Board's assessment, almost all (n=70) expressed that they wished to be adopted. Two opinions were neutral, and one did not express a wish to be adopted if this meant reduced contact with the biological father. An example of the County Board's characteristics of an opinion of a 15-year-old girl is the following:

> She wants to be a full member of a family she is happy with and who cares a lot for her. The security of living in a predictable home, and a future with the people she appreciates, weighs heavily (NA42).

Another girl's opinion, age nine years, was reiterated in the following way:

---

6   With the new law of 2017, it is specified that consent must be provided in writing, whereas the previous legislation of 1986 did not specify this requirement.

> The child calls her foster parents mum and dad. I tell her that if they become her adoptive parents, she will be their child forever. She says she is aware of this, and this is what she wants (NA75).

A boy's view, age 15 years, was referred to like this:

> The perhaps most important argument in favour of adoption, in this case, is still the boy's clear and well-reflected wish to be adopted. He wants to be fully integrated into the family, take their name, and be like "other children" (NA145).

Quote from the child, age nine years, who did not wish to be adopted:

> In his last conversation with the spokesperson, Child x expressed that he did not want to be adopted if this means a reduction in contact with his father. The County Board interprets this statement as an indication that continued contact with father is more important to Child x than adoption (NA43).

5.5 Assigning Weight to the Child's Opinion

The County Board has an obligation to give the child's opinion due weight according to the age and maturity of the child. We have found that a total of 73 children's views (41 per cent of the total sample) are included in the County Board's reasoning, see Table 4 below, and of these the County Board states that they rely on the child's view for 53 children (73 per cent) in their decision-making.

TABLE 4   Overview of the weight the County Board has given the opinion of the child. N=73 children

Code	Result	Number of children	% of N
The boards' weighing of the child's opinion or views in their decision N=73	Yes	53	73%
	Yes – unspecified	34	47%
	Yes – a lot	14	19%
	Yes – some	5	7%
	Not mentioned	11	15%
	No	9	12%

For 11 out of 73 children (15 per cent), the County Board does not mention any weighing of the child's view, and for 9 children out of 73 (12 per cent), the County Board states expressly that it will not assign the child's opinion any weight.

Focusing on the 53 children for which the County Board relies on the child's view, the County Board in most instances (n=34) just states that it will assign the child's view weight, without specifying *how much*, as this quote about a nine-year-old child illustrates: 'The child is nine years old, and the County Board has assigned his opinion weight'. The County Board can also express its reliance on the child's opinion in a general way, as this quote about an eight-year-old child illustrates: 'The County Board relies on the fact that the child has spoken about adoption, both with the social worker and with the foster parents.' For 13 children, the County Board states that the child's opinion is assigned a lot of weight, as these two illustrative examples about a 12-year-old and a 10-year-old, respectively, show:

> Child x has stated his opinion in this case, as stated above. He wants to be adopted, and his wish will be assigned considerable weight (NA44).

> According to the spokesperson, the child has expressed that, 'she would very much like to be adopted because then it will be for real, she is eager and repeats this several times'. The child sticks to this, even though this means stopping contact with the biological mother. The statement relates naturally to the impression the child gives of her attachment to the foster family and her consciousness of her own situation there. In light of this, the Board considers that her opinion should be assigned considerable weight, even though she is only ten years old (NA102).

For five children, their opinion is assigned some weight by the County Board, as this statement about an 8-year-old child illustrates:

> The child has stated to the spokesperson that he wants to live with the foster parents until he is grown up. He wants someone to say that this is where he will stay. The board will assign this opinion some weight, due to the child's age (NA106).

For 11 children, there is no mention by the County Board if the opinion is relied upon, as illustrated by the following quotes from a case about a six-year-old boy and an eight-year-old girl:

> The boy has been appointed a spokesperson. In conversation with the spokesperson, the boy explained that he wants to continue to live in the foster home until he is an adult (NA16).

In conversation with the County Board members, the girl has stated that she wants to live with mum forever. She knows she is a foster child, but does not remember meeting her biological parents (NA101).

For nine children, their opinion is not assigned weight by the County Board, either by explicit statement or because the opinion is devalued.

We have already seen that age is an important marker for involvement, and there is a distinct difference in age groups as to the degree to which the Board will rely on the opinions of the children, see Table A in the Appendix. For the children that are aged four up to seven years old and the very few that had their views mentioned, just over half (n=7) of these were relied upon by the Board in their decision, whereas for the remaining (n=5), the assigned weight was not mentioned. None of these opinions were discarded by the Board.

In 23 per cent (n=9) of the decisions concerning children aged 7 up to 12 years old, the County Board discarded the child's view. The County Board justified discarding all of these with the child's lack of understanding of what adoption entails, even though the child indicated a positive attitude towards adoption. This is illustrated by the following quotes:

> The child's opinion will be taken into account in view of the child's age and maturity, cf. CWA Section 6-3. ... The expert, Psychologist 1, has spoken to Boy (8) about his views towards this case. Boy was very clear in that he wants to live in his current home, and he does not want to move to either of his biological parents. Psychologist 1 tried to explain to the boy the difference between adoption and a foster placement, but the Board finds that Boy did not understand the implications of this and that he did not express any clear views in relation to this. Boy expressed that contact with both parents is okay, and the amount of contact is fine (NA17).

> Girl's (seven) wish to stay in the foster home and to have the same last name as the foster family, will not be decisive. She stated where she wanted to live, not that she wanted to be adopted (NA21).

For the children aged 12 years or older, no opinions were disregarded by the Board, whereas for 2 (10 per cent), the County Board does not mention weighing the opinion, as the following quotes illustrate:

Girl (12) has told the spokesperson that she does not actually think she will have to move, but she is still afraid of this. She has repeatedly expressed a wish to be adopted by her foster parents in the last years (NA59).

Girl (12) has become more aware and has expressed a wish to be adopted by her foster parents. As the situation is today, she does not want contact with her grandmother. She does not want to be confronted by her grandmother with questions on why she wants adoption. She wants to see her biological brother (NA23).

In sum, the County Board states that it assigns weight to the children's opinion for the majority of the children that have their view included, and in some judgments, the County Board also qualifies the weight given to the views of the child.

5.6 Characteristics of the Child and/or the Opinion and Correlated with the Weight Given by the County Board

Examining if and what features and characteristics the County Board mentions when considering the weight to assign to the views of the included children, we find three main areas of consideration (see Table 5): characteristics of the child, such as understanding, age, maturity, and the constitution of the child (if sick, disabled etc.); features of the opinion-formation process, including if sufficient clarity around the opinion is displayed, no exercise of pressure, and sufficient information; finally, there is an emphasis on the opinion itself, if the opinion is rational and the opinion is in line with the best interest of the child. Although we cannot make a direct link between the impact of these various characteristics and the decisions made, our findings show us that the characteristics of the child are the most important factor (age, understanding, maturity), and the other factors are mentioned much less.[7] For the few decisions in which the County Board has explicitly assigned a great deal of weight to the child's opinion (see Table 4 above), the County Board seems to focus on the quality of the opinion and the formation process, and less on various proxy terms such as age and maturity. From an example of an opinion that was assigned 'considerable weight' by the Board (in our coding scheme, this would equal 'a lot of weight'), we see that the opinion is valued as well reasoned, strong, and held over time:

---

[7] A detailed overview of all factors mentioned, by weight can be found in Table B in the Appendix.

> The girl (17) will turn 18 this year. She has a strong wish to be adopted by the foster parents. She has held this wish over a long period of time, and she has elaborated and accounted for this in meetings before the board. The board has assigned the girl's wish considerable weight (NA134).

For the children where the Board simply states that it has assigned weight to their opinion, but not specified how much, we see a high emphasis on the child's understanding. For these children, the Board points to their lack of understanding, or their limited understanding of the adoption question (n=10), and only two of the children are deemed to understand:

> It may be doubtful whether she understands the full implications of what adoption entails, but the County Board's assessment is nonetheless that she sees it as something positive, and a declaration of trust towards the foster parents (NA123).

In those cases where the opinion has only been assigned some weight, the emphasis is almost exclusively on age, more precisely that the child's (young) age implies the opinion should be assigned less weight:

> The child's opinion should be assigned weight. The girl (8) has told the spokesperson that she wants to be adopted. Considering her age, the majority will not assign the child's opinion decisive weight (NA80).

This is true for all five children whose opinion is assigned 'some weight'. Four of these children were eight years old, and one was ten years old. While this is a very small sample, it is still interesting how the Board finds that these children are of such a young age that their opinion should only be assigned some weight, especially because age alone is the conclusive factor.

In an example of an opinion in which the County Board does not mention whether it has assigned the opinion any weight, the emphasis is on whether the child has understood, with the conclusion that this has not been clarified – thus, the Board finds no conclusive indicator of capacity:

> In conversations with the spokesperson, the boy (seven) is clear that he wants to live in the foster home, without there being any further indication of whether he has understood the difference between adoption and a continued foster placement (NA122).

As in the example above, for the 11 children for whom it is not possible to determine if the County Board assigns weight to their views, only a few characteristics are mentioned by the County Board. This includes the child's understanding (in one case, that the child does not appear to understand the difference between adoption and foster placement, in one case, that the child has shown consciousness around adoption); and that the opinion is consistently held over time. An example of the latter is a child aged 12 years: "The boy has expressed his wish to be adopted by his foster parents repeatedly over the years' (NA59).

When the County Board disregarded nine children's views, this was justified by their lack of understanding (eight out of nine children). In addition, age, the child's maturity, clarity of opinion, or opinion formed under pressure, were mentioned by the County Board. By way of example:

> The board relies on the fact that the boy (seven) is immature for his age, and that he does not understand what adoption is in the actual and legal sense (NA79).

The girl (eight) had no clear perception of what adoption entails but clearly expressed that she belongs in the foster home and the network around them and that this is where she wants to grow up and belong (NA76).

5.7 *The Sample of Cases Not Resulting in Adoption*

Five per cent of the cases did not result in an adoption, involving eight children ranging in age from four to nine years old. Five of these children did not have their views mentioned by the Board, of which two were four years old, one was five, and one was six, and only for one of them did the County Board give a reason for excluding them: the child (aged four years) was too young. Three children aged six, seven and nine years had their views mentioned by the Board. Two were positive towards adoption. The Board emphasised the child's wish to have contact with the biological mother in one case (six years old), and the child's lack of understanding of the adoption question in the second case (seven years old). The nine-year-old child was negative towards adoption, mainly due to concern that adoption would entail less contact with the biological father.[8] The Board interpreted this as an expressed view that contact with the biological father was more important to the child than adoption, and concluded further that the child had not been sufficiently informed of the consequences of adoption. The adoptive applicants, in this case, had, in fact, agreed to post-adoption contact.

---

8 This was the only child found in our sample expressing a negative view towards adoption.

TABLE 5 Factors of importance when considering the child's opinion and its weight. N=73 children

Weight assigned to the child's opinion N=number of children	Factors the Board relies upon to assess the capacity of the child (in parentheses number of children in which a factor is mentioned at least once)
Yes N=53 (73%)	Child's age (21) Child's understanding (19) Clarity of opinion/reflection (13) Opinion held over time (10) Child's maturity (6) Opinion is coherent/well thought out (6) Sufficient information (4) Whether opinion formed under pressure (3) Features of the child/child's constitution (2) Opinion is consistent with what is in the child's best interests (1)
Not mentioned 11 (15%)	Child's understanding (2) Opinion held over time (1)
No 9 (12%)	Child's understanding (8) Child's age (3) Child's maturity (1) Clarity of opinion/reflection (1) Whether the opinion is formed under pressure (1)

6 Discussion

We are examining decisions that are of direct importance to the concerned children, namely, if they should be adopted or if they should continue to remain in public care. Findings from an English study reveal that many children are worried and highly concerned about these types of court proceedings (Thomas et al., 1999), and the importance for the children is clear as this statement from one of the children shows: 'I was worried whether I would be allowed to get adopted or not. And if I was not, what would I do and where would I go?' (Thomas et al., 1999: 69). Our analysis of all adoption cases concerning children four years and older over a six-year period reveals some interesting and intriguing findings.

First, young children do not have any type of agency in their own case. An overwhelming number of children have not had their capacity assessed, and these children are more or less absent from the decision-makers' considerations and justification for the decision. Although it can be argued that on average, four-, perhaps five- and six-year-olds, often may not have the necessary capacity, this cannot be *ex ante* taken for granted. In our view, this finding shows a clear violation of the legal requirement that children's capabilities to form an opinion should be the determinant of involvement. Similar findings have been shown in studies of care order decisions in the Norwegian County Boards (Magnussen and Skivenes, 2015), child protection frontline (Vis *et al.*, 2010), Swedish child protection (Heimer *et al.*, 2017; Hultman *et al.*, 2019), as well as in other countries (Berrick *et al.*, 2019; Porter, 2019). The judicial decision-makers have overall used the seven-year age limit to determine inclusion of children and are thus behaving in the way the CRC committee warned against. The discretionary authority delegated to the judiciary decision-makers to assess children's capabilities has not been applied and, as a result, only a handful of the youngest children have had their capacity to form an opinion and to have agency in their case considered. Even though the CRC is implemented in Norwegian law, it is clearly not followed in practice. This also indicates a lack of awareness that Article 5 of the CRC is, in fact, relevant to decision-makers and other authorities, and is not a duty placed on parents alone, despite the article's wording. States, and by extension state authorities, have a duty to ensure that children are being supported in exercising their rights under the CRC in accordance with their evolving capacities.

Second, and related to the first, our findings support previous research showing how the Norwegian justice system strongly relies on age as a proxy for maturity and competency in child protection cases (Magnussen and Skivenes, 2015). Age is the main explanation for why children's opinions are given weight, or the reason given in the few cases that children's capacities are assessed and children are excluded. The use of an age limit in the law, although a guide, is probably the explanation for why most children aged seven years have their opinion mentioned in the judgments, while most children below this age do not. Other systems, as in the UK, do not set an age limit for children's involvement, and we recommend that Norway do the same.

Third, a deficit in regard to the consent criteria is revealed. Consent is a statutory requirement for children aged 12 years and older, and consent should be mentioned in all the decisions that concern children in that age group. When only very few decisions mention consent – there is a cause for concern. As to why consent is not a focus, we can only speculate. One possible explanation is that adoption is regulated both by the Child Welfare Act as well as the Adoption

Act. While the Child Welfare Act and the Adoption Act have relatively similar provisions in relation to the child's opinion and involvement, only the Adoption Act mentions and requires the child's consent after age 12 years. As cases under the Child Welfare Act make up most of the Boards' caseload, they may not be as familiar with the requirements of the Adoption Act. It is possible that decision-makers assume that the adoption application is in accordance with the child's wishes. However, they still have a duty to ensure that proper procedure is followed and everyone's rights are protected. While one can also assume that any foster parent seeking to adopt *wants* to do so, adoption decisions will nonetheless include a statement of the foster parents' suitability and wish, and the biological parents consent or objection (Helland and Skivenes, 2019). This would indicate that, nonetheless, adults' rights, for example to consent or object, are still taken more seriously than those of the child. Recently, a template has been introduced for decisions in adoptions from care that explicitly requires a check of consent from children aged 12 years or older, and we hope that this development can lead to greater awareness on this issue.

Fourth, the assessment of capabilities and the County Boards' approach to children seem simplistic. This is evident when decision-makers are assessing children because either age or the child's ability to understand is used as a proxy for maturity and competency. Only a few times do we find the County Board's assessment of consistency and strength (see Archard and Skivenes, 2009), and almost never is the child's meaning formation process an issue. This may be a result of the limited information offered to the County Board to assess the ability of the child; information on whether the child was subject to pressure, or whether the child had sufficient information. Because the Board rarely meets the child, decision-makers will have limited opportunity to seek additional information on the capacity of the child should they need it. However, it may also be due to a lack of focus and interest from the decision-makers because children's involvement does not seem high on the agenda in child protection cases (Vis *et al.*, 2010; Hultman *et al.*, 2019; Porter, 2019). A lack of guidelines and clear political aims to follow the CRC are two likely explanations of why the system is like this. Furthermore, decision-makers may feel they lack the competency to assess children's capacity, and that lack of training on children's development explains why there is a relatively low focus on children in these cases. However, we wish to point out that in the County Boards one of the decision-makers is an expert on children and their development, but we do not see this expertise reflected in the judgments. Possibly this is related to the working form of the County Boards, where the legal chair is responsible for organising and writing the judgments. However, the expert members have opportunities to bring in their viewpoints during the hearing process as well as into the written judgments, so possibly they also have a low focus on children in the cases. As we will return to below, the County Boards' interaction with children has so far been indirect via a spokesperson and the written material, and this is about to change from 2019 and onward.

Fifth, and closely related, is the issue of what the child's capacity is measured against. Although there are only a few children in our material in which the decision-makers provide information about how they have weighted a child's opinion, it is sometimes clear that an opinion is disregarded because the issue of adoption and its legal implications is not understood (and possibly the decision-makers also believe this cannot be understood by children overall). In some other situations, it is the child's opinion about his/her life situation and their wish to belong in the family that is considered. Thus, the County Boards vary in their perceptions of what the child should be providing their view about: some focus on the legal implications of adoption, others on the child's view on their present living situation. Some decision-makers even indicate that it is a burden for children to be involved and that young children should be shielded from involvement without a further assessment of the child's capacity and their right to have agency in their own case. This seems to be a disenabling form of paternalism in the sense that it is not given a specific justification for the paternalistic act. Possibly, the reason for this is the County Boards' lack of information about the child. They rarely meet with the child directly, and the findings from our analysis show that the child's views often are only briefly presented. However, the County Board has a choice to ask for more information, and they may extract it from the case files as well as from the spokesperson (see Enroos *et al.*, 2017). While the County Board has a duty to ensure the child can participate and have their views heard, it is also a duty to consider the child's best interest (see Archard and Skivenes, 2010 for a discussion of this, cf. also Hultman *et al.*, 2019), and they likewise have a duty to protect the child from undue duties and burdens. This requires a type of paternalism towards the child that is enabling, for example, in the format that *explicit and elaborate justifications* are provided in terms of why an opinion is disregarded or why a child is not involved in the case.

Sixth, our analysis shows that in very few cases due weight to the child's opinion is explained and elaborated on, and in the majority of the cases, it is not specified. This is also detected elsewhere, as Daly (2018) points out a lack of common ground amongst decision-makers in terms of giving weight to children's opinion. In her view, the concept of 'giving due weight' has been an obstacle to children's participation, and has promoted decision-makers to give weight to opinions that concur with their opinion and neglecting those that disagree. Training in providing reasons, and increased awareness on why and how an argument is important for a decision-making outcome, may be two solutions that the County Board may pursue (see Porter (2019)).

Our findings coincide with a notion of disenabling paternalism towards younger children and a more enabling paternalism towards the older. Although only indicative findings, younger children's (below age 12 years) ability to form an opinion seems to be assessed by their age and their ability to understand, while older children's (12 years and older) ability seems to be judged by their capacity to form a well-reasoned and consistent opinion – i.e. qualities of the decision-formation process, rather than simply features of the child. A study of a representative sample of the populations in England and Norway reveals a significantly higher portion of the Norwegians being willing to act paternalistically towards children compared with the English population (Cappelen *et al.*, in preparation).

7 Concluding Remarks

Our results are discouraging because overall, children's role and place in cases about adoption from care are minimal. These children are not given agency, and they are not the main person in these cases. In itself, this raises a question about legitimacy, and we doubt this would happen with an adult person's case. We can conclude that the law is not followed, and children's rights as laid out in the CRC are not respected, which is surprising and disappointing, bearing in mind that the County Board is led by a lawyer and is a decision-making body operating as a court. However, new guidelines are in place for the County Boards, and involvement of children is not impossible nor difficult to realise, as there are very good examples of in our analysis and a point clearly made by Experts by Experience (2019). We end this chapter with an excerpt from the judgment about a 15-year-old child that we believe had agency in her case:

> Something which in this case speaks especially in favour for adoption is Girl's own strong wish to be adopted, as well as research indicating it is better for children to grow up as adoptive children rather than foster children. Girl will soon turn 16 years old, and her opinion must weigh heavily. She has stuck by this wish over time. She is familiar with what adoption entails and has provided good reasons for her wish.

She wants to be a full member of a family she is happy with, and who cares a lot for her. The security of living in a predictable home, and a future with the people she appreciates, weighs heavily (NA42).

Acknowledgements

We owe great thanks to PhD student Barbara Ruiken and research assistant Florian Wingens for reliability testing our coding and to Trond Helland for checking our translations. The paper was presented at the "CRC-IP Colloquium on Article 5" at Cambridge University, Robinson College, in July 2019, and furthermore at the seminar Rights, Democracy and Welfare in August 2019: We are grateful for the feedback and comment we received from the participants. Many thanks for constructive and insightful comments from an anonymous reviewer.

Funding

This project has received funding from the European Research Council (ERC) under the European Union's Horizon 2020 research and innovation program (grant agreement no. 724460).

References

Archard D., "Children" in LaFollette H. (ed), *The Oxford Handbook of Practical Ethics* (New York NY: Oxford University Press, 2005). DOI: 10.1093/oxfordhb/9780199284238.001.0001.

Archard, D. and Skivenes M., "Balancing a Child's Best Interests and a Child's Views", *The International Journal of Children's Rights* 2009 (17 (1)), 1–21. DOI: 10.1163/157181808X358276.

Archard, D. and Skivenes M., "Hearing the Child", 14 *Child & Family Social Work* 2009a (14(4)), 391–399. DOI: 10.1111/j.1365-2206.2008.00606.x.

Berg, T., "Adopsjon som barneverntiltak – Hvordan gikk det med barna? Rapport fra praksis" (in Norwegian, Adoption as a child welfare measure – How were the children?), *Tidsskriftet Norges Barnevern* 2010 (87(1)), 48–59.

Berrick, J., Dickens, J., Pösö, T. and Skivenes, M., "Children's and parents' involvement in care order proceedings: a cross-national comparison of judicial decision-makers' views and experiences", *Journal of Social Welfare and Family Law* 2019 (41), 188–204. DOI: 10.1080/09649069.2019.1590902.

Cappelen, A., Skivenes, M. and Tungodden, B., *Responsibility and autonomy – an experimental study of adults view on children's freedom to make choices* (in preparation).

Coffey, A. and Atkinson, P., "Making sense of qualitative data: Complementary research strategies" (Thousand Oaks, CA, US: Sage Publications, Inc., 1996).

Committee on the Rights of the Child (CRC), General Comment No. 12 2009, *The Right of the Child to Be Heard* CRC/C/GC/12.

Daly, A., "No Weight for 'Due Weight'? A Children's Autonomy Principle in Best Interest Proceedings", *The International Journal of Children's Rights* 2018, 26(1) 61–92. DOI: 10.1163/15718182-02601012.

Enroos, R., Helland, H.S., Pösö, T., Skivenes, M. and Tonheim, M., "The role and function of spokesperson in care order proceedings: a cross-country study in Finland and Norway", *Children and youth service review* 2017 (74), 8–16. DOI: 10.1016/j.childyouth.2017.01.017.

Eriksen O. E. and Weigård J., *Kommunikativ Handling Og Deliberativt Demokrati* (Bergen: Fagbokforlaget, 1999).

Eriksen O. E. and Weigård J., *Understanding Habermas Communicative Action and Deliberative Democracy* (London: Bloomsbury Publishing PLC, 2004).

Forandringsfabrikken (The Change Factory), Rett og sikkert: om anmeldelse, avhør i barnehus og rettssak. Fra unge som har opplevd vold eller overgrep (in English: Just and safe: on pressing charges, testimony in children's houses and trials. From young persons who have experienced violence or abuse. Expert by Experience Report.) (Forandringsfabrikken Kunnskapssenter: 2019).

Falch-Eriksen, A. and Skivenes, M., "Article 19 – Children's right to protection in Norway" in Langford, M., Skivenes, M. and Søvig, K. (eds.), *Child rights in Norway: Measuring Compliance* (Oslo: Universitetsforlaget, 2019).

Fenton-Glynn, C., "The Child's Voice In Adoption Proceedings: A European Perspective", *The International Journal of Children's Rights* 2013 (21(4), 590–615. DOI: 10.1163/15718182-55680018.

Gal, T. and Duramy, B. (eds.), *International Perspectives and Empirical Findings on Child Participation: From Social Exclusion to Child-Inclusive Policies* (Oxford: Oxford University Press, 2015).

Habermas, J., *The Theory of Communicative Action* (Boston: Beacon Press, 1981).

Hart, R., "Children's Participation: From Tokenism to Citizenship", *Innocenti Essays* 1992: https://www.unicef-irc.org/publications/pdf/childrens_participation.pdf. Accessed 28 August 2019.

Heimer, M., E. Näsman and Palme, J., "Vulnerable children's rights to participation, protection, and provision: The process of defining the problem in Swedish child and family welfare" in *Child & Family Social Work*. 2018; 23: 316–323.

Helland, H. S. and Skivenes, M., *Adopsjon som barneverntiltak* (in Norwegian, Adoption as a schild welfare measure), (University of Bergen; Centre for Research on Discretion and Paternalism: Bergen, 2019).

Helland, H. S. and Skivenes, M., "Adoption from care in Norway" in Pösö T., Skivenes M. and Thoburn J. (eds.), *Adoptions from Care in an international perspective* (in press).

Hultman, E., Höjer, S. and Larsson, M., "Age Limits for Participation in Child Protection Court Proceedings in Sweden", *Child & Family Social Work* 2019, 1–9. DOI: 10.1111/cfs.12686.

Lansdown, G., "The Evolving Capacities of the Child", UNICEF *Innocenti Research Centre*, 2005.

Leeson, C., "My life in care: Experiences of non-participation in decision-making processes", *Child and Family Social Work* 2007 12(3), 268–277. DOI: 10.1111/j.1365-2206.2007.00499.x.

Le Grand, J. and New, B., *Government Paternalism: Nanny state or helpful friend?* (Princeton NJ: Princeton University Press, 2015).

Magnussen, A-M. and Skivenes, M., "The Child's Opinion and Position in Care Order Proceedings: An Analysis of Judicial Discretion in the County Boards' Decision-Making", *The International Journal of Children's Rights* 2015 23(4), 705–723. DOI: 10.1163/15718182-02304001.

Miller, P. H., *Theories of Developmental Psychology* (New York, NY: Worth Publishers Inc., 2016).

Palacios, J., Adroher, S., Brodzinsky, D. M., Grotevant, H. D., Johnson, D.E., Juffer, F., Martínez-Mora, L., Muhamedrahimov, R. J., Selwyn, J., Simmonds, J., Tarren-Sweeney, M., Adoption in the service of child protection: An international interdisciplinary perspective, *Psychology, Public Policy, and Law* 2019 25, 57–72. DOI: 10.1037/law0000192.

Porter, R. B., Recording of Children and Young People's Views in Contact Decision-Making, *The British Journal of Social Work* 2019. DOI: 10.1093/bjsw/bcz115.

Shier, H., "Pathways to Participation: Openings, Opportunities and Obligations", *Children & Society* 2001 15(2), 107–117. DOI:10.1002/chi.617.

Skivenes, M., "Norway: Toward a Child Centric Perspective" in Neil Gilbert, Nigel Parton and Marit Skivenes (eds.), *Child Protection Systems: International Trends and Orientations* (New York, NY: Oxford University Press, 2011).

Skivenes, M., "Barneperspektiv i fokus" (Child perspective in focus, in Norwegian) in Steinrem, I. and Toresen, G. (eds.), *Barnas Barnevern* (*Children's Child Protection, in Norwegian*) (Oslo: Universitetsforlaget, 2018).

Skivenes, M. and Søvig, K., "Judicial Discretion and the Child's Best Interest – The European Court of Human Rights on Child Protection Adoptions" in E. Sutherland and L. Macfarlane (eds.), *Implementing Article 3 of the United Nations Convention on the Rights of the Child: Best Interests, Welfare and Well-being* (Cambridge: Cambridge University Press, 2016).

Skivenes, M. and Søvig, K. H., "Norway: Child welfare decision-making in cases of removals of children" in Burns, K., Pösö, T. and Skivenes, M. (eds.), *Child Welfare*

Removals by the State: A Cross-Country Analysis of Decision-Making Systems (New York, NY: Oxford University Press, 2017).

Skivenes, M. and Thoburn, J., "Pathways to Permanence in England and Norway: A Critical Analysis of Documents and Data", *Children and Youth Services Review* 2016 (67), 152–160. DOI: 10.1016/j.childyouth.2016.05.020.

Skivenes, M. and Tonheim, M., "Deliberative Decision-Making on the Norwegian County Social Welfare Board: The Experiences of Expert and Lay Members", *Journal of Public Child Welfare* 2017 (11), 108–132. https://doi.org/10.1080/15548732.2016.1242447.

Smith, P. K., Cowie, H. and Blades, M., *Understanding Children's Development* (Trento: John Wiley & Sons, 2015).

Thomas, C., Lowe, N. V., Lowe, N., Beckford, V. and Murch, M., *Adopted Children Speaking: A Whole New World* (British Association for Adoption and Fostering (BAAF): 1999).

Tregeagle, S., Moggach, L., Trivedi, H. and Ward H., "Previous Life Experiences and the Vulnerability of Children Adopted from Out-of-Home Care: The Impact of Adverse Childhood Experiences and Child Welfare Decision Making", *Children and Youth Services Review* 2019 (96), 55–63. DOI: 10.1016/j.childyouth.2018.11.028.

Varadan, S., "The Principle of Evolving Capacities under the UN Convention on the Rights of the Child", *The International Journal of Children's Rights* 2019, (27(2)), 306–338. DOI: 10.1163/15718182-02702006.

Vis, S. A., Holtan, A. and Thomas, N., "Obstacles for child participation in care and protection cases – why Norwegian social workers find it difficult", *Child Abuse Review* 2010, 21(1), 7–23. DOI: 10.1002/car.1155

Legislation

Convention on the Rights of the Child 1989, United Nations, Treaty Series, vol. 1577, p. 3.

European Convention on the Adoption of Children (Revised) 2008, CETS No. 202, Strasbourg.

Lov 17. mai 1814 Kongerikets Noregs Grunnlov (The Constitution of the Kingdom of Norway 1814).

Lov 28. februar 1986 om adopsjon (adopsjonsloven) (The Norwegian Adoption Act 1986).

Lov 17. juli 1992 om barneverntjenester (barnevernloven) (The Norwegian Child Welfare Act 1992).

Lov 17. Juni 2005 om mekling og rettergang i sivile tvister (tvisteloven) (The Norwegian Dispute Act 2005).

Lov 16. juni 2017 om adopsjon (adopsjonsloven), (The Norwegian Adoption Act 2017).

CHAPTER 10

Children's Views, Best Interests and Evolving Capacities in Consenting to Their Own Adoption

A Study of NSW Supreme Court Judgements for Adoptions from Care

Judy Cashmore, Amy Conley Wright and Sarah Hoff

1 Children's Views, Best Interests and Evolving Capacities about Their Own Adoption

Adoption marks a momentous change in the lives of children, severing legal ties with their birth family, and establishing them with their adoptive family. In most jurisdictions, the 'best interests' of the child is the paramount consideration but in determining 'best interests', some assessment of the child's wishes, views or feelings may be required. How these decisions take into account children's wishes or views about the adoption and how this relates to the concept of the child's 'evolving capacities' as defined in Article 5 of the UN Convention on the Rights of the Child is the focus of this chapter. It is based on the published judgments in one Australian jurisdiction in relation to the adoption of children from out-of-home care, and the way in which the court recognises and respects children's 'evolving capacity' in relation to children's expressed wishes.

Lansdown (2005) conceptualised children's evolving capacities in terms of three frameworks: as a developmental concept, a participatory or emancipatory concept, and a protective concept. In essence, these involve the recognition by parents, carers and the state that as children develop, their increasing capacity, insights and abilities mean the gradual transfer of agency and autonomy rights from adults to children in line with children's evolving capacities. At the same time, children still need to be protected 'from participation in or exposure to activities likely to cause them harm' including decision-making that they do not feel ready for or do not wish to be involved in (Lansdown, 2005, p. x; Tobin, 2019). As the UN Committee stated in general Comment 14:

> The evolving capacities of the child (art. 5) must be taken into consideration when the child's best interests and right to be heard are at stake. ... the more the child knows, has experienced and understands, the more the parent, legal guardian or other persons legally responsible for him or her

have to transform direction and guidance into reminders and advice, and later to an exchange on an equal footing. Similarly, as the child matures, his or her views shall have increasing weight in the assessment of his or her best interests. Babies and very young children have the same rights as all children to have their best interests assessed, even if they cannot express their views or represent themselves in the same way as older children. States must ensure appropriate arrangements, including representation, when appropriate, for the assessment of their best interests; the same applies for children who are not able or willing to express a view. (paragraph 44)

Recognition of children's evolving capacities is therefore central to the balance between participation and protection. Children's experience in exercising agency is also key to developing capacity.

2   Different Legal Frameworks

Following Lansdown's discussion of various legal frameworks, Fenton-Glynn (2014) examined the adoption laws of European countries and their approach to taking children's views into account. The most common approach, with age alone as the criterion in 30 European countries at that time, was a 'strict fixed age limit' such that when a child reaches the prescribed age, 'his or her consent is a necessary condition for granting an adoption order' (p. 139). The prescribed age varied, ranging from 10 to 15 years. Lansdown, and subsequently the Committee on the Rights of the Child (General Comment no 12 paras 20–21), criticised the rigidity of a fixed age limit on the grounds that it 'fails to comply with the principle of respecting the right of children to participate in decision-making in accordance with their evolving capacities ... and to allow for flexibility depending on the levels of risk involved and the degree of protection needed' (p. 50). It is therefore restrictive and also potentially harmful but the simplest to implement.

Other legal approaches involve some assessment of the child's age and maturity – applying age limits with exceptions for capable children or exceptions for 'best interests' – or having no fixed age of consent or no legal requirement for the child's consent. In England, for example, the child's ascertainable wishes and feelings must be considered taking into account the child's age and understanding, but 'at no time are the child's wishes legally determinative' (p. 149). Fenton-Glynn (2014) concluded that there was 'no clear consensus about the age at which children should give consent to an adoption order, the weight to be given or even whether his or her views should be considered at all' (p. 136).

Fenton-Glynn's (2014) analysis provides an interesting framework for the analysis of the role of children's wishes and room for 'evolving capacities' in the Australian State and territory jurisdictions, and in particular, adoption proceedings in New South Wales which is the focus of this chapter. The next section provides some contextual background in relation to adoption in Australia, and legislative requirements concerning children's wishes and feelings, and the age at which children can consent to their own adoption.

3   Adoption in Australia

Adoption in Australia, particularly 'local' or domestic adoption, has a problematic history, reflecting the trauma, pain and grief of generations of child removals of Aboriginal children in the *Stolen Generations* and the 'forced adoptions' of the babies of unmarried women in the from the 1940s to the 1970s (Human Rights and Equal Opportunity Commission, 1997; Kenny et al., 2012; Wright et al., 2021). The adoption of children continues to be a contentious issue, and is not favoured as a permanency option for children in out-of-home care in the same way as in the US and UK (Huntington, 2014; Ross and Cashmore, 2016; Sloan, 2018; Whitt-Woosley and Sprang, 2014). The number of adoptions of children from out-of-home care in Australia is extremely low compared with the US and UK. In 2018–19, only 142 children were adopted by their carers across Australia; at that time, there were approximately 44,900 children in out-of-home care in Australia (as at 30 June 2019) (Australian Institute of Health and Welfare, 2020, p. 48). Nearly all of these adoptions occurred in one state, New South Wales (NSW).

Child protection and adoption are governed by state-based legislation and policy in Australia, and the states have different legislative and policy frameworks for the adoption of children from out-of-home care. Legislative changes in NSW in 2014 prioritised 'open adoption' for non-Indigenous children in foster care, whom the Children's Court determines cannot be safely returned to their parents. Adoption matters are considered by the NSW Supreme Court, under the NSW Adoption Act 2000. This legislation allows the Court to dispense with parental consent in matters where the child's current authorised (foster carer) is applying for an adoption order, where there is an established relationship, and the court is satisfied that this is in the best interests of the child and clearly preferable to any other action (ss 67 and 90 NSW Adoption Act 2000 No 75). For Aboriginal children, the NSW Adoption Act 2000 notes that the Aboriginal Child Placement Principle must be applied, which emphasises the participation of children's families, families and communities in placement decisions and asserts the importance of keeping children connected to their culture by preferencing placements within their Kinship networks or other Indigenous carers. Adoption of Aboriginal children is strongly opposed by Aboriginal community organisation and peak representative bodies (Family Matters, 2019).

Australian adoption legislation also differs across jurisdictions in relation to children's consent but, in most jurisdictions, clearly specifies that children's wishes or views should be sought in relation to the adoption application for children who are 'able to form and express a view' (see, for example, Queensland Adoption Act 2009 s 6(d). In several states (Victoria and Queensland), this is tied to a requirement that the child has received age-appropriate information or counselling (Institute of Open Adoption Studies, 2018). In NSW, the Supreme Court must not make an adoption order without being satisfied that, 'as far as practicable and having regard to the age and understanding of the child, the wishes and feelings of the child have been ascertained and due consideration given to them' (Adoption Act 2000 No 75 s 90 (1)(b)). The Act also includes a participation principle (s 9) and requirements that are commensurate with those under Article 12 of the UN Convention of the Rights of the Child that place responsibility on the decision maker for providing the child with:

(a) adequate information, in a manner and language that the child can understand, concerning the decision,
(b) the opportunity to express his or her views freely, according to his or her abilities,
(c) information about the outcome of the decision and an explanation of the reasons for the decision,
(d) any assistance that is necessary for the child to understand the information and to express his or her views,
(e) appropriate counselling when the child's consent is required to his or her adoption.

In addition to the requirements about children's views or wishes, several jurisdictions including NSW require children of 12 years of age and older to give consent to their adoption, unless that consent is dispensed with – in line with Fenton-Glynn's category of a fixed (minimum) age limit. The child's consent can also serve as sole consent, removing the need for the consent of the birth parents for a child from age 12 in NSW and from age 16 in Western Australia. In NSW, children are able to give sole consent to being adopted by their carers, if they have been in their care for at least two years (s 54(2)) and have 'been counselled' (s 55). In other states, such as Victoria and Queensland, the fixed age limit in earlier legislation and the requirement for a child from the age of 12 to consent to their adoption were replaced with current requirements that include the provision of information to children, counselling (mandatory in Victoria) and the court's consideration of the child's wishes with no age limit specified (VLRC, 2017, paras 3.38 – 3.44).

The most common means of presenting children's wishes or views in Australia, and in particular in NSW, is via the report of an authorised adoption assessor as well as a report or affidavit from the principal officer of the State statutory department or the accredited adoption service provider (s 91(2) of the NSW Adoption Act 2000). The authorised adoption assessor may be appointed by or employed by the designated agency managing the casework for the child and the adoptive family but cannot be their caseworker. These 'assessments' and reports are commonly undertaken by clinical psychologists, social workers or former caseworkers. Their assessment is based on meeting with the child, visiting the child's home, and interviewing the birth parents and other family members and the prospective adoptive parents. The assessor's report involves making an assessment of the best interests of the child and also presenting the child's wishes to the Court. Their role is similar to that of the spokesperson in care order proceedings in Finland (Enroos et al., 2017) or the children's guardian in adoption matters in England and Wales.

In Australia, children do not participate directly in the court process for adoption or the preceding child protection proceedings and have no direct interaction with the decision-maker, although there have been occasions where children have written a note or letter to the judge (noted in their adoption file or decision). This is unlike adoption from care matters in Norway, outlined by McEwan-Strand and Skivenes (2020), where children aged 15 and older can be a party in the case and may be legally represented and directly heard by the County Board. The reservations of judicial officers in Australia about talking with children during the hearing are very similar to the concerns of English judges; they are concerned about their own skill and training to conduct such interviews and the importance of transparency and procedural fairness in any evidence-gathering process (Fenton-Glynn, 2014). It is also rare in adoption matters in Australia for children to be legally represented, although NSW adoption legislation specifies instances when children should be given legal representation and/or a *guardian ad litem* (eg s 122 of the NSW Adoption Act 2000). This is in contrast to child protection or juvenile justice proceedings in NSW and in Commonwealth family law proceedings, where children are routinely legally represented. In essence, this means that few children have direct legal representation and must instead rely upon professionals to interview them to ascertain their views. The advantages and disadvantages of such indirect means of presenting the child's views to the court are outlined by Fenton-Glynn (2014) and Kilkelly (2010). The advantages include the application and value of the skills and training of professionals, and the disadvantages, children's possible dissatisfaction with how their views are interpreted and represented by others.

This chapter focuses on the consideration of the wishes of children from out-of-home care in NSW, the only state in Australia with significant numbers of these adoptions. The term 'wishes' rather than 'views' is used because that is the term used in the legislation.

4 Methodology

This study involved an analysis of 80 published judgements of the Supreme Court of New South Wales during the 13 year period from 2008–2020 in which the court was deciding whether an adoption order should be made for children in out-of-home care by their carers. Published judgements are anonymised and publicly available on the NSW Caselaw website (https://www.caselaw.nsw.gov.au/) and Austlii (http://www.austlii.edu.au/). The judgements were located in Caselaw NSW, AUSTLII and the Judicial Information Research System of the Judicial Commission of NSW, using the search terms, 'adoption', 'adopt*', 'child*', 'contact' and *Adoption Act*.

New South Wales (NSW) is the only jurisdiction in Australia that routinely publishes judgements concerning the adoption of children; it is also the only state in which there are substantial, though still small, numbers of children adopted from out-of-home care. Judgements are not available for all cases in NSW, and mostly focus on contested matters and those with particular points of interest in law to place on record important considerations in decision-making. The published judgements generally follow a set format that outlines the background facts, the legal principles, procedure and evidence under the Adoption Act, the evidence, submissions and consideration and finally the orders.

The research team analysed references in the published judgements to the child's 'wishes and feelings' about the adoption, and the consent of children aged 12 years and older. These references were found in the Judge's summary of the evidence and their comments on the Secretary's submissions (principal officer of the statutory department and applicant for the adoption), the s 91 report by an authorised assessor, affidavits from the adoptive parents and the birth parents, and judicial considerations. These were coded by the research team, using the qualitative data analysis software NVivo.

A set of deductive codes were developed, drawing on the NSW Adoption Act, which specifies that the court is required to be satisfied before making an adoption order that 'as far as practicable and having regard to the age and understanding of the child, the wishes and feelings of the child have been *ascertained* and *due consideration* given to them' (s 90(1)(b)). Accordingly, judgements were categorised according to the assessment of children's views (no judicial reference, minimal to substantial assessment/reference) and the weight given to children's views by judges (no or minimal weight to considerable weight). In addition to the adoption decision, other key decisions around the child's name and contact arrangements with birth family were also considered and coded.

There were 116 children and adolescents involved in these cases. There were 24 siblings groups of 2 to 5 children; most sibling groups (15/24) were two siblings; 57 were single child adoptions. The children ranged in age from 15 months to 17 years; 22 were under 5 years, 34 were aged 5 to 7 years, 37 aged 8 to 11 years, and 23 aged 12 and older.

5 Findings

There were four broad categories of cases based on how the child's views were assessed and considered by NSW Supreme Court judges. The majority of the cases (80%) involved children under the age of 12 so their consent was not required but their wishes and feelings were required to be ascertained where possible and given due weight (s 90). The following discussion outlines the way children's wishes were referred to, and the weight that was attached to them in judicial considerations, as articulated in these published judgements.

5.1 *Reference to or Assessment of the Child's Wishes*

5.1.1   No Reference to the Child's Wishes

In five judgements concerning children aged 3 to 6 years, there was no specific reference to the child's wishes apart from citing s 8 of the Act which listed 'any wishes expressed by the child' as one of the factors to be considered in determining what was in the child's best interests. The consideration was instead concerned with the child's 'feelings' and their attachment to the prospective adoptive parents, based in several cases on the submissions of the statutory department or the s 91 report writer's assessment. In one case, for example, involving a five year-old who had been living with his adoptive parents since he was 3 weeks old, the judge accepted the report writer's assessment that the child had 'a strong and secure attachment' and determined that it was in the child's best interests that 'he become legally what he is in fact already: a member of their family'.

5.1.2   Child is Too Young – 'However'…

The most common category of cases (23 judgments) was that in which the children were considered, in the opinion of the judge, the Department or the report writer, to be 'too young' to be able to ascertain their wishes or too young to understand the adoption process and what it means. In 13 cases, the judge considered or accepted without qualification the opinion of the department or the report writer that the children were 'too young' or that it was inappropriate to ascertain their wishes or views. These children were all under the age of 8, with the exception of one 9 year-old with a disability, and mostly under 5. For example:

> Since Samuel is only 6 years of age, the Department submits that he is too young for his views to be sought. I accept that submission and the defendant does not contend otherwise. (*Re Samuel* [2013] NSWSC 550)

> M is too young to express any wishes. Because of his age, the proposed adoption has not been discussed with him. Thus, in this case, this is a presently irrelevant consideration. [Child was 7 and had lived with the provisional adoptive parents almost since birth] (*Re M* [2011] NSWSC 369)

In 11 cases where children were deemed too young to ascertain their wishes (or their wishes had not been ascertained) or too young 'to understand the adoption process', the judge inferred what the children's wishes and feelings were on the basis of the s 91 report or other evidence before the court about the children's reported sense of belonging, 'attachment', contentment or behaviours. The children in these cases ranged in age from 3 to 9 years. Typically:

> His age ('nearly 7') does not permit him to have complete understanding of the adoption process. ... All that can really be inferred is that he appears to be content to become more closely bound into the family in which he is now living [the only family he has ever known]. (*A Child Proposed for Adoption* [2019] NSWSC 1654 at 169)

> Whilst the children have not reached an age and level of maturity [6 and 5 years] at which they can fairly be expected to express their wishes or to have a detailed understanding of all of the background and circumstances in which the adoption application is made or what adoption means in terms of their legal relationships with their birth parents, siblings, half-siblings and proposed adoptive parents, it is clear from the evidence that they have developed a strong sense of emotional attachment to and belonging with the proposed adoptive parents. (*Adoption of X and Y (anonymised)* [2020] NSWSC 918)

5.2 Weight Given to Child's Wishes

Where children had expressed their wishes about the adoption in some form, the weight that judges gave to those wishes varied from 'minimal' to 'considerable', as coded by the research team. Most of the children in these judgements were 7 to 11 year-olds, below the age of 12 at which their consent was required or at which they could consent to their own adoption.

5.2.1 'Little Weight'

At one end of the spectrum, judges' comments indicated that the child's wishes did not carry much weight in their determination of the child's 'best interests': were 'not a major factor' or given 'some weight'.

In other cases, it was not clear what weight was applied, since the judges simply indicated that they had taken the child's wishes into account or had given them 'due consideration' or 'due weight' – in line with the wording of s 8(1)(d) of the Act.[1] In some cases, 'due consideration' clearly meant 'little':

> As is required by s 8(1)(d) of the Act, I took into account the children's views, giving them 'due weight in accordance with the developmental capacity of the children and the circumstances'. Because of their age [9 and 8 years], I have given their views minimal weight in exercising the Court's discretion to make an adoption order. (*Secretary*, NSW *Department of Communities and Justice v Gabrielle; Re Olivia and Ava* [2020] NSWSC 281 at 14).

In several cases, the children were not necessarily deemed to have a 'full understanding of adoption' but their wishes were reportedly given 'some weight'. Their wishes were also often considered in relation to related issues such as any proposed change of their name (as required by s 101(2) of the Act) or post-adoption contact arrangements with the members of their birth family, primarily their parents.

5.2.2 'Considerable Weight'

At the other end of the spectrum, children's 'wishes and feelings' were accorded more importance, and for example, 'regarded as "a strong factor" ... especially when expressed so clearly and deliberately'. Being an important or 'strong factor' did not mean 'determinative'. In the words of one judge:

> I should make plain that I do not consider even a strong expression of wishes to be determinative of the application. In my respectful view, on

---

1　S 8 (1)(d): ... if the child is able to form his or her own views on a matter concerning his or her adoption, he or she must be given an opportunity to express those views freely and those views are to be given **due weight** [bold added] in accordance with the developmental capacity of the child and the circumstances.

the proper construction of the Act, even a strong wish by a child to be adopted is no more than a very important factor among those matters which the Act requires a decision maker to take into account. (*The Secretary, NSW Dept of FACS v Hanna* [2018] NSWSC 77)

In determining that adoption was the preferred option and in the best interests of the 10 year-old child involved, the judge evaluated the child's wishes as being 'free, informed and rational':

> In dealing with this consideration, s 8(2) of the Act makes mandatory as the first consideration of the decision maker in determining the best interests of the child 'any wishes expressed by the child'. For the reasons and by reference to the evidence which I have set out above, I am satisfied that Evie has a clear wish, which is free, informed and rational, to be adopted by Penny. (*The Secretary, New South Wales Department of Family and Community Services v Zara* [2018] NSWSC 580, at 68).

Further he explained, in relation to 'rationality' and the child's wishes not being determinative:

> ... as any parent or teacher knows, in some circumstances even the rational wishes of a child are not in the child's best interests. That is a judgment which a parent, teacher or, in this case the Court, is familiar with having to make on a child's behalf. Sometimes that decision must be made notwithstanding, and in anticipation of, the strongly expressed objection of the child. (*The Secretary, New South Wales Department of Family and Community Services v Hanna* [2018] NSWSC 77 at 73).

In others, 'due weight' appears to mean 'considerable' but 'not absolute weight'. One judge said, for example, that '"due weight" is not 'absolute weight' or determinative; another referred to the child's wishes being 'accorded the respect they deserve':

> Although she is not quite twelve, J by all accounts is an astute and intelligent person whose views in my view should be given appropriate weight. Of course, once she turns twelve subject to the provisions of the Act being complied with, she would be legally able to give consent. Her views are very important but not determinative. Nonetheless they are to be accorded the respect they deserve. (*Adoption of J K (anonymised)* [2020] NSWSC 789)

It appears that even judges may not be entirely clear what 'due weight' means; in the words of one:

> The weight to be attached to these wishes is not made clear, particularly where the child in question is over the age of 12 years. The legislation, in s 54, provides the minimum age at which a child is likely to be of sufficient maturity to express informed views. Of course, ... that will vary according to the intelligence, characteristics, background and maturity of the individual child and the circumstances of the case. (*Department of Family and Community Services and LH; Re R* [2011] NSWSC 551)

5.3 *Children Aged 12 and Older and Sole Consent*

Children aged 12 and older are in a separate category because an adoption order must not be made for children of this age 'who are capable of giving consent' without their consent, and after they have been counselled and certified to understand the effect of their consent (s 55). Their consent alone is sufficient even if their parents object to the adoption. Even so, the Court must still be satisfied that the adoption is 'clearly preferable in the best interests of the child' to alternative actions (s 90 (3)). The wishes and consent of children of this age are therefore very important but again not determinative, although the way in which judges express their considerations of the child's wishes are considerably stronger for children of this age. One judge, for example, stated that he considered the wishes of four children aged 15, 14, 12 and 9 in one family group to be 'extremely important' and that:

> 'it would be misconceived to ignore their clear and informed wishes' ... 'when they have been living in the same home for nearly their whole lives, where their primary psychological bonds are clearly with the proposed adoptive parents, and when they have expressed their views about the adoption. (*Secretary, Dept of Communities and Justice v OA* [2019] NSWSC 1457 para 91)

In relation to the adoption of a 12 year-old, another judge stated:

> Notably, in the context of the *Adoption Act* and the emphasis it places on the wishes of a child, adoption will accord with PS's wishes. If the Act means anything in directing the Court to take into account his wishes – which have now been formed over some period of time and repeatedly articulated – at least some good reason for not giving weight to those wishes would need to be advanced or apparent, and I cannot see one. (*Adoption of PS* [2015] NSWSC 2159)

5.4 Other Aspects of the Adoption: Birth Family Contact and Change of Name

Other aspects of the adoption that generally need to be considered include whether or not to change the child's (last) name and what contact children will have post-adoption with their birth parents and siblings living elsewhere. The presumption in NSW, unlike other jurisdictions in US and UK, is that adoption will be 'open' and involve face-to-face contact for children with members of their birth family, and particularly with their parents, as long as it is determined to be in the child's best interests. Post-adoption contact largely reflects and continues the arrangements that were in place prior to the adoption, and adoptive parents need to show 'willing' in adoption plans; contact may also be part of the negotiations as to whether birth parents oppose the adoption in some matters (Luu et al., 2019; Wright et al., 2021).

As the following discussion indicates, judicial considerations and report writers' comments about children's wishes and understanding in relation to their name and birth family contact were similar to the assessment of their wishes and the weight given for the adoption per se; in most cases, these comments aligned with those about the adoption.

5.4.1 Child's Last Name

Judges' decisions and comments about children's wishes involved considerations of the child's wish to have the same last name as their adoptive parents to avoid the need to explain why it was different from that of the family they were living with and to help them feel fully part of their adoptive family. The general presumption, citing the general comments of s 91 report writers, was expressed by one Judge in the following terms:

> In my view, it is clear that they should have the family name of the family of which, upon adoption, they will become legal as well as de facto members. They have expressed a clearly articulated desire to have their adoptive mother's name or family recognised in their name in place of the second names that they were given at birth. If that be done, they will continue to bear and be known by the first names which their birth parents gave them. (*Adoption of BJW, JWW, CMW and LW* [2015] NSWSC 2084)

In this case, the children were older than 12 but the wishes of younger children about changing their name were considered and the weight given to their wishes was greater in some cases than in relation to the adoption per se. In one case, for example, the judge indicated the child's wishes in relation to their name change should be given 'full weight' in a significant departure for a child of this young age:

> In my view, a seven year old child would be likely to have the maturity to make that decision, and would be likely to understand the decision if its ramifications were explained. The evidence establishes that P has been asked about the proposed change to her name by her ... Case Manager and has discussed the change more than once with her proposed adoptive parents. I am satisfied that she understands it and that full weight should be given to her wish to share the same name as her proposed adoptive family. (*Adoption of P* [2017] NSWSC 1483)

Similarly, another judge said in relation to an 8 year-old:

> So far as is practicable having regard to the age and understanding of the child, I have, as recorded above, ascertained and given due consideration to his wishes and feelings. ... [In relation to the proposed change of the child's last name] There is no reason to depart from that approach in this case. Insofar as any wishes of the child in this respect can be ascertained, the interest in a new birth certificate is some evidence of a wish on the part of the child to have the surname of the proposed adoptive parents. The child is to have the surname J. [*Adoption of BS* (No.3) [2013] NSWSC 2033]

5.4.2 Birth Family Contact

Judicial comments about children's birth family contact reflected the presumption that open adoption and face-to-face contact is generally beneficial for children; that view tended to outweigh the assessment and weight given to the wishes of younger children. One judge commented, for example, that:

> Developments in adoption law and practice over the last couple of decades have made reasonably clear that contact between an adopted child and birth parents is normally beneficial for the child. Such contact is most likely to work best in the child's interests when it accords with arrangements made between the parties. (*Re TVK* [2012] NSWSC 1629)

The same judge went further in several cases to state that:

> a significant element in meeting the identity needs of a child who does not reside with his or her birth family is birth parent contact...Further, the arrangements for birth parent contact are relevant to whether an adoption order should be made, because they bear on whether the child's identity needs will be addressed, and thus whether adoption is in the

child's best interests. (*Adoption of KH* [2015] NSWSC 274 at 40, 41, *Adoption of* RCC *and* RZA [2015] NSWSC 813 at 88-89, *Adoption of BS*, 25).

Judicial considerations about children's wishes concerning contact with their birth family were largely in response to children's resistance to contact, both for younger children and adolescents. Some judges expressed some concern about leaving it up to children to decide whether contact should take place. In some cases, this was because they saw it as inappropriate to 'cede responsibility' to children in these circumstances; in others it was because of concern that this might 'too easily provide an excuse for adoptive parents not to pursue the question of contact'. In one case, the judge did not support the adoption plan for a child who was nearly seven that included the provision that 'contact will occur only with C's agreement' on the grounds that it was not appropriate and not in the child's longer term best interests to 'effectively ... give a child of six or so years of age the ability to veto contact'. Despite recognising the de-stabilising impact and the child's fear and emotional distress, the judge indicated that continuing contact with the mother was more important for the child's identity issues in the longer term, given there was seen to be no *actual* physical risk to the child:

> ... the child finds his relationship with his birth mother very difficult, destabilising and distressing. However, there is nothing to suggest that contact poses any physical danger, nor any actual risk, as distinct from fear, of abduction. The solution is not to avoid the distress by ceasing contact; as severing the relationship with the birth mother in that way is likely to exacerbate identity issues in later years, but to persevere in working through it. (*Adoption of NG (No 2)* [2014] NSWSC 680)

On the other hand, the same judge considered it appropriate for three older children (aged 16, 15 and 10) who had been distressed by their first contact with their mother in a number of years to 'largely be the arbiters of contact' saying:

> Given the age of the children, I think it is almost inevitable that they will at some stage, express a wish to see their birth mother on further occasions. But in the context of this case, I also think it is important that they largely be the arbiters of that.' (*Director-General, Department of Family and Community Services; re* MAP, SRP *and* BCP [2013] NSWSC 2004, 20).

Similarly, while reflecting on the importance of contact, the judge prioritised the 'very clear and not irrational views' of older children (aged 12 to 17 years):

> Clearly, all four boys do not want any form of contact with [their birth family] and their reasons are clear and considered. While it may be tempting for the Court to consider an order for some alternate form of contact in this case, I have considered this matter deeply, and in the context of my well documented professional record of promoting contact between young people and their birth families in over 100 current cases, I have concluded that to force any form of contact in the face of such considered statements to the contrary by these boys would be to minimise their feelings and concerns in a potentially damaging manner as it could be seen by them as prioritising the requests of [their mother] over their own heartfelt requests. (*Adoption of BJW, JWW, CMW and LW* [2015] NSWSC 2084)

Some judges also indicated that they recognised children's evolving capacity, highlighting the fact that the contact arrangements needed to take account of changes in children's development, and associated changes in their views, activities and lives. For example:

> The plan acknowledges that, as the child grows older, he will begin to have a significant input regarding the way that contact occurs, and the adopting parents agree to support the child in his wishes regarding contact frequency and structure. The plan also makes provision for an exchange of letters, information and photographs, and contemplates telephone and/or email contact. (*Re TVK* [2012] NSWSC 1629)

6   Discussion

References to the child's 'age and understanding' are common in judicial considerations about the proposed adoption, in line with the legislation. There were also other related considerations including: concerns about the impact on children of expressing their wishes, the influence of their parents (birth and adoptive) and others on children's expressed views, and the role of expert reports in the assessment of children's wishes.

Before making an adoption order, judges need to consider whether adoption is 'clearly preferable to other actions'. One option or 'other action' considered by judges in some cases was the possibility of delaying the decision until children are 12 or older and can provide their own consent. This option is sometimes raised by a parent to delay the adoption but may also be considered by the agency which has carriage of the matter because the child's sole consent can then dispense with the need for parental consent so pre-empting a contested hearing. In all the judgements in which this possibility was raised, it was rejected on the grounds that it would unnecessarily delay the decision and because it would shift or cede responsibility for this important decision to the child, with the risk of placing them in a difficult position with their parents. One judge in rejecting the mother's proposal to defer a decision in an adoption involving her 7 year-old son stated:

> ... it seems to me that to take that approach, and effectively leave it to K to decide whether or not he wished to be adopted in five years' time, would contravene the principle in s 8(1)(e1) of the Act, which provides that undue delay in making a decision in respect of the adoption of a child is likely to prejudice the child's welfare, and also that it is not in the interests of K effectively to cede responsibility for making a decision that the court is charged with making about his best interests to him – and potentially place him, who may well then have developed a very good relationship with his birth parents, as well as the adoptive applicants – in the invidious position of having to risk offending one or the other by making a choice. (*Adoption of KH* [2015] NSWSC 274 at 58)

A second and related consideration, for judges and report writers, was whether children's expressed wishes or reluctance to express a view were influenced by their concern about upsetting their parents if they indicated they did wish to be adopted. In one case involving two children aged 10 and 9 who had been living with their adoptive family for over six years, the judge relied upon the evidence of the prospective adoptive mother, as well as the s 91 report writer. The adoptive mother said that the mother had 'whispered something' to the older child and also said to him 'you don't want to be adopted, do you?' and that the child had later said 'words to the effect "I don't want to upset anyone about the adoption" and also "That's why you don't let kids decide".' The judge stated:

> I accept this evidence. ... I am satisfied that, despite what N said to Ms O'D (perhaps in an endeavour to avoid a confrontation with someone he loves) both he and his younger brother do wish to be adopted by Mr and Mrs J. ...

The judge went on to comment on the child's statement:

> N's observation that '[t]hat's why you don't let kids decide' showed remarkable insight on his part. (*Adoption of N and J* [2017] NSWSC 662)

A third and related judicial consideration was whether the child's views were genuine and not influenced by those with a vested interest in the decision. That consideration was often based on the evidence of the s 91 report writer who assesses and reports upon the child's circumstances and wishes, explicit or inferred. In a contested matter in which the child's mother challenged her 14 year-old's sole consent to her own adoption, the judge indicated that he was 'satisfied well beyond the civil standard of proof that Jennifer unequivocally wishes to be adopted by Mary and that Jennifer's consent to her adoption, over and above its formal validity under the Act, is free, informed and rational'. He commented on the s 91 report writer's evidence about the genuineness of the child's views in the following terms:

> I accept that evidence, particularly from a witness such as Ms H who made it clear that she respected and felt concerned for each of Jennifer [child], [adoptive parent and birth mother]. In cross-examination by Ms D, Ms H gave her opinion that Jennifer's expression of desire to be adopted was very much Jennifer's own and not the product of outside pressure or anything similar. Her evidence (which I accept) was that she had 'formed the view that I think Jennifer would like her view to ... hold much more weight than anybody else's'. She's ... very strong — "why aren't people listening to me?" (*The Secretary, NSW Dept of FACS v Hanna* [2018] NSWSC 77 at 66).

Some judges were explicit about the value of the expert evidence and their reliance on it. They were clear in their evaluation of the evidence and indicated their acceptance of it. One judge, for example, indicated that he was 'fortified in his view by the opinions of all three experts'. 'Unaided by them I would not have come to a different view upon all the evidence having had the opportunity of seeing each of the relevant major participants'. Another stated:

> Strictly speaking I am not bound to accept the expert evidence. However, I am in entire agreement with them. They were both informed and highly experienced and each has, from somewhat different vantage points, thoroughly examined the issues and come to similar conclusions. I accept their opinions.

As indicated earlier, children rarely have any direct participation in the court proceedings but in a recent case, a child who was nearly 12, and not yet able to consent to her own adoption, wrote a note that was presented to the court to explain her position. Her note was 'in clear support of adoption: "Dear Judge, I do want to be adopted by [prospective adoptive parents] ... I DO NOT want O [birth parent] to stop that in anyway". The judge noted:

> l am satisfied on the evidence that J does have a sufficient understanding of adoption and the consequences and she should be heard. The evidence supports the conclusion J wants to be adopted. She has said so on numerous occasions, especially to her psychologist, Ms M. She has, however, sometimes wavered in that view. Ms P [Independent Assessor] says, in my view plausibly, that her conduct in that regard appears to be as a result of wishing to appease her mother and avoid conflict. She has written a note to be presented in these proceedings quite clearly expressing that view. (*Adoption of J K (anonymised)* [2020] NSWSC 789).

In another case, the judge said he had considered interviewing an 11 year-old, the oldest of four siblings, who reportedly wanted the adoption to proceed but the judge stated that 'all parties were against that in view of his mental age' (*The Director General Department of Human Services by her delegate, the Principal Officer, Adoptions, Barnardos Australia* [2011] NSWSC 1438). It is quite common now, however, in New South Wales for the judge to meet the child together with their family and friends in a celebratory 'hearing' after the adoption order is made.

7 Conclusions

So what conclusions can be drawn, on the basis of these published judgements, about judicial considerations of children's wishes and evolving capacities in these adoption-from-care matters? To what extent are children's views taken into account, how are they assessed, and what reliance is placed on those assessments?

First, some judges explicitly articulated comments that indicated clear recognition of children's evolving capacities – but references to children's 'age', 'capacity' or 'maturity' were much more common. This is not surprising since the legislation specifically refers to children's 'age and developmental capacity' (s 9(2)) and 'age and understanding' (s 90(1)(b)) so judges are directly using that language.

Age 12 is a clear marker in judicial considerations, largely because that is the age at which an adoption order cannot be made without the child's consent and at which children can provide sole consent to their own adoption. Even at age 12 and older, however, some judges clearly indicated that the child's wishes about the adoption or birth family contact were not necessarily determinative. Given the comments some judges made in deciding that deferring the adoption until the child was 12 was not in the child's best interests, it seems likely their intent was protective – to take the burden and responsibility of the decision from them, in line with Lansdown's (2005) observation that children need to be protected from decisions that may place them under undue burden. Certainly, the published cases indicate that judges recognise that asking a child of 12 or older to provide sole consent to their adoption may place them in an uncomfortable situation, where they are in effect 'choosing' the prospective adoptive parents over their birth parents.

Second, there was a clear overall trend to privilege the wishes of older children, and particularly those over the age of 12 and into middle adolescence. Some judges, for example, referred to it as being 'disrespectful' and 'misconceived' to ignore the 'clear and informed' wishes of children of that age. On what basis did judges determine that the child's wishes were 'clear and informed' or 'free, informed and rational', terms that do not appear in the legislation? Authorised assessors did not use these terms in their s 91 reports either, though in several cases they did address the issue of whether the children's wishes were 'genuine' in response to a parent's challenge. The strength and consistency of the child's wishes were not necessarily a guarantee that judges would deem those wishes and feelings to be 'rational' or to be in the child's best interests. As Daly (2018) commented, courts prefer the 'rational' rather than the 'emotional' when it comes to children's reasons, but more importantly Daly was concerned about the circularity and self-referential reasoning in judges' appraisal of the child's 'maturity' and the rationality or 'goodness' of their wishes. As Daly argues:

> It seems then, that children will be competent/mature if their views on their situation concur with that of the judge, which renders weight for their wishes a moot point. What is the purpose of weighing wishes, if all that means is that the question will in effect be: how similar to the judge's determination are the wishes of the child? (p. 72)

In jurisprudential terms, this is an example of Julius Stone's category of concealed circular reference. As Aroney (2008) explained: 'It occurs when a legal category prescribes as an essential part of its own principle what is actually a restatement or reformulation of the very question in issue, with the result that the principle which should give an answer to the question in issue merely restates the same question in a different way' (p. 115). Is it rational and informed simply because it agrees with the judge's view? Is it likely that judges would see a choice that they would not make as one that could still be rational and informed?

Third, on a related question, what can we conclude about how judges weigh the wishes of children, and particularly younger children who are not yet of an age to consent to their own adoption? Clearly the bar is set higher for children consenting to their own adoption but the Court is required to be satisfied before making an adoption order that 'as far as practicable and having regard to the age and understanding of the child, the wishes and feelings of the child have been ascertained and *due consideration* given to them' (s 90(1)(b). 'Due consideration' or 'due weight' are vague and uncertain terms and seem to mean different things in different matters – ranging from 'very little' to 'a lot'. The vague and indeterminate nature of this term has been criticised by Daly (2018) for not being transparent or consistent, and for providing 'few opportunities for holding decision-makers, usually with enormous discretion, accountable via appeals or other avenues' (Daly, 2018: 288–292). In jurisprudential terms, it is an example like 'due care' and 'reasonableness' of Julius Stone's (1964) 'category of indeterminate reference' calling for 'judicial evaluation on the basis of an indeterminate concept ... predicated on fact-value complexes, not on mere facts' (Stone, 1964, 263–264 cited by Aroney, 2008). In non-legal terms, it is perhaps a term that Humpty Dumpty might be comfortable with: 'It means just what I choose it to mean—neither more nor less'. On the other hand, Lundy, Tobin and Parkes (2019) defend the term 'due weight' in article 12 of the UN CRC in accordance with children's 'age and level of maturity' as 'a practical and justified restraint on the deference to be accorded to children's views given that many children will lack the knowledge, wisdom, and experience to sufficiently understand the implications of their views on some matters affecting them'.

Fourth, it is clear that judges relied on the s 91 reports of the authorised adoption assessors and on the evidence provided in submissions and affidavits by the statutory department or designated adoption agency. Their judgements routinely cited this evidence and indicated agreement with it though several judges indicated that they were not bound by 'these opinions'. The way in which judges referred to children's wishes reflected some of the language of the s 91 reports, including comments about children having 'sufficient maturity and understanding of the emotional and legal effects of an adoption order being made'. Judges routinely referred to the length of time that children had been living with their adoptive family, using terms such as 'virtually their whole lives', and referring to children's 'sense of emotional attachment to and belonging with the proposed adoptive parents'. These were, not surprisingly, correlated: the longer the child had lived with the family, the stronger their 'psychological bond' or 'sense of emotional attachment'.

It is of course to be expected that judges will rely on and cite the s 91 reports of assessors who have met with the child, usually on more than one occasion at their adoptive home. The assessor has the benefit of seeing the child in person and observing how they interact with the members of that family in that setting, as well as talking with them about their awareness, understanding, feelings and wishes about the adoption and related issues such as birth family contact. The court has to rely on the evidence before it, and on the basis of these judgements, the different sources of evidence do appear to be largely consistent even in contested matters. The 80 published judgements which are the basis of this chapter provide a second-hand account of that evidence, as summarised by the judge. Another current study of all 89 Supreme Court adoption from care court files in one calendar year includes both reported/published and unreported matters, and provides much more detail about the reports and affidavits; analyses to date indicate that conflicting evidence between the 'advice' provided to the court in s 91 reports and affidavits is rare; the birth parents' evidence may, however, differ. Further analysis of the full text of these affidavits and s 91 reports will provide deeper insights into the presumptions underlying the 'advice' in these reports and affidavits.

Given their influence on judicial considerations, the quality of these assessments and the nature of the evidence before the court is crucial, particularly since independent legal representation of children in these matters is rare. Since the s 91 report writer may be employed by the designated adoption agency, though not a caseworker, there are concerns about possible conflicts of interest for this agency and that of the statutory department. In its review of the Adoption Act in the next most populous state in Australia, the Victorian Law Reform Commission (VLRC) recommended that all children in adoption matters should have independent legal representation because the Secretary or principal officer of that department is conflicted; those agencies have already made key decisions affecting the child's removal, placement with the prospective adoptive family, and the adoption plan prior to filing the adoption application (VLRC, 2017, para 14.122).

Finally, how do these findings align with those of a comparable study of the decisions of Country Boards in Norway by McEwan-Strand and Skivenes (2020)? That study involved the adoptions of 179 children from public care over a six year period (2011–2016) with the decisions made a by a three-member County Board. McEwan-Strand and Skivenes stated that Norwegian legislation provides extensive and cohesive guidance and requirements concerning children's involvement in these processes; it does not set out a strict age limit but 'a combination of age, capacity and maturity to be considered when assessing whether the child should be involved', with ages 7 and 12 years as key markers in assessing the maturity of the child (p. 642).

McEwan-Strand and Skivenes (2020) concluded that their findings were 'discouraging' for several reasons: because the child's opinion or capacity was assessed for only half the children, and then generally 'a shallow assessment at best'; because age was 'commonly used as a proxy for competency and maturity', and because it was unclear what role the children's opinion played in the cases as well as in the decision-making' (p. 632). Accordingly, the children were 'not given agency' and 'the law was not followed' in many of the cases, despite the clear guidance and requirements for children's involvement in the Norwegian Constitution and the Norwegian Children Act 1981 (p. 661).

In the current study of adoption judgements in NSW, there is no evidence that the law was not followed but as indicated, there are concerns about the assessment of children's wishes and feelings and the lack of independent legal representation in these matters. In all other proceedings affecting children's care, residence and time with parents, children are legally represented, but not in adoption apart from some exceptional circumstances. While the difficult decisions in relation to the child's removal from their family and the determination that there is no realistic possibility that the child will be restored home are made prior to the adoption application, severing the child's legal relationship with their birth family is a crucial decision with life-long effects.

As McEwan-Strand and Skivenes (2020) also found, there was clearly some variability in the approach of judges in NSW in relation to children's wishes. There was also some indication of change over time with fewer children younger than 6 or 7 years being deemed too young to take account of their wishes in the more recent judgements. As in the Norwegian study, it does appear that children under 12 were assessed more in terms of their age and understanding whereas older children, at the age at which their consent was required and at which they could give sole consent to their adoption, were assessed more in terms of their capacity to 'form a well-reasoned and consistent opinion' (p. 660). For some children who were deemed too young to ascertain their wishes and understanding of adoption, the s 91 assessment and evidence spoke to their feelings of emotional security and belonging in the adoptive family.

In relation to possible reforms to adoption in Australia, it is well worth noting the recommendation of the VLRC's review of adoption that:

(1) 'there should not be a fixed age for a child's participation in adoption decisions. The combined effect of the CRC's article 12 (right to be heard) and article 5 (recognition of a child's evolving capacity) requires that a case-by-case approach be taken ... and 'acknowledges that capacity exists

on a spectrum, rather than a hard-line separation between capacity and incapacity.' (para 3.84);
(2) that children should be legally represented throughout the adoption process (para 14.125); and
(3) that judicial reasons be publicly available to provide greater understanding of adoption practice and jurisprudence, and facilitate and support much-needed open adoption research (para 93).

Judicial reasons would also close the feedback loop for children informing them, then and when they are older, why the decision was made and how their wishes and feelings were considered. There are examples of judges in NSW and elsewhere writing their judgements as 'a letter to the child', explaining in a personal and age-appropriate way how they came to their decision (*Re A: Letter to a Young Person* [2017] EWFC 48 in a longstanding relocation dispute in England; Barnes Macfarlane, 2018). In a recent NSW case, for example, the judge systematically explained the views and considerations of the various people involved in the birth and adoptive family, including siblings, and reflected the child's own views:

> As a Judge, I have to be satisfied of two things in an adoption matter. First, I have to be satisfied that there is a kid who is special, and I have to be satisfied that there is a family who loves him.
>
> I have read all of the evidence in this matter.
>
> I can see that C has chosen very well. He has lived with his adoptive family since he was five-months old and so he knows them all very well. ...
>
> So what does C think? Well, C, you are now old enough to give consent, and you have consented to this adoption. You said,
>
> "Yes, I don't get taken away from this family. They are a good family, they love me, I will feel even more a part of the family. They love me and I love them." (*Adoption of X* (Supreme Court (NSW), Rees J, 16 June 2020, unreported).

The longer-term outcomes for children and their reflections on how adoption has worked for them is, of course, the most important link in closing the feedback loop.

Acknowledgements

This chapter is based on the paper presented at the 'CRC-IP Colloquium on Article 5' at Cambridge University, Robinson College, in July 2019. The data analysis was funded by a grant from the NSW Government.

References

Adoption Act 2000 No 75. (NSW) (Austl.). Retrieved from https://www.legislation.nsw.gov.au/#/view/act/2000/75.

Aroney, N., 'Julius Stone and the End of Sociological Jurisprudence: Articulating The Reasons for Decision in Political Communication Cases', *UNSW Law Journal* 2008 (31(1)), 107–135.

Australian Institute of Health and Welfare (AIHW). (2019). *Adoptions Australia 2018–19*. Child welfare series no. 71. Cat. no. CWS 71. Canberra: AIHW.

Australian Institute of Health and Welfare. *Child Protection Australia 2018–19*. Child Welfare Series 2020 no. 72. Cat. no. CWS 74. Canberra: AIHW. https://www.aihw.gov.au/getmedia/3a25c195-e30a-4f10-a052-adbfd56d6d45/aihw-cws-74.pdf.aspx?inline=true

Barnes Macfarlane, L-A. 'Patrick v Patrick Re a Letter to a Young Person: Judicial Letters to Children - an Unannounced, but Not an Unwelcome, Development', *Edinburgh Law Review* 2018 (22), 101–107.

Daly, A., 'No Weight for 'Due Weight'? A Children's Autonomy Principle in Best Interest Proceedings', *The International Journal of Children's Rights* 2018, 26(1) 61–92. doi: 10.1163/15718182-02601012.

Enroos, R., Helland, H.S., Pösö, T., Skivenes, M. and Tonheim, M., 'The role and function of spokesperson in care order proceedings: a cross-country study in Finland and Norway', *Children and Youth Service Review* 2017 (74), 8–16. doi: 10.1016/j.childyouth.2017.01.017.

Family Matters, *Measuring trends to turn the tide on Aboriginal and Torres Strait Islander child safety and removal* 2019. https://www.familymatters.org.au/wp-content/uploads/2020/02/1097_F.M-2019_LR.fupdated.pdf.

Fenton-Glynn, C., 'The Child's Voice in Adoption Proceedings: A European Perspective', *International Journal of Children's Rights* 2013 21(4), 590–615. doi: 10.1163/15718182-55680018.

Human Rights and Equal Opportunity Commission, Commonwealth of Australia, *Bringing them home: Report of the National Inquiry into the Separation of Aboriginal and Torres Strait Islander Children from their Families.* (Sydney: Australian Government, 1997).

Huntington, C., 'The Child-Welfare System and the Limits of Determinacy', *Law and Contemporary Problems* 2014 (77), 221–234.

Institute of Open Adoption Studies, University of Sydney, Response to the House of Representatives Standing Committee on Social Policy and Legal Affairs Inquiry into Local Adoption, May 2018.

Kenny, P., Higgins, D., Soloff, C. and Sweid, R., *Past Adoption Experiences: National Research Study on the Service Response to Past Adoption Practices* (Research Report No. 21, 2012).

Kilkelly, U. (2010). *Listening to Children About Justice: Report of the Council of Europe Consultation with Children on Child-Friendly Justice* (5 October 2010) CJ-S-CH(2010) 14 rev., https://rm.coe.int/168045f81d.

Lansdown, G., *The Evolving Capacities of the Child.* (UNICEF Innocenti Research Centre, Florence).

Luu, B., Wright, A.C., and Cashmore, J., 'Development of Adoption Plans in New South Wales: Post-adoption Contact Arrangements and the Views of Children, Birth Families and Adoptive Families', *Australian Social Work* 2019 (72(4)), 404–418.

Lundy, L. Tobin, J. and Parkes, A. 'Art.12 The Right to Respect for the Views of the Child', in J. Tobin (ed.), *The UN Convention on the Rights of the Child: A Commentary.* Oxford Commentaries on International Law (Oxford, 2019).

McEwan-Strand, A. and Skivenes, M., 'Children's Capacities and Role in Matters of Great Significance for Them: An Analysis of the Norwegian County Boards' Decision-making in Cases about Adoption from Care', *International Journal of Children's Rights* 2020 (28), 632–665. doi:10.1163/15718182-02803006.

Palacios, Jesus et al., 'Adoption in the Service of Child Protection: An International Interdisciplinary Perspective' *Psychology, Public Policy, and Law* 2019 (25(2)), 57–72.

Re A: Letter to a Young Person [2017] EWFC 48 https://www.bailii.org/ew/cases/EWFC/HCJ/2017/48.html.

Ross, N. and Cashmore, J., 'Adoption Reforms New South Wales style: A Comparative Look' *Australian Journal of Family Law* 2016 (30), 51–75.

Sloan, B. 'Adoption versus Alternative Forms of Care' in J. G. Dwyer (ed.), The *Oxford Handbook of Children and the Law* (Oxford Handbooks Online, 2018).

Stone, J. *Legal System and Lawyers' Reasonings* (Stanford: Stanford University Press, 1964).

Victorian Law Reform Commission, *Review of the Adoption Act 1984: Report* (Melbourne, Victorian Government Printer, 2017).

Whitt-Woosley, A. and Sprang, G., 'When Rights Collide: A Critique of the Adoption and Safe Families Act from a Justice Perspective'. *Child Welfare* 2014 (93(3)), 111–134.

Wright, A.C., Luu, B. and Cashmore, J., 'Adoption in Australia: Past, Present and Considerations for the Future', *Australian Law Journal* 2021 (95), 67–80.

CHAPTER 11

Article 5 of the Convention on the Rights of the Child and the Involvement of Fathers in Adoption Proceedings: A Comparative Analysis

Brian Sloan

1   Introduction

Adoption has profound consequences for the child concerned, since it will often[1] produce a severance of the legal relationship between parent and child, and the creation of new legal relationships between the child and a new set of parents. This chapter considers the involvement of fathers[2] in decisions about adoption, particularly in circumstances where a mother resists such involvement. The paper is largely a response to the work of Jill Marshall (2012; 2018), who has forcefully argued in favour of anonymous birth and adoption for children (without involvement of their fathers) as a choice that can be validly exercised by mothers. The argument of this chapter is that Marshall's views are not obviously consistent with the requirements of Article 5 of the UN Convention on the Rights of the Child (CRC), requiring states to 'respect the responsibilities, rights and duties of parents … to provide … appropriate direction and guidance in the exercise by the child of the rights recognized in the present Convention', and other provisions of the CRC such as Articles 7 and 8.

The paper begins by engaging in a detailed policy discussion on issues surrounding the involvement of fathers in the adoption process with reference to Article 5 and other CRC provisions, including whether Article 5 has much to say about adoption at all. With reference to the policy conclusions drawn, it

---

1   Cf. 'simple adoption', a form of adoption available in France and some other civil law jurisdictions, which 'does not sever the relationship with the family of origin so that the adopted child is not entirely integrated into his or her adoptive family': (Council of Europe (2008: [63]).
2   Similar issues could apply to other legal parents who have not given birth to the child. That said, in the United Kingdom, for example, it seems unlikely (albeit not impossible) that a second female parent who has complied with the agreed female parenthood conditions (Human Fertilisation and Embryology Act 2008, s. 44) could end up without parental responsibility, and it will be seen that such responsibility is key to involvement in the adoption process.

goes on to consider the substantive treatment of the issue in the law of England and Wales, Scotland and Ireland respectively.[3]

2   The CRC, Fathers and Adoption: Policy Issues

2.1   *The Core Scenario*

The typical scenario considered in this chapter is where a child is born, perhaps following a fleeting or essentially non-existent relationship (involving sexual intercourse only) between the biological parents, to a mother who wants the child to be adopted by strangers swiftly and without the involvement, or perhaps even the knowledge, of the father. Depending on the facts or the legal system in question, the mother may also have succeeded in, purported to or wished to give birth "anonymously" "in secret", such that no link is even recorded between the child and the mother, let alone between the child and the father. The implications of the CRC for such a scenario, irrespective of the particular national legal system involved, must now be considered.

2.2   *Fathers and the Relevance of Article 5 or Other CRC Provisions*

Article 5 of the CRC requires states to:

> respect the responsibilities, rights and duties of parents or, where applicable, the members of the extended family or community as provided for by local custom, legal guardians or other persons legally responsible for the child, to provide, in a manner consistent with the evolving capacities of the child, appropriate direction and guidance in the exercise by the child of the rights recognized in the present Convention.

The first question to be addressed is whether this particular article has any relevance to the involvement of fathers in the adoption process.

It could be argued that Article 5 has little explicitly to say about adoption. At the very least, it is significantly less relevant to the issue than other provisions of the Convention, particularly Article 21 with its express reference to adoption. I suggest, however, that a key phrase in Article 5 for present purposes is 'in

---

[3] The law in Northern Ireland largely mirrors that in England and Wales on the allocation of parental responsibility (Children (Northern Ireland) Order 1995), but on adoption it is somewhat modelled on the older law in the English Adoption Act 1976, which did not treat child welfare as the paramount consideration and did not apply a straightforward welfare test to dispensing with consent (Adoption (Northern Ireland) Order 1987). This could have varying consequences for both CRC compatibility and involvement of fathers in adoption.

the exercise by the child of the rights recognized in the present Convention'. Whatever the inherent difficulties in apparently recognising parental rights in a children's rights convention, then (see, e.g., McGoldrick, 1991), Article 5 really has any impact only when read alongside the rest of the Convention. Much of the Convention self-evidently does address adoption. Most obviously, Article 21 requires states that recognise the concept of adoption to ensure that 'best interests of the child' 'shall be the paramount consideration', but also requires that the adoption is 'permissible in view of the child's status concerning parents, relatives and legal guardians' and refers to the 'informed consent to the adoption' of relevant persons.

Other potentially relevant CRC obligations include protecting a child's right, 'as far as possible, ... to know and be cared for by ... her parents' (Article 7), respecting a child's right to her identity and 'family relations' (Article 8), ensuring that 'a child shall not be separated from ... her parents against their will, except when competent authorities subject to judicial review determine, in accordance with applicable law and procedures, that such separation is necessary for the best interests of the child' (Article 9), treating a child's best interests as a primary consideration and ensuring 'such protection and care as is necessary for his or her well-being', but 'taking into account the rights and duties of his or her parents' (Article 3), and rendering 'appropriate assistance to parents and legal guardians', who 'have the primary responsibility for the upbringing and development of the child', 'in the performance of their child-rearing responsibilities' (Article 18). All of these are in principle rights *of the child*. Thus, while the phrasing may sometimes be awkward, and these articles may well have more force in the adoption context if considered on a stand-alone basis, by being involved in the adoption process a father is arguably providing 'direction and guidance' to the child (or in practice her representatives where she is too young to form a view) in ensuring that (for example) her rights to have her welfare treated as the paramount consideration (particularly given the uncertainty attached to that concept: Sloan, 2013), to know and be cared for by her parents, or to establish her identity, are respected. While much of the focus of the literature on Article 5 is inevitably on 'evolving capacities' (as evidenced by many of the contributions to this volume), it would surely go too far to suggest that a child has no Article 5 rights where she has yet truly to develop any relevant capacities. Significantly, moreover, it is in its chapter on Article 5 that Unicef's *Implementation Handbook* (Hodgkin and Newell, 2007: 75) notes that '[i]n no sense is the Convention "anti-family", nor does it pit children against their parents', that 'the Preamble upholds the family as "the fundamental group of society and the natural environment for the growth and well-being of all its members and particularly children"', and that '[s]everal articles emphasize the primary responsibility of parents and place strict limits on state intervention and any separation of children from their parents'. Despite the initial impression, then, I suggest that read in its context Article 5 is highly relevant to the situation considered in this chapter, even if it remains less relevant than other articles.

2.3   Mothers and Article 5 etc.

Of course, on particular facts, a swift adoption *could* secure the Convention rights of the child, whether facilitating the paramountcy (Article 21) or primacy (Article 3) of her best interests, protecting the child from 'all forms of physical or mental violence, injury or abuse, neglect or negligent treatment, maltreatment or exploitation' while in the care of parents, legal guardians or others (Article 19), providing 'special protection and assistance' and alternative care where she cannot remain in her home environment (Article 20), protecting the child's 'inherent right to life' and ensuring 'to the maximum extent possible the survival and development of the child' (Article 6), granting her 'the enjoyment of the highest attainable standard of health' (Article 24), 'a standard of living adequate for the child's physical, mental, spiritual, moral and social development' (Article 27), education (Article 28) and special protection if he or she is disabled (Article 23). It could be argued that, in at least some circumstances, a *mother* could invoke Article 5 to say that she is providing 'appropriate direction and guidance' in relation to the exercise of these rights by the child by advocating a swift adoption without the involvement of the father (or potentially other, wider, family members). Conversely, she could argue that any 'direction and guidance' provided by the father if involved would not be 'appropriate'.

As is inevitable much of the time with the Convention (Alston, 1994), then, the question is how to resolve a conflict of norms, or potentially a conflict of the same norm invoked from different perspectives leading to conflicting conclusions.

2.4   Marshall on the CRC and Identity

It is now necessary to summarise the views of Marshall on the core scenario addressed in this chapter, critiquing them with reference to the interpretations of the CRC put forward in the previous sub-sections. For Marshall, any conflict between legal norms relating to the core scenario in this chapter, which on my analysis would include differing interpretations of Article 5, should apparently always be resolved in favour of the mother's wishes, leading to a situation where a father and child may not even be aware of, let alone meet or live with, each other.

In an important initial qualification to her work, however, Marshall (2018: 168) advocates 'a conceptual separation between the one who gives birth and the mother'. Similarly, in her view (2018: 171, n. 25), 'the man who contributes sperm to create the child is not a father by this act alone', such that she 'would like', albeit does not use, 'a different word to denote the distinction between this and genuine fatherhood'. Significantly, Marshall elsewhere (2012) uses quotation marks around the word "father" to reflect her preference. This in itself is potentially problematic for the purposes of Articles 7 and 8.

Much of her view on the nature of motherhood and fatherhood and other points is coloured by the fact (Marshall, 2018: 176) that there is 'no explicit reference in these provisions [of the CRC, among others] ... to the biological family and, although the family in which the child is raised will commonly be the genetic/biological family, this will not always be so, including in secret birth situations'. On Marshall's (2018: 177) analysis, Articles 7 and 8 'were ... drafted to deal with situations of forced removals, quite unlike voluntary secret births and so to which different considerations should apply'.

She expresses concern that (2018: 179): 'the idea of identity presented by ... some interpretations of children's identity rights (... which highlight genetics and biology), depends on an idea of identity based on an unchanging foundational core of the human person', which equates a right to identity with knowledge of genetic or biological origins'. For Marshall (*ibid.*), this has the potential for oppression, in that it 'can be used to justify the state making people feel that they have to bring to fruition and liberate some inner core, to "find out" who they "truly" are'. She fears that (2018: 180) '[p]erpetuating genetic and biological views of what constitutes a child's identity right pits the child against a woman who wishes not to reveal her own identity and/or the identity of the father', and 'risks making the adopted child, who might otherwise have been content, feel he or she is living an inauthentic life, and that his or her right to identity is being contravened and damaged in some way'. This (*ibid.*) 'could also be used, not only to argue for revelation of this information, but to make the woman feel her decision to relinquish a child is inauthentic and impermissible'. Marshall (177) places much emphasis on the qualification, 'as far as possible' in the wording of Article 7 on the right to know one's parents, but that is open to interpretation and does not necessarily *reduce* the extent of protection of informational rights. As Fenton-Glynn (2014: 188) puts it, 'Geraldine Van Beuren [(1995)] rightly argues that this phrase should be read as relating to the practicality of providing the information, not the legality'.

In Marshall's (2018: 179) view, however, '[i]dentity rights pursuant to the CRC ... can ... be interpreted differently' to the focus on genetic origin, in that '[r]ather than focusing on the past, on needing to know everything about other people's lives, including those of one's father and birth giver in a unfairly gendered world, and reducing our identity to blood or genes, it is possible to explore different ways in which we can gain a strong sense of our identity through lived existence and belonging from birth'. Her preference for 'lived existence' may derive some support from Ronen (2004), who argues that the CRC does not go far enough in allowing children to maintain ties meaningful to them.

Marshall (2018: 178) appears to advocate a 'more fluid idea of identity focusing on self-determination through lived experience.' In her view (*ibid.*: 179), 'any human right to identity must be related to care and encourage an environment of belonging and inclusion for any newborn and birth giver', which 'has potential to be a more empowering, positive and kinder way to proceed in this context of secrecy in pregnancy and birth and to help lead to a more gender-equal world'. Further (*ibid.*: 180), '[t]he law could, and should, instead enable everyone to be safe, well, and enabled to have a private life through the provision of care and support', encouraging 'a sense of belonging for both birth giver and children born secretly'. Marshall (2018: 184) considers 'it ... worth reflecting as to why [sympathetic] attitudes towards anonymity [for mothers] are so sparse in times of peace and beyond the case of rape'. In her view, '[f]amily love and connection from birth are ongoing activities and experiences throughout our lives, forming part of the creation of our identity as a project within relationships', and '[s]afe relinquishment can ... safeguard children from infanticide and abuse, abortion, and abandonment on the street'. This is despite the fact that Fenton-Glynn (2014: 193) finds 'no indication that either anonymous birth or baby-boxes have had any effect on the number of abortions or children illegally abandoned or killed', although a more nuanced empirical picture may have emerged since Fenton-Glynn was writing (see, e.g., Klier *et al.*, 2013).

In contrast to her preference, Marshall (2018: 179) cites 'a shift in judicial attitudes' towards openness about genetic origins, apparently in England and Wales, 'that risks being exploited and manipulated, for example, by biological fathers claiming that they should have a relationship with the child despite the opposition of the mother'. It might surely be questioned, however, whether it is really 'manipulation' when having a relationship with her father would be consistent with the child's welfare and rights, or whether there is not equally a risk of 'manipulation' where a mother successfully convinces a judge that it would be undesirable for a child to have a relationship with the father, potentially because the mother simply wants nothing further to do with him (see, e.g., Sloan, 2009).

Ultimately, Marshall (2018: 185) concludes that '[a] sense of identity can be developed based on the encouragement and support provided to a newborn child, infant and young person through love, care and nurturance and building a sense of their own identity throughout life, through the development of self-esteem and self-confidence'. She (2018: 185) asserts that:

> Showing care and respect by listening to, and acting upon, a girl's or woman's choice to relinquish and to keep her pregnancy and birth secret can coincide with a child's best interests and identity rights by assisting the child to live in security and to be cared for by those who love, want, support, and are capable of looking after the child. Providing social conditions to improve care and belonging for both the child born secretly and the secret birth giver can be part of a process to bring about such freedom.

There is clearly much of merit in Marshall's arguments. There is certainly a case for suggesting that "identity" rights for the purposes of Article 8 would be overly narrowly interpreted if they were said to relate solely to biological or genetic origins. The reference to creating the impression of an "inauthentic life" for someone not raised by the biological family arguably reflects Robert Leckey's (2015) critique of arguments in favour of greater access to genetic information for those who are donor-conceived or adopted. On Leckey's (*ibid.*: 527) analysis, such arguments 'oppose the incomplete, insecure identity of adopted or donor-conceived individuals to the ostensibly complete, secure identity of those raised by their putatively genetic parents', such that they 'exaggerate what is distinct, and harmful, about being adopted or donor-conceived'. But there is surely a significant risk of social engineering if the state uses "lived experience" or "lived existence" to justify the de-emphasis of biological origins as aspects of identity, particularly since the child will not have much in the way of lived experience at the time of relinquishment in the core scenario considered in this chapter. As for Article 7, Bainham (1999: 38) forcefully argues that, because of the history and context of the CRC, '"parents" in the Convention was intended to mean genetic parents and ... the onus is very firmly on those who would argue for an unconventional interpretation'. Moreover, the United Kingdom entered a declaration on ratification of the CRC to the effect that it interprets the references in the Convention to "parents" to mean only those persons who, as a matter of national law, are treated as parents' (United Nations, 2019). While this declaration could cause difficulty *after* adoption in relation to knowledge or contact with birth parents (Sloan, 2014), it surely adds weight to the view that in the core scenario under discussion in this chapter, "parents" must mean biological parents, who are *prima facie* the legal parents under English law. Otherwise, a child could be rendered legally parentless for the purposes of the CRC, and deprived of Article 7 rights, unless and until adopted. Similar considerations would also apply to references to parents in Article 5, *inter alia*, albeit that Article 5 clearly encompasses the right to receive appropriate direction and guidance from those who are not "parents" but otherwise have legal or de facto responsibility for the child, which may include prospective adopters on particular facts.

It must be recognised that Marshall is arguing that genetic origins should be lessened as an aspect of identity. This is in contrast to what the Committee on the Rights of the Child says about anonymous birth, and access to information. Marshall (2018: 171) notes, with apparent concern, that 'there appears to be a growing assumption that fathers, and wider family members, ought to know of the child's existence', noting (177) that the CRC Committee has 'expressed concern at what it describes as the "alarming spread" of the use of baby boxes in certain parts of Europe', citing Ramesh (2012). Such boxes, as Fenton-Glynn (2014: 186) puts it, 'allow parents to leave children in the care of the state anonymously'. They 'commonly take the form of an incubated crib in a hospital or child welfare centre'. When a child is placed by the mother in the crib, 'a bell is rung, and the mother can leave anonymously before a carer comes to take the child. After a waiting period ranging from two to eight weeks, depending on the jurisdiction, the child is then placed for adoption'. In a Concluding Observation relating to the Czech Republic, the Committee on the Rights of the Child (2011: [49]-[50]) expressed itself 'seriously concerned about the State party's so-called "Baby Box" programme, which is in violation of, *inter alia*, Articles 6, 7, 8, 9 and 19 of the Convention' and:

> ...strongly urge[d] the State party to undertake all measures necessary to end the "Baby Box" programme as soon as possible and expeditiously strengthen and promote alternatives, taking into full account the duty to fully comply with all provisions of the Convention. Furthermore, the Committee urge[d] the State party to increase its efforts to address the root causes which lead to the abandonment of infants, including the provision of family planning as well as adequate counseling and social support for unplanned pregnancies and the prevention of risk pregnancies.

Concern has also been expressed by the UN about the exclusion of fathers from adoption processes. The *Handbook* (Hodgkin and Newell, 2007: 296) opines that '[s]tates should reconsider ... laws that do not permit fathers of children born outside marriage to have any potential rights in adoption procedures', and the Committee on the Rights of the Child (2004: [42]) has referred to the need for 'both legal parents' to consent to adoption. The UN Guidelines on the Alternative Care of Children (UN General Assembly, 2010: [10]), moreover, provide that '[s]pecial efforts should be made to tackle discrimination on the basis of any status of the child or parents', including, *inter alia*, 'birth out of wedlock' and 'all other statuses and circumstances that can give rise to relinquishment, abandonment and/or removal of a child'.

As Hodgkin and Newell (2007: 296) put it, the Committee has 'made clear that adopted children have the right to be told they are adopted and to know the identity of their biological parents, if they so wish, which implies keeping accurate and accessible records of the adoption'. The Committee (2004: [40]) has expressed 'concern at [a] practice of keeping the identity of biological parents of the adoptee secret'. Hodgkin and Newell (2007: 107) assert that 'children's right to know their parentage could only be refused on the grounds of best interests in the most extreme and unambiguous circumstances', and advises states to ensure that 'information about genetic parents is preserved to be made available to children if possible'. Their *Handbook* (*ibid.*: 108) appears to suggest that states should facilitate the collection of information for future distribution even where the mother faces a risk of 'extreme forms of social condemnation, such as ostracism, injury or death'. This is an extreme proposition (Besson, 2008), and while the *Handbook* is endorsed by the Chairs of the Committee and aims to synthesise the Committee's views, it does not cite a specific source for its assertion. But even if it is possible to argue that the *Handbook* states the position too strongly, if genetic/biological aspects are still *part* of a child's identity to some extent, there should surely be some scrutiny as to the reasons why such secrecy is necessary on the particular facts. It should be borne in mind that the child did not choose to be born at all, or indeed to be relinquished and brought up outside the biological family. The mother, by contrast, except in the very difficult case of rape, did choose to engage in an activity (namely sexual intercourse) that could (even if this was not intended) produce a child. It is not immediately clear that the mother's interest in keeping that choice secret should automatically prevail over the child's interest when she desires it, even if on particular facts Marshall is correct to say that those interests might coincide. There is surely a distinction between saying that a mother must raise a child and is not permitted to relinquish him or her (which none of the legal systems to be considered in the next section of this chapter do), and saying that the mother can simply decide that there should be no link whatsoever between her (and/or the father) and the child. On Fenton-Glynn's (2014: 190) analysis, 'anonymous birth and relinquishment allow the mother to unilaterally decide the extent to which a child's rights can be exercised'. While there may be a limited justification for this phenomenon within Article 5, as she notes it 'deprives the child and his or her father from establishing any relationship, denying the father the chance to care for the child if he so wishes'.

Further (*ibid.*: 191), '[t]he right of a child to be cared for by his or her parents is not predicated on the sex of that parent' (see Sloan, 2019 on Article 2 and discrimination between parents as regards parental responsibility), and 'there is no reason why the mother should be permitted to choose the involvement of the father in the child's life, even if she has been the one who has given birth'.

There is also a paradox in Marshall's argument: she (quite reasonably to a significant degree in the practical sense) denies the obligation of the person who has given birth to be a "mother", but at the same time advocates the right of that person to determine conclusively whether the resulting child should have any relationship at all with the biological family. In any event, as Fenton-Glynn (2014: 191) puts it, chiming with what I have argued above, rights 'to refuse motherhood, and to escape defined societal roles and the moral and legal obligations imposed on parents ... are not predicated on anonymity, but can be achieved simply through placing the child for adoption in a conventional manner'.

In my view, Article 5, *inter alia*, means that a biological father should be presumptively entitled, for the benefit of the child, to know that his child exists and have some level of involvement in the adoption proceedings. Where it is proposed that this should not occur (and Fenton-Glynn (2017) accepts that there can be no absolute duty to involve the father even when writing from a children's rights perspective, agreeing to that extent with Marshall), it should be by virtue of a clear judicial finding that, exceptionally, it would be contrary to the best interests of the child for the father to be informed or involved, and the father should not be excluded based on the mere whim or preference of the mother alone. In the language of Article 5, there must be some independent evaluation of which parent's (likely) 'direction and guidance' is most 'appropriate' or consistent with the child's best interests. While Article 8 identity-based rights should not be limited to the biological/genetic manifestations of the concept, they should certainly *include* those elements, and it should be no answer to an allegation that Article 8 has been breached that the "identity" of a particular child has been artificially adjusted by the state at the behest of the mother such that it no longer includes that child's biological parents. Convention rights mean that "anonymous" or "secret" births are potentially problematic and should be subject to regulation if permitted. Presumptively, then, the biological parents should be the parents for the purposes of Articles 7 and 5 *inter alia*. For Marshall's argument prioritising the choice of mothers to be considered valid, such that there is no real scrutiny of what constitutes a child's best interests on particular facts, I would suggest that a route would have to be found outside the corners of the CRC (given its emphasis on child welfare). It must be conceded, however, that matters may be more complicated in circumstances where the mother herself is a child (meaning under the age of 18 by virtue of UNCRC, Article 1) at the time she gives birth. The next section of this chapter measures the legal approaches within the British Isles against these suggested implications of the CRC.

3 Substantive Law

3.1 *England and Wales*

Unlike the situation in France and several other jurisdictions (Marshall, 2018; Fenton-Glynn, 2014), the person who gives birth to a child in England and Wales is obliged to register the birth within 42 days (Births and Deaths Registration Act 1953, s. 2). If she is married to the father, that obligation is shared with her husband, but if not, the mother has it alone and is not currently obliged to provide any information about the father on registration (Births and Deaths Registration Act 1953, s. 10; cf. Welfare Reform Act 2009, Sch. 6, considered further below). Despite the obligation to register and be registered in the first instance, the mother will nevertheless be able to consent to the placement of the child for adoption (Adoption and Children Act 2002, s. 19), and to give advance consent to the adoption itself (Adoption and Children Act 2002, s. 20) by virtue of her automatic parental responsibility (see further Sloan, 2019), albeit that the process cannot be completed without a court order made when treating the child's welfare as the paramount consideration (Adoption and Children Act 2002, ss. 1, 46), with that welfare significantly including the effect throughout the child's life of ceasing to be a member of the birth family (Adoption and Children Act 2002, s. 1(4)(c)).

On Marshall's (2018: 172) analysis, the English case law, 'indicates that the father has no right to know of the child's existence or, if there is a right, it can be lawfully interfered with'. There is, however, an obligation in secondary legislation, 'where the father of the child does not have parental responsibility for the child and the father's identity is known to the adoption agency' (Adoption Agencies Regulations 2005/389, r. 14(3)), and where the agency 'is satisfied it is appropriate to do so', to provide counselling, explain to him the legal effect of adoption and related processes, ascertain his wishes and feelings on the adoption, and ascertain whether he wishes to apply for parental responsibility and/ or another relevant order (Adoption Agencies Regulations 2005/389, r. 14(4)). But it is clear that there is much local authority discretion.

The leading case on involvement of fathers in adoption is now *Re A, B and C (Adoption: Notification of Fathers and Relatives)* [2020] EWCA Civ 41 (see Fenton-Glynn, 2017 and Sloan, 2009, 2013, 2017 and 2018 for discussion of previous relevant case law, including *Re C (A Child) (Adoption: Duty of Local Authority)* [2007] EWCA Civ. 1206). In *Re A, B and C*, the Court of Appeal considered three separate appeals on the issue and conducted a comprehensive review of the law. Somewhat controversially, and not necessarily consistently with Article 21 of the CRC, it held that child welfare is not paramount on the question whether a father or other relatives should be notified about a child's existence or proceedings that could ultimately lead to the child's adoption. The matter was held to be neither a decision 'relating to the upbringing of a child' for the purposes of section 1(1) of the Children Act 1989 or 'relating to the adoption of a child' for the purposes of section 1(1) of the Adoption and Children Act 2002, but rather one about 'who should be consulted about such a decision' (*Re A, B and C*, [83]). As such, the correct approach was to balance the interests of the various parties involved in a fact-sensitive manner.

In expounding the balancing approach, the Court of Appeal noted that where a mother desires confidentiality, her right to respect for private life under the European Convention on Human Rights is engaged and can be infringed only when necessary to protect the rights of others. That said, the 'profound importance' of adoption is clearly capable of overriding the mother's request ([85]), depending on the circumstances. The Court noted the pitfalls of the 'often limited and one-sided nature of the information available', emphasising that '[t]he confidential relinquishment of a child for adoption is an unusual event and the reasons for it must be respectfully scrutinised so that the interests of others are protected' ([85]). In achieving a fair balance on the facts, relevant factors would include: parental responsibility, whose possession by the father would cause 'compelling reasons' to be required before confidentiality could be justified, Article 8 rights, the substance of the relationships between the protagonists, the likelihood of a family placement, the impact on the mother and others of notification, cultural and religious factors, the availability and durability of the confidential information and the impact of delay. Ultimately, 'maintenance of confidentiality is exceptional' ([85]).

In each of the three cases before it, the Court of Appeal refused to sanction confidentiality. In the *A* case, the mother and father were students who previously had a 4½-year relationship. *Inter alia*, the judge had attached undue weight to the alleged impact of disclosure on the mother and her view that the father was unlikely to have anything to offer, failing to achieve an appropriate balance. His decision was overturned. In *B*, paternity was uncertain and the mother had been abused. But a family placement was possible, the judge had appropriately balanced the factors and the local authority should continue its enquiries. In the *C* case, the parents were married with other children but the mother alleged that the child concerned had been conceived as a result of rape and she was worried about the reaction of the father if he found out about the child. Despite the circumstances, confidentiality would be an 'extremely strong course to take' in light of the father's parental responsibility automatically conferred by marriage. The parental responsibility meant that the father's consent was *prima facie* required to any adoption, albeit that it could be dispensed with where the child's welfare 'require[d]' it (Adoption and Children Act 2002, s. 52). Disclosure was held to be appropriate on the facts.

The framework set out in *Re A, B and C* clearly runs contrary to Marshall's preference and is closer to according with the interpretation of Article 5 put forward in the last section of this chapter. It remains the case, however, that on particular facts a mother may still be given an effective veto. It is highly significant, for example, that the Court of Appeal regarded *Re C (A Child) (Adoption: Duty of Local Authority)* [2007] EWCA Civ. 1206) as 'plainly correctly decided' (*Re A, B and C*, [5]). *Re C* involved a mother who had become pregnant after a one-off sexual encounter, and who made it clear that she wished the resulting child to be adopted shortly after birth. She kept the pregnancy secret from her own parents and the biological father, who did not have parental responsibility, and refused to identify him. The local authority charged with the child's care and eventual adoption sought judicial guidance on whether it should attempt to identity the father (it being likely that it could do so if independent enquiries were made), inform him of the child's birth and possible adoption and assess him as a potential carer even though he did not have parental responsibility. The Court of Appeal ordered the local authority not to take any steps to identify the father. The priority was held to be finding a permanent home for the child, who was four months old by the time of the hearing, without any further delay. This, on the court's analysis, was the course of action most compatible with the child's best interests, and there was no evidence that the father could care for her based on what the mother had told the court. But the precise nature of the parents' relationship is not given detailed consideration in the Court of Appeal's judgments, which is problematic. This may simply have been a case where the mother, irrespective of the child's interests, did not disclose the resulting pregnancy to the father simply because she wanted nothing further to do with him, although it does reflect Marshall's preference. In *A, B and C*, however, the Court of Appeal described *Re C* as:

> ...a strong case on its facts, there being no reason to doubt the mother's account that her relationship with the father had been a fleeting one, with the consequence that her wish for privacy was always likely to prevail ([66]).

I would respectfully, suggest, however, that it is not necessarily clear that *Re C* is consistent with the Court of Appeal's own approach in the later case of *Re A, B and C*, and particularly its concern about the potentially one-sided nature of the information provided by the mother.

The focus on the relationship between the parents is also shown by the significance of the presence or absence of parental responsibility, and its impact on consent. This, in turn, is reflected in the Court of Appeal's conclusion in the C element of the *Re A, B and C* decision. Since most fathers not married to the mother of their children obtain parental responsibility (usually through registration on the child's birth certificate (Children Act 1989, s. 4(1)(a); only 5.2 per cent of births were registered by the mother alone in 2016 (Office for National Statistics, 2017: 8)), it would be an exaggeration to say that English law excludes unmarried fathers from a *prima facie* requirement to consent to adoption as a rule. But the key point is that parental responsibility for an unmarried father requires either co-operation from the mother or a court order. In this paper's core scenario, the mother is actively trying to prevent the father from having any involvement in the child's life, and if a father does not even know about the child's existence, he is hardly likely to seek a court order that he does not realise he needs.

Schedule 6 to the Welfare Reform Act 2009 could in principle have ameliorated this effect. Somewhat consistently with several other jurisdictions (Sloan, 2017) it would have obliged mothers not married to the fathers of their children to register those fathers as such, except in ostensibly limited, albeit arguably exploitable, circumstances (Department for Children, Schools & Families 2010). But it seems that it will not be brought into effect (Clifton, 2014). It is arguable that, even following *Re A, B and C*, the law should attach greater importance to the child's likely de facto relationship with the father, rather than (at times formalistically) the relationship between the parents per se.

In an overall sense, English law rhetorically complies with the requirements of Article 5 by presumptively at least involving fathers irrespective of parental responsibility and excluding them only in "exceptional" circumstances, even if it is ultimately possible to order adoption against the wishes of fathers. It remains to be seen, however, whether this "exceptionality" will always be truly present even in light of *Re A, B and C*. There may still be scope (*inter alia* because of the unsatisfactory law on parental responsibility allocation) for judges simply to act according to the personal preference of the mother in excluding the father, largely in a manner advocated by Marshall but in my view unfavourable in the light of the requirements of the CRC.

3.2 Scotland

It is claimed that the adoption of children looked after by the state in Scotland 'does not happen very often' (Kidner, 2012:10), and the policy context of adoption in England and Scotland may therefore differ (Sloan, 2016). There are also apparently fewer reported cases on the subject of this chapter. The basic structure of Scots law's response to this paper's core scenario, however, is essentially the same as in England, including on birth registration (Registration of Births, Deaths and Marriages (Scotland) Act 1965; cf. Scottish Government 2018, Part 12) and the paramountcy of welfare (Adoption and Children (Scotland) 2007, s. 14).

In Scotland, a "parent" whose consent is *prima facie* required for a child's adoption means a parent who 'has any parental responsibilities or parental rights in relation to the child' or does not have them 'by virtue of a permanence order which does not include provision granting authority for the child to be adopted' (Adoption and Children (Scotland) 2007, s. 31(15)). As in England, the consent of even such a father can still be dispensed with on the basis that child's welfare 'requires' it (Adoption and Children (Scotland) Act 2007, s. 31(3)(d) of the 2007 Act, even if the grounds for dispensing with consent 'are specified in greater detail than in sec 52(1) of the [English] 2002 Act' (*S v. L* [2012] UKSC 30, [25]). The 'welfare requires' provision in section 31(3)(d) of the 2007 Act applies only where the parent has parental responsibilities or rights or is likely to be given them in the future (Adoption and Children (Scotland) 2007, s. 31(5)), and it cannot be said that the parent is 'unable satisfactorily' to discharge or exercise those rights or responsibilities and 'is likely to continue to be unable to do so' (Adoption and Children (Scotland) 2007, s. 31(4)). It has thus been described as 'a residual ground' (*S* [2014] CSIH 42, [28]). Section 31(3)(d) is narrower in scope in the context than the equivalent ground in the English 2002 Act. While it directs a court to consider the extent to which a parent can look after a child effectively (now or in the future) before dispensing with consent, it also underlines the fact that consent can in principle be dispensed with even where no such finding can be made (see further Sloan, 2016).

While the father will have parental rights and responsibilities where he is 'married to the mother at the time of the child's conception or subsequently' (Children (Scotland) Act 1995, s. 3), if he is unmarried he will have such rights and responsibilities if he has been registered as the father on the child's birth certificate (from May 2006 under s. 3) (including re-registration, unlike in England and Wales), by registered agreement with the mother (Children (Scotland) Act 1995, s. 4) or by court order (Children (Scotland) Act 1995, s. 11). Importantly, as Norrie (2013: [6.09]) describes and as reflects the current situation in England and Wales, '[t]he father must have the co-operation of the mother to be registered [on the birth certificate], and so, in the absence of any court decree, the mother is the "gatekeeper" to the father's entitlement to parental responsibilities and parental rights', albeit that (again broadly consistently with England and Wales), only 4.3 per cent of birth registrations in 2016 were sole ones (National Records of Scotland, 2017). The obligations of an adoption agency under secondary legislation towards a father without parental rights and responsibilities are also notably similar to those in England (Adoption Agencies (Scotland) Regulations 2009/154, r. 14). Scots law therefore raises similar issues to English law in relation to the scenario under discussion for the purposes of CRC compatibility, however much relevant case law is lacking.

3.3   Ireland

Adoption has had a controversial history in Ireland, involving extreme secrecy (cf. now Adoption (Information and Tracing) Bill 2016, not yet passed at the time of writing) and stigmatised unmarried mothers cruelly treated in mother and baby homes and essentially forced to agree to the child's adoption (McCaughren and Lovett, 2014). Conversely, *married* parents were unable voluntarily to have their child placed for adoption until a change to the Constitution (Irish Constitution, article 42A.3) and the implementation of the Adoption (Amendment) Act 2017 (see further Sloan, 2018a). It must be noted at the outset that an adoption order may be made by the *quasi*-judicial Adoption Authority rather than a court in Ireland, but it will be seen that courts do have a role to play in the scenario with which this chapter is concerned. The welfare of the child is now the 'paramount' consideration (Adoption (Amendment) Act 2017, s. 9), rather than the 'first and paramount' one (Adoption Act 2010, s. 19 (pre-amendment)), consistently with both England and Scotland and Article 21 of the CRC.

In its Concluding Observations on Ireland's initial report, the Committee on the Rights of the Child (1998: [17]) was concerned 'about the disadvantaged situation of children born of unmarried parents due to the lack of appropriate procedures to name the father in the birth registration of the child', which 'also has an adverse impact on the implementation of other rights in relation to adoption which, under current regulations, can take place without the consent of the father'. Whatever the general obligations placed on parents in relation to birth registration (Civil Registration Act 2004, s. 19), it remains true that information about the unmarried father is not required to be registered (Civil Registration Act 2004, s. 22). While reforms were enacted to require information about the father to be recorded except in limited circumstances (Civil Registration (Amendment) Act 2014), these have yet to be commenced and do not grant substantive rights in relation to adoption in any event.

As regards adoption specifically, the basic position (subject to the ability to dispense with consent) is now that an adoption order cannot be made 'without the consent of every person, being the child's mother or guardian or other person having charge of or control over the child' (Adoption Act 2010, s. 26). This may exclude a father who is not a guardian, albeit that the relevant Authority is under a basic duty to 'take such steps as are reasonably practicable to ensure that every relevant non-guardian of the child is consulted in relation to the adoption', except in limited circumstances (Adoption Act 2010, s. 30). One such circumstance is where the adoption authority is satisfied that, 'having regard to' 'the nature of the relationship between the relevant non-guardian of a child and the mother or guardian of the child', or 'the circumstances of the conception of the child', 'it would be inappropriate for the Authority to consult the relevant non-guardian in respect of the adoption of that child' (Adoption Act 2010, s. 30(3)). There, with court approval, the adoption can proceed without consultation with that non-guardian. A 'relevant non-guardian' includes a father who is not a guardian (Adoption Act 2010, s. 3), and a father (in turn) includes a person who 'believes himself to be the father of the child' (Adoption Act 2010, s. 30(1)). Where the father 'is unknown to the Authority and the mother or guardian of the child will not or is unable to disclose the identity of that father', the Authority is obliged to 'counsel the mother or guardian of the child, indicating' 'that the adoption may be delayed', 'the possibility of that father of the child contesting the adoption at some later date', 'that the absence of information about the medical, genetic and social background of the child may be detrimental to the health, development or welfare of the child', and 'such other matters as the Authority considers appropriate in the circumstances' (Adoption Act 2010, s. 30(4)). After it has done so, the Authority 'may, after first obtaining the approval of the High Court, make the adoption order without consulting [the] father' if 'the mother or guardian of the child either refuses to reveal the identity of that father of the child, or provides the Authority with a statutory declaration that he or she is unable to identify that father', and 'the Authority has no other practical means of ascertaining the identity of that father' (Adoption Act 2010, s. 30(5)).

It can be seen that, for reasons of practicality, the mother retains much control over the process, and much will depend on the exercise of a value judgment by the adoption authority and the court. A possible advantage of the Irish position for the purposes of Article 5, however, is that the circumstances in which a father need not be consulted (alongside what is to be done where the mother will not cooperate) are fairly clearly set out in primary legislation, rather than being the subject of an open-ended assessment and/or weak obligations in secondary legislation. The 'counselling' obligation imposed on the Adoption Authority displays an admirable understanding of the notion of identity and other matters as understood by the Convention and the Committee.

It should nevertheless be noted that the consent to the adoption of a(n unmarried) father who is not a 'guardian or other person having charge of or control over the child' is still not required in the first place (Adoption Act 2010, s. 26(1)), albeit that fathers are more likely to have guardianship by virtue of the reforms introduced by the Children and Family Relationships Act 2015 (Guardianship of Infants Act 1964, s. 2(4A)). As in both England and Scotland, unmarried fathers do not, as a category, automatically acquire "guardianship" (equivalent to parental responsibility or parental responsibilities and rights) for their children. Unlike in those jurisdictions, however, even an unmarried father can in some circumstances obtain guardianship without either the mother's agreement or a court order (see further Sloan, 2019). At first glance, this is encouraging for the purposes of Article 5 etc., albeit that it is still predicated on a relatively substantial relationship between the parents that may not be present in this paper's core scenario. The final Children and Family Relationships Act's formulation is that an unmarried father will be a guardian if he 'and the mother of the child concerned have been cohabitants for not less than 12 consecutive months occurring after the date on which [the relevant] subsection comes into operation, which shall include a period, occurring at any time after the birth of the child, of not less than three consecutive months during which both the mother and the [father] have lived with the child' (Guardianship of Infants Act 1964, s. 2(4A)), and it is expressly provided that '"cohabitant" shall be construed in accordance with' the Civil Partnership and Certain Rights and Obligations of Cohabitants Act 2010 (Children and Family Relationships Act 2015, s. 2). The new provision is clearly an improvement on the previous law (similar to that in England and Scotland), though it still places much control for the automatic granting of guardianship in the hands of the mother (Treoir, 2014: [2.1.1]).

Under the 2010 Act as amended in 2017, the consent *prima facie* required of a relevant parent can be dispensed with (with court approval) where, *inter alia*, parents have failed in their duty towards the child for 36 months 'to such extent that the safety or welfare of the child is likely to be prejudicially affected', that there must be 'no reasonable prospect that the parents will be able to care for the child in a manner that will not prejudicially affect his or her safety or welfare', and that the child must have been in the 'custody' of the applicants for at least 18 months (Adoption (Amendment) Act 2017, s. 24). There is a new requirement (alongside the pre-existing one that 'by reason of the failure, the State, as guardian of the common good, should supply the place of the parents') that 'the adoption of the child by the applicants is a proportionate means by which to supply the place of the parents' (Adoption (Amendment) Act 2017, s. 24).

Overall, despite (or perhaps because of) its difficult history with adoption, in many ways Ireland takes an approach that is likely to be consistent with the interpretation of the CRC put forward in this chapter. Conversely, Irish Law is not fully consistent with the approach advocated by Marshall.

4 Conclusion

There are, of course, legitimate debates to be had about whether children's rights and welfare should be prioritised to the extent that appears to be undertaken by the CRC. It is also arguable that the stance taken by this chapter risks simply furthering the interests of one parent (the father) over another (the mother) in the adoption process, which is not necessarily any more conducive to furthering the interests of the child. But within the confines of the CRC, it is doubtful whether the secrecy advocated by Marshall on adoption can be justified. The jurisdictions under scrutiny in this chapter offer a preferable approach. It must be emphasised that, even where a father is involved in the adoption process and objects to adoption, it remains perfectly possible to dispense with his consent, essentially on the basis of child welfare, in England, Scotland and Ireland. Moreover, there is still value in involving fathers from an informational perspective even if they prove unsuitable to care for or even have a relationship with the child: while this was rejected in the English case of *Re C* (still regarded as correctly decided In *Re A, B and C*), Fenton Glynn (2017) has criticised the Court of Appeal for the purposes of the CRC for taking an unduly narrow view of welfare there. From an Article 5 perspective, it seems preferable that neither fathers nor mothers should have essentially uncontested authority either to cause or prevent an adoption, even if this chapter has had to concede that Article 5 has less to say on adoption than other provisions of the Convention.

Acknowledgement

The author is grateful, subject to the usual disclaimer, for the comments of participants at the CRC-IP Article 5 colloquium in Cambridge and the anonymous reviewer on an earlier version of this chapter.

References

Alston, P., "The Best Interests Principle: Towards a Reconciliation of Culture and Human Rights", *International Journal of Law and the Family* 1994 (8(1)), 1–25. DOI: https://doi.org/10.1093/lawfam/8.1.1.

Bainham, A., "Parentage, Parenthood and Parental Responsibility: Subtle, Elusive Yet Important Distinctions" in A. Bainham, S. D. Sclater and M. Richards (eds.), *What is a Parent? A Socio-Legal Analysis* Oxford: Hart Publishing, 1999. DOI: 10.5040/9781472561961.ch-002.

Besson, S., "Enforcing the Child's Right to Know her Origins: Contrasting Approaches under the Convention on the Rights of the Child and the European Convention on Human Rights", *International Journal of Law, Policy and the Family* 2007 (21(2)), 137–159. DOI: https://doi.org/10.1093/lawfam/ebm003.

Clifton, J., "The Long Road to Universal Parental Responsibility: Some Implications from Research into Marginal Fathers", *Family Law* 2014, 44(6), 858–861.

Committee on the Rights of the Child, "Consideration of Reports Submitted by State[ ] Parties under Article 44 of the Convention – Concluding Observations: Ireland" (Initial Report), CRC/C/15/Add.85, 1998.

Committee on the Rights of the Child, "Consideration of Reports Submitted by State[ ] Parties under Article 44 of the Convention – Concluding Observations: Papua New Guineau" (Initial Report), CRC/C/15/Add.2294, 2004.

Committee on the Rights of the Child, "Consideration of Reports Submitted by State[ ] Parties under Article 44 of the Convention – Concluding Observations: Uzbekistan" (Second Report), CRC/C/UZB/CO/2, 2006.

Committee on the Rights of the Child, "Consideration of Reports Submitted by State[ ] Parties under Article 44 of the Convention – Concluding Observations: Czech Republic" (Third and Fourth Reports), (CRC/C/CZE/CO/3–4, 2011.

Council of Europe, "Explanatory Report to the European Convention on the Adoption of Children (Revised)", 2008.

Department for Children, Schools & Families, *The Registration of Births (Parents Not Married And Not Acting Together) Regulations 2010: A Consultation*, 2009.

Fenton-Glynn, C., "Anonymous Relinquishment and Baby-Boxes: Life-Saving Mechanisms or a Violation of Human Rights?" in K. Boele-Woelki, N. Dethloff and W. Gephart (eds.), *Family Law and Culture in Europe Developments, Challenges and Opportunities* (Cambridge: Intersentia, 2014). DOI: 10.1017/9781780685274.015.

Fenton-Glynn, C., "Court of Appeal (England and Wales): *Re C v XYZ County Council*" in H. Stalford, K. Hollingsworth and S. Gilmore (eds.), *Rewriting Children's Rights Judgments: From Academic Vision to New Practice* (Oxford: Hart Publishing, 2017). DOI: 10.5040/9781782259282.ch-006a.

Hodgkin, P. and Newell, R., *Implementation Handbook for the Convention on the Rights of the Child* (3rd edn., New York: Unicef, 2007).

Kidner, C., *SPICe Briefing: Child Protection* (Scottish Parliament, 2012).

Klier, C., Chryssa, G., Amon, S., Fiala, C., Weizmann-Henelius, G., Pruitt, S., Putkonen, H., "Is the introduction of anonymous delivery associated with a reduction of high neonaticide rates in Austria? A retrospective study", *BJOG*, 2013 (120), 428–434. DOI: 10.1111/1471-0528.12099.

Leckey, R., "Identity, law, and the right to a dream", *Dalhousie Law Journal*, 2015 (38(2)), 525–548.

Marshall, J., "Concealed Births, Adoption and Human Rights Law: Being Wary of Seeking to Open Windows into People's Souls", *Cambridge Law Journal*, 2012 (71(2)), 325–354. DOI: https://doi.org/10.1017/S0008197312000517.

Marshall, J., "Secrecy in births, identity rights, care and belonging", *Child and Family Law Quarterly*, 2018 (30(2)), 167–185.

McCaughren, S. and Lovett, J., "Domestic adoption in Ireland: a shifting paradigm?", *Adoption & Fostering*, 2014 (38(3)), 238–254. DOI: https://doi.org/10.1177/0308575914543233.

McGoldrick, D., "The United Nations Convention on the Rights of the Child", *International Journal of Law and the Family*, 1991 (5(2)), 132–169. DOI: https://doi.org/10.1093/lawfam/5.2.132.

National Records of Scotland, "Table 3.02: Live births, numbers and percentages, by marital status of parents and type of registration, Scotland, 1974 to 2016" (Edinburgh, 2017).

Norrie, K. McK., *The Law Relating to Parent & Child in Scotland* (3rd edn., Edinburgh: W Green, 2013).

Office for National Statistics, "Statistical Bulletin: Births by parents' characteristics in England and Wales: 2016" (London, 2017).

Ramesh, R., "Spread of 'baby boxes' in Europe alarms United Nations", *The Guardian*, 10 June 2012, www.theguardian.com/world/2012/jun/10/unitednations-europe-news.

Ronen, Y., "Redefining the Child's Right to Identity", *International Journal of Law, Policy and the Family*, 2004 (18(2)), 147–177. DOI: https://doi.org/10.1093/lawfam/18.2.147.

Scottish Government, *Review of Part 1 of the Children (Scotland) Act 1995 and creation of a Family Justice Moderation Strategy. A Consultation* (Edinburgh, 2018).

Sloan, B., "*Re C (A Child) (Adoption: Duty of Local Authority)* – Welfare and the Rights of the Birth Family in 'Fast Track' Adoption Cases", *Child and Family Law Quarterly*, 2009 (21(1)), 87–103.

Sloan, B., "Conflicting Rights: English Adoption Law and the Implementation of the UN Convention on the Rights of the Child", *Child & Family Law Quarterly*, 2013 (25(1)), 40–60.

Sloan, B., "Post-Adoption Contact Reform: Compounding the State-Ordered Termination of Parenthood?", *Cambridge Law Journal*, 2014 (73(2)), 378–404. DOI: https://doi.org/10.1017/S0008197314000439.

Sloan, B., "Primacy, Paramountcy and Adoption in England and Scotland" in E. Sutherland and L. Barnes Macfarlane (eds.), *Implementing Article 3 of the United Nations Convention on the Rights of the Child: Best Interests, Welfare and Well-being* (Cambridge: Cambridge University Press, 2016). DOI: https://doi.org/10.1017/S0008197314000439.

Sloan, B., "Commentary on *Re C v XYZ County Council*" in H. Stalford, K. Hollingsworth and S. Gilmore (eds.), *Rewriting Children's Rights Judgments: From Academic Vision to New Practice* (Oxford: Hart Publishing, 2017). DOI: 10.5040/9781782259282.ch-006a.

Sloan, B., "Finality Versus Fathers: Undoing Adoption to Recognise Biological Ties". *The Cambridge Law Journal*, 2018 (77(2)), 258–261. DOI: https://doi.org/10.1017/S000819731800051X.

Sloan, B., "A New Approach to Adoption in Ireland", *Zeitschrift für das gesamte Familienrecht*, 2018a (18), 1391–1392.

Sloan, B., "Illegitimate Consequences of 'Illegitimacy'?: Article 2 UNCRC and Non-Marital Children in the British Isles. Child Rights and International Discrimination Law" in M. Skivenes and K. H. Søvig (eds.), *Implementing Article 2 of the United Nations Convention on the Rights of the Child* (Oxon: Routledge, 2019).

Treoir, "Submission to the Oireachtas Committee on Justice, Defence and Equality on the General Scheme of a Children and Family Relationships Bill 2014" (Dublin, 2014).

United Nations, "Multilateral Treaties Deposited with the Secretary-General" ch. IV, no. 11, http://treaties.un.org/Pages/ViewDetails.aspx?src=TREATY&mtdsg_no=IV-11&chapter=4&lang=en.(2019).

United Nations General Assembly, "UN Guidelines on the Alternative Care of Children", A/RES/64/142, 2010.

Van Bueren, G., "Children's Access to Adoption Records—State Discretion or an Enforceable International Right?", *Modern Law Review*, 1995 (58(1)): 37–53. DOI: https://doi.org/10.1111/j.1468-2230.1995.tb01993.x.

PART 5

Case Studies on the Application of Article 5

CHAPTER 12

Article 5: The Role of Parents in the Proxy Informed Consent Process in Medical Research Involving Children

Sheila Varadan

1   Introduction

Children have been called the 'little medical heroes' of science (Lenz, 1940; Lederer, 2003; Lederer and Grodin, 1994). James Phipps, an eight-year old boy, was among the first human subjects to test the smallpox vaccine (Lentz, 1940; Lederer, 2003: 2–4). James Greenlees, an 11-year old boy, was the first human subject to undergo a carbolic acid treatment to prevent wound infection, after he suffered a compound leg fracture (Lentz, 1940; Lederer, 2003: 2–4). Joseph Meister, a ten-year old boy, was the first human subject to receive a rabies vaccination, after he had been bitten 14 times by a rabid dog (Lentz, 1940; Lederer, 2003: 2–4). But, for each of these scientific breakthroughs, there have been countless other instances in which a child was subjected to undignified treatment and unnecessary suffering for the purposes of advancing medical knowledge for the benefit of others (Lederer and Grodin, 1994; Jonsen, 1999; Wiendling, 2016).

At the crux of human subject research is the tension it poses between the pursuit of knowledge for the benefit of human progress, and the need to preserve the inviolability, and dignity of all persons. Informed consent represents an attempt to negotiate that tension through a process that seeks to respect, as widely as possible, the autonomy of persons, expressed in the voluntary, uncoerced and fully informed consent of the human subject in research. It is likely for this reason that informed consent remains among the most important ethical requirements in medical research and the *sine qua non* of all research involving human subjects (Perley *et al.*, 1992; Emanuel *et al.*, 2000; Emanuel *et al.*, 2004). However, it is also for this reason that medical research involving a child, who may be unable to give informed consent, presents an ethical dilemma for researchers seeking to further knowledge of child-related illness and disease (Beecher, 1959; McCormick, 1974; Perley et al., 1992; Katz, 1992).

Children stand to benefit significantly from advances made through medical research and experimentation. The exclusion of children from medical research has been said to render child-related illnesses the 'therapeutic orphans' of medicine, and deny children as a class of persons, access to the collective benefits of medical progress (Nuffield Council, 2015: xvi). Moreover, relying on adult data to inform the clinical care of children, even on everyday matters such as drug-dosing, places the individual child at risk, given the differences in children's pharmacokinetic and pharmacodynamic profiles from adults (Spriggs and Caldwell, 2011: 664; Nuffield Council, 2015: xvi).

To resolve the ethical impasse, children have been categorised as 'vulnerable' subjects in research with additional ethical protections imposed on research involving them (Belmont Report, 1979; Declaration of Helsinki 2000, 2004, 2008, 2013). Amongst these protections, consent by proxy provides the basis to obtain informed consent on behalf of the child in medical research (Draft Code of Ethics on Human Experimentation, 1962; Declaration of Helsinki, 1964, 1975, 1983, 1989, 1996, 2000, 2004, 2008, 2013). Because children below 18 years of age are generally presumed incompetent under the law, and a young child may lack sufficient understanding and independence to say "no" to adult researchers, consent by a parent or legal guardian ("proxy") provides an added layer of protection for the vulnerable child participant, while also serving as the legal basis to authorise the child's enrolment in a study (Belmont Report, 1979; Spriggs and Caldwell, 2011: 665).

However, the concept of proxy consent and the framework for its implementation present significant practical and ethical challenges for researchers. What are the parameters of proxy decision-making authority? What is the role of the child in the informed consent process? To what extent should a child's autonomy be recognised and enabled in the proxy informed consent process? The absence of any standardised regulatory framework for proxy informed consent and the resultant variations that have emerged in ethical guidelines have led to uneven approaches in how children are recognised, supported and enabled in the proxy informed consent process.

There are no straightforward answers to these questions, and this chapter does not seek to resolve them. What it considers is the extent to which the framework of the United Nations Convention on the Rights of the Child (UNCRC), and more specifically Article 5, may offer a different vantage point for researchers contemplating these issues in the research setting.

For clarity, and to avoid the use of contested terms such as "therapeutic" and "non-therapeutic" research, this chapter defines medical research as follows: a subset of health research that deals specifically with human subject experimentation, undertaken for the primary purpose of acquiring generalisable scientific or medical knowledge to further understanding of the causes, development and effects of human disease and improve preventive, diagnostic and therapeutic interventions (Declaration of Helsinki, 2013, principle 6; CIOMS 2016, Preamble).

This chapter does not focus on parental consent in medical treatment or experimental treatment in the clinical care of a child. Its aim is to consider the complexities surrounding proxy informed consent, where a parent (or legal guardian) is designated to authorise a child's enrolment in research that does not envisage a direct medical benefit to the child. It contemplates the relevance of the UNCRC, and Article 5, as a complementary framework for researchers, navigating the relationship between parents and children in the informed consent process.

What follows is a three-part analysis which expounds upon Article 5 and its potential relevance in the proxy informed consent process in medical research involving children. Part I provides a brief history of informed consent and an overview of proxy informed consent provisions in existing international ethical guidelines and instruments. Part II considers the relevance of the UNCRC in medical research and the unique vantage point that Article 5 may provide in respect of the parent-child relationship in proxy informed consent. Part III examines how Article 5 could be used to guide researchers navigating the proxy informed consent process. This chapter posits that Article 5 and the UNCRC framework may be useful in three respects. First, it introduces boundaries around how proxy authority should be exercised in the informed consent process. Second, it promotes a model for parent-child decision-making that is participatory, collaborative and linked with the child's enjoyment of rights under the UNCRC. Third, it fosters respect for and support of children's autonomy by recognising the child's evolving capacities to provide informed consent in medical research. The paper concludes that greater consideration should be given to Article 5 as a complementary framework in medical research involving children.

2 Part I – Overview of Informed Consent in Medical Research Ethics

2.1 *History of Informed Consent in Human Subject Medical Research*

That human subjects should voluntarily consent to medical research was not widely accepted when it was codified under Principle One of the Nuremberg Code (Katz, 1992: 229; Jonsen, 1999; Lederer, 2003; Faden and Beauchamp, 1986: 152). Because medical experimentation tended to take place within the context of medical treatment, the rights and protection of human subjects were viewed through the prism of the physician-patient relationship, as part of the physician's duty to act in the patient's best interest (Faden and Beauchamp, 1986:

152). A participant's consent was seen as more of a practical consideration, to facilitate cooperation, rather than an ethical duty to respect the autonomy of the participant (Katz, 1992; Beecher, 1966: Lederer, 2009).

The gravity and magnitude of atrocities committed during the Nazi era under the guise of medical experimentation (Wiendling, 2016) was a reckoning for the medical profession (Perley *et al.*, 1992; Faden and Beauchamp, 1986; Lederer, 2009). As the Nazi Doctors' Trial (*United States v. Karl Brandt*) unfolded, the ethical practices of the international medical community came under scrutiny: the accused defendants drew attention to the use of prisoners, institutionalised children and the mentally-ill in human experimentation, and challenged the assertion that voluntary participation was a common practice that 'generally occurred' in human subject research (Faden and Beauchamp, 1986: 155; Katz, 1992). In rejecting these claims, the Tribunal pronounced a set of ten 'basic principles' to 'satisfy moral, ethical and legal aspects' of research, which placed central importance on the voluntary participation of the human subject in research (Lederer, 2009; Faden and Beauchamp, 1986: 155). That the Nuremberg Code focused on experimentation with prisoners (unrelated to medical treatment) did not diminish the universality of its principles or the stature of the Code (Faden and Beauchamp, 1986: 156; Annas and Grodin, 1992). The Nuremberg Code was a watershed moment for the autonomy and dignity of human participants in scientific and medical experimentation, and to this day, remains the most influential statement on the rights of human subjects in research (Katz, 1992).

By the late 1950s, however, concerns began to emerge over the practicability and enforceability of the Code, particularly in a rapidly expanding field of drug development and clinical research (Beecher, 1959; Perley *et al.*, 1992: 157; Faden and Beauchamp, 1986: 156; Lederer, 2003). There were fears that strict adherence to the informed consent requirements under the Nuremberg Code would 'effectively cripple' research in mental illness and 'render experimentation on children impossible' (Beecher, 1959; Lederer, 2003: 10). There were also doubts over practicability and enforceability of an absolute requirement of informed consent, after it was revealed that physician-researchers were not consistently implementing the Code's informed consent requirements in clinical research settings (Beecher, 1966).

In the early 1960s, the World Medical Association (WMA) began a process to develop a code of professional ethics (drafted by physicians for physicians) to provide guidance to physician-researchers across a wider range of clinical research settings (Lederer, 2003: 10). Led by the British Medical Research Council, Harvard Medical School, and the British Medical Association, a draft code was drawn up in 1961. It replicated the structure and aims of the Nuremberg

Code (Katz, 1992: 233; Perley *et al.*, 1992). However, the WMA delegates could not agree on the draft and a protracted period of revisions ensued between 1962 and 1964 (Beauchamp and Faden, 1986; Lederer, 2003). When the draft code was finally adopted at the 18th WMA Assembly in Helsinki, Finland in 1964, its provisions on informed consent had significantly changed (Katz, 1992: 232; Ethics of Human Experimentation, 1964).

The Declaration of Helsinki departed from the Nuremberg Code in a number of important respects. It introduced the possibility of conducting research on persons incapable of providing voluntary, free and informed consent, breaking from the absolute requirement under Principle One of the Nuremberg Code (Declaration of Helsinki, 1964, part II, principle 1, part III, principle 3a). It proposed a concept of "consent by proxy" for persons incapable of providing informed consent to enable their participation in research (Declaration of Helsinki, 1964, part II, principle 1, part III, principle 3a). It introduced a distinction between medical research combined with clinical care (therapeutic research), for which informed consent was not strictly required (Declaration of Helsinki, 1964, part II, principle 1), and medical research undertaken for the purpose of accruing scientific knowledge for the benefit of others (non-therapeutic research) for which free and fully informed consent was required (Declaration of Helsinki, 1964, part III, principle 3a) (Katz, 1992). The upshot of these changes was to introduce a concept of informed consent (by proxy) that departed from the autonomy-based model of consent envisaged under Principle One of the Nuremberg Code.

The Declaration of Helsinki has since been revised eight times – 1975, 1983, 1989, 1996, 2000, 2004, 2008, 2013 – and continues to be recognised as the foundational instrument in medical research ethics, from which all other international guidelines and national regulatory frameworks are based.

2.2 *International Ethical Guidelines on Informed Consent in Medical Research*

2.2.1 The Ethical Dilemma of involving Children in Medical Research
When the Declaration of Helsinki introduced the notion of proxy consent into medical research, it did so without explicating how such an informed consent process should be understood or implemented in the research setting. Who had the moral legitimacy to act as the proxy? On what basis did a proxy have moral authority to volunteer a child in research? What were the parameters of proxy decision-making authority? What was the child's role in the proxy informed consent process? To what extent should a child's preferences and views be elicited and prioritised in the proxy decision-making process? The uncertainty surrounding these questions led ethicists to debate the morality

of involving children in medical research, particularly where the research did not overlap with the clinical care of the child (Jonsen, 2006; McCormick, 1974; Ramsey, 1976). Many of these questions remain unanswered, and the concept of proxy informed consent continues to stir unease among ethicists, who have characterised it as an "insoluble dilemma" in human subject research (Moser, 1974: 433; McCormick, 1974: 19; McLean, 1992; Spriggs and Caldwell, 2011).

2.2.2 International Ethical Guidelines on Proxy Informed Consent in Medical Research

In the meantime, international ethical guidelines and instruments have evolved myriad frameworks for proxy informed consent which confer wide authority on parents (or legal guardians) to act as decision-makers on behalf of their children in medical research. A brief survey of international ethical guidelines and instruments (Table 1), reveals some notable differences in how children are recognised, supported and enabled in the proxy informed consent process.

These differences are further magnified at the national level where an estimated 1,100 laws and regulations inform human subject research across 131 countries (OHRP, 2019). A recent survey of informed consent provisions in 27 European countries revealed significant differences in age requirements, legal definitions for consent and assent, and proxy requirements (Lepola *et al.*, 2016). What we are left with, then, is an uneven ethical and regulatory framework for proxy informed consent that provides little assurance to the child that her rights and autonomy will be respected and supported in the informed consent process in medical research.

3 Part II – The UNCRC and Informed Consent in Medical Research

3.1 *The Role of the UNCRC in Medical Research with Children*

Despite its adoption over 30 years ago, the UNCRC seldom appears in international ethical guidelines and instruments. The Declaration of Helsinki – revised five times since 1989 – makes no reference to the UNCRC or the rights of children in its preamble or principles (Declaration of Helsinki, 1996, 2000, 2004, 2008, 2013). The technical guidelines for clinical practice issued during the International Conference on Harmonisation (ICH-GCP) also make no reference to the UNCRC (ICH-GCP, 1995, 2016). The Guidelines of the Council for International Organizations of Medical Sciences (CIOMS), developed in collaboration with the WHO in 1982 and subsequently revised in 1993, 2002 and 2016, also make no reference to the UNCRC, despite mentioning the 'evolving

TABLE 1   Informed Consent under International Medical Research Ethical Codes and Guidelines

Instrument	Recognition of the child	Disclosure and participation in decision-making	Respect for child's agreement ('assent')	Respect for child's refusal ('dissent')	Weight given to child's preferences / authority of proxy
Declaration of Helsinki (2013) World Medical Association Principles 28, 29	Children identified as persons 'incapable of giving informed consent'	No. There is no explicit requirement for engaging or involving children in decision-making	Yes. If a child is able to agree to participate, physicians must obtain assent alongside consent	Yes. A child's dissent or refusal must be respected	The child's refusal is **determinative** Assent is required alongside informed consent from the legally authorised representative
CIOMS *Guidelines* (2016) Council for International Organizations of Medical Sciences Guidelines 9, 15 and 17	Children and adolescents recognised as having 'evolving capacities to give informed consent'	Yes. Age-appropriate information must be provided to children, and they must be involved in discussions in accordance with their evolving capacities	Yes. Agreement must be obtained in keeping with the child's evolving capacities	Yes. Refusal must be respected over parents'/guardian permission, unless participation in research is the best medical option for the child	The child's refusal is **determinative** if it does not interfere with his or her best interests in clinical care Assent is required alongside permission from a parent or legally authorized representative
Good Clinical Practice: Consolidated Guidance (1995, 2006, 2016) ICH Paras 4.8.12	Children identified as 'vulnerable subjects'	Yes. Children should be informed about the nature of the research to the extent of their understanding	Yes. If the child is deemed capable of assenting, he or she may sign the informed consent form	No. Only parent or guardian may withdraw a child, and only if she or he appears unduly distressed.	The child's refusal is **not** recognised and **not** determinative Informed consent is required from a legally acceptable representative Assent may be obtained if the child is capable.

TABLE 1   Informed Consent under International Medical Research Ethical Codes and Guidelines (cont

Instrument	Recognition of the child	Disclosure and participation in decision-making	Respect for child's agreement ('assent')	Respect for child's refusal ('dissent')	Weight given to child's preferences / authority of proxy
UNESCO *Declaration on Bioethics and Human Rights* (2005) UNESCO Article 7	Children identified as 'persons without capacity to consent'	Yes. The child should be involved to the greatest extent possible in decision-making	Not required	Yes. If research does not envisage a direct benefit, a child's refusal must be respected	The child's refusal is **determinative** Authorisation is required from a parent or legal guardian
Regulation (EU) No 536/2014 on clinical trials on medicinal products (2014) European Parliament Article 32	Children identified as 'minors' incapable of providing informed consent	Yes. The child must be engaged in a way adapted to their age and mental maturity	Not explicit. However, deference is given to national laws to determine where and when a child may give 'assent'	Yes. If a child refuses to participate or wishes to withdraw, his or her views must be respected	The child's refusal is **determinative** Informed consent is required from legally designated representative
Oviedo Convention, (1997) Council of Europe Arts 5, 6, 17	Children identified as 'minors'	Yes. The child must be engaged in discussions and informed of his or her rights as prescribed by law	Not explicit. However, the child's views will be afforded increasing weight subject to age and maturity	Yes. If the child refuses, her or his wishes must be respected	The child's refusal is **determinative** Informed consent is required from parent or legal representative
Add'l Protocol on Biomedical Research (2005) Council of Europe Arts 14, 15	Children identified as 'minors'	Yes. The child must be engaged in discussions and informed of his or her rights as prescribed by law	Not explicit. However, the child's views will be afforded increasing weight subject to age and maturity	Yes. If the child refuses, her or his wishes must be respected	The child's refusal is **determinative** Informed consent is required from parent or legal representative

capacities of the child' in its provisions on informed consent (CIOMS 2016, Guideline 17).

The Convention on Human Rights and Biomedicine (Oviedo, 1997) mentions the UNCRC in its preamble, but the rights of the child are not explicitly referenced in its provisions. The Convention has been criticised for failing to recognise 'children's evolving capacities' and 'right to be heard and participate in decision-making' in the informed consent process (Liefaard, Hendriks and Zlotnik, 2017: 4, 5, 27, 28).

For its part, the Committee on the Rights of the Child has stated that the UNCRC applies in the medical research setting, and '...academics, private companies and others, undertaking research involving children [must] *respect the principles and provisions of the Convention*' alongside ethical guidelines and codes (emphasis added) (CRC General Comment No. 15: para 85).

The CRC Committee has further emphasised the importance of respecting children's rights in the research setting:

> Children have been subjected to unnecessary or inappropriately designed research with little or no voice to either refuse or consent to participation. In line with the child's evolving capacities, consent of the child should be sought and consent may be sought from parents or guardians if necessary, but in all cases consent must be based on full disclosure of the risks and benefits of research to the child (General Comment No. 3, para. 29).

Yet, the UNCRC does not explicitly address consent to medical research or treatment within its provisions. The UNCRC Working Group considered the issue late in the drafting process during its 1989 Working Group Session (Legislative History, Vol. 2, 2007: 601). A draft paragraph was tabled during the discussions on the right to health (Article 24), which stated, 'that a child shall not be subject to any medical or scientific experimentation or treatment unless it is with the free and informed consent of the child or where appropriate that of the child's parents' (Legislative History Vol. 2, 2007: 601). A number of delegates strongly supported the inclusion of the paragraph. However, as discussions ensued, complex issues emerged, raising concerns about adopting such a provision without further consultation with experts (Van Bueren, 1995: 310–312). Given the late stage in the drafting process, it was decided that the proposed paragraph should be rejected (Legislative History Vol. 2, 2007: 601).

That the UNCRC did not address children's consent in medical research has been lamented as a missed opportunity to re-evaluate the issue of proxy informed consent: 'This Convention might have strengthened procedures, reassessed the whole issue of proxy consent and encapsulated tests to which all jurisdictions would be expected to subject proxy decisions were they to be authorised' (McLean, 1992: 189). Whether the proposed paragraph would have fulfilled these expectations will never be known. In the absence of any such a provision, this chapter considers the extent to which Article 5 may offer guidance to researchers navigating these questions in the proxy informed consent process.

3.2 Article 5 – A Unique and Necessary Provision of the UNCRC

Article 5 is unique to the UNCRC, having no antecedent and no subsequent equivalent in any other international and regional instrument on the rights of the child (Tobin and Varadan, 2019: 159; Kamchedzera, 2012). When the Working Group began discussing Article 5, they were motivated by two equally important concepts: the child as a rights holder with evolving capacities, and the duties, responsibilities and rights of parents, and legal guardians (Working Group Report, 1987). The ambition of Article 5 was to bring together these two important general concepts under one provision, striking a delicate balance between empowering the child in the exercise of her rights, while also respecting the role of parents and guardians in the upbringing of their children (Working Report, 1988: para. 28, 30; Tobin and Varadan, 2019: 160).

An important aspect of Article 5 was its recognition of autonomy and rights as relational concepts under the UNCRC. As Tobin writes:

> Rights for children under the CRC are not to be enjoyed in isolation from their parents and family ... the realization of children's rights will be deeply connected to, and interdependent with, the exercise of parental rights and responsibilities (Tobin, 2017: 21).

Because children are born in a state of dependency, there will be a period in a child's life, in which she will need to rely on parents and others to provide direction and guidance to enable her realisation and enjoyment of rights under the Convention (Eekelaar, 1994; Tobin and Varadan, 2019: 161). Respecting a child's autonomy as a rights-holder will thus require giving consideration to the involvement of parents in the child's life, not only to ensure the child's protection, but also to support and enable her exercise of rights under the Convention. Viewed in this way, the UNCRC introduces a conception of rights that does not abandon children to their autonomy but rather recognises the important role that relationships will play in supporting and enabling children's autonomy as rights-holders (Daly, 2017: 190). That said, Article 5 does not envisage a role for parents and family that is indeterminate or indefinite. The reference to the 'evolving capacities of the child' recognises that as a child grows, respect for her autonomy should concurrently increase, and a time will come when parental guidance and direction will no longer be needed (Tobin, 2013; Peleg, 2018: 18). In this respect, Article 5 should be understood as 'an enabling or scaffolding provision that is designed to protect the rights of the child, *not parents*, by demanding that parents and carers provide the direction and guidance necessary for children to enjoy their rights' (Tobin and Varadan, 2019: 177).

For this reason, Article 5 is also somewhat radical. It promotes a model of the parent-child relationship that departs from historical conceptions of the parent-child relationship, which were framed in terms of ownership over the child (Lansdown, 2005; Tobin, 2017). It introduces a conception of parenthood which should be understood as 'a form of stewardship … or trusteeship' that 'perceives [the] child not as an object subject to the control and subjugation of an adult but rather an independent subject with discreet entitlements, the realisation of which is dependent on the assistance of adults' (Tobin, 2005). It promotes a parent-child decision-making relationship that is 'co-operative and interdependent', with emphasis on 'a dialogue of participation and mutual respect' (Tobin, 2005: 41). From the child's perspective, it reframes the role of parents as 'first and foremost duty-bearers expected to fulfil their obligation in the upbringing of the child', rather than 'rights-holders vis-à-vis the child' (Peleg, 2018: 18). Article 5 thus introduces a model for parent-child decision-making that places the child at the centre of the process, with a right to receive appropriate guidance and direction from his or her parents, rather than a right of parents to have their authority respected by the State (Tobin and Varadan, 2019: 161; Peleg, 2018).

This chapter suggests that Article 5 could offer guidance to researchers, where ethical guidelines and instruments have been unable.

4 Part III – Article 5 and Proxy Informed Consent in Medical Research

This section examines how Article 5 could be applied in the research setting to support researchers navigating the relationship between parents (or legal guardians) and child subjects in the proxy informed consent process. It suggests that Article 5 may be useful in three respects: (1) it introduces boundaries around how proxy decision-making authority is exercised; (2) it promotes a model for parent-child decision-making that fosters participation, dialogue and collaborative decision-making in the proxy informed consent process; (3) it places an obligation on parents and legal guardians to support and enable a child's autonomy by recognising her evolving capacities for decision-making in the research setting. Each of these aspects of Article 5 is considered below.

4.1   Boundaries around Proxy Decision-Making Authority

For the most part, research ethical guidelines and instruments do not explicate the boundaries of proxy decision-making authority in informed consent. This was likely a deliberate decision to ensure respect for the authority of parents (or legal guardians) acting on behalf of their child in the research setting. However, situations can arise when a proxy's exercise of authority will not be consistent with the child's enjoyment of rights in the research setting. For example, Spriggs and others (2015) observed a practice in which parents withheld information from their children in the informed consent process. In some cases, parents misrepresented the purpose of the research to the child. Spriggs and others (2015) found that while, '[t]hese kinds of situations were … troubling for researchers', '[r]esearch ethics guidelines and regulations in the UK, Australia and the USA [had] nothing specific to say about the deception of children' by their parents (Spriggs *et al.*, 2015: 179, 180).

Article 5 may offer guidance to researchers on this point. While it respects the role of parents and adult carers to provide guidance and direction to their children, this authority is not unbounded. The nature of the 'responsibilities, rights and duties of parents' is informed by the other provisions of the UNCRC, specifically those relating to the responsibilities of parents (Articles 18, 27, 14 and 5). Any direction and guidance provided to children must also be "appropriate", which in the context of the UNCRC framework, is understood as consistent with the child's enjoyment of other rights under the Convention (Tobin and Varadan, 2019: 171, 172). Finally, guidance and direction provided by parents must take into account, 'the evolving capacities of the child', recognising that as children grow, the role of a proxy will need to be adjusted to enable more respect for the autonomy and agency of the child subject in the research setting.

4.2   The Parent-Child Relationship in Proxy Informed Consent

Remarkably, ethical guidelines and instruments have struggled to find an ethical basis to justify children's participation in the proxy informed consent process that is not linked with the determinative outcome of providing consent. This is due, in part, to individualistic conceptions of autonomy that have dominated the discourse on informed consent (Ramsey, 1974; McCormick,

1976; Faden and Beauchamp, 1986; Emanuel *et al.*, 2000). However, it is also due to traditional understandings of parent-child relationships, in which parents have been historically conferred with wide and unfettered authority to determine how and to what extent their child should be involved in decision-making in informed consent (Sibley *et al.*, 2016; Gaylin and Macklin, 1982).

The advent of concepts such as "assent", which appear in some ethical guidelines and instruments (Declaration of Helsinki, 2000, 2004, 2008, 2013; CIOMS 2016; ICH-GCP 2016) and not others (UNESCO 2005; EU Regulation 2014; Oviedo 1997; Additional Protocol 2005) has been widely criticised for introducing more confusion rather than clarity over children's participation in the proxy informed consent process.

The concept of "assent" and its use in the research setting are problematic for a number of reasons. First, there is no agreed definition for "assent" in medical research ethics (Nuffield Council, 2015: 60). This has led to uneven understandings of what assent means, and how it should be obtained, which in some cases has resulted in age restrictions or other barriers being placed on children's participation (Wendler and Shah, 2003; Shah, 2004; Ungar, Jofee and Kodish, 2006). Second, variations in the assent process have resulted in disagreements over its role and function, prompting some to question the value of children's participation in the informed consent process (Baines, 2011). Third, the binary framework of "assent" and "dissent" has reduced children's participation to either "agreement" or "refusal", overlooking the wide range of perspectives in between, and undermining the value of children's expression in the proxy decision-making process.

These practical challenges have fed broader debates around the value and weight that should be given to children's participation in the proxy informed consent process. These perspectives have yielded a number of ethical approaches, which may be summarised as follows: (1) attributing value to a child's views to support and foster her developing autonomy in decision-making in informed consent (Bartholome, 1976; Nelson and Miller, 2006, 27; Navin and Wasserman, 2019; Nuffield Council, 2015; Joffe, 2003; Nelson, 2003; Diekema, 2003; Miller and Nelson, 2006; Sibley *et al.*, 2012); (2) attributing value to a child's views as a pedagogical exercise to nurture moral growth and development (Sibley *et al.*, 2016; Nelson and Miller, 2006; Joffe, 2003); (3) attributing value to a child's views as a show of respect for the individual child and her moral worth in the research setting (Sibley *et al.*, 2016: 6; Nuffield Council, 2015; Navin and Wasserman, 2019); (4) attributing value to a child's views as a reflection of the fluidity in the parent-child decision-making process, and the gradual devolvement of decision-making authority from the proxy to the child (Joffe, 2003; Diekema, 2003; Fisher, 2003; Rossi *et al.*, 2003).

The Nuffield Council on Bioethics, in its 2015 report, *Children and clinical research: ethical issues*, recognised the importance of involving children in the informed consent process, as a show of respect for the individual child 'regardless of their age or capacity' (Nuffield Council, 2015: 102). Navin and Wasserman (2019) agree with this approach, recognising that there is 'moral value' in involving a child that is 'not reducible to considerations of either autonomy or best interests' (Navin and Wasserman, 2019: 44). Sibley *et al.* (2016) have put forward an ethical justification for children's participation that is based on the 'moral worth' of the child, recognising the inherent value of involving a child even if she is 'not considered to have the necessary and cognitive capacities to give fully informed consent' (Sibley *et al.*, 2012; Sibley *et al.*, 2016; Navin and Wasserman, 2019).

Article 5 and the UNCRC framework could offer additional guidance to researchers on these issues. First, the UNCRC reinforces the notion that the child has moral worth and her participation has inherent value, through its rights-based framework. Articles 5 and 12 together affirm that all children are holders of rights, with voice and agency, which, even if not determinative, must be listened to and respected by those adults, exercising influence over the child (Tobin, 2013: 407; Archard, 2004: 58; Tobin and Varadan, 2019: 173).

Second, Article 5 introduces a model for parent-child decision-making, which demands that, 'parents concede that they are not always the sole arbiters of a child's best interests' (Tobin, 2017: 24). It requires that parents work with their children to create decision-making systems that allow the child's views to be heard, taken into account and treated seriously in decision-making processes (Tobin, 2017: 24). This collaborative decision-making model promotes a relationship that is based on dialogue and participation, in which parents must not only involve the child in decision-making, but also explain to her why certain decisions are made (Tobin, 2017: 24). The Article 5 framework thus challenges the traditional proxy-child relationship, in which the child is designated as "vulnerable" and the proxy (parent or guardian) empowered as "protector". It replaces it with a framework that recognises the evolving capacities of the child and, importantly, 'demands that parents (or guardians) support the child to develop her decision-making capacities' (Tobin, 2015: 177).

Third, Article 5, Article 12 and Article 18 provide a framework to guide researchers in how they attribute weight to the child's views in the proxy informed consent process. Article 18 requires that parents make the child's best interests their basic concern, while Article 5 requires parents to provide guidance and direction that is appropriate and in a manner consistent with the child's evolving capacities. However, Articles 5 and 18 together recognise the importance of respect for the views and preferences of a child in the assessment of her best interests. As the CRC Committee explains:

> Assessment of a child's best interests must include respect for the child's right to express his or her views freely and due weight given to said views in all matters affecting the child. ... The two articles have complementary roles: the first aims to realize the child's best interests, and the second provides the methodology for hearing the views of the child ... in all matters affecting the child, including the assessment of his or her best interests (CRC General Comment No. 14: para. 43).

The CRC Committee further adds:

> The evolving capacities of the child (art. 5) must be taken into consideration when the child's best interests and right to be heard are at stake ... as the child matures, his or her views shall have increasing weight in the assessment of his or her best interests (CRC General Comment No. 14: para. 44).

Thus, as a child grows and her capacities evolve, greater weight must be attributed to her views and preferences in proxy decision-making setting. In this respect, Articles 5, 12 and 18 offer guidance to researchers faced with situations, in which a parent's use of proxy authority does not respect the views and preferences of the child subject in the research setting. Applying Articles 5, 12 and 18, if a child has sufficient understanding, capacity and maturity to express free and voluntary consent to participate in medical research, her views should be determinative in an assessment of her best interests (Tobin, 2019: 1417). This position aligns with the recommendations of the Nuffield Council which state, that 'where [children] are capable of understanding what is involved in taking part in a particular piece of research ... professionals have an ethical obligation to actively seek their consent ... regardless of any additional requirements of national legislation' (Nuffield Council, 2015: 150, 151). Thus, while the UNCRC does not directly resolve the issue of children's right to consent in medical research, Articles 5, 12 and 18 at the very least, provide a framework that assures the views and preferences of the child will not be overlooked or disregarded in the informed consent process.

4.3 *The Evolving Capacities Principle and the Autonomy of the Child*

For the most part, ethical guidelines and instruments have generally presumed that all children under 18 years of age are incapable of providing informed consent, deferring to national laws and regulations to determine when and under what conditions a child may provide informed consent in medical research (Declaration of Helsinki, 2013: Principles 28, 29; CIOMS, 2016: Guideline 15, 17; ICH-GCP, para 4.8; UNESCO, 2005: Article 7; EU Regulations 2014: Article 32; Oviedo Convention, Article 5; Additional Protocol (2005), Article 14). However, because a young child may also lack sufficient understanding, and independence to engage in autonomous decision-making, children, as a group, are designated as 'vulnerable subjects' in medical research (Belmont Report, 1979; Declaration of Helsinki, 2000, 2004, 2008, 2013; CIOMS 2016, Guideline 15). This combination of presumed incompetence and vulnerability has essentialised children as 'non-autonomous' beings, in need of protection rather than empowerment in the informed consent process (Emanuel et al., 2000; Ramsey, 1974; McCormick, 1976).

Yet, there is an emerging body of qualitative research and empirical data that challenges the notion of children as non-autonomous, incapable and vulnerable in the research setting. Hein and others (2015) suggest that a child may be capable of autonomous decision-making through 'shared' or 'co-consent' as early as 12 years of age (Hein et al., 2015). Alderson and others have shown that children are able to engage in various levels of decision making at all ages (Alderson et al., 2006; Alderson et al., 2005; Alderson, 1990; Alderson, 1993) and are often able to express free and informed consent well before the age of legal competency (Alderson, 1993; Alderson and Montgomery, 1996). Although these perspectives are finding more support in the discourse on research ethics (Nuffield Council, 2015; Navin and Wasserman, 2019; Miller and Nelson, 2006), researchers continue to grapple with how to balance respect for parental authority with recognition of children's autonomy in the informed consent process.

Article 5 may provide guidance on this point. As Peleg observes, '[a]rticle 5 and the evolving-capacities principle is, essentially, a mechanism to achieve balance between autonomy and protection' (Peleg, 2019: 207). As the CRC Committee further elaborates, 'parents (and others) have a responsibility to continually adjust the levels of support and guidance they offer to a child' to 'take account of a child's interests and wishes as well as the child's capacities for autonomous decision-making and comprehension of his or her best interests' (CRC Committee, General Comment No. 7, para. 17). In other words, as a 'child grows and develops, respect for her autonomy should concurrently increase' and a time will come when the child has sufficient capacity that she will no longer need to rely on her right to parental guidance and direction to secure the enjoyment of her rights under the Convention (Tobin, 2013; Peleg, 2018: 18; Tobin and Varadan, 2019: 177).

In this respect, Article 5 and the evolving-capacities principle are not dissimilar to the often cited judgment of the House of Lords in *Gillick v. West Norfolk and Wisbech Area Health Authority* ([1986] 1 AC 112) (*Gillick*), in which reference was made to parental rights as a 'dwindling right' which terminates once a child has achieved sufficient understanding, intelligence and discretion to enable her to make a wise choice in her own interests (*Gillick*). Though *Gillick* predated the UNCRC, it embodied a vision of children's rights that aligns with the UNCRC, and Article 5 (Tobin, 2009: 600). It is likely for this reason that it is often cited as a basis to recognise children's right to consent in medical research (Alderson, 2007; Alderson, 2012; Alderson, 2018; Nuffield Council, 2015). However, the decision in *Gillick* focuses on children's consent in medical treatment, and its authority is confined to common law jurisdictions; whereas Article 5 provides a framework that is accessible to any researcher working in medical research across all of the 196 State Parties of the UNCRC.

It is important to emphasise that Article 5 does not 'render the involvement of ... parents mute or displace their authority' (Tobin, 2005: 32). It requires, and indeed expects, parents to provide, 'appropriate levels of protection' to prevent the child from being forced to make decisions in circumstances when they themselves do not feel competent or comfortable doing so (Tobin and Varadan, 2019: 174). In this respect, Article 5 adopts a conception of autonomy that is relational and supported. It challenges individualistic notions of autonomy in the discourse on informed consent, which have historically characterised children as incompetent and 'non-autonomous'. Article 5 offers, in its place, a concept of 'supported autonomy' which Daly explains as, '[c]hildren [able] to have their autonomy respected without being given the same status as adults and without being abandoned to harmful fates unaided' (Daly, 2017: 132).

At the same time, the evolving capacities principle is not without concerns for the proxy informed consent process. The question of how a child's 'evolving capacities' will be assessed, and the process by which decision-making authority will devolve from the parent to the child are not addressed within Article 5 or practically considered by the CRC Committee. Making a child's exercise of autonomy conditional on her evolving capacities potentially 'opens up adults' discretion to decide who is capable' (Alderson, 2018), enabling paternalism through the rhetoric of rights (Tobin, 2009; Freeman, 2005). While there will be legitimate situations where a child's autonomy in decision-making will need to be constrained (Daly, 2017; Tobin, 2009; Gaylin, 1982), without further elaboration on how a child's "evolving" capacities will be recognised and practically enabled, there remains a risk that Article 5 could be used to undermine rather than support the autonomy of child subjects in the medical research setting.

Notwithstanding these concerns, Article 5 and the evolving-capacities principle may nonetheless offer guidance to researchers, providing a framework that fosters respect for a child's autonomy as she grows and develops (Peleg, 2018: 18), and places responsibility on parents (or legal guardians) to exercise their authority in a manner that supports and enables the child's capacities to engage in autonomous decision-making in the informed consent process.

5 Conclusion

In the mid-1970s, two leading bioethicists – Paul Ramsey and Richard McCormick – were invited to discuss the morality of medical research involving children, in what would become the pivotal debate on the ethics and regulation of proxy informed consent in medical research. As McCormick and Ramsey laid out their arguments, a remarkably blunt conception of the child was revealed. For Ramsey, the child was not a moral agent (Ramsey, 1976: 25). For McCormick, the child was neither legally competent nor factually capable of consent (McCormick, 1974: 2). In essentializing the child as 'vulnerable', 'non-autonomous' and 'incapable', Ramsey and McCormick effectively robbed children of voice and agency in the informed consent process, laying the foundation for a proxy consent process that prioritized protection over empowerment in the research setting.

In the 45 years since Ramsey and McCormick, research with children has challenged this narrow understanding of informed consent. Alderson and others offer evidence that children, from a very young age, are able to engage in various forms of decision-making at varying levels (Alderson, 1993; Alderson and Montgomery, 1996; Alderson, Sutcliffe and Curtis, 2006; Alderson, Hawthorne and Killen, 2005). Increasingly, it is recognised that child acquire capacities over a dynamic and evolving process that encompasses multiple dimensions – psychological, cognitive, emotional, social, cultural and spiritual.

Yet, the ethical framework for proxy informed consent in medical research remains unchanged, and the image of the child as vulnerable and non-autonomous continues to influence how children are viewed, recognised and supported in the proxy informed consent process in medical research.

This chapter contemplated how Article 5 and the UNCRC framework could be applied to medical research to recognise, support and enable children's voice and agency in the proxy informed consent process. It is suggested that Article 5 may offer guidance to researchers in three broad respects. First, it introduces boundaries around how proxy authority is exercised, ensuring parental decision-making is undertaken in a manner that respects and supports the child's enjoyment of rights in the research setting. More practically, it provides a set of guiding principles to evaluate when and under what circumstances the exercise of parental authority will be inappropriate in the proxy informed consent setting. Second, it promotes a model for parent-child decision-making that values participation, dialogue and collaborative decision-making in the proxy informed consent process, ensuring that a child's views and preferences are respected and taken seriously at each stage of the decision-making process. Third, it places an obligation on parents to respect and support children's autonomy by recognising the evolving capacities of the child in the medical research setting.

It is undeniable that medical research has yielded advances in medicine that have dramatically improved the health, well-being and life expectancy of all human beings. This is particularly true for children, whose lives have been transformed over the past century as a result of medical progress in the prevention, diagnosis and treatment of child-related illness and disease. Inclusion of children in research has been and will remain essential if further gains are to be made in children's health, and well-being. Yet, ethical guidelines and instruments continue to grapple with how to involve children in research, in a manner that respects and supports the autonomy of the child participant. This chapter did not set out to resolve the ethical dilemmas and legal uncertainties surrounding children's consent in medical research. What it sought to do is introduce a conception of the child as a rights holder in the medical research setting, whose voice and agency, even if not determinative, must be listened to, respected and supported by parents and researchers in the proxy informed consent process.

Acknowledgement

I would like to thank Elaine Sutherland, Claire Fenton-Glynn and Brian Sloan for the opportunity to attend the CRC-IP Colloquium on Article 5 (17–18 July 2019) in Cambridge. I would also like to thank Priscilla Alderson, Ton Liefaard and Jaap Doek for their helpful comments and encouragement. All errors and omissions are my own.

References

International Research Ethical Codes and Guidelines

Nuremberg Code (1947), Judgement, *Trial of War Criminals before the Nuremberg Military Tribunals under Control Council Law No. 10, Nuremberg Germany*, October 1946 – April 1949, available at: https://history.nih.gov/research/downloads/nuremberg.pdf.

Draft Code of Ethics on Human Experimentation (1962), World Medical Association, reprinted in *British Medical Journal*, 2(5312), 1119.

Declaration of Helsinki (1964), World Medical Association, adopted by the 18th World Medical Assembly, Helsinki, Finland, June 1964.

Declaration of Helsinki (1975), World Medical Association, revised by the 29th World Medical Assembly, Tokyo, Japan, October 1975.

Declaration of Helsinki (1983), World Medical Association, revised by the 35th World Medical Assembly, Venice, Italy, October 1983.

Declaration of Helsinki (1989), World Medical Association, revised by the 41st World Medical Assembly, Hong Kong, September 1989.

Declaration of Helsinki (1996), World Medical Association, revised by the 48th General Assembly, Somerset West, Republic of South Africa, October 1996.

Declaration of Helsinki (2000), World Medical Association, revised by the 52nd WMA General Assembly, Edinburgh, Scotland, October 2000.

Declaration of Helsinki (2004), World Medical Association, revised by the 55th WMA General Assembly, Tokyo, Japan, October 2004.

Declaration of Helsinki (2008), World Medical Association, revised by the 59th WMA General Assembly, Seoul, Korea, October 2008.

Declaration of Helsinki (2013), World Medical Association, revised by the 64th WMA General Assembly, Fortaleza, Brazil, October 2013.

Belmont Report (1979), National Commission for the Protection of Human Subjects and Biomedical and Behavioural Research, Office of the Secretary, Department of Health, Education and Welfare, Baltimore: United States of America.

International Ethical Guidelines for Health-related Research Involving Humans, CIOMS Guidelines (2016), Council for International Organizations of Medical Sciences (CIOMS) in collaboration with the World Health Organization (WHO), Geneva: Switzerland.

Handbook for Good Clinical Research Practice (1995, 2005), World Health Organization, Geneva: Switzerland.

Good Clinical Practice: Consolidated Guidance (1995, 2016), International Conference on Harmonisation of technical requirement for registration of pharmaceuticals for human use, Geneva: Switzerland.

Declaration on Bioethics and Human Rights (2005), UNESCO, adopted by acclamation at the 33rd session of the General Conference of UNESCO, 19 October 2005.

Regulation (EU) No. 536/2014 on clinical trials on medicinal products for human use, European Parliament and of the Council, 16 April 2014.

Convention on Human Rights and Biomedicine (Oviedo Convention), Council of Europe, entered into force on 1 December 2009.

Additional Protocol to the Convention on Human Rights and Biomedicine, Concerning Biomedical Research, Council of Europe, entered into force on 1 September 2007.

UN Committee on the Rights of the Child

UN Committee on the Rights of the Child, General Comment No. 3 (2003), *HIV/AIDS and the rights of the child*, 17 March 2003, CRC/GC/2993/3.

UN Committee on the Rights of the Child, General Comment No. 7 (2005), *Implementing child rights in early childhood*, 20 September 2006, CRC/C/GC/7/Rev.1.

UN Committee on the Rights of the Child, General Comment No. 12, *The right of the child to be heard* (2009), 20 July 2009, CRC/C/GC/12.

UN Committee on the Rights of the Child, General Comment No. 14 (2013) on *The right of the child to have his or her best interests taken as a primary consideration* (Art. 3, para. 1), 29 May 2013, CRC/C/GC/14.

UN Committee on the Rights of the Child, General Comment No. 15 (2013) on *The right of the child to the enjoyment of the highest attainable standard of health* (Art. 24), 17 April 2013, CRC/C/GC/15.

UN Committee on the Rights of the Child, General Comment No. 20 (2016) on The implementation of the rights of the child during adolescence, 6 December 2016, CRC/C/GC/20.

UN Working Group Session Reports on Drafting the UNCRC

United Nations Commission on Human Rights, "Report of the Working Group on a draft convention on the rights of the child" (1987), E/CN.4/1987/25.

United Nations Commission on Human Rights, "Report of the Working Group on a draft convention on the rights of the child" (1988), E/CN.4/1988/28.

Secondary Sources
Books

Alderson, P., *Choosing for Children: Parents' Consent to Surgery* (Oxford: Oxford University Press, 1990).

Alderson, P., *Children's Consent to Surgery* (Buckingham: Open University Press, 1993).

Alderson, P. and Montgomery, J., *Health Care Choices: Making decisions with children*, (London: Institute for Public Policy Research, 1996).

Archard, D., *Children, Rights and Childhood* (2nd edn., London: Routledge, 2004).
Daly, A., *Autonomy and the Court: Beyond the Right to Be Heard* (Stockholm: Brill, 2017).
Faden, R. and Beauchamp, T. with King, N., *A History and Theory of Informed Consent* (Oxford: Oxford University Press, 1986).
Jonsen, A., *A Short History of Medical Ethics* (Oxford: Oxford University Press, 1999).
Lansdown, G., *The Evolving Capacities of the Child* (Florence: UNICEF, 2005).
Liefaard, T., Hendriks, A. and Zlotnik, D., *From Law to Practice: Towards a Roadmap to Strengthen Children's Rights in the Era of Biomedicine* (Leiden: Leiden University/ The Committee on Bioethics of the Council of Europe, 2017).
Nuffield Council of Bioethics, *Children and clinical research: ethical issues* (London: Nuffield Council, 2015).
Office of the United Nations High Commissioner for Human Rights, *Legislative History of the Convention on the Rights of the Child*, Vols. 1 and 2, (New York/Geneva: United Nations, 2007).
Office for Human Research Protections, U.S. Department of Health and Human Services, *International Compilation of Human Research Standards*, 2019 edn., accessed at: https://www.hhs.gov/ohrp/sites/default/files/2019-International-Compilation-of-Human-Research-Standards.pdf (15 October 2019).
Peleg, N., *The Child's Right to Development* (Cambridge: Cambridge University Press, 2019).
Van Bueren, G., *The International Law on the Rights of the Child* (London: Martinus Nijhoff Publishers, 1995).

Book Chapters

Alderson, P., "Children's Consent and 'Assent' to Healthcare Research'" in M. Freeman (ed.), *Law and Childhood Studies* (Oxford: Oxford University Press, 2012).
Gaylin, W., "Competence: No Longer All or None" in W. Gaylin and R. Macklin (eds.), *Who Speaks for the Child: The Problems of Proxy Consent* (New York: Hastings Center, 1982).
Kamchedzera, G., "Article 5 – The Child's Right to Appropriate Direction and Guidance" in A. Alen and others, *A Commentary on the United Nations Convention on the Rights of the Child* (The Netherlands: Martinus Nijhoff, 2012).
Katz, J., "The Consent Principle of the Nuremberg Code: Its Significance Then and Now" in G. Annas and M. Grodin (eds.) *The Nazi Doctors and the Nuremberg Code* (New York: Oxford University Press, 1992).
Lederer, S. and Grodin, A., "Historic Overview: Pediatric Experimentation" in M. Grodin and L. Glantz (eds.), *Children as Research Subjects: Science, Ethics & Law* (Oxford: Oxford University Press, 1994).
Lederer, S., "Chapter 49: The Ethics of Experimenting on Human Subjects" in R. B. Baker and L. B. McCullough (eds.), *The Cambridge World History of Medical Ethics* (Cambridge: Cambridge University Press, 2009).

McLean, S., "Medical Experimentation with Children" in P. Alston, S. Parker and J. Seymour (eds.), *Children, Rights and the Law* (Oxford: Clarendon Paperback, 1992).

Peleg, N., "International Children's Rights Law: General Principles" in T. Liefaard and U. Kilkelly (eds.), *International Human Rights of Children*, Singapore: Springer Nature Singapore, 2018).

Perley, S., Fluss, S., Bankowski, Z. and Simon, F., "The Nuremberg Code: An International Overview" in G. Annas and M. Grodin (eds.), *The Nazi Doctors and the Nuremberg Code* (New York: Oxford University Press, 1992).

Tobin, J., "Chapter 4: Fixed Concepts but Changing Conceptions: Understanding the Relationship Between Children and Parents under the CRC" in M. D. Ruck, M. Peterson-Badali, and M. Freeman (eds.), *Handbook of Children's Rights: Global and Multidisciplinary Perspectives* (London: Routledge Taylor & Francis Group, 2017).

Tobin, J., "Article 36: Protection against All Other Forms of Exploitation" in J. Tobin and P. Alston (eds.), *The UN Convention on the Rights of the Child: A Commentary* (Oxford: Oxford University Press, 2019).

Tobin, J. and Varadan, S., "Article 5: The Right to Parental Direction and Guidance Consistent with a Child's Evolving Capacities" in J. Tobin and P. Alston (eds.), *The UN Convention on the Rights of the Child: A Commentary*, (Oxford: Oxford University Press, 2019).

Peer-reviewed Journal Articles

Unsigned, "Ethics of Human Experimentation", *British Medical Journal* 1964 (2(5402)) 135–136.

Alderson, P., Hawthorne, J., Killen, M., "The Participation Rights of Premature Babies", *The International Journal of Children's Rights* 2005 (13) 31–50.

Alderson, P., Sutcliffe, K. and Curtis, K., "Children's Competence to Consent to Medical Treatment", *Hastings Center Report* 2006(36(6)) 25–34.

Alderson, P., "Giving Children's Views 'Due Weight' in Medical Law", *The International Journal of Children's Rights* 2018(26) 16–37. DOI:10.1163/15718182-02601001.

Baines, P., "Assent for children's participation in research is incoherent and wrong", *Archives of Disease in Childhood* 2011(96) 960–962. DOI: 10.1136/adc.2011.211342.

Bartholome, A., "Parents, Children, and the Moral Benefits of Research", *Hastings Center Report* 1976 44–45.

Beecher, H., "Experimentation in Man", *Journal of the American Medical Association* 1959(169) 461–478.

Beecher, H., "Ethics and Clinical Research", *The New England Journal of Medicine* 1966(274(24)) 1354–1360.

Caplan, A., "Informed Consent: A History and Theory of Informed Consent" by Ruth R. Faden and Tom L. Beauchamp", *Journal of the American Medical Association* 1987 (257(3)) 386.

Dorscheidt, J. H. H. M., "Medical Research Involving Children – Giving Weight to Children's Views", *The International Journal of Children's Rights* 2018(26) 93–116. DOI:10.1163/15718182-02601006.

Diekema, D., "Taking Children Seriously: What's so Important about Assent?", *American Journal of Bioethics* 2003(3(4)) 25–26.

Eekelaar, J., "The Interests of the Child and the Child's Wishes: The Role of Dynamic Self-Determinism", *International Journal of Law, Policy and the Family* 1994(8) 42–61.

Emanuel, E., Wendler, D., and Grady, C., "What Makes Clinical Research Ethical?", *Journal of the American Medical Association* 2000 (283(20)) 2701–2711.

Emanuel, E., Wendler, D., Killen, J. and Grady, C., "What Makes Clinical Research in Developing Countries Ethical? The Benchmarks of Ethical Research", *Journal of Infectious Diseases* 2004(189) 930–7.

Fisher, C., "A Goodness-of-Fit Ethic for Child Assent to Nonbeneficial Research", *American Journal of Bioethics* 2003 (3(4)) 27–28.

Freeman, M. D., "Rethinking Gillick", *The International Journal of Children's Rights* 2005(13(1–2)) 201–218.

Hanson, K. and Lundy, L., "Does Exactly What it Says on the Tin? A Critical Analysis and Alternative Conceptualisation of the So-called 'General Principles' of the Convention on the Rights of the Child", *The International Journal of Children's Rights* 2017(25(2)) 285–306. DOI:10.1163/15718182-02502011.

Hein, I., De Vries, M., Troost, P., Meynen, G., Van Goudoever J. B. and Lindauer, R., "Informed consent instead of assent is appropriate in children from the age of twelve: Policy implications of new findings on children's competence to consent to clinical research", *BMC Medical Ethics* 2015(16(76)) 1–7. DOI: 10.1186/s12910-015-0067-z.

Joffe, S., "Rethink 'Affirmative Agreement', but Abandon 'Assent'", *American Journal of Bioethics* 2003 (3(4)) 9–11.

Jonsen, A., "Non-therapeutic research with children: the Ramsey versus McCormick Debate", *Journal of the American Medical Association* 2006 S12–S14.

Lederer, S., "Children as Guinea Pigs: Historical Perspectives", *Accountability in Research* 2003(10) 1–16.

Lentz, J., "Little Medical Heroes", *Hygeia* 1940 (18) 888.

Lepola, P., Needham, A., Mendum, J., Sallabank, P., Neubauer, D. and de Wildt, S., "Informed consent for pediatric trials in Europe", *Archives of Disease in Childhood* 2016(101) 1017–1025.

McCormick, R., "Proxy consent in the experimentation situation", *Perspectives in Biology and Medicine* 1974 (18(12)) 2–20.

Miller, V. and Nelson, R., "A Developmental Approach to Child Assent for Nontherapeutic Research", *Journal of Pediatrics* 2006 S25–30. DOI:10.1016/j.peds.2006.04.047.

Moser, R. H., "An Anti-Intellectual Movement in Medicine?", *Journal of the American Medical Association* 1974(227(4)) 432–434.

Navin, C. and Wasserman, J., "Capacity for Preferences and Pediatric Assent", *Hastings Center Report* 2019(49(1)) 43–51. DOI: 10.1002/hast.980.

Nelson, R., "We Should Reject Passive Resignation in Favor of Requiring the Assent of Younger Children for Participation in Nonbeneficial Research", *American Journal of Bioethics* 2003(3(4)), 11–13.

Ramsey, P., "The enforcement of morals: non-therapeutic research on children", *Hastings Centre Report* 1976(6(4)) 21–30.

Rossi, W., Reynolds., W. and Nelson, R., "Child Assent and Parental Permission in Pediatric Research", *Theoretical Medicine* 2003 (24) 131–148.

Rothmier, J., Lasley, M. and Shapiro, G., "Factors Influencing Parental Consent in Pediatric Clinical Research", *Pediatrics* 2003 (11(5)) 1037–1041.

Shepherd, L., Read, K. and Chen, D., "Children Enrolled in Parents' Research: A Uniquely Vulnerable Group in Need of Oversight and Protection", *IRB Ethics and Human Research* 2013(35(3)) 1- 8.

Sibley, A., Pollard, A., Fitzpatrick, R. and Sheehan, M., "Developing a new justification for assent", *BMC Medical Ethics* 2016(17(2)) 1–9. DOI: 10.1186/s12910-015-0085-x.

Sibley, A., Sheehan, M. and Pollard, A., "Assent is not consent", *Journal of Medical Ethics* 2012 (38(1)) 3.

Spriggs, M. and Caldwell, P., "The ethics of paediatric research", *Journal of Paediatrics and Child Health* 2011(47) 664–667.

Spriggs, M. and Gillam, L., "Deception of children in research", *Journal of Medical Ethics* 2015(41) 179–182.

Tobin, J., "Parents and Children's Rights under the Convention on the Rights of the Child: Finding Reconciliation in a Misunderstood Relationship", *Australian Journal of Professional and Applied Ethics* 2005 (7(2)) 31–46.

Tobin, J., "Judging the Judges: Are They Adopting the Rights Approach in Matters Involving Children?", *Melbourne University Law Review* 2009 (33) 579–625.

Tobin, J., "Justifying Children's Rights", *The International Journal of Children's Rights* 2013 (21(3)) 395–441. DOI: 10.1163/15718182-02013004.

Tobin, J., "Understanding Children's Rights: A Vision Beyond Vulnerability", *Nordic Journal of International Law* 2015(84) 155–182. DOI: 10.1163/15718107-08402002.

Ungar, D., Joffe, S. and Kodish, E., "Children are not small adults: Documentation of assent for research involving children", *Journal of Pediatrics* 2006 S31-S33. DOI: 10.1016/j.peds.2006.04.048.

Varadan, S., "The Principle of Evolving Capacities under the UN Convention on the Rights of the Child", *The International Journal of Children's Rights* 2019(27(2)) 306–338. DOI:10.1163/15718182-02702006.

Weindling, P., von Villiez, A., Loeweneau and Farron, N., "The victims of unethical human experiments and coerced research under National Socialism", *Endeavour* 2016(40(1)), 1–6.

Wendler, D., "Assent in paediatric research: theoretical and practical consideration", *Journal of Medical Ethics* 2004(32) 229–234.

Wendler, D. and Shah, S., "Should Children Decide Whether They are Enrolled in Non-beneficial Research?", *American Journal of Bioethics* 2003 (3(4)), 1–7.

CHAPTER 13

Scotland's Named Person Scheme

A Case Study of Article 5 of the United Nations Convention on the Rights of the Child in Practice

Gillian Black

1   Introduction

This chapter considers the impact of Article 5, UNCRC on the proposed Named Person scheme in Scotland – legislated for in 2014 and abandoned in 2019, without ever having been implemented. The core premise of this scheme was that every child in Scotland should be allocated a Named Person: an adult who would be a single identified point of contact, who knew the child, and could help support and advise the child and parents. Despite laudable aims, the scheme was dogged by controversy, including a successful challenge in 2016 in the UK Supreme Court (*The Christian Institute and Others v. The Lord Advocate* [2016] UKSC 51). Yet in addition to the many criticisms levied against the proposals, a further question can be asked: to what extent would the appointment of a Named Person have supported or hindered the 'responsibilities, rights and duties' of parents under Article 5? Despite the scheme being cancelled, it nevertheless offers a valuable case study on a legislative proposal which was designed to improve support for children and parents, but which did not apparently take into account the provisions of Article 5.

After setting out the core elements of the Named Person scheme, I will briefly outline the controversy and litigation that hampered its introduction, before exploring the ramifications of Article 5 in this context.

2   The Scheme and Its Background

2.1   *The Scheme*

The Named Person scheme was introduced in the Children and Young People (Scotland) Act 2014 (hereafter the "2014 Act"), although the relevant part of the statute was never brought into force and, in September 2019, the Deputy First

Minister announced the Scottish Government would not be proceeding with the scheme (Scottish Parliament Business, 2019). If it had been implemented, the scheme would have seen a Named Person appointed to *every* child in Scotland. "Child" here was defined as a child or young person up to 18 years old (2014 Act, s. 97(1)).[1] Typically, the local authority would have been responsible for making arrangements for provision of a Named Person (2014 Act, s. 21), unless the child was still of pre-school age (2014 Act, s. 20), or was of school age but attended an independent school, or was in secure accommodation, or in legal custody, in which case other specified organisations would have appointed a Named Person in respect of the child (2014 Act, s. 21). As a general rule, the Named Person would typically have been the local Health Visitor for the first five years of the child's life and then, when the child moved to school, a teacher or the school headteacher. There was no reference in the 2014 Act to what happened when a 16- or 17-year old got married: presumably they (and their spouse, if also 16 or 17) would still have a Named Person.[2]

The Named Person was intended to exercise specified statutory functions, all in order to 'promote, secure or safeguard the wellbeing of the child or young person' (2014 Act, s. 19(5)). These functions were:

1. Advising, informing or supporting the child or young person, or a parent of the child or young person,
2. Helping the child or young person, or a parent of the child or young person, to access a service or support, or
3. Discussing, or raising, a matter about the child or young person with a service provider or relevant authority, and
4. Such other functions as are specified by [the 2014] Act or any other enactment as being functions of a Named Person in relation to a child or young person (2014 Act, s. 19(5)(a) and (b)).

In order to fulfil these functions, the service provider (encompassing the Named Person) and the local authority were to have a right to share information where, in the opinion of the information holder, it would be relevant for the exercise of the Named Person functions, ought to be provided, and would not otherwise

---

[1] The only exception, whereby no Named Person was to be appointed, was for children who are members of any of the regular forces. Thus, a 16-year old in the Army would not have an appointed Named Person: s. 21(1) and (4). Moreover, where a child was in the reserve forces, the 2014 Act would not apply when the child was subject to service law: s. 19(6). These were both grounds for concern in themselves.

[2] Of course, the fact that Scots law permits 16- and 17-year olds to get married is a separate issue. In its most recent Concluding Observation, the UN Committee on the Rights of the Child recommended that, 'The State party raise the minimum age of marriage to 18 years across all devolved administrations': CRC/C/GBR/CO/5: 5, para. 19.

prejudice any criminal investigation or prosecution of crime (2014 Act, s. 26(1)-(4)). This information sharing could of course have comprised the personal data of the child or young person and parents and, as framed in the 2014 Act, the consent of the child, young person or parent would not be required – although in providing any information, the information holder (not necessarily the Named Person), was directed to 'ascertain and have regard to the views of the child', with regard to the child's age and maturity (2014 Act, s. 26(5) and (6)).

One of the critical factors was that the scheme was designed to apply to *every* child, whether previously identified as "at risk" or not. While the 2014 Act did not seek to impose an obligation on children or parents to use their allocated Named Person, there was also no facility to opt out of the scheme. This blanket operation was intended to ensure the scheme operated without distinction: this was a valid aim in its own right, to treat all children alike and thereby reduce stigma. To this extent it was comparable to other schemes, such as the Health Visitor scheme, whereby every pre-school child has an allocated health visitor to help address any queries or concerns. Likewise, the Scottish "baby box" scheme offers every mother-to-be a box of essential supplies for her newborn child. Because it is offered to all mothers, there is no stigma attached to dressing your baby in the baby box clothes, for example, or using the other provisions.[3]

2.2   *The Rationale*

The rationale for the Named Person scheme was set out in the Government's Policy Memorandum. There were at least three benefits sought to be achieved. First, the Named Person could act as an identified source of help when no other source is obvious: 'Where children and young people face issues that are not easily addressed by the practitioners with whom they and their families are in regular contact, it is not always clear who they can turn to for help' (Scottish Parliament Policy Memorandum, 2013: para. 66). By providing a Named Person, every child and their family would have an identifiable point of contact and support. Second, a Named Person was intended to be able to identify the need for early intervention in the lives of children who need support, with the hope that the earlier the intervention, the better the outcome. This was one reason why the scheme was to apply to all children, and not just those identified as being at risk: by the time they have come to the attention of the local authority, the window for early intervention would typically have closed.

Thirdly, the scheme aimed to ensure that children did not "fall through the cracks" – typically where different agencies were involved, but there was no

---

[3] Details of the scheme and the contents of the baby box are available at: https://www.mygov.scot/baby-box/.

collaboration between them, to work together for the child. Thus, schools, the police, and the General Practitioner service might all be involved with the same child, but there will not always be an established pathway for communication, or any overarching strategy for the child. Having a Named Person as a single point of communication and support was designed to help close this gap, by ensuring improved communication and collaboration:

> The Named Person will usually be a practitioner from a health board or an education authority, and someone whose job will mean they are already working with the child. They can monitor what children and young people need, within the context of their professional responsibilities, link with the relevant services that can help them, and be a single point of contact for services that children and families can use, if they wish. The Named Person is in a position to intervene early to prevent difficulties escalating. The role offers a way for children and young people to make sense of a complicated service environment as well as a way to prevent any problems or challenges they are facing in their lives remaining unaddressed due to professional service boundaries. Their job is to understand what children and young people need and quickly make the connection to those services that can help when extra help is needed. (Scottish Parliament Policy Memorandum, 2013: para. 68)

Numerous reviews into the tragic deaths of children at the hands of their parents or carers had identified both a failure to act timeously and a lack of communication between agencies as key failings (Sutherland, 2017: 295–296). The evidence therefore pointed to the fact that, even where there was involvement in a child's life by a range of services, this was not always sufficient to protect them (Sutherland, 2017: 303). The Named Person service was intended to tackle these failings and, in doing so, to promote a 'change in the culture and practice of all services that affected the lives of children, young people and their families' (*Petition of the Christian Institute and Others for Judicial Review of the Children and Young People (Scotland) Act 2014* [2015] CSOH 7: para. 30.)

Prior to the introduction of the 2014 Act, the scheme had already been trialled in a number of areas within Scotland, such as the Highland Pathfinder Project, which had been positively received (Scottish Parliament Policy Memorandum, 2013: para. 86; Sutherland, 2017: 304). There had also been a consultation on the scheme, again with generally positive results – albeit with some concerns about the guidance to Named Persons on sharing information between different bodies:

> *The proposal to provide a Named Person for every child and young person was strongly supported by stakeholders, both through the public consultation and the engagement undertaken.* However, concern was expressed about the existing legal framework for information sharing. This was felt to be confusing and potentially insufficient to enable the role of the Named Person to operate as well as anticipated. In particular, there were concerns regarding the sharing of information about children where consent is not given, both between others and the Named Person, and the Named Person and other professionals. It was felt that this could lead to professionals being unsure as to when information should be shared (Scottish Parliament Policy Memorandum, 2013: 75, emphasis added).

Despite these concerns regarding what was (at the time) viewed as a fairly technical issue, there certainly did not appear to be anything to prevent the 2014 Act being implemented. There can be no doubt that the scheme it envisaged had a clear and worthy rationale on the face of it, and had been the subject of lengthy and detailed planning, consultation and testing. Why then was it abandoned without ever being applied?

3 Concerns with the Scheme: Controversy and Litigation

Concerns about the operation of the scheme were present from when the draft bill was first introduced. These typically reflected the competing concerns of parents, on the one hand, and those likely to be Named Persons on the other. From the service provider perspective, concerns included resourcing and training of the employees to be Named Persons and, critically, liability. The 2014 Act made clear that 'responsibility for the exercise of the Named Person functions lies with the service provider rather than the Named Person' (2014 Act, s. 19(8)) A further apprehension was whether an employee of the state can truly hold the state to account, in situations where a dispute arises between the child or family and the local authority. If, for example, the child's complaint was with the school, and the Named Person was a teacher at the school, would that teacher be able to act as an independent advocate for the child and family? And, perhaps most significantly given the existing failings in state support for children at risk, 'disquiet was occasioned by the prospect of resources being diverted to monitor vast numbers of children who have no demonstrable need for state intervention, when over-stretched social work departments are unable to fulfil their responsibilities to children who are already on their radar due to concerns about their care' (Sutherland, 2017: 305). In a particularly distressing twist, one of the children killed by his parents in the year the 2014 Act was introduced, Liam Fee, had been in a local authority area where a precursor of the Named Person scheme was in place (Sutherland, 2017: 303–4). Would there have been sufficient resources allocated to the new scheme to implement it effectively? Absent such resources, the death of Liam Fee suggested that failings would continue.

Opposition also came from parents and groups representing parents. Despite the clearly stated aim of the scheme, to support children and families and secure early intervention to maximise beneficial outcomes, there were strong critics from the outset. The focus of the concerns were on the unwanted – and allegedly unwarranted – state interference with family life that could result from the powers of the Named Person. A campaign group, No2NP, was formed to contest the legislation, arguing that, 'The Scottish Government's planned Named Person scheme will undermine parents' responsibility for their own children and allow state officials unprecedented powers to interfere with family life.'[4]

A legal challenge was mounted, contesting the appointment of a Named Person to every child in Scotland: *Petition of the Christian Institute and Others for Judicial Review of the Children and Young People (Scotland) Act 2014* ([2015] CSOH 7). There were seven petitioners, comprising both charities and individuals: The Christian Institute; Family Education Trust (an English charity which researches the causes and consequences of family breakdown); The Young ME Sufferers ("TYMES") Trust; Care (Christian Action Research and Education); James and Rhianwen Mcintosh; and Deborah Thomas. They claimed that they were 'acting in the public interest as responsible members of and participants in civil society... and concerned about what they perceive to be an excess or misuse of power reflected in the [Named Person] provisions...' (*Petition of the Christian Institute and Others for Judicial Review of the Children and Young People (Scotland) Act 2014* [2015] CSOH 7: para. 7). Two of the petitioners were parents who argued that, in accordance with their Christian beliefs, raising their family is a God-given responsibility placed upon them and not the State (*Petition of the Christian Institute and Others for Judicial Review of the Children and Young People (Scotland) Act 2014* [2015] CSOH 7: para. 8).

The challenge was rejected at first instance in the Outer House of the Court of Session and again on appeal to the Inner House (*The Christian Institute and Others v. The Scottish Ministers* [2015] CSIH 64). The campaigners appealed to

---

4   https://no2np.org/ (accessed 19 June 2019).

the UK Supreme Court (*The Christian Institute and Others v. The Lord Advocate* [2016] UKSC 51). Despite the impetus being their objection to state interference in family life, the petitioners' legal claim focused on whether the scheme was beyond the competence of the Scottish Parliament. The petitioners alleged the 2014 Act was not lawful because it breached the European Convention on Human Rights and European Union law, specifically regarding the data sharing provisions. Thus, the challenge was that the powers of the Named Person to share personal data about children with a range of other agencies were not compliant with the (then) data protection regime and Article 8, ECHR privacy rights.[5] Despite the Scottish Government's success at the first two hearings, the petitioners reversed their fortunes at the third attempt. The UK Supreme Court held that the scheme, as drafted, would not be compliant with data protection legislation:

> In summary, we conclude that the information-sharing provisions of ... the Act ... are incompatible with the rights of children, young persons and parents under article 8 of the ECHR because they are not 'in accordance with the law' as that article requires ... [and] may in practice result in a disproportionate interference with the article 8 rights of many children, young persons and their parents, through the sharing of private information (*The Christian Institute and Others v. The Lord Advocate* [2016] UKSC 51: para. 106).

The Supreme Court therefore referred the data sharing proposals back to the Scottish Government, to review and revise the data sharing guidance.

Following the Scottish Government defeat in that case in 2016, the Named Person scheme was put on hold, pending revised data sharing provisions which would comply with Article 8, ECHR and the new GDPR regime for data protection. In an attempt to achieve this compliance, the Scottish Government introduced the Children and Young People (Information Sharing) (Scotland) Bill in September 2017.[6] The Scottish Government also established a GIRFEC

---

5   A third strand of argument advanced on behalf of the petitioners was that the 2014 Act was outside the legislative competence of the Scottish Parliament, as a devolved legislature, as it legislated on a matter reserved to Westminster, being data protection. The UKSC concluded that the purpose of the legislation, being to promote the wellbeing of children and young people, did not 'relate to' data protection: [2016] UKSC 51: paras. 63–66.

6   The Scottish Parliament's Education and Skills Committee heard evidence on the draft bill from a wide range of parties, including the Law Society of Scotland and the Faculty of Advocates (20 September 2017); Dr Ken Macdonald, Head of ICO Regions; and Maureen Falconer, Regional Manager, the Information Commissioner's Office (4 September 2017). The written

Practice Development Panel in late 2017, with the objective of developing a data sharing Code of Practice. The Panel was due to report in September 2018, but its final report was delayed. Eventually, in August 2019, minutes from the GIRFEC Practice Development Panel meeting of 21 March 2019 were published (GIRFEC Practice Development Panel, 2019). These indicated that the Panel would not be delivering a data sharing Code: 'a statutory Code of Practice that must be applied in all situations is not the right thing to do at this time, which is brave'. Although such a Code could be produced, 'it would not be desirable as the complexity of this would mean it would not be easy to understand or apply in practice' (GIRFEC Practice Development Panel, 2019). Just weeks after the publication of these Minutes, the Deputy First Minister announced:

> We will now not underpin in law the mandatory named person scheme for every child. We will withdraw the Children and Young People (Information Sharing) (Scotland) Bill and repeal the relevant legislation. Instead, existing voluntary schemes that provide a point of contact for support will continue, under current law (Scottish Parliament Business, 2019).

From a data protection perspective, the primary impediment to implementing the scheme was the need for a lawful basis for processing the personal data of children (and their parents). The comprehensive nature of the intended scheme, in applying to all children, meant that many lawful bases were unsuitable (General Data Protection Regulation 2018, articles 6, 7 and 9; Data Protection Act 2018, ss. 8, 10 and 11). Seeking consent from children or parents was simply not relevant for a scheme which was meant to apply on a blanket basis, rather than an opt-in one. Even if consent had been appropriate to provide a lawful basis, there would have been complexities in seeking consent from children, and determining whether they have capacity. There is a presumption that children over 12 have capacity, but this can be rebutted (Data Protection Act 2018, s. 208). Other grounds for processing, such as the vital interests of the data subject, were also effectively excluded by the blanket application: it would not be in the *vital* interests of every child to have a Named Person appointed. Instead, "vital interests" would be likely to be limited to those identified as "at risk". In the absence of some other broad "public interest" justification, securing a lawful basis for processing the relevant data of (almost) all children in Scotland, appears to have been an insurmountable hurdle.

---

evidence of the Faculty of Advocates acknowledged that the issues raised by the UKSC were not 'easy to resolve': http://www.advocates.org.uk/media/2498/final-faculty-response-15-aug-2017-named-person.pdf.

However, the focus of this chapter is not on the challenges of ensuring a data protection compliant regime, nor on the litigation itself. Instead, this chapter aims to explore the Article 5, UNCRC dimension to the proposed scheme. Two aspects of the judgments will therefore be considered: the views of the judiciary on the impact of the Named Person scheme on family life; and the implications of Article 5 UNCRC for the scheme.[7]

4 The Named Person Scheme and Family Life: The Judicial Perspective

At every stage of the legal proceedings, the judiciary gave explicit recognition to the extensive work that had gone in to developing the scheme, and its positive aims. In the words of Lord Pentland:

> the policy behind the named person service has been developed carefully over more than a decade. The process of policy development has been informed by a high level of input from experts in child welfare, education, health and care. The basic aim of the policy and the legislation giving effect to it is that the wellbeing of children will be promoted and safeguarded by providing for every child and his or her family a suitably qualified professional who can, if necessary, act as a single point of contact between the child and any public services from which the child could benefit. The named person will be in a position to identify any emerging challenges for the child at an early stage and to provide information about and coordinate access to any necessary services for the child. The named person service is based on the GIRFEC philosophy [Getting It Right For Every Child]. As the policy documents explain, that approach is grounded in putting the best interests of every child at the heart of decision-making; it encourages professionals to work together; and it advocates preventative work and early intervention to support children, young persons and their families (*Petition of the Christian Institute and Others for Judicial Review of the Children and Young People (Scotland) Act 2014* [2015] CSOH 7: para. 39).

On appeal, the Inner House of the Court of Session rejected claims about excessive state interference with the role of parents:

---

7 An examination of the proposals in the scheme against the UNCRC as a whole, including key articles such as Articles 3 (best interests), 12 (views of the child) and 16 (privacy), is beyond the scope of this chapter.

> The mere creation of a named person, available to assist a child or parent, no more confuses or diminishes the legal role, duties and responsibilities of parents in relation to their children than the provision of social services or education generally. It has no effect whatsoever on the legal, moral or social relationships within the family. *The assertion to the contrary, without any supporting basis, has the appearance of hyperbole* ... The legislation does not involve the state taking over any functions currently carried out by parents in relation to their children (*The Christian Institute and Others v. The Scottish Ministers* [2015] CSIH 64: para. 68, emphasis added.)

The Supreme Court too was apparently supportive of the intentions of the Scheme:

> The public interest in the flourishing of children is obvious. The aim of the Act, *which is unquestionably legitimate and benign*, is the promotion and safeguarding of the wellbeing of children and young persons ... the policy of promoting better outcomes for individual children and families is not inconsistent with the primary responsibility of parents to promote the wellbeing of their children. Improving access to, and the coordination of, public services which can assist the promotion of a child's wellbeing are legitimate objectives which are sufficiently important to justify some limitation on the right to respect for private and family life (*The Christian Institute and Others v. The Lord Advocate* [2016] UKSC 51: para. 91, emphasis added).

The fact that the Supreme Court approved the aim of the Act, whilst holding that it did not comply with Article 8, ECHR and the data protection regime, led to the curious position whereby *both* sides claimed the Supreme Court decision as a victory: the petitioners because the scheme was defeated on the data sharing side; the Scottish Government because the defeat was *only* on the data sharing side, with the express recognition that it would be lawful, benign and unexceptionable if the data sharing guidance was lawful (Sutherland, 2017: 306).

However, in reaching their conclusion, the Supreme Court explicitly acknowledged that the aim of improving public services to promote child wellbeing can justify some limit on the right to respect for private and family life. Is this an implication that the Named Person scheme would indeed have impinged on that right? And did it also engage Article 5, UNCRC?

5 Is the Named Person Scheme Compliant with Article 5, UNCRC?

5.1 Assessing Article 5 and the Named Person Scheme

Article 5 states:

> Parties shall respect the responsibilities, rights and duties of parents or, where applicable, the members of the extended family or community as provided for by local custom, legal guardians or other persons legally responsible for the child, to provide, in a manner consistent with the evolving capacities of the child, appropriate direction and guidance in the exercise by the child of the rights recognized in the present Convention.

To what extent did the proposed Named Person scheme respect the 'responsibilities, rights and duties of parents' to provide 'in a manner consistent with the evolving capacity of the child' the appropriate 'direction and guidance' in the child's exercise of his or her Convention rights?

In fact, rather unusually for domestic litigation in Scotland, the petitioners referred to Article 5, UNCRC, briefly, in their pleadings. The judge, Lord Pentland, summarised their submissions on this point:

> In support of their claims of infringement of [ECHR] Convention rights, the petitioners maintained that the enactment of the provisions in Part 4 of the Act was also incompatible with the rights enjoyed by the fifth to seventh petitioners under a number of international instruments, namely
>
> 1. article 16(3) of the Universal Declaration of Human Rights 1948;
> 2. article 23(1) of the International Covenant on Civil and Political Rights 1966 (reference was also made to article 17);
> 3. article 10(1) of the International Covenant on Economic, Social and Cultural Rights 1966;
> 4. and articles 3(2) and 5 of the UN Convention on the Rights of the Child 1969. [sic]
>
> *Although differently expressed, all these measures aim to safeguard the family and the home against disproportionate interference by the State; they recognise the family as having the primary role in the upbringing and education of children.*

One might also refer to article 24(1) of the Charter of Fundamental Rights of the European Union ('the CFR'); this provides that children have the right to such protection and care as is necessary for their wellbeing (*Petition of the Christian Institute and Others for Judicial Review of the Children and Young People (Scotland) Act 2014* [2015] CSOH 7: para. 41, emphasis added).

It seems to have been accepted that all these international provisions were relevant to the dispute and, as Lord Pentland said, 'informed the proper interpretation and application of the [ECHR] Convention rights of the fifth to seventh petitioners' (*Petition of the Christian Institute and Others for Judicial Review of the Children and Young People (Scotland) Act 2014* [2015] CSOH 7: para. 41). But having sprinkled a medley of Declarations, Conventions, Covenants and Charters into their case, no specific line of argument was predicated on any of them:

> The petitioners did not, however, advance any stand-alone line of argument based on the terms and effect of the international measures. Rather, they submitted that they formed part of the backdrop against which their claims of infringement of [ECHR] Convention rights should be evaluated (*Petition of the Christian Institute and Others for Judicial Review of the Children and Young People (Scotland) Act 2014* [2015] CSOH 7: para. 41).

Thus, while accepting that Article 5, UNCRC was relevant, the nature of its relevance and its application to the issue at hand were not further explored. There was also no consideration of Article 5 in the context of the UNCRC as a whole, nor the possible impact of other Convention articles, such as Article 3 (best interests of the child) or Article 16 (privacy).

The Supreme Court also reflected on the role of the UNCRC here:

> As is well known, it is proper to look to international instruments, such as the UNCRC, as aids to the interpretation of the ECHR. The Preamble to the UNCRC states:
> 'the family, as the fundamental group of society and the natural environment for the growth and wellbeing of all its members and particularly children, should be afforded the necessary protection and assistance so that it can fully assume its responsibilities within the community.'
> Many articles in the UNCRC acknowledge that it is the right and responsibility of parents to bring up their children ...; article 5 requires States

Parties to respect the responsibilities, rights and duties of parents ... to provide appropriate direction and guidance to the child in the exercise of his or her rights under the Convention (*The Christian Institute and Others v. The Lord Advocate* [2016] UKSC 51: para. 72).

Again, no specific challenge to the Named Person scheme was advanced on the back of Article 5, UNCRC. However, the Supreme Court did explore the need for Article 5, UNCRC and the imperative for the state to allow families freedom in how they function. The Court recognised that: 'There is an inextricable link between the protection of the family and the protection of fundamental freedoms in liberal democracies' (*The Christian Institute and Others v. The Lord Advocate* [2016] UKSC 51: para. 73.) Article 5, UNCRC plays a fundamental role in ensuring the state cannot interfere without good cause in the life of the family, as a guard against oppression:

Different upbringings produce different people. The first thing that a totalitarian regime tries to do is to get at the children, to distance them from the subversive, varied influences of their families, and indoctrinate them in their rulers' view of the world. Within limits, families must be left to bring up their children in their own way (*The Christian Institute and Others v. The Lord Advocate* [2016] UKSC 51: para 73; see also *In Re B (Children)* [2008] UKHL 35: para. 20).

But there is another side to this coin. The very real concerns expressed by the Supreme Court have to be balanced against the potential harm to children which can occur behind closed doors: parents cannot plead privacy to inflict cruelty or neglect with impunity. As the Committee on the Rights of the Child observed in a report from a 1994 Discussion Day:

Children are often abused, neglected, and their right to physical integrity ignored, on the assumption that the privacy of the family automatically confers on parents the ability to make correct and informed judgments with respect to 'the responsible upbringing of future citizens' (General Day of Discussion Report, 1994: 194–195).

To what extent would the Named Person scheme have succeeded in balancing these conflicting risks: over-interference in private life vs the risk of abuse in private? Had it been implemented, would it have interfered with the 'responsibilities, rights and duties' of parents? It is also important to remember that the Article 5 rights of parents are given in the context of the child exercising

Convention rights. It specifies that these responsibilities, rights and duties are given to parents to enable them 'to provide, in a manner consistent with the evolving capacities of the child, appropriate direction and guidance' to the child (Sutherland, 2021). Thus, both elements must be considered: the rights of parents, and the evolving capacity of the child.

5.2 The Responsibilities and Rights of Parents

Opposition to the scheme was frequently framed in terms of interference with the "rights of parents". However, it is arguable that these objections stemmed from a misconceived understanding of parental responsibilities and rights, both under the UNCRC and domestic legislation, whereby parents at times focus on the notion of their "rights" without understanding the substance of those rights, or the relationship to their parallel responsibilities. Parental rights in Scotland – as in many jurisdictions – are there to enable parents to fulfil their parental responsibilities. Section 1 of the Children (Scotland) Act 1995 sets out the parental responsibilities, and section 2 the corresponding parental rights, shaped to ensure they can meet these responsibilities. (Even the ordering of these sections underlines the importance of responsibilities, given that they are set out first, in section 1, with the rights flowing therefrom in section 2.)

The responsibilities imposed on parents include the duties to 'safeguard and promote the child's health, development and welfare' (Children (Scotland) Act 1995, s. 1(1)(a)) and to 'to provide, in a manner appropriate to the stage of development of the child (i) direction; (ii) guidance to the child' (Children (Scotland) Act 1995, s. 1(1)(b)). The appointment of a Named Person, who would also be able to provide advice and support, would not automatically interfere with the responsibility of the parents to do so. Moreover, the reference here to the 'stage of development' reflects the evolving capacity of the child, which is also an important part of Article 5, UNCRC. The parental rights are specifically given to parents to enable them to fulfil their responsibilities (Children (Scotland) Act 1995, s. 2): they go no further than that. And one of the rights is the right 'to control, direct or guide, in a manner appropriate to the stage of development of the child, the child's upbringing' (Children (Scotland) Act 1995, s. 2(1)(b)). Again, this requires parents to take account of the evolving capacity of their child.

5.3 Evolving Capacity of the Child

It is arguable that the Named Person scheme sought to reflect and respect the evolving capacity of the child – a core element of Article 5. By providing a source of support and advice to the child, the scheme would have allowed children to decide as and when they were ready to seek help themselves, without having to rely on (or be constrained by) their parents. It therefore attempted to encourage children to take responsibility for raising any issues with the Named Person, and presumably as children develop, and their capacity evolves, they would be able to seek assistance that reflects their own needs and abilities.

When the significance of evolving capacity is recognised, the true impact of Article 5 becomes clear. No parent has an absolute and unfettered right to raise their child: parenting must be seen in the framework of parental responsibilities and rights, and against the background of the child's evolving capacity. The Named Person would have been there to support the child through providing guidance and support, and also help support the parents in fulfilling *their* responsibilities and rights. To this extent, the proposals in the Named Person scheme could certainly be viewed as in keeping with parental responsibilities and rights and Article 5, rather than in conflict.

6   Concluding Comments

As this chapter has shown, the Named Person scheme had the potential to support both parents and children in the context of Article 5. However, the concern remains that the scheme would nevertheless have encroached on Article 5 because of its blanket application. While this had a clear rationale in facilitating early intervention – and in avoiding stigma – it is at the heart of all the problems that were faced by the initiative. By imposing the scheme on all children, it became arguable that the state was no longer respecting their evolving capacity, through denying them the right to choose to opt in. Public opposition to the scheme also centred round this wholesale application. Moreover, this was the key factor causing problems for the Scottish Government in finding a lawful basis for processing and sharing personal data – a critical element of the Named Person proposals. While the emphasis of this chapter has been on Article 5, the ultimate stumbling block for the Scottish Government was the data sharing element. Nevertheless, with the scheme now abandoned, there is a real risk that children are denied the support they need, which will also fail to respect their evolving capacity in choosing to seek guidance from others as well as parents. The Scottish Government must therefore seek another way to protect children, through enhanced early intervention and guidance – while also respecting the responsibilities of parents and, critically, the evolving capacity of the child. Further developments in this fraught field are awaited with interest.

Acknowledgements

My thanks are due to Professor Elaine E. Sutherland and to the anonymous reviewer for their very helpful insights on a draft of this chapter, and to all the participants at the UNCRC-IP Colloquium in Cambridge in July 2019 for their constructive comments in response to my paper on the Named Person scheme. The usual disclaimer applies.

References

General Day of Discussion Report, "Role of the Family", 1994, CRC/C/34: https://www.ohchr.org/Documents/HRBodies/CRC/Discussions/Recommendations/Recommendations1994.pdf.

GIRFEC Practice Development Panel, Minutes of 21 March 2019, published on 8 August 2019 at: https://www.gov.scot/publications/girfec-practice-development-panel-minutes-march-2019/.

Scottish Parliament Business Report, 19 September 2019: http://www.parliament.scot/parliamentarybusiness/report.aspx?r=12260&i=110854.

Scottish Parliament Policy Memorandum on the Children and Young People (Scotland) Bill (2013): https://www.parliament.scot/S4_Bills/Children%20and%20Young%20People%20(Scotland)%20Bill/b27s4-introd-pm.pdf.

Sutherland, Elaine E., "Proactive Child Protection: A Step Too Far?" in Margaret Brinig (ed.), *The International Survey of Family Law 2017 Edition* (Cambridge: Intersentia, 2017).

Sutherland, Elaine E., "The Enigma of Article 5 of the United Nations Convention on the Rights of the Child: Central or Peripheral?" in Brian Sloan and Claire Fenton-Glynn (eds.), *Parental Guidance, State Responsibility and Evolving Capacities* (Leiden: Brill, 2021).

CHAPTER 14

New Zealand Case Studies to Test the Meaning and Use of Article 5 of the 1989 United Nations Convention on the Rights of the Child

Mark Henaghan

1   Introduction

Article 5 of the 1989 United Nations Convention on the Rights of the Child brings together in one article all the natural tensions that inevitably flow through the Convention.

To what degree and when should children have rights to be autonomous and make their own decisions and their own mistakes? How do parental rights and responsibilities to bring up their children in a way the particular parent sees appropriate relate to and interact with their children's rights? When is it applicable for members of the extended family or community or legal guardians or other persons legally responsible for the child to step into the shoes of parental responsibilities? What is the role of the State in protecting children from harm, even within their family or from external forces? What is the role of the State in supporting parents to exercise their rights, responsibilities and duties as set out in Article 5? What is the role of the State in ensuring that the rights children have in the UN Convention on the Rights of the Child are fully implemented and how and on what principles does the State arbitrate between emancipatory rights and protectory rights?

The case study on a child's right to maintain their dignity and identity through the length of hair they prefer, illustrates both the evolving capacity of the child to make the decision and the importance of parental direction in making it. The case study on wider family member's rights to give appropriate directions in regard to the child's cultural identity helps understand an important recognition in Article 5 that such directions are not limited just to parents but where appropriate, wider family are recognised as being able to give such directions. The issue of breastfeeding a child is central to the welfare and wellbeing of the evolving child. This case study shows how other articles in the Convention on the Rights of the Child were used by a judge to overcome the importance of the attachment between a breastfeeding mother and her child. The final case study confronts the dilemma which runs throughout Article 5, namely the tension between giving the evolving child the maximum autonomy to make their own choices and protecting them from things that are harmful to them.

2   International Debate on the Role and Purpose of Article 5

Hanson and Lundy argue that Article 5, particularly its use of the phrase, the "child's evolving capacities", has been formulated in direct relation to the other rights recognised in the UN Convention on the Rights of the Child. Based on this observation, Hanson and Lundy propose that Article 5, particularly the concept of the child's evolving capacities, is best called "a crosscutting standard" which means that it applies to many other articles in the Convention. (Hanson and Lundy, 2017: 301). Sheila Varadan says that when evolving capacities of a child appeared in the text of UNCRC, 'it represented a distinct break from previously held conceptions of childhood and children under International law' (Varadan, 2019: 307). Lansdown argues that the term "evolving capacities of a child" gave the child visibility under international law and showed clearly that the role of parents is to adjust how they bring up their children and guide them in order for children to be able to exercise their own agency in relation to their lives. (Lansdown, 2005: 6). As Varadan says, 'this was a somewhat radical departure from traditional parent–child relationship, in which parents were the primary rights-holders and the child was a passive recipient of protection and care' (Varadan, 2019: 307).

A number of scholars have seen the recognition of the ability of children to evolve in capacity as 'innovative, unique' (Kamchedzera, 2012: 6, 13), 'new and profound' (Van Bueren, 1995: 51, 137).

Varadan, in her research on the evolving capacities of a child, found it appears over 80 times in the General Comments of the Convention on the Rights of the Child (Varadan, 2019: 306, 333). Varadan concludes her article with a view that Article 5 should not be recognised as a general principle of the UN Convention on the Rights of the Child without due consideration given to the manner in which evolving capacities has come to be used and understood by the Committee (*ibid.*: 332). Varadan argues that the term "evolving capacities", if it is to be a broader principle that applies across the whole of the Convention on the Rights of the Child, needs to be delinked from Articles 5 and 14(2) (*ibid.*: 332). Varadan rightly indicates that when the phrase "evolving capacities" of a child was first discussed in the early drafts of the UNCRC, it was seen as a counterbalance to the wide liberties given to parents, particularly in respect of their child's right to freedom of religion.

The concept of evolving capacities in Article 5 has attracted the most limelight in relation to the exposure and use of Article 5. This chapter wants to take a broader view of Article 5 based primarily on the work of Ya Ir Ronen. Ronen takes the view that Article 5 creates 'a new basis for the relationship between the child, the family and state... namely that the State's primary responsibility is to respect the role of the nuclear and extended family and of the community in the child's life rather than to intervene in order to protect the child from them' (Ronen, 2004: 161). Ronen recognises that particularly when children are young, they depend very much on their family life to begin forming their identity (*ibid.*). That identity is at the core of a person's dignity and why we have rights for individuals in the first place. The assumption is that each child needs to be able to construct their own unique identity (*ibid.*: 149). The development of an authentic, self-actualising individual is based on the idea of human dignity and the basic justification for the attribution of human rights (see for example, Taylor 1994: 41–2; Rockefeller, 1994: 87; Erbele, 2002: 256; Freeman, 1992; Freeman, 1997).

Lansdown takes Ronen's view a step further by arguing that the conventional view of protecting children has been a one-sided process with adults as the primary agents and children as mere recipients (Lansdown, 2005: 41). Lansdown goes on to say, 'the reality is more complex, involving a dynamic process that recognises children's capacities to contribute towards their own protection and allows them to build on their strengths' (*ibid.*).

Ronen rightly points out that identity does not incur in a vacuum but evolves through dialogue, struggles with significant others, until it finds its own path and becomes the person's own unique self ((Ronen 2004: 19; see also Eekelaar, 2004)).

3 The Four Case Studies and Why They Have Been Chosen

The case studies have been chosen because they illustrate different pressure points with regard to the interpretation and application of Article 5 to situations which have ended up in court because of clear differences of opinion, either between the child and the State, between parents and other caregivers, or between parents themselves. Underlying the analysis of these case studies is the position set out above, that an interpretation and application of the Article should always be given in a way that best enables the individual child to maximise their opportunity to develop and find their own unique individual identity in the world.

Before a detailed analysis of the case studies is undertaken it is important to understand the key phrases and wording in Article 5 to see how they can be interpreted in a manner which best ensures the child's capacity to become a free, dignified, individual human being.

3.1 *The Wording of Article 5*

3.1.1 State Parties *Shall Respect* the Responsibilities, Rights and Duties of Parents

The word "respect" is the key word here. It is defined in different ways (Oxford English Dictionary): one is a 'feeling of deep admiration for someone elicited by their abilities, qualities or achievements'; another is 'due regard for the feelings, wishes or rights of others'. The second meaning is the most likely one here. Oxford gives it synonyms: 'show consideration for', 'show regard for', 'take into consideration', 'take into account', 'make allowances for', and be 'mindful of'.

In itself the word "respect" does not appear to require the State to do anything in terms of action but be considerate and mindful. But, what about families impacted by poverty or that have limited resources (Concluding Observations on Australia, 2002: para. 50; Concluding Observations on Switzerland: para. 52); families where parents are in prison (Concluding Observations on Norway: para. 21; Concluding Observations on Sweden: para. 36; Concluding Observations on Great Britain and Northern Ireland: para 54), families which are in the indigenous minority and who have been disinherited and disempowered (Concluding Observations on Bulgaria: para. 35; Concluding Observations on Ireland: para. 43; Concluding Observations on New Zealand: para. 27; Concluding Observations on Norway: para. 21; Concluding Observations on Romania: para. 28) or families where children are head of the household and there are no parents present (Concluding Observations on South Africa: para. 42). What does being "considerate" and giving "due regard" to these families mean in terms of their responsibilities, rights and duties as "parents?" It cannot simply mean being "mindful" of these families as that does nothing about their current status quo, but recognises it.

If Article 5 is to have any global impact, which is an underlying goal of the 1989 Convention on the Rights of the Child, and if it is going to enhance the individual identity and dignity of each child, then 'respecting responsibilities, rights and duties of parents' with limited and sometimes no resources means providing those resources so that these parents can take part in all that Article 5 has to offer. Even parents who have the economic resources may not necessarily understand what Article 5 asks of them. How many parents, for example, would be aware of the United Nations Convention on the Rights of the Child and what it contains? Very few, I suspect, unless states run campaigns to educate them fully on the Convention, so they can exercise their responsibilities, rights and duties in relation to it. If we really believe that the Convention will enhance each child's rights, if its provisions are carried out, then the word "respect" must be given a strong meaning of not only "consider" or have "due regard" but also ensure that all parents are armed with the appropriate understanding of the Convention and are supported in their efforts to give directions to their children about the Convention.

Kamchedzera rightly argues that while there is a duty on parents and wider family members to provide appropriate direction and guidance, the child has a fundamental right to such appropriate direction and guidance. (Kamchedzera, 2012: 26). Some States have recognised the duty to give guidance by parents and caregivers in their Constitution. For example, the Constitution of Poland says:

> parents shall have the right to rear their children in accordance with their own convictions. Such upbringing shall respect the degree of maturity of the child and his freedom of conscience and belief and also his convictions (Constitution of Poland, 1997).

Similarly in Ireland, the Irish state has undertaken in its Constitution, to 'respect the inalienable and duty of parents to provide, according to their means, for the religious and moral, intellectual, physical and social education of their children' (Constitution of Ireland, 1937).

Kamchedzera puts a strong emphasis on the State's role. First by saying that parents do not have a blanket autonomy to exercise their duties and responsibilities, as children can be the victims of physical, emotional or sexual abuse within their family structures (Kamchedzera, 2012: 28). Secondly, States have the obligation to raise awareness and understanding of the child's right to receive appropriate direction (*ibid.*). Thirdly, the State needs to ensure an appropriate environment for appropriate parental guidance and directions to thrive – 'this may require support and appropriation to civil society organisations that are able to provide parental education' (*ibid.*: 29) To its credit, the UN Convention on the Rights of the Child Committee has proposed to States to implement programmes that would enable families to obtain knowledge and understanding of children's rights (Concluding Observations on Bulgaria, 1997: para. 28; Concluding Observations on Panama, 1997: para. 30; Concluding Observations on Sierra Leone, 2000: para. 49; Concluding Observations on Oman, 2006: para. 37; Concluding Observations on Saint Lucia, 2005: para. 37).

3.1.2   Article 5 Allows for Extended Family, or Community as Provided For by a Local Custom, Legal Guardians or Other Persons' Legally Responsibilities of the Child to Give Guidance on the United Nations Convention on the Rights of the Child 'Where Applicable'

Kamchedzera makes this point, elegantly emphasising that this part of Article 5 recognises the 'legal and moral roles' for community members regarding the upbringing of a child. (Kamchedzera, 2012: 20). Article 5 is about the rights of the child to receive direction from a wide range of extended family members within the child's community. This places a duty on all members of the extended family when interacting with the child to give appropriate guidance and direction. This gives a child a rich source of information upon which to build their unique identity in a manner consistent with the evolving capacity of the child.

Does it mean when the parents are not available to do it, or when the parents are not doing it, or when the parents are doing a bad job explaining the Convention? Or that they should do this together with the parents? If the enhancement of the individual child's unique identity is the goal of the Convention, then all of the above should be 'applicable'. The more children are aware of their rights in the Convention the better. The more family members that exercise the responsibility to inform children of their rights in the Convention, the more children are likely to grow up in an environment where their rights will be enhanced and their unique identity will be built on rich and diverse sources of guidance.

3.1.3   In a Manner Consistent with the Evolving Capacities of the Child

A manner means "in a way" which is best for the particular child. For example, with a young child it would be best done by example and giving direction for the child. As the child grows older it would be best done with the child and once the child reaches the stage of making their own decision it would be best done by letting the child make that decision themselves. In the New Zealand Care of Children Act 2004, section 16 recognises that guardians of children are to make decisions for the children when they are very young, to work with them as they get older and to be a backstop for them once they begin to make their own decisions. Because Article 5 is in the context of the UN Convention on the Rights of the Child, the directions and guidance needs to be consistent with a Convention-based image of childhood (Kamchedzera, 2012: 22). Lansdown rightly argues that because Article 5 requires direction and guidance across the whole of the Convention it should be recognised as a principle for the realisation of a child's rights (Lansdown, 2005).

The development of a unique identity is enhanced by working with children so they are all able eventually to make their own choices and decisions on their own terms. The concept of "evolving capacity" acknowledges that this is a process that happens over time by first being a good example and then working alongside until eventually the young person is able to make their own decisions.

3.1.4 Appropriate Directions

The word "appropriate" and what it means in any particular context is inevitably going to be debatable around the margins of how far and to what degree of detail and in what manner direction should be given. This is never easy to encapsulate, given the busy lives people have and the myriad of demands which are on them. What is needed is a simple, easily understandable touchstone for parents and caregivers to check their behaviour and actions in relation to their children. That touchstone can be, 'is what I am doing right now enhancing the child's capacity to develop their unique identity and capacities now and into the future?' There is and always will be differences of opinion as to what actions do or do not enhance the development of a child's unique identity. The key is that each child's identity is different, so adjustments need to be made to each particular child in terms of how they are developing and what will enhance their unique characteristics into the future. So there are no universal templates as to what is best. The preamble to the Convention gives insight into the environment a child should live in for the 'full and harmonious development of his or her personality', namely an atmosphere of 'happiness, love and understanding'. Those are the keys to enabling unique and authentic identity to develop and are a good further measure as to whether or not the directions given to a particular child are given in such an atmosphere.

4 Case Studies on Article 5

This section uses four case studies to analysis how Article 5, with its central emphasis on children' s rights and children's agency, provides an important litmus test of how best to make decisions that involve children.

4.1 *Case Study 1*

> *A child and a mother working together to hold the State to respecting the right of the child to preserve his identity*

James Hunt is a 12-year old boy who is starting secondary school at an all-boys school called Auckland Grammar in Auckland, New Zealand. As a tribute to his grandfather, who was expelled from Auckland Grammar 50 years earlier, James has grown his hair long down to his shoulders. The school rule at Auckland Grammar is that a student's hair needs to be clean and short enough to ensure it does not touch his shirt collar, should be no longer than a "number 2" and 'should not be long enough to be tied up in any form'.

The case received media attention on Stuff.co.nz (*New Zealand Herald*, 23 March 2017), when the school required James to have his hair cut. James' mother, Heidi, is quoted in the story as saying: 'It's his identity ... I wouldn't allow James to attend a school that still applies the same rule that resulted in his grandfather's expulsion 50 years ago' (*ibid.*). Eventually James had his hair cut so that he could attend the school but he and his mother are mounting a legal challenge against the school as to whether or not they can legally require James to have his hair cut in order to attend school.

There have been two previous cases in New Zealand where the issue of hair length and being able to attend the school have been the primary issue. In the case of *Edwards v. Onehunga High School* ([1974] 2 NZLR 238 [CA]), the New Zealand Court of Appeal ruled that it would not interfere with the Principal's decision that the student behaviour of having long hair and refusing to have it cut, was an 'injurious or dangerous example to other pupils' (which is a ground for suspending a pupil), unless the Principal could not have reasonably reached that view. There was no mention of the pupil's rights in 1974.

In 2014 the case of *Battison v. Melloy and the Board of Trustees of St John's College* ([2014] NZHC 1462) came before the New Zealand High Court. Lucan Battison had been suspended from St John's College in Hastings in New Zealand for failing to comply with a request from the school's Principal (Mr Melloy) that Lucan cut his hair.

Collins J. began his analysis of the decision to suspend Lucan by saying that, 'Courts in New Zealand and cognate jurisdictions have been more willing to ensure the rights of a student are given proper weight when revisiting schools disciplinary decisions' (*ibid.*: para. 50) The primary reason given for this change by Collins J. was the introduction of and the signing of the UN Convention on the Rights of the Child by the New Zealand Government (*ibid.*) Collins J. sited Priestley J. in *P v. K* ([2003] NZLR 787), where Priestly J, said, 'this important Convention establishes International Law norms relating to children and their rights. Where possible New Zealand's domestic law should be interpreted in such a way as to accord with the Convention ... Furthermore, Courts should strive to uphold the norm of the Convention when possible' (*ibid.*: para. 72).

Section 14(1)(c) of the Education Act 1989 gives a Principal of a State School in New Zealand the discretion to stand down or suspend a student if satisfied on reasonable grounds that the student's gross misconduct or continual disobedience is a harmful or dangerous example to other students at the school. Collins J. took the view that the suspension of Lucan was not warranted as the conduct was not 'so egregious that it seriously impacts on the welfare and attitude of other students at the school to the point where the Principal is left with no alternative other than to suspend or stand down the student in question' (*Battison*: para. 55).

Collins J. then looked at the hair rule of the school. Lucan argued that the hair rule breached his common law right to personal autonomy and integrity and was contrary to his freedom of expression in Section 14 of the New Zealand Bill of Rights Act 1990. Collins J. said that the breach of Lucan's rights argument raises 'a number of legal issues' but said he would 'resist the temptation to try and resolve these issues because the hair rule as presently worded does not comply with the common law requirement that it needs to be certain' (*ibid.*: para. 83).

The school rule said that hair is to be, 'short, tidy and of natural colour. Hair must be off the collar and out of the eyes. [Extremes including plait, dreads and mohawks are not acceptable]'. Collins J. held the rule 'was capable of being interpreted differently by students, parents, teachers, the Principal, and the Board' (*ibid.*: para, 92) and therefore it was unlawful because of uncertainty.

Collins J. went on to conclude whether or not it is necessary for the school to continue to have a hair rule, saying: 'the school will need to give very careful consideration as to whether or not any hair rule would breach a student's right to autonomy, individual dignity and his rights to freedom of expression affirmed by section 14 New Zealand Bill of Rights Act' (*ibid.*: para. 94) and I would add his right to identity under Article 8 of the Convention on the Rights of the Child.

Hair is a deeply personal part of us all. It goes to the core of our identity and how we see ourselves and how we want to be seen. Dr Dean Knight of Victoria University, Wellington, New Zealand said in a media statement that rules about hair length are 'ripe for being challenged' in Court. (Newshub 31/01/2019). Dr Knight asks, 'which educational purpose do these rules serve? Conformity is not a blank cheque for discipline'. His primary concern is that the hair rules have a reach outside the school – 'unlike a uniform which can be taken off, the student has to have short hair on week nights and weekends too. It breaches rights of personal autonomy'.

Dr Knight argues that hair rules are discriminatory both on the grounds of gender, where girls can have long hair at school, and religions and culture where Sikh men traditionally do not cut their hair and long hair is in several Polynesian cultures.

James Hunt's case is yet to be decided by the New Zealand Courts. It is a good example of a parent exercising her responsibilities, rights and duties under Article 5 to work with her son to give him appropriate direction in terms of his rights to identity, freedom of expression and personal autonomy and dignity. Collins J. has pointed the way in the *Battison* case that hair rules have the potential to breach such rights. This is an excellent example of an agent of the State, namely the courts, playing their role in taking the Convention seriously. It is a good example of a parent exercising her responsibilities, rights and duties under Article 5 in supporting her son's choice in making his own decisions about his hair choices.

In terms of the questions at the start of this chapter, this case study provides examples of the way they can be answered. James' mother in this case supports her son in his exercise of his rights consistent with his own identity, an important part of which is to emulate the long hair his grandfather once had. The State provides a court system to referee disputes where the children's rights came into conflict with a school's expectations and rules. Schools play a major role in a child's life. The United Nations Convention on the Rights of the Child in Articles 28 and 29 has important statements about education of children. Article 28(2) of the Convention says that State parties 'shall' take all appropriate measures to ensure that school discipline is administered in a manner consistent with the child's human dignity and in conformity with the Convention. Article 29(1)(a) of the Convention emphasises that the crucial goal of education is the development of the child's personality, talents and mental and physical abilities to their fullest potential. There is a strong emphasis on developing the unique, authentic identity and personality of the particular child. Added to that is Article 29(1)(b) which directs that education is required to develop respect for human rights and fundamental freedoms and for the principles enshrined in the Charter of the United Nations. The best way to develop respect in children for rights is to respect children's own values. Article 29(1)(c) of the Convention requires State parties to develop respect for the child's 'own ... values'.

4.2   Case Study 2

When is it Applicable for Members of the Extended Family of the Child to give Guidance and Directions under Article 5?

Rhonda Nikau is the third child of her parents Esther and Colin Nikau, and their only daughter (all the names in this case study are fictional names provided by the Family Court). Colin is of Maori descent (Maori are the indigenous people of New Zealand), and his wife Esther, is pakeha (Pakeha is the Maori term for European New Zealanders). Colin agreed to place Rhonda with his sister Wendy, who is of Maori descent and her partner Winston, who is also of Maori decent, in accordance with matua whangai – a Maori concept whereby children are placed with other family members who cannot have children of their own to be brought up but they still maintain regular contact with their birth parents. Wendy and Winston were not able to have children of their own, so Rhonda was placed with them to be raised as their daughter. In terms of the principles of tikanga Maori and of matua whangai, whilst Wendy and Winston raised Rhonda, Esther and Colin, the birth parents were to be fully and deeply involved in Rhonda's life.

Unfortunately for Rhonda the relationship between her birth parents and the whangai parents broke down. Esther wanted Rhonda back in her care to live with her brothers Toby and Mitchell.

Esther made allegations that Rhonda had been abused in the care of Wendy and Winston. Oranga Tamariki[1] – the state child welfare agency – removed Rhonda from Wendy and Winston and placed her in the care of Esther's parents, Mr and Mrs Tatchell, who were Rhonda's grandparents. The grandparents lived a distance from where Rhonda had been living with Wendy and Winston, with Esther and Colin living nearby. Esther and Colin moved closer to where Rhonda was with the grandparents.

The case came before the courts – with both Esther and Colin, and Wendy and Winston, seeking to have Rhonda returned to their care. The allegations of abuse had been dismissed, and the only question therefore was where the child should live (*Nikau v. Tatchell* [2018] NZFLR 276 (*'Nikau* (Family Court')). Rhonda's birth parents Esther and Colin wanted Rhonda back in their care and Wendy and Winston wanted Rhonda back in their care and to be appointed additional guardians of Rhonda.

At this point, Rhonda is eight years old. Judge Coyle says that the evidence shows that Rhonda sees herself as having two mums and dads. Judge Coyle put primary emphasis on the fact Rhonda was a child of Maori decent:

> The principles of the Treaty of Waitangi (a treaty between the indigenous people of New Zealand and the settlers signed in 1840) require the Courts

---

1 Oranga Tamariki is the Maori words for life for children and they have replaced what used to be called Social Welfare.

to give particular importance to the preservation and strengthening of whanau relationships (whanau relationships include both family and wider family) and identity to Maori children over and above that of other cultures (*Nikau*, 2018: para. 100).

Judge Coyle emphasised the crucial importance of Rhonda's Maori heritage:

> The Family Court in recognition of its Treaty obligations should embrace Te Ao Maori (Te Ao Maori means Maori world view) and afford to Maori children ... a particular and careful focus in ensuring that ... a child's sense of identity as Maori can be particularly and specially both preserved and strengthened (*Nikau* (Family Court): para. 102).

Judge Coyle decided that it was best if Rhonda went back to the original town she had lived in with Wendy and Winston, the whangai parents, as most of Rhonda's whanau (Maori word for extended family) lived there. Judge Coyle listened to Rhonda's view that she has two 'mums and dads' and said that if Esther and Colin move back to the original town they would share the care of Rhonda with the whangai parents as they had in the early years of Rhonda's life. Wendy and Winston were appointed additional guardians for Rhonda. This means they had equal rights and responsibilities in terms of the upbringing of Rhonda with the birth parents, Esther and Colin.

The primary emphasis in the Family Court decision of Judge Coyle was to preserve and strengthen Rhonda's Maori identity. Article 8 of the UNCRC requires State parties to respect the right of a child to preserve his or her identity. This is consistent with s. 4(1)(f) of the New Zealand Care of Children Act 2004, which requires the Family Court to take into account the cultural identity of the child in deciding what is best for the child.

Judge Coyle was strongly of the view that there were aspects of Maori culture which it is not possible to teach from afar, but can only be learnt through lived experiences, through osmosis so they become an integral part of Rhonda's life.

The birth parents, Esther and Colin, appealed the decision to the New Zealand High Court (*Nikau and Nikau v. Nikau and Hohepa v. Tatchell and Tatchell* [2018] NZHC 162 (('*Nikau* (High Court)')) as they did not want to move back to the original town they had lived in before, nor share the care with Wendy and Winston. By the time the appeal was heard in the New Zealand High Court, Rhonda's life history was as follows – for the first four and a quarter years, Rhonda was in the primary care of her whangai parents, Wendy and Winston, with considerable involvement of her birth parents, Esther and Colin. For the next two and a quarter years Rhonda was in the shared care of both sets of parents. For the 18 months leading up to the appeal in the High Court, Rhonda was in the primary care of her grandparents, Mr and Mrs Tatchell, with considerable involvement from her birth parents, Esther and Colin.

Woolford J. in the High Court upheld the appeal. The view was taken that Judge Coyle had put too much weight on cultural identity and relationships with whanau and extended family and not sufficient weight on the principle that a child's care and development and upbringing should be *primarily* the responsibility of his or her parents or guardians. Woolford J. described this principle as 'important' (*Nikau* (High Court): para. 57) and not given sufficient weight in the Family Court. Woolford J. also emphasised that continuity of care, set out in s 4(1)(d) of the New Zealand Care of Children Act 2004, was also 'important' (*Nikau* (High Court): para. 57). Rhonda was doing very well at school and had many new friends – 'she had a particularly good relationship with her teacher whom she adores' (*ibid.*) Rhonda was said to have made 'real progress in terms of maturity and the development of her personality' (*ibid.*) in her current environment living with her grandparents and having frequent contact with her birth parents and brothers who were said to have 'contributed to a positive environment' (*ibid.*) Woolford J. expressed concern and risk if Rhonda went back to the environment she was in when younger, particularly when there was still tension between the birth and whangai parents. Esther, the birth mother, made it clear to the High Court that she would not return to the original location because she felt intimidated by the environment. Woolford J. was concerned that if the primary care of Rhonda was with her whangai parents in the original environment, that she, her birth parents, her brothers and her maternal grandparents would see much less of her. They were described by Woolford J. as a 'significant part of her family group' (*ibid.*: para. 60).

Woolford J. accepted that if Rhonda stayed in her current location with her birth parents rather than return to the original location where there were more whanau, and extended family, that Te Ao Maori 'will be less accessible to Rhonda if she was to remain with her birth parents' (*ibid.*: para. 65). Her birth father, Colin, told the High Court that he was 'committed to Te Reo and acknowledges a duty to pass on his knowledge of Te Ao Maori to Rhonda' (*ibid.*).

The High Court placed Rhonda in the day-to-day care of her birth parents, Esther and Colin, and the whangai parents would have care of Rhonda one weekend every month and one week during each school term holiday and half the Christmas holiday. The order of the Family Court granting additional guardianship to the whangai parents was quashed so they would not have a say in the important matters in Rhonda's life such as which school she went to.

They would still have influence on Rhonda's life through exposing her to Te Ao Maori, and through their own values and world views.

Wendy and Winston appealed the decision to the New Zealand Court of Appeal (*Nikau and Nikau v. Nikau and Hohepa v. Tatchell and Tatchell* [2018] NZCA 586 ('*Nikau* (Court of Appeal)')). The Court of Appeal did agree that whether or not whangai parents counted as parents for the purposes of the Care of Children Act – and one could also say the UN Convention on the Rights of the Child – was a bona fide arguable point but did not think this was the case in which such an issue could be resolved. The Court of Appeal concluded that the parenting orders made in the High Court were in the best interests and welfare of Rhonda and the interpretation of the word "parent" would have made no difference to the outcome, and they refused leave for the appeal.

This case study shows how through the agency of the Courts, decisions are made as to who will be the primary directors of a child's understanding of the world and which environment it is best for the child to thrive in and develop their identity. Woolford J. in the High Court (*Nikau* (High Court): para. 37) said that he noted Rhonda's view that she wished to remain in the original location with her parents and have the arrangements with her birth parents and her whangai parents restored 'to be the same as before' (*ibid.*: para. 37). Woolford J. took Rhonda's view into account as required by s. 6 of the Care of Children's Act 2004, but was of the opinion that it was 'not possible' (*ibid.*) to do what Rhonda wanted. This was based on the psychologist's report that Rhonda was at risk 'of developing physical adjustment problems under her birth parents, and her whangai parents if unable to resolve their differences or learn to encapsulate their conflict' (*ibid.*). Research was presented to the Court that 'it is often better to prioritise one solid attachment then to have the transfer of attachment' (*ibid.*).

This case study shows that there are different concepts of what "family" means for the purposes of Article 5. Article 5 recognises wider family and whanau as part of the group who may have the rights, duties, responsibilities to give direction to the child about the Convention, but only when 'applicable', not as of right. Justice Williams, speaking extra-judicially, said that for Maori, 'all economic social and political rights and obligations are organised and controlled through kinship' (Williams, 2017); the child is part of a wider whanau and according to Maori values all of whom should be part of the upbringing of the child. A recent review of the New Zealand Family Court (Te Korowai Ture a-Whanau, 2019), found that the Family Court has not been responsive to Maori values and Maori have felt alienated by the Court. This case study shows that a Family Court Judge made major efforts to understand a Maori world view for

Rhonda but was overturned by the High Court decision which emphasised a more European birth parent view of what would be best for Rhonda.

The case study also shows that Rhonda was constructing a clear view of her own unique identity by wanting to be shared by both sets of parents as she had been for the first four years of her life. Her right to be able to do that, which Article 5 protects, has been interrupted both by Court processes and by changes of arrangements.

4.3   *Case Study 3*

A Breastfed five-month old Girl and Contact with her Father

The issue in this case, (*MT v. AK* [Interim Parenting Orders] [2010] NZFLR 613), was the appropriate contact for a father of a five-month-old female child who is being breastfed. The father wanted contact on Tuesday, Wednesday and Thursday each week from 8.30 a.m. to 5.30 p.m. The mother was agreeable to Monday and Thursday contact each week for one and half hours, moving to three days a week for one and half hours. The reason for the offer of fewer hours was that the baby was fed on demand and was fed every one and half hours. The parents lived close to each other so it was very easy and took little time to transfer the baby back and forwards. The mother had breastfed her other four daughters and wanted to do the same with this baby daughter.

Evidence was given to the Family Court by a mid-wife who said there were risks to the baby of illness, greater possibility for hospital admissions, gastrointestinal infections, risk of asthma, eczema and obesity if the baby was not breastfed (*ibid.*: para. 23). Judge Coyle said he found this evidence to be 'not helpful' as there was no statistical analysis of the risk to the child if not breastfed. Is it 'one chance in two of developing these symptoms or one chance in 10 billion' (*ibid.*)?

The mid-wife said that breastfeeding was optimal for the first year of a child's life and essential that the baby be fed exclusively with breast milk for the first six months (*ibid.*: para. 24) Judge Coyle accepted that the view was consistent with the view expressed by the World Health Organisation, and referred to Article 24(2)(d) of the UN Convention on the Rights of the Child:

> State parties shall take appropriate measures to ensure that all segments of society, in particular parents and children, are informed, have access to education and are supported in the use of basic knowledge of child

health and nutrition, the advantages of breastfeeding, hygiene and environmental sanitation and the prevention of accidents.

Judge Coyle interpreted Article 24(2)(d) of the Convention to mean that the State should ensure caregivers of children have access to education about the advantages of breastfeeding but does not go as far as supporting the use of breastfeeding (*ibid.*: para. 34).

The mother refused to express breast milk but indicated a willingness to breastfeed the baby when she was in her father's care (*ibid.*: para. 36).

Judge Coyle took the view that the mother was using the breastfeeding to keep the child at arm's length from the father. The child had been conceived when the mother had a break from her husband and had a sexual relationship with the father of the baby. The mother and the husband were now back together. Judge Coyle said the mother wanted to keep the father at arm's length and did not want to be reminded that there was a baby in the family with a different father than her husband (*ibid.*: para. 27).

Judge Coyle goes on to say that the mother's 'desire to maintain breastfeeding while laudable is subject to the welfare and basic best interest of the child. In the absence of evidence of clear risk to [the child], breastfeeding should not operate as a barrier to contact between the child and her father' (*ibid.*: para. 31).

Judge Coyle emphasises that the mother and father of the baby are encouraged to work together to discuss how the baby can continue to be breastfed whilst in her father's care. A warning was given to the mother that if she is not willing to work with the father to ensure that the baby is able to be breastfed when she is in her father's care, then 'bottle-feeding will be the only option and if [the mother] continues with her view that she refuses to express breast milk [the father] has no option but to use formula' (*ibid.*).

An order was made that the father was to have care of the child every Tuesday and Wednesday from 10.30 a.m. till 2.00 p.m. and some additional time as could be agreed between the father and the mother (*ibid.*: para. 34).

Judge Coyle based his decision on the importance of 'preserving' and 'strengthening' family relationships and saw those words in section 4(d) of the Care of Children Act as very important (*ibid.*: para. 16). 'Strengthening' was said to mean 'building upon' and 'growing' of family relationships. Articles 5, 7(1), 8(1) 14(2) and 18(1) of the Convention on the Rights of the Child are cited by Judge Coyle as supporting his analysis that strengthening and growing of family relationships was the most significant factor in the case. What is common about all the above articles in the Convention is that they focus on the rights and duties of parents, the preservation of family relations, and the responsibility of both parents for the upbringing and development of a child. There is no mention of Article 5 which is focussed on child's rights and parental duties. As Kamchedzera points out, Article 5 has been interpreted in an adult-centred approach to the notions of family and parenthood which ignores the content of the child's rights in Article 5 (Kamchedzera, 2012: 14).

Judge Coyle was of the view that the sooner the relationship between parent and child is established the better for the child in terms of building their family relationships for the future. In an ideal world, the baby would be breastfed and would also build a relationship with her father through regular contact. This is why Judge Coyle encouraged this as the best option. But if there was a choice to be made between breastfeeding and good contact with the father, contact with the father was seen as more important in the child's long-term welfare.

A case such as this is highly contestable. Those who strongly believe in breastfeeding and the significance of it for the child will deeply disagree with the result. Those who believe the earlier the father becomes involved in a meaningful relationship with the child, the better for the child, will see the case as positive for the child. Article 5 and the Convention do not provide ready-made answers to such disagreements.

The Convention cannot be too prescriptive of what is best for a child as knowledge and understanding of what is best for children changes over time. For example, there was a massive debate between social scientists in the field as to whether or not overnight stays for young children under three were beneficial or harmful to children. In the end, a compromise was reached (Pruett, MacIntosh and Kelly, 2014). Judge Coyle did his best in reaching a compromise in this case by strongly encouraging the mother to do her breastfeeding when the baby was with the father. This is not an easy compromise for a mother who is deeply attached to breastfeeding and would have to visit the father's house every one and a half hours to breastfeed her baby. A different approach to breastfeeding is taken by Judge Ellis in the case of *SAQ v. LRER* (FAM-2009-091-000618, 12 November 2010, Family Court Wellington), who said this about the need of young babies:

> That is a perfectly natural progression in any child's life, commencing from the most intimate attachment with the mother and the womb, through the processes of fundamental, maternal bonding and breastfeeding and then toddling towards dad and beginning to explore the world outside with him. These are perfectly natural processes which need, for the best interests of the children, to be achieved, to be supported, nurtured and carefully managed by the parents (*ibid*.: para. 69).

Fiona Mackenzie in her PhD thesis on "Motherhood and Family Law" (Mackenzie, 2016) wrote an alternative judgment *B v. C* (2016) to the *MT v. AK* (2010) [Interim Parenting Orders] judgment of Judge Coyle. In her judgment, Mackenzie says:

> A is nearly five months old and she is currently fully breastfed by her mother. She is of an age where she is clearly entirely dependent upon the adults around her, particularly her mother, to meet all her needs and for her support. Mrs C too is in a circumstance as a breastfeeding mother, where she is more vulnerable than during other periods of her life, and therefore also requires the care and support of the adults around her to be able to respond well to the immediacy and the intimacy required by A's present, complete dependency upon her. A is at the genesis of a lifetime of opportunity to develop and strengthen her relationships with her parents, beginning with her relationship with her mother. As her primary relationship, this must be preserved and strengthened (Mackenzie, 2016: second schedule, para. 12).

Mackenzie makes it clear in her judgment that the baby's welfare and best interests are not based on the rights of the father as her biological father but 'in the quality and network of the relationships that are available and able to be developed in the future for A' (*ibid.*: para. 15).

Mackenzie assessed the evidence differently, finding that the mother was not using her breastfeeding relationship to keep the father at arm's length but rather, 'the fact is the gendered nature of the role and function of a mother towards the child through breastfeeding means that the father cannot participate in this' (*ibid.*: para. 35).

Mackenzie ordered contact on Monday, Thursday and Friday from 10.30 a.m. until 12 noon and other times that 'can be agreed between the mother and father'. She also ordered special counselling to help the parents to communicate well over the future of the child.

Mackenzie's hypothetical judgment places more weight on the importance of the child to receive breastfeeding from its mother in a way that the mother is comfortable and supported to ensure that the child whose rights are at stake receives the best possible environment to develop this child's unique identity and wellbeing in the world.

This case shows the interplay between parental rights and the child's rights in Article 5. When a child is young as in this case, it is tempting to put the major emphasis on parenting, as was done by the Court; however, Article 5's reason for existence is to enable the rights of each particular child to be enhanced. The lens must focus on what is happening to this particular child, enabling the child to fully develop.

4.4 Case Study 4

> Two girls 11 and 13 who were described as 'vulnerable to sexual exploitation' had been sexually abused while in their parent's care (not by their parents). They were placed in State care and now wanted to return home to live with their parents

Both children were described as 'strongly' bonded with their parents, more particularly with their mother. The 13-year-old had been sexually abused by four different people while in the parents' home. Judge Ingle QC said in the matter of the *S Children* ([1994] NZFLR 971), the evidence indicated that 'the child does not seem to have any idea that sexual conduct with her (such as sodomy) are in fact sexual abuse'. Judge Ingle QC made a finding that neither parent had 'any real idea' of the kind of training a child needs to avoid sexual abuse and that they were unable to protect the children from sexual abuse. 'My finding is that the parents are either unwilling or unable to appreciate that a problem exists'. (*ibid.*: 973) For example the parents had rented out a sleepout on their property to a boarder who then sexually abused the older girl.

Judge Inglis QC turned to the United Convention Rights of the Child for guidance as to what principles in it were applicable to the two young girls.

First, the best interests of the child was said to be a recurring theme in Article 3(1), 9(2) and 18(1).

Second, respect for the interests of the child's natural family unit and in particular, 'recognition of the nurturing responsibility of the children's parents and the child's right to be nurtured by his or her parent' were said to be at the core of Articles 5, 9 and 18. (*ibid.*: 977–978)

This case study presents a choice between the parents' rights and responsibilities to nurture the best interests of these two young girls so that they can develop their unique identities, and the State's interests in protecting children from harm and abuse as required by Article 19 of the Convention on the Rights of the Child. Article 9(1) of the Convention says that children may only be separated from the parents or family if 'such separation is really in the best interests of the child'. While it is important for children in maintaining relationships and contact with their parents, it is also clear that children have an interest in being protected from abuse or neglect.

The two young girls were placed in the custody of the Director-General of Social Welfare who was given additional guardianship of both girls. Discretion was given to the Director-General to when the girls would have access with their parents and the degree of supervision that would be appropriate.

Judge Inglis QC said he felt some sympathy for the parents who had a 'tried to do what was asked of them' and also resented the interference by the State. (*ibid.*: 985)

The outcome for the two young girls is that they were placed in State care with the State deciding the degree of contact they will have with their parents. It is assumed that State care will protect the two young girls from future sexual abuse, but this cannot be guaranteed as children can be abused in State care. Currently New Zealand is carrying out a major inquiry into the abuse of children and young people who have been in State care. (State Care Abuse Inquiry, 2019) The girls close bond with their parents, particularly their mother will be put at risk as they will spend far less time with their parents.

The former Commissioner for Children in New Zealand, Russell Wills, brought out a report on Children in State Care (State of Care, 2015). The outcome was very sobering. Children in State care in the matters of wellbeing and educational attainment were at the very bottom statistically.

There has to be better ways to ensure the development of the unique identity of these two young girls. They clearly wanted to remain with their parents as it was an important part of their development of who they were. Their family needed intensive support and help to look after their daughters, rather than removal of them. The intensive support and help would provide the protective factor but they would still be able to maintain their strong bond with their parents. This is more likely to give them a chance of constructing their own unique personal identities rather than removing them totally and placing them in a totally different context.

5   Conclusion

Article 5 recognises the importance of parents and wider family members in ensuring that children are given appropriate directions on all their extensive rights in the UN Convention on the Rights of the Child. At the core of Article 5 is the right of the child to be able to be nurtured, informed, encouraged, and enabled to develop their own unique individual identity and capacity.

Article 5 is not prescriptive as to how both the State and the family members should carry out their duties to inform and allow children and young people to understand and develop their own unique capacities in terms of the rights the Convention gives to them. Article 5 places a duty on the State to support parents and other family members in carrying out their important responsibilities under Article 5, particularly where families have very limited resources and some may have no resources at all.

Underlying Article 5 and all the other articles in the Convention is the importance of recognising each child's individual personal identity. The case study of James Hunt and his mother Heidi Hunt exemplifies that personal dignity is very closely attached as to how the particular child sees themselves. We all have our unique view of who we are and this case study shows that to date the Court takes the right to personal dignity very seriously which gives hope for the future application of Article 5.

Children exist in a wide matrix of family members Article 5 recognises that, by acknowledging the applicability of wider family members to give direction and guidance to children. When this is done in the right spirit it inevitably enriches the child's particular life and gives them a wider source of constructing their own unique and authentic identity, which is the primary purpose of Article 5. The case study about Rhonda shows this can be easily overlooked if too much focus is placed on adult's disputes and concerns and not sufficient on the child's unique world view.

Clashes between family members as to what is best for a child are inevitable. In case study three breastfeeding was the sore point that created conflict between the parents not because either parent was opposed to breastfeeding but because the father wanted to see his daughter on terms that were more favourable to him. This was a further example where adult concerns overrode the perspective and situation of the particular young baby. It was perfectly possible to both enable the child to be breastfed in a comfortable and loving environment and also see her father, if the focus had been more strongly on the young baby's rights rather than the parents' concerns.

The final case study addresses a core issue regarding children when there appears to be a clash between protection and autonomous decisions. Protection never exists in isolation and removing children from their homes in the eyes of protection can create different risks for children. Ultimately the question must be asked what consequence does the protective method engaged in have in terms of the child or young person developing their unique identity and is it possible for them to maintain the relationships they want to but with oversite and support for their safety.

Article 5 when looked at with the purpose of fostering a child's right to establish his or her own unique identity provides a powerful principle and interpretative technique to ensure that the particular child's uniqueness and dignity is not lost in State and family arguments as to what is best for the child.

Acknowledgement

This chapter is based on a presentation to a Symposium (17–18 July 2019) on Article 5 of the 1989 UN Convention on the Rights of the Child, organised by Drs Claire Fenton-Glynn and Brian Sloan from the University of Cambridge Law Faculty. Thank you to all those who took part for their wise and helpful comments.

References

Articles

Eekelaar, J., (2004) 'Children between Cultures' *International Journal of Law, Policy and the Family* 2004 (18) 178–94.

Erbele, E.J, *Dignity and Liberty: Constitutional Visions in Germany and the United States* (Westport: Praeger Publishers, 2002).

Freeman, M., *Children, Their Families and the Law: Working with the Children Act*, (Basingstoke: Macmillan, 1992).

Freeman, M., *The Moral Status of Children: Essays on the Rights of the Child* (Hague: Kluwer Law International, 1997).

Hanson, K. and Lundy, L., 'Does Exactly What it Says on the Tin? A Critical Analysis and Alternative Conceptualisation of the So-Called 'General Principles' of the Convention on the Rights of the Child' *International Journal of Children's Rights* 2017 (25(2)) 285–306.

Williams, J., 'Address' (New Zealand Law Society Family Law Conference Rotorua, 20 October 2017), https:\\www.lawyerseducation.co.nz.

Kamchedzera, G., *Article 5: The child's right to appropriate direction and guidance: A Commentary on the United Nations Convention on the Rights of the Child* (Leiden: Martinus Nijhoff Publishers, 2012).

Lansdown, G., *The Evolving Capacities of the Child* (Florence: UNICEF Innocenti, 2005).

Pruett, M., MacIntosh J., and Kelly J., 'Parental Separation and Overnight Care of Young Children' *Family Court Review* 2004 (52), 240–255.

Rockefeller, S.C., 'Comment' in A. Gutmann (ed), Multiculturism: *Examining the Policy Recognition* (Princeton: Princeton University Press, 1994).

Ronen, Y., 'Redefining the Child's Right to Identity' *International Journal of Law, Policy and the Family* 2004 (18) 147–177.

Taylor, C., 'The politics of recognition' in A. Gutmann (*ed*) *Multiculturism: Examining the Politics of Recognition* (Princeton: Princeton University Press, 1994).

Van Bueren, G., *The International Law on the Rights of the Child* (Dordrecht: Martin Nijhoff Publishers, 1995).

Varadan, S., 'The Principle of Evolving Capacities under the UN Convention on the Rights of the Child', *International Journal of Children's Rights* 2019 (27) 306–338.

Concluding Observations from the CRCC

United Nations Committee on the Rights of the Child, *Concluding Observations on Australia* CRC/C/AUS/CO/4, 28 August 2012.

United Nations Committee on the Rights of the Child, *Concluding Observations on Switzerland* CRC/C/CHE/CO/2-4, 26 February 2015.

United Nations Committee on the Rights of the Child, *Concluding Observations on Bulgaria* CRC/C/BGR/CO/3-5, 21 November 2016.

United Nations Committee on the Rights of the Child, *Concluding Observations on Ireland* CRC/C/IRL/CO/3-4, 1 March 2016.

United Nations Committee on the Rights of the Child, *Concluding Observations on New Zealand* CRC/C/NZL/CO/5, 30 September 2016.

United Nations Committee on the Rights of the Child, *Concluding Observations on Norway* CRC/C/NOR/CO/5-6, 4 July 2018.

United Nations Committee on the Rights of the Child, *Concluding Observations on Romania*, CRC/C/ROU/CO/5, 13 July 2017.

United Nations Committee on the Rights of the Child, *Concluding Observations on Bulgaria* CRC/C/15/Add.66, 24 January 1997.

United Nations Committee on the Rights of the Child, *Concluding Observations on Panama* CRC/C/15/Add.68, 24 January 1997.

United Nations Committee on the Rights of the Child, *Concluding Observations on Sierra Leone*, CRC/C/15/Add.116, 24 February 2000.

United Nations Committee on the Rights of the Child, *Concluding Observations on Oman* CRC/C/OMN/CO/2, 29 September 2006.

United Nations Committee on the Rights of the Child, *Concluding Observations on Saint Lucia* CRC/C/15/Add.258, 21 September 2005.

United Nations Committee on the Rights of the Child, *Concluding Observations on Norway* CRC/C/NOR/CO/5-6, 4 July 2018.

United Nations Committee on the Rights of the Child, *Concluding Observations on Sweden* CRC/C/SWE/CO/5, 6 March 2015.

United Nations Committee on the Rights of the Child, *Concluding Observations on United Kingdom of Great Britain and Norther Ireland*: CRC/C/GBR/CO/5, 12 July 2016.

United Nations Committee on the Rights of the Child, *Concluding Observations on South Africa*CRC/C/ZAF/CO/2, 27 October 2016.

Constitutions

Article 48(1) of the *Constitution of Poland* (1997), accessible through https://confinder.richmond.edu/.

Article 42(1) of the *Constitution of Ireland* (1937), accessible through https://confinder.richmond.edu/.

Definitions

The definitions here are taken from the Oxford English Dictionary (originally published 1st February 1884, taken from the March 2010 edition).

Media

Bateman, S., (2019, January 31) Boys should be allowed to have long hair at school – Victoria Uni law professor Dr Dean Knight. *Newshub*. Retrieved from newshub.co.nz.

Martin, M., (2019, March 23). Mum goes head-to-head with top Auckland school over length of son's hair. *Stuff*. Retrieved from stuff.co.nz.

Reports

Te Korowai Ture a-Whanau: The Final Report of the Independent Panel Examining the 2014 Family Justice Reforms (2019), https:\\justice.govt.nz.

Royal Commission of Inquiry into Historical Abuse in State Care and in the Care of Faith Based Institutions (2019), https:\\orangatamariki.gov.nz.

State of Care 2015, *What We Learnt From Monitoring Child Youth and Family* (Office of the Commissioner for Children August 2015). https:\\www.occ.org.nz.reports.

Thesis

Dr Fiona Mackenzie Motherhood and Family Law submitted to the University of Otago in New Zealand in June 2016 and is stored in the Otago University Library https:\www.otago.ac.nz>library.

Index

Abortion   55, 58
Adolescence   68, 89
Adoption
   Age Limits   *see* Age Limits, Adoption
   Birth Parents' Consent   235, 264, 267, 269, 271
   Changing Surname   *see* Changing Surname
   Child Participation   207-208, 210-222, 226, 233, 235-242, 249-
   Child's Consent To   205, 216, 224, 233, 235, 242, 248-250
   Contact with Birth Family   205, 207, 217, 222, 243-246, 333-337
   Father's Involvement   257-275
   Generally   26, 189-190, 199, 204, 206, 234, 258-259, 333
   Information about Birth Parents to Child   265
   'Simple'   257n1
Age and Maturity   121, 180, 200, 203, 207-208, 225, 246, 249, 251, 309
   Age LimitsAdoption   204-205, 207-208, 216, 224, 233, 235, 246, 249
   Criminal Responsibility   93-94, 99-100
   Generally   44-46, 89-90, 200
Alternative Dispute Resolution   *see* Mediation
Apartheid   148
Appropriate Direction   329, 332
Armed Forces   46, 308n1
Assault   151, 160
Assent   293
Autonomy Support   70, 71

Baby Box, Scottish   309
Baby Boxes, Adoption   262, 264
Best Interests
   of a Medical Patient   283
   Paramountcy of   153, 155, 157-159, 181, 184, 187, 232, 259
   Principle of   41, 72, 94-95, 129-130, 133, 142, 174, 179, 226, 266, 269, 294, 341 *see also* CRC Article 3(1)

Birth Certificate   185, 270-272
Birth Registration   267, 270, 272
Breastfeeding   337-341

Capacity
   Generally   83-84, 90, 92-94, 108, 202
   Legal   54-55
   Mental   54-56, 58-59, 73
   to Make Decisions   224-225, 232
   see also Evolving Capacity of the Child
Care, State
   Child Participation in Proceedings   199
   Generally   199-200, 342
Changing First Name   189
Changing Surname   217, 243
Child Abuse   *see* Children, Harm to
Child Autonomy   38, 42, 60-63, 91, 94, 202, 232, 290, 294-298, 331
Child Development   43, 47, 71, 75, 99, 108, 320
Child Protection   26-27, 144, 205-207, 234, 236
Child's Views, Taking into Account   117-119, 122, 132, 134, 200-201, 226-227, 236, 295, 336
Children Act 1989   72
Children and Family Courts Advice and Support Service (Cafcass)   139-141, 143
Children as Parents   267
Children
   as Heads of Household   23
   as Property   41
   Harm to   135, 153, 156-157, 180, 310, 312, 319, 341-342
   Legal Representation   57, 97, 100, 110, 121, 236, 252
Cohabitation   274
Cold Decision Making   74, 92
Concrete Operational Stage   67
Consent By Proxy   282, 286, 289-295, 298
Contact   109, 119, 135, 337-341
Convention on the Rights of the Child (CRC)
   Article 2: Child's Non-Discrimination   14, 37, 64

Convention on the Rights of the
    Child (CRC) (cont.)
  Article 3: Best Interests   14, 21-22, 29, 31,
    41, 72 *see also* Best Interests
  Article 6: Child's Right to Life, Survival and
    Development   14, 30, 47
  Article 7: Right to Know Parents   261, 263
  Article 8: Cultural Identity   330, 334-335
  Article 9: Non-separation from
    Parents   341
  Article 12: Child's Participation Rights   14,
    32, 39-40, 62-64, 95, 104-106, 111, 120, 186,
    199, 202, 289
  Article 18: Both Parents Should Bring up
    Child   129, 135, 144, 294
  Communications and Complaints
    Procedure   21, 28, 32
  General Principles   14, 29, 85, 157
Corporal Punishment   *see* Physical
    Punishment
Criminal Justice   87-88, 92-9100
Criminal Responsibility   46, 73-74, 83-84,
    89-93
Custody   *see* Residence

Declaration of Helsinki   285-287
Declaration of the Rights of the Child   14
Delict   151
Depression   177
Deprivation of Liberty   87, 95
Developmental Psychology   66-68, 200
Disability   26, 37-38, 47, 65, 70
Discrimination
  Disability   37-38
  Gender   23-24, 29, 37-38
  Non-   14, 37, 64-65
  Race   37
Divorce
  Financial Arrangements   138
  Generally   23, 104, 109, 112-117, 129-131, 135
Donor Conception   263

ECHR Article 8: Right to Respect for Private
    Life   268, 313, 316
Emerging Adulthood   68
Evolving Capacity of the Child
  Legal Concept   17-18, 25, 27, 28, 30-32, 36,
    38-39, 42-43, 45, 59-60, 75, 83-86, 89,
    91-93, 107, 155, 182, 201-202, 232, 249,
    289, 320-321, 324, 328-329

Mental Capacity   66, 291-292, 294-298
    see also Capacity
Extended Family   19, 41, 273, 328,
    333-337

Fair Trial, Right to   97, 100
Family Law, Reform   131-132, 141-142
Family Law, State Intervention   144
Father
  Biological   261-262, 265
  Registration   271-272
Formal Operational Stage   68
Foster Care   26 *see also* Care, State
Foster Parents   205, 225, 234

Gender Dysphoria   177, 186
Gender Identity   185
Gender Reassignment Surgery   *see* Sex
    Alteration Surgery
Gender Reveal Parties   172
General Data Protection Regulations   313-314,
    316
Gillick Competence   52, 54-55, 58, 65, 72, 75,
    181, 297
Guardian Ad Litem   236
Guardianship   111, 274, 333
Guidelines on Child-Friendly Justice   93,
    96-97, 100

Hair Length   330-331
Hermaphrodites   *see* Intersex
Homosexuality   *see* Sexual Orientation
Hot Decision Making   74, 92

Indigenous Groups   *see* Minority Groups
Informed Consent Doctrine   185, 188, 281,
    296-298
Intelligence Quotient   66
International Covenant on Civil and Political
    Rights   16
International Covenant on Economic, Social
    and Cultural Rights   16
Intersex   172-177, 181-185, 188-189

Lawyers, Conflict of Interests   143
Legal Parents   263
Lived Existence   262-263, 334

Macarthur Competence Assessment Tool for
    Treatment   57, 59

INDEX

Marriage   39, 45, 308
Mediation   110, 133, 136, 143
Medical Consent   53-58, 64-65, 181, 188, 191, 281
Medical Experimentation   283-284, 289
Medical Research   282-289, 295, 297, 299
Medical Treatment   68, 71-72, 74, 135, 181, 184, 281, 283, 289, 297
Mens Rea   90
Mental Capacity Act 2005   54-59, 70, 73
Mental Illness   47
Minority Groups   22, 65-66, 234-235, 333-337
Mother and Baby Homes   272
Mother, Biological   261, 266

Name   see Changing First Name and Changing Surname
Named Person Scheme   307-322
Nuclear Family   22
Nuremberg Code   283-284

Parental Guidance   83, 86, 93-98, 100, 104, 106-109, 174, 183, 266, 290-291, 327, 331-332
Parental Influence   111, 134
Parental Responsibility   206, 267-270
Parents
    Incarceration   23
    Ownership of Children   178, 182, 187, 291
    Primacy of   40
Paternalism   226-227
Physical Punishment
    at School   149, 152
    Generally   30, 148-150, 152, 157, 163-165
    in Criminal Justice System   148
    in the Home   149-150, 159
Positive Parenting   156, 164
Poverty   22, 47, 158
Pre-Nuptial Agreements   142
Prefrontal Cortex   74
Preoperational Stage   67
Proxy Informed Consent   see Consent by Proxy
Puberty   68

Reasonable Chastisement   149-152, 158, 160-161, 164-166

Reconciliation   136
Reduced Culpability   93, 99
Religion   18, 72, 158, 160, 163-165, 312, 331
Residence   109, 130, 138, 141
Respect   326-327

Scaffolding   108-109, 291
Secret Births   258, 261, 263, 265-266, 268
Sensorimotor Stage   67
Separation
    Informal Arrangements   141-142
    see also Divorce
Sex Alteration Surgery   173, 182, 184-185, 188
Sexual Abuse   341-342
Sexual Orientation   176, 185
Special Needs   26, 180
Special Procedure   136

Third Optional Protocol   see CRC Communications Procedure
Transgender   185, 189
Triangular Relationship   13, 20, 36, 42, 86, 154-155

UN Committee on the Rights of the Child   14, 27, 29
UN Convention on the Rights of the Child   see Convention on the Rights of the Child
UN Standard Minimum Rules for the Administration of Juvenile Justice   73-74

Voting   39, 44

Welfare
    Generally   138, 140-141, 156, 179-180, 267, 268, 320, 338
    Paramountcy of   260, 271-272
Whangai Parents   333-337
Working   45-46

Youth Justice   see Criminal Justice

Printed in the United States
by Baker & Taylor Publisher Services